Macromedia® NAKED

DREAMWEAVER® MX 2004

Sherry Bishop and Piyush Patel

THOMSON
COURSE TECHNOLOGY

Naked Macromedia® Dreamweaver® MX 2004

Sherry Bishop and Piyush Patel

Executive Editor:
Nicole Jones Pinard

Product Manager:
Karen Stevens

Associate Product Manager:
Emilie Perreault

Editorial Assistant:
Abigail Reider

Production Editors:
Summer Hughes/ Megan Belanger

Composition House:
GEX Publishing Services

QA Manuscript Reviewers:
Ashlee Welz, Chris Carvalho

Development Editor:
Ann Fisher

Text Designer:
Ann Small

Illustrator:
Philip Brooker

Cover Design:
Ryan O'Donnell

Naked Series Vision

Naked Macromedia Dreamweaver MX 2004. Naked? Just a ploy to get you to pick up this book? Not at all. "Naked" describes exactly the approach taken in this series. No extra fluff just to fill pages. No bells and whistles. Just clutter-free, pure instruction that helps you master Dreamweaver MX 2004 quickly and easily. Books in the *Naked* series serve as your guides to today's hottest multimedia applications. These comprehensive books teach the skills behind the application, showing you how to apply smart design principles to multimedia products, such as dynamic graphics, animation, Web sites, software authoring tools, and video.

A team of design professionals including multimedia instructors, students, authors, and editors worked together to create this series. The result is a series that:

- Gives you comprehensive step-by-step instructions
- Offers in-depth explanation of the "why" behind a skill
- Includes creative projects for additional practice
- Explains concepts clearly using full-color visuals

It was our goal to create a book that speaks directly to the multimedia and design community—one of the most rapidly growing computer fields today.

This series was designed to appeal to the creative spirit. We would like to thank Philip Brooker for developing the inspirational artwork found on each chapter opener. We would also like to give special thanks to Ann Small of A Small Design Studio for developing a sophisticated and instructive book design.
—The *Naked* Series

Acknowledgments:

This book represents a great team effort by a group of dedicated and talented professionals. The Course Technology team is creative, energetic, and insightful. Karen Stevens, as Product Manager, skillfully guided the team from beginning to end with a cheerful, upbeat attitude. She never encountered difficulties during the process; rather, opportunities to enhance and improve. She is one of those rare people who, although extremely busy, makes you feel that she has all the time in the world for you whenever you call her.

Ann Fisher is the ideal editor. She can edit your work so skillfully that you think you did it all by yourself! She successfully juggled two editing projects, packing, and moving her home without ever losing her sweet nature and finely honed organizational skills.

Thank you to Chris Carvalho and Ashlee Welz for their exceptional feedback as they reviewed each chapter. They helped us to see each project through students' eyes. This part of the publishing process is truly one of the real strengths of Course Technology. Summer Hughes did an excellent job coordinating the many details and deadlines. She made sure everyone stayed on track to insure that the book was completed on schedule.

Piyush Patel was the creator of the Super Bug Zapper Web site. It is difficult to design a Web site that provides simple real-life examples for learning, yet is creative and fun for readers. He accomplished this with ease.

Special thanks go to Nicole Pinard, the Executive Editor. She is an extremely talented individual who brings out the best in those who are fortunate enough to work with her. I will always be grateful to her for inviting me to join her team. It is hard to keep up with her, but I've enjoyed trying!

Typically, your family is last to be properly thanked. My husband, Don, has always been my most fervent supporter. He has made my life a joy for the last thirty-three years. My children Christy, Michael, and Jonathan are as encouraging to me with my projects as I hope I have been to them with theirs. Lastly, our companion of the past sixteen years, Buster, didn't quite make it through the completion of this book. He taught us well in the lessons of unconditional love, as only a rat terrier can. We miss him.
— Sherry Bishop

Introduction

Welcome to *Naked Macromedia® Dreamweaver® MX 2004*. This book offers creative projects, concise instructions, and complete coverage of basic to intermediate Dreamweaver MX 2004 skills, helping you to create and publish Dreamweaver Web sites.

This text is organized into fourteen chapters. In these chapters, you will learn many skills you need to create dynamic Dreamweaver Web sites.

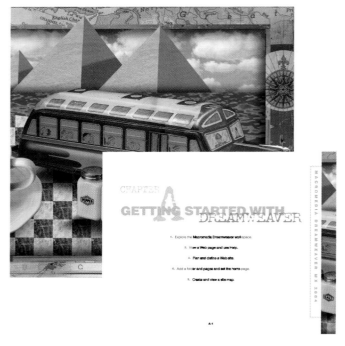

What You'll Do

A What You'll Do figure begins every lesson. This figure gives you an at-a-glance look at the skills covered in the chapter and shows you the completed data file for that lesson. Before you start the lesson, you will know—both on a technical and artistic level—what you will be creating.

Comprehensive Conceptual Lessons

Before jumping into instructions, in-depth conceptual information tells you "why" skills are applied. This book provides the "how" and "why" through the use of professional examples. Also included in the text are tips and sidebars to help you work more efficiently and creatively, or to teach you a bit about the history behind the skill you are using.

Step-by-Step Instructions

This book combines in-depth conceptual information with concise steps to help you learn Dreamweaver MX 2004. Each set of steps guides you through a lesson where you will apply tasks to a Dreamweaver data file. Step references to large colorful images and quick step summaries round out the lessons.

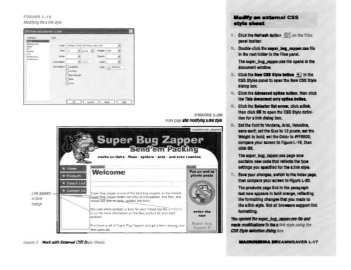

Projects

This book contains a variety of end-of-chapter materials for additional practice and reinforcement. The Skills Review contains hands-on practice exercises that mirror the progressive nature of the lesson material. The chapter concludes with four projects: two Project Builders, one Design Project, and one Group Project. The Project Builders require you to app ly the skills you've learned in the chapter to create powerful Web sites. Design Projects explore design principles by sending you to the Web to view Dreamweaver in action. Group Projects encourage group activity as readers use the resources of a team to create a Web site.

CHAPTER A　GETTING STARTED WITH DREAMWEAVER

CONTENTS

CHAPTER B   DEVELOPING A WEB PAGE

CHAPTER C   WORKING WITH TEXT AND GRAPHICS

CHAPTER D   WORKING WITH LINKS

CHAPTER J CREATING AND USING TEMPLATES

CHAPTER M WORKING WITH LIBRARY ITEMS AND SNIPPETS

CHAPTER A

GETTING STARTED WITH DREAMWEAVER

1. Explore the Macromedia Dreamweaver workspace.

2. View a Web page and use Help.

3. Plan and define a Web site.

4. Add a folder and pages and set the home page.

5. Create and view a site map.

CHAPTER A

GETTING STARTED WITH DREAMWEAVER

Introduction

Macromedia Dreamweaver MX 2004 is **Web design software** that lets you create dynamic, interactive Web pages containing text, images, hyperlinks, animation, sounds, video, and other elements. You can use Dreamweaver to create an individual Web page or a complex Web site consisting of many Web pages. A **Web site** is a group of related Web pages that are linked together and share a common interface and design. You can use Dreamweaver to create some Web page elements such as text, tables, and interactive buttons, or you can import elements from other software programs. You can save Dreamweaver files in many different file formats including HTML, JavaScript, or XML to name a few. **HTML** is the acronym for Hypertext Markup Language, the language used to create Web pages.

> **QUICK**TIP
>
> You use a browser to view your Web pages on the Internet. A **browser** is a program, such as Microsoft Internet Explorer or Netscape Communicator, that lets you display HTML-developed Web pages.

Using Dreamweaver Tools

Creating a good Web site is a complex task. Fortunately, Dreamweaver has an impressive number of tools that can help. Using Dreamweaver design tools, you can create dynamic and interactive Web pages without writing a word of HTML code. However, if you prefer to write code, Dreamweaver makes it easy to enter and edit the code directly and see the visual results of the code instantly. Dreamweaver also contains organizational tools that help you work with a team of people to create a Web site. You can also use Dreamweaver management tools to help you manage a Web site. For instance, you can use the **Files panel** to create folders to organize and store the various files for your Web site. You also use the Files panel to add pages to your Web site, and to set the **home page** in Dreamweaver, the first page that viewers will see when they visit the site. You can also use the **site map**, a graphical representation of how the pages within a Web site relate to each other, to view and edit the navigation structure of your Web site. The **navigation structure** is the way viewers navigate from page to page in your Web site.

Tools You'll Use

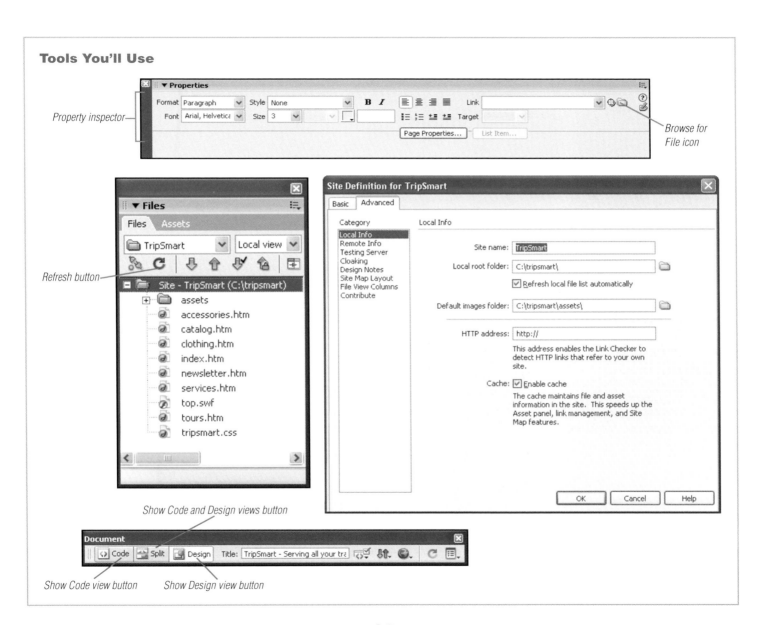

Property inspector

Browse for File icon

Refresh button

Show Code and Design views button

Show Code view button

Show Design view button

EXPLORE THE DREAMWEAVER WORKSPACE

What You'll Do

 In this lesson, you will start Dreamweaver, examine the components that make up the Dreamweaver workspace, and change views.

Examining the Dreamweaver Workspace

The **Dreamweaver workspace** is designed to provide you with easy access to all the tools you need to create Web pages. Refer to Figure A-1 as you locate the components described below.

The **document window** is the large white area in the Dreamweaver program window where you create and edit Web pages. The **menu bar**, located above the document window, includes menu names, each of which contains Dreamweaver commands. To choose a menu command, click the menu name to open the menu, then click the menu command. Directly below the menu bar is the Insert bar. The Insert bar includes seven categories displayed as tabs. They are Common, Layout, Forms, Text, HTML, Application, and Favorites. Clicking a tab on the Insert bar displays the buttons and menus associated with that category. For example, if you click the Layout tab, you will find the Table button, used for inserting a table, and the Frames menu, used for selecting one of thirteen different frame layouts.

QUICKTIP

You can also display the categories using tabs, as in previous versions of Dreamweaver, by clicking the current Insert bar list arrow, then clicking Show as Tabs.

The **Document toolbar** contains buttons you can use to change the current work mode, preview Web pages, debug Web pages, and view file-management options. The **Standard toolbar** contains buttons you can use to execute frequently used commands also available on the File and Edit menus. The Standard toolbar is not part of the default workspace setup and might not be showing on your screen.

QUICKTIP

To hide or display the Standard, Document, or Insert toolbars, click View on the menu bar, point to Toolbars, then click Document, Standard, or Insert.

The **Property inspector**, located at the bottom of the Dreamweaver window, lets you view and change the properties of a selected object. The **status bar** is located below the document window. The left end of the status bar displays the **tag selector**, which shows the HTML tags used at the insertion point location. The right side displays the window size and estimated download time for the current page.

A **panel** is a window that displays information on a particular topic or contains related commands. **Panel groups** are sets of related panels that are grouped together. To view the contents of a panel in a panel group, click the panel tab you want. Panel groups can be collapsed and docked on the right side of the screen, or undocked by dragging the gripper

on the left side of the panel group title bar. To collapse or expand a panel group, click the expander arrow on the left side of the panel group title bar, as shown in Figure A-2 or just click the name of the panel group. When you use Dreamweaver for the first time, the Design, Code, Application, Tag Inspector, and Files panel groups are open by default.

Working with Dreamweaver Views

You view a Web page in the document window using one of three different views. A **view** is a particular way of displaying page

content. **Design view** shows the page as it would appear in a browser, and is primarily used for designing and creating a Web page. **Code view** shows the underlying HTML code for the page; use this view to read or edit the underlying code. **Code and Design view** is a combination of Code view and Design view. Code and Design view is the best view for **debugging** or correcting errors because you can see immediately how code modifications will change the appearance of the page. The view buttons are located on the Document toolbar.

FIGURE A-1
Dreamweaver MX 2004 workspace

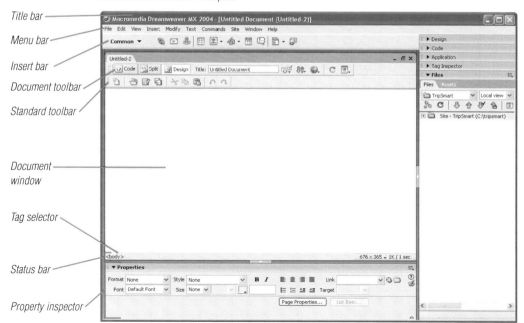

Title bar
Menu bar
Insert bar
Document toolbar
Standard toolbar

Document window

Tag selector

Status bar

Property inspector

FIGURE A-2
Panels in Files panel group

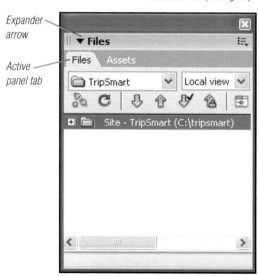

Expander arrow

Active panel tab

Start Dreamweaver (Windows)

1. Click the **Start button** 🏁 start on the taskbar.

2. Point to **Programs** or **All Programs**, point to **Macromedia**, then click **Macromedia Dreamweaver MX 2004**, as shown in Figure A-3.

You started Dreamweaver MX 2004 for Windows.

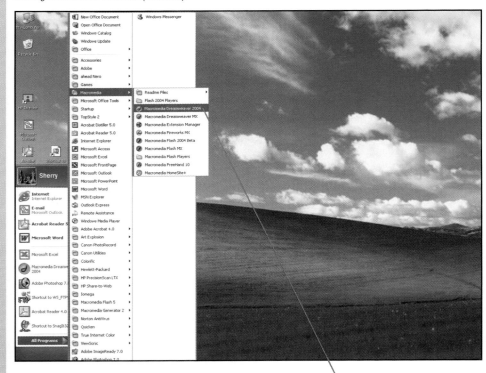

*Click Macromedia
Dreamweaver MX 2004*

Choosing a workspace layout (Windows)

If you are starting Dreamweaver in Windows for the first time after installing it, you will see the Workspace Setup dialog box, which asks you to choose between the Designer or Coder layout. Both layouts are built with an integrated workspace using the Multiple Document Interface (MDI). The **Multiple Document Interface** means that all document windows and panels are positioned within one large application window. In the Designer workspace layout, the panels are docked on the right side of the screen and the Design view is the default view. In the Coder workspace layout, the panels are docked on the left side of the screen and the Code view is the default view.

FIGURE A-4

Starting Dreamweaver MX 2004 (Macintosh)

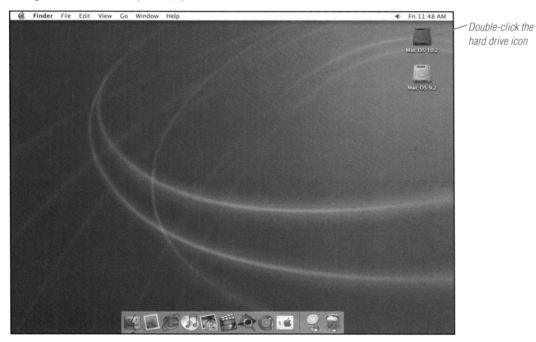

Double-click the
hard drive icon

1. Double-click the **hard drive icon**, as shown in Figure A-4.

2. Double-click the **Macromedia Dreamweaver MX 2004 folder**.

   > TIP   Your Macromedia Dreamweaver folder might be in another folder called Applications.

3. Double-click the **Macromedia Dreamweaver MX 2004 program icon**.

You started Dreamweaver MX 2004 for Macintosh.

Change views and view panels

1. Click the **Create New HTML link** on the Dreamweaver Start screen.

   The Dreamweaver Start screen provides shortcuts for opening files or for creating new files or Web sites.

2. Click the **Show Code view button** [⟨⟩ Code] on the Document toolbar as shown in Figure A-5.

   The HTML code for an untitled, blank document appears in the document window.

3. Click the **Show Code and Design views button** [Split] on the Document toolbar.

4. Click the **Show Design view button** [Design] on the Document toolbar.

   (continued)

FIGURE A-5
Code view for blank document

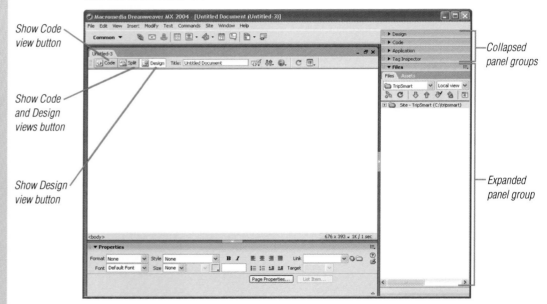

Show Code view button

Show Code and Design views button

Show Design view button

Collapsed panel groups

Expanded panel group

FIGURE A-6
Displaying a panel group

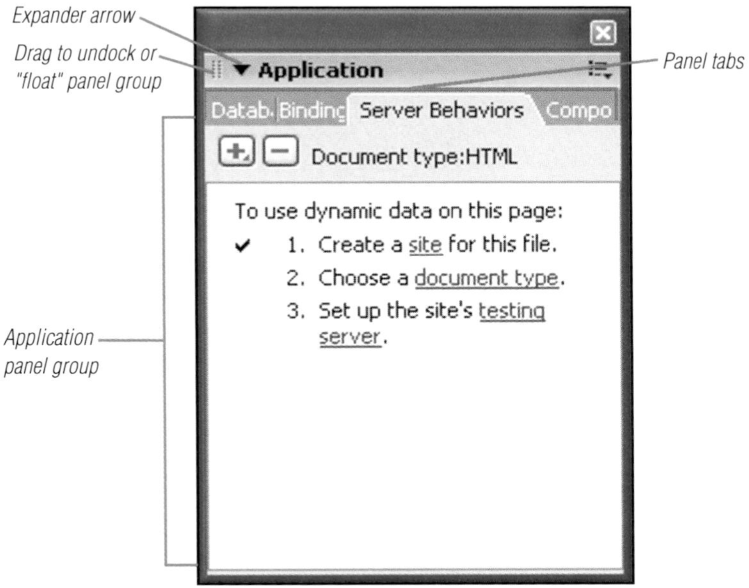

Expander arrow

Drag to undock or "float" panel group

Panel tabs

Application panel group

▼ **Application**

Datab. Binding **Server Behaviors** Compo

[+] [−] Document type:HTML

To use dynamic data on this page:

✓ 1. Create a <u>site</u> for this file.
2. Choose a <u>document type</u>.
3. Set up the site's <u>testing server</u>.

5. Click **Application** on the panel group title bar, then compare your screen to Figure A-6.

> TIP If the Application panel group is not displayed, click Window on the menu bar, then click Server Behaviors.

6. Click each panel name tab to display the contents of each panel.

7. Click **Application** on the panel group title bar to collapse the Application panel group.

8. View the contents of the Code and Files panel groups, then collapse the Code panel group.

> TIP If you are a Mac user, you first need to open the panel groups. To open each panel group, click Window on the menu bar, then click Server Behaviors (for the Application panel group), or Assets (for the Files panel group).

9. Close the open HTML document.

You viewed a blank Web page using three views, opened each panel group and displayed the contents of each panel, then closed each panel group.

VIEW A WEB PAGE AND USE HELP

What You'll Do

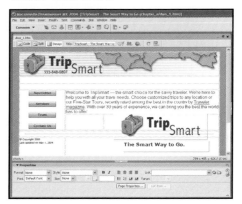

 In this lesson, you will open a Web page, view several page elements, and access the Help system.

Opening a Web page

After starting Dreamweaver, you can create a new Web site, create a new Web page, or open an existing Web site or Web page. The first Web page that appears when viewers go to a Web site is called the **home page**. The home page sets the look and feel of the Web site and directs viewers to the rest of the pages in the Web site.

Viewing Basic Web Page Elements

There are many elements that make up Web pages. Web pages can be very simple, and designed primarily with text, or they can be media-rich with text, graphics, sound, and movies. Figure A-7 is an example of a Web page with several different page elements that work together to create a simple and attractive page.

Most information on a Web page is presented in the form of **text**. You can type text directly onto a Web page in Dreamweaver or import text created in other programs. You can then use the Property inspector to format text so that it is attractive and easy

to read. Text should be short and to the point to prevent viewers from losing interest and leaving your site.

Hyperlinks, also known as **links**, are graphic or text elements on a Web page that users click to display another location on the page, another Web page on the same Web site, or a Web page on a different Web site.

Graphics add visual interest to a Web page. The saying that "less is more" is certainly true with graphics, though. Too many graphics will cause the page to load too slowly and discourage viewers from waiting for the page to download. Many pages today have **banners**, which are graphics displayed across the top of the screen that can incorporate a company's logo, contact information, and links to the other pages in the site.

Navigation bars are bars that contain multiple links that are usually organized in rows or columns. Sometimes navigation bars are used with an image map. An **image map** is a graphic that has been divided into sections, each of which contains a link.

Flash button objects are objects created in Macromedia Flash that can serve as links to other files or Web pages. You can insert them onto a Web page without requiring the Macromedia Flash program to be installed. They add "pizzazz" to a Web page.

Getting Help

Dreamweaver has an excellent Help feature that is both comprehensive and easy to use. When questions or problems arise, you can use the commands on the Help menu to find the answers you need. Clicking the Using Dreamweaver command on a Windows computer opens the Using Dreamweaver MX 2004 window that contains four tabs you can use to search for answers in different ways. The Contents tab lists Dreamweaver Help topics by category. The Index tab lets you view topics in alphabetical order, and the Search tab lets you enter a keyword to search for a specific topic. You can use the Favorites tab to bookmark topics that you might want to view later. On a Macintosh you can choose between Index or Table of Contents view and the Search field is always present at the top of the window. You can also use the Tutorials command on the Help menu to get step-by-step instructions on how to complete various tasks. Context-specific help can be accessed through the Property inspector.

FIGURE A-7
Common Web page elements

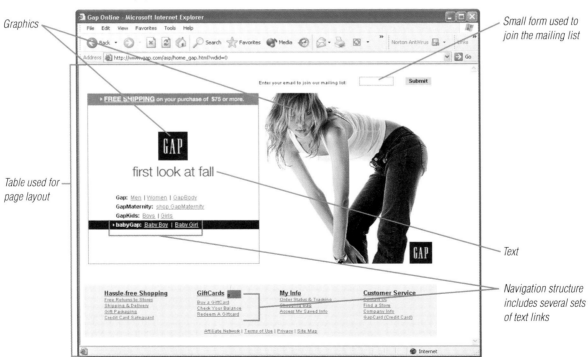

Graphics

Small form used to join the mailing list

Table used for page layout

Text

Navigation structure includes several sets of text links

Open a Web page and view basic page elements

1. Click the **Open link** on the Dreamweaver Start screen.

   | TIP If you do not want to use the Start screen shortcuts, click the Don't show again check box.

2. Click the **Look in list arrow** (Win), or **From list arrow** (Mac), locate the drive and folder where your Data Files are stored, then double-click the chapter_a folder (Win), or click the chapter_a folder (Mac).

3. Click dwa_1.htm, then click **Open**.

4. Locate each of the Web page elements shown in Figure A-8.

5. Click the **Show Code view button** to view the code for the page.

6. Scroll down to view all the code, then click the **Show Design view button** to return to Design view.

   | TIP To view the code for a particular page element, select the page element in Design view, then click the Show Code view button.

7. Click **File** on the menu bar, then click **Close** to close the page without saving it.

You opened a Web page, located several page elements, viewed the code for the page, then closed the Web page without saving it.

FIGURE A-8
TripSmart Web page elements

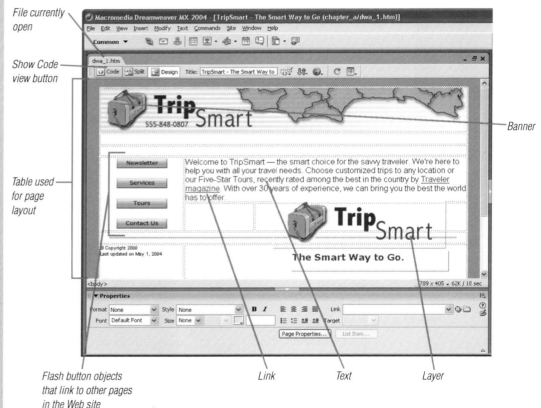

File currently open

Show Code view button

Table used for page layout

Banner

Flash button objects that link to other pages in the Web site

Link

Text

Layer

Use Dreamweaver Help

1. Click **Help** on the menu bar, then click **Using Dreamweaver**.

2. Click the **Search tab** (Win).

3. Type **saving** in the Type in the keyword to find text box (Win) or the Ask a Question text box (Mac).

4. Click **List Topics** (Win) or press **[return]** (Mac), then scroll down to view the topics.

5. Continue to Step 6 (Win) or close the Help window (Mac).

6. Select saving in the Type in the keyword to find text box, type **"save files"**, (be sure to type the quotation marks), then press **[Enter]**.

   Because you placed the keywords in quotation marks, Dreamweaver shows only the topics that contain the exact phrase "save files."

7. Double-click the first topic in the topic list.

   Information on accessing sites, servers, and local drives appears in the right frame, as shown in Figure A-9.

8. Scroll down and scan the text.

   The search words you used are highlighted in the Help text.

9. Close the Help window.

You used the Dreamweaver Help files to read information about connecting to a server to edit files.

FIGURE A-9
Using Dreamweaver Help

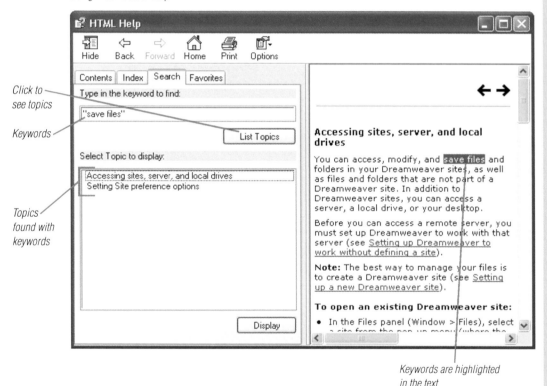

Click to see topics

Keywords

Topics found with keywords

Keywords are highlighted in the text

PLAN AND DEFINE A WEB SITE

What You'll Do

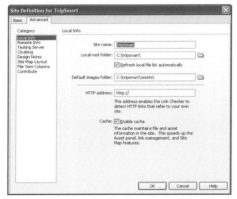

 In this lesson, you will review a Web site plan for TripSmart, a full-service travel outfitter. You will also create a root folder for the TripSmart Web site, and then define the Web site.

Understanding the Web Site Creation Process

Creating a Web site is a complex process. It can often involve a large team of people working in various roles to ensure that the Web site contains accurate information, looks good, and works smoothly. Figure A-10 illustrates the steps involved in creating a Web site.

Planning a Web Site

Planning is probably the most important part of any successful project. Planning is an *essential* part of creating a Web site, and is a continuous process that overlaps the subsequent phases. To start planning your Web site, you need to create a checklist of questions and answers about the site. For example, what are your goals for

Understanding IP addresses and domain names

To be accessible over the Internet, a Web site must be published to a Web server with a permanent IP address. An **IP address** is an assigned series of numbers, separated by periods, that designate an address on the Internet. To access a Web page, you can enter either an IP address or a domain name in the address text box of your browser window. A **domain name** is a Web address that is expressed in letters instead of numbers, and usually reflects the name of the business represented by the Web site. For example, the domain name of the Macromedia Web site is *www.macromedia.com*, but the IP address would read something like 123.456.789.123. Because domain names use descriptive text instead of numbers, they are much easier to remember. Compare an IP address to your Social Security number and a domain name to your name. Both your Social Security number and your name are used to refer to you as a person, but your name is much easier for your friends and family to use than your Social Security number. You can type the IP address or the domain name in the address text box of the browser window to access a Web site.

the Web site? Who is the audience you want to target? Teenagers? Senior Citizens? How can you design the site to appeal to the target audience? The more questions you can answer about the site, the more prepared you will be when you begin the developmental phase. Because of the public demand for "instant" information, your plan should include not just how to get the site up and running, but how to keep it current. Table A-1 lists some of the basic questions you need to answer during the planning phase for almost any type of Web site. In addition to a checklist, you should also create a timeline and a budget for the Web site.

Setting Up the Basic Structure

Once you complete the planning phase, you need to set up the structure of the site by creating a storyboard. A **storyboard** is a small sketch that represents every page in a Web site. Like a flowchart, a storyboard shows the relationship of each page in the Web site to all the other pages. Storyboards

FIGURE A-10
Steps in creating a Web site

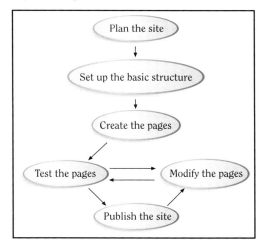

TABLE A-1: Web Site Planning Checklist

question	examples
1. Who is the target audience?	Seniors, teens, children
2. How can I tailor the Web site to reach that audience?	Specify an appropriate reading level, decide the optimal amount of multimedia content, use formal or casual language
3. What are the goals for the site?	Sell a product, provide information
4. How will I gather the information?	Recruit other company employees, write it myself, use content from in-house documents
5. What are my sources for multimedia content?	Internal production department, outside production company, my own photographs
6. What is my budget?	Very limited, well financed
7. How long do I have to complete the project?	Two weeks, 1 month, 6 months
8. Who is on my project team?	Just me, a complete staff of designers
9. How often should the site be updated?	Every 10 minutes, once a month
10. Who is responsible for updating the site?	Me, other team members

are very helpful when planning a Web site, because they allow you to visualize how each page in the site is linked to others. You can sketch a storyboard using a pencil and paper or using a graphics program on a computer. The storyboard shown in Figure A-11 shows all the pages that will be contained in the TripSmart Web site that you will create in this book. Notice that the home page appears at the top of the storyboard, and has four pages linked to it. The home page is called the **parent page**, because it is at a higher level in the Web hierarchy and has pages

linked to it. The pages linked to it below are called **child pages**. The Catalog page, which is a child page to the home page, is also a parent page to the Accessories and Clothing pages. You can refer to this storyboard as you create the actual links in Dreamweaver.

QUICKTIP

You can create a storyboard on a computer using a software program such as Word, PowerPoint, Paint, Paintshop Pro, or Macromedia Freehand. You might find it easier to make changes to a computer-generated storyboard than to one created on paper.

In addition to creating a storyboard for your site, you should also create a folder hierarchy for all of the files that will be used in the Web site. Start by creating a folder for the Web site with a descriptive name, such as the name of the company. This folder, known as the **root folder**, will store all the Web pages or HTML files for the site. Then create a subfolder called **assets** in which you store all of the files that are not Web pages, such as images and video clips. You should avoid using spaces, special characters, or uppercase characters in your folder names.

FIGURE A-11
TripSmart Web site storyboard

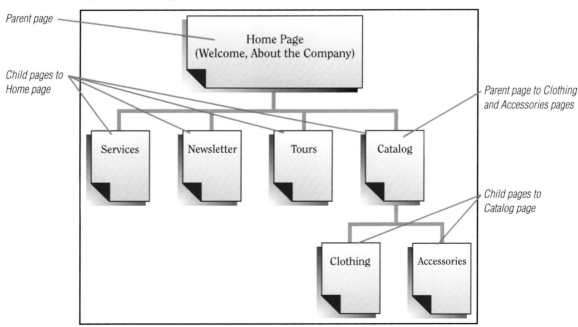

Getting Started with Dreamweaver

After you create the root folder, you need to define your Web site. When you **define** a Web site, the root folder and any folders and files it contains appears in the **Files panel**, the panel you use to manage your Web site's files and folders. Using the Files panel to manage your files ensures that the site links work correctly when the Web site is published. You also use the Files panel to add or delete pages.

Creating the Web Pages and Collecting the Page Content

This is the fun part! After you create your storyboard, you need to gather the files that will be used to create the pages, including text, graphics, buttons, video, and animation. Some of these files will come from other software programs, and some will be created in Dreamweaver. For example, you can create text in a word-processing program and insert it into Dreamweaver or you can create and format text in Dreamweaver. Graphics, tables, colors, and horizontal rules all contribute to making a page attractive and interesting. In choosing your elements, however, you should always carefully consider the file size of each page. A page with too many graphical elements might take a long time to load, which could cause visitors to leave your Web site. Before you actually add content to each page, however, you need to use the Files panel to add all the pages to the site according to the structure you specified in your storyboard. Once all the blank pages are in place, you can add the content you collected.

Testing the Pages

Once all your pages are completed, you need to test the site to make sure all the links work and that everything looks good. It is important to test your Web pages using different browser software. The two most common browsers are Microsoft Internet Explorer and Netscape Navigator. You should also test your Web site using different versions of each browser. Older versions of Internet Explorer and Netscape Navigator do not support the latest Web technology. You should also test your Web site using a variety of screen sizes. Some viewers may have small monitors, while others may have large, high-resolution monitors. You should also consider modem speed. Although more people use cable modems or DSL (Digital Subscriber Line) these days, some still use slower dial-up modems. Testing is a continuous process, for which you should allocate plenty of time.

Modifying the Pages

After you create a Web site, you'll probably find that you need to keep making changes to it, especially when information on the site needs to be updated. Each time you make a change, such as adding a new button or graphic to a page, you should test the site again. Modifying and testing pages in a Web site is an ongoing process.

Publishing the Site

Publishing a Web site means that you transfer all the files for the site to a **Web server**, a computer that is connected to the Internet with an IP (Internet Protocol) address, so that it is available for viewing on the Internet. A Web site must be published or users of the World Wide Web cannot view it. There are several options for publishing a Web site. For instance, many Internet Service Providers (ISPs) provide space on their servers for customers to publish Web sites and some commercial Web sites provide limited free space for their viewers. Although publishing happens at the end of the process, it's a good idea to set up Web server access in the planning phase. You use the Files panel to transfer your files using the FTP (**File Transfer Protocol**) capability. **FTP** is the process of uploading and downloading files to and from a remote site. Dreamweaver MX 2004 also gives you the ability to transfer files using the FTP process without creating a Web site first. You simply enter login information to an FTP site to establish a connection by clicking New in the Manage Sites dialog box, then clicking the FTP & RDS server option.

Create a root folder (Windows)

1. Click the **Start button** 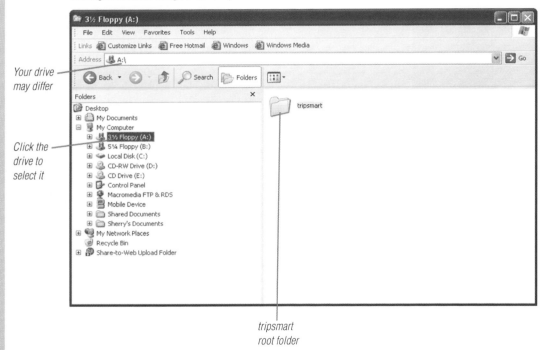 on the taskbar, point to **All Programs**, point to **Accessories**, then click **Windows Explorer**.

2. Navigate to the drive and folder where you will create a folder to store your files for the TripSmart Web site.

3. Click **File** on the menu bar, point to **New**, then click **Folder**.

4. Type **tripsmart** to rename the folder, then press **[Enter]**.

   The folder is renamed tripsmart, as shown in Figure A-12.

   | TIP Your desktop will look different than Figure A-12 if you are not using Windows XP.

5. Close Windows Explorer.

You created a new folder to serve as the root folder for the TripSmart Web site.

FIGURE A-12
Creating a root folder using Windows Explorer

Your drive may differ

Click the drive to select it

tripsmart root folder

Setting the Home Page

The home page of a Web site is the first page that viewers see when they visit your Web site. Most Web sites contain many other pages that all connect back to the home page. Dreamweaver uses the home page that you have designated as a starting point for creating a **site map**, a graphical representation of the Web pages in a Web site. When you **set** the home page, you tell Dreamweaver which page you have designated to be your home page. The home page filename usually has the name index.htm.

Adding Pages to a Web Site

Web sites might be as simple as one page or might contain hundreds of pages. When you create a Web site, you need to add all the pages and specify where they should be placed in the Web site folder structure in the root folder. Once you add and name all the pages in the Web site, you can then add the content, such as text and graphics, to each page. It is better to add as many blank pages as you think you will need in the beginning, rather than adding them one at a time with all the content in place. This will enable you to set up the navigation structure of the Web site at the beginning of the development process, and view how each page is linked to others. When you are satisfied with the overall structure, you can then add the content to each page.

Using the Files panel for file management

You can use the Files panel to add, delete, move, or rename files and folders in a Web site. It is very important that you perform these file maintenance tasks in the Files panel rather than in Windows Explorer (Win) or in the Finder (Mac). Dreamweaver will not recognize any changes you make to the Web site folder structure outside the Files panel. You use Windows Explorer (Win) or the Finder (Mac) only to create the root folder or to move or copy the root folder of a Web site to another location. If you move or copy the root folder to a new location, you will have to define the Web site again in the Files panel, as you did in Lesson 3 of this chapter.

Add a folder to a Web site (Windows)

1. Right-click the **TripSmart site** in the Files panel, then click **New Folder**.

2. Type **assets** in the folder text box, then press **[Enter]**.

3. Compare your screen with Figure A-16.

You used the Files panel to create a new folder in the tripsmart folder, and named it assets.

Add a folder to a Web site (Macintosh)

1. Click **Window** on the menu bar, click **Files** to open the Files panel (if necessary), press and hold **[control]**, click the **tripsmart folder**, then click **New Folder**.

2. Click the triangle to the left of the tripsmart folder to open it (if necessary), then click untitled on the new folder, type **assets** as the folder name, then press **[return]**.

   TIP   You will not see the new folder until you expand the tripsmart folder by clicking the triangle to the left of the tripsmart folder.

3. Compare your screen with Figure A-17.

You used the Files panel to create a new folder under the tripsmart folder, and named it assets.

TripSmart site in Files panel with assets folder created (Windows)

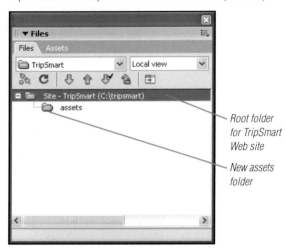

Root folder for TripSmart Web site

New assets folder

TripSmart site in Files panel with assets folder created (Macintosh)

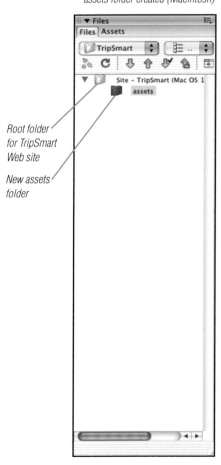

Root folder for TripSmart Web site

New assets folder

FIGURE A-18

Site Definition for TripSmart with assets folder set as the default images folder

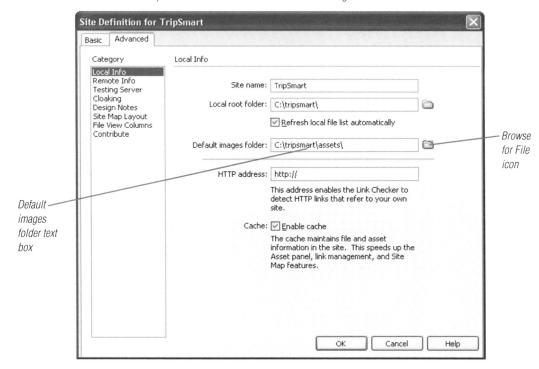

Default images folder text box

Browse for File icon

1. Click the **Site list arrow** next to TripSmart on the Files panel, click **Manage Sites**, then click **Edit**.

2. Click the **Browse for File icon** 📁 next to the Default images folder text box.

3. Navigate to the folder where your Web site files are stored, double-click the **tripsmart folder** (Win), or click the **tripsmart folder** (Mac), double-click the **assets folder** (Win), or click the **assets folder** (Mac), then click **Select** (Win) or **Choose** (Mac).

   Compare your screen to Figure A-18.

4. Click **OK**, then click **Done**.

You set the assets folder as the default images folder so that imported images will be automatically saved in it.

Set the home page

1. Open dwa_2.htm from the location where your Data Files are stored.

2. Click **File** on the menu bar, click **Save As**, click the **Save in list arrow** (Win) or the **Where list arrow** (Mac), navigate to the tripsmart folder, type **index.htm** in the File name text box (Win), or Save As text box (Mac), then click **Save**.

   | TIP   If you are asked if you want to update links, click Yes.

   As shown in Figure A-19, the title bar displays the page title, TripSmart - The Smart Way to Go, followed by the root folder (tripsmart) and the name of the page (index.htm) in parentheses. The information within the parentheses is called the **path**, or location of the open file in relation to other folders in the Web site.

3. Right-click (Win) or [control] click (Mac) the **index.htm** filename in the Files panel, then click **Set as Home Page**.

   | TIP   If you want your screen to match the figures in this book, make sure the document window is maximized.

You opened a file, saved it with the filename index.htm, then set it as the home page.

FIGURE A-19
index.htm placed in the tripsmart root folder

Page title and path for file

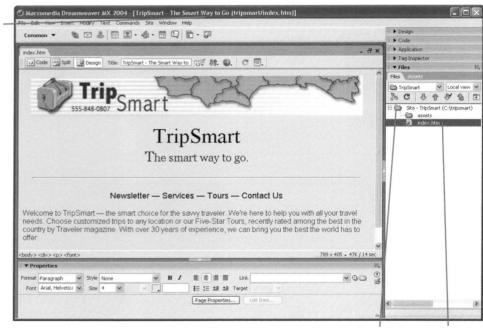

Root folder   index.htm

FIGURE A-20
Property inspector showing properties of the TripSmart banner

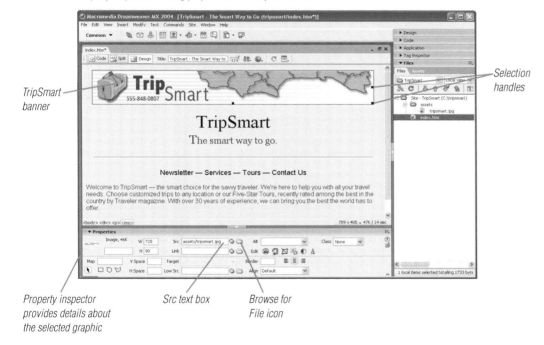

TripSmart banner

Selection handles

Property inspector provides details about the selected graphic

Src text box

Browse for File icon

1. Click the **TripSmart banner** to select it.

   The Src text box in the Property inspector displays the current location of the selected banner.

2. Click the **Browse for File icon** next to the Src text box in the Property inspector, click the **Look in list arrow** (Win) or **From list arrow** (Mac), navigate to the assets folder in your Data Files folder for this chapter, click **tripsmart.jpg**, then click **OK** (Win), or **Choose** (Mac).

   The TripSmart banner is automatically copied to the assets folder of the TripSmart Web site, the folder that you designated as the default images folder. The Src text box now shows the path of the banner to the assets folder in the Web site.

3. Compare your screen to Figure A-20.

   > **TIP** If you do not see the tripsmart.jpg file listed in the Files panel, click the Refresh button on the Files panel toolbar.

   Until you copy a graphic from an outside folder to your Web site, the graphic is not part of the Web site and the image will appear as a broken link on the page when the Web site is copied to a remote site.

You saved the TripSmart banner in the assets folder.

Add pages to a Web site (Windows)

1. Click the **plus sign** to the left of the assets folder (if necessary) to open the folder and view its contents, tripsmart.jpg.

   | TIP   If you do not see any contents in the assets folder, click the Refresh button 🔁 on the Files panel toolbar.

2. Right-click the **tripsmart root folder**, click **New File**, type **catalog.htm** to replace untitled.htm, then press **[Enter]**.

   | TIP   If you create a new file in the Files panel, you must type the filename extension (.htm or .html) manually.

3. Repeat Step 2 to add five more blank pages to the TripSmart Web site, then name the new files **services.htm**, **tours.htm**, **newsletter.htm**, **clothing.htm**, and **accessories.htm**.

   | TIP   Make sure to add the new files to the root folder, not the assets folder. If you accidentally add them to the assets folder, just drag them to the root folder.

4. Click the **Refresh button** 🔁 on the Files panel to list the files alphabetically, then compare your screen to Figure A-21.

You added the following six pages to the TripSmart Web site: catalog, services, tours, newsletter, clothing, and accessories.

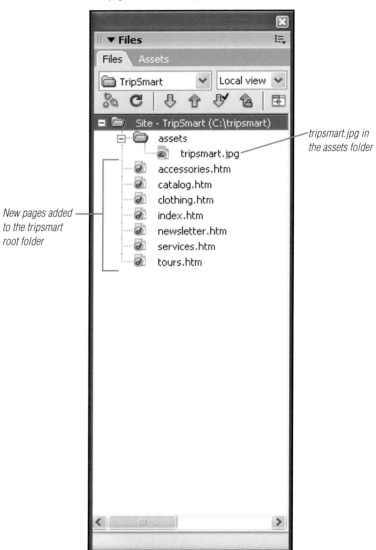

tripsmart.jpg in the assets folder

New pages added to the tripsmart root folder

FIGURE A-22

New pages added to the TripSmart Web site (Macintosh)

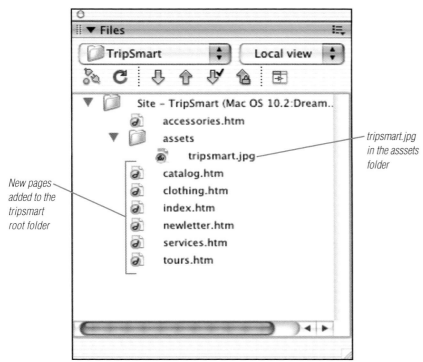

New pages added to the tripsmart root folder

tripsmart.jpg in the asssets folder

Add pages to a Web site (Macintosh)

1. Click **Window** on the menu bar, then click **Files** to open the Files panel.

2. Click the triangle to the left of the assets folder to open the folder and view its contents.

   TIP   If you do not see any contents in the assets folder, click Site on the menu bar, then click Refresh.

3. [control] click the **tripsmart root folder**, click **New File**, type **catalog.htm** to replace untitled.html, then press **[return]**.

   TIP   If you create a new file in the Files panel, you must type the filename extension (.htm or .html) manually.

4. Repeat Step 3 to add five more blank pages to the TripSmart Web site, then name the new files **services.htm**, **tours.htm**, **newsletter.htm**, **clothing.htm**, and **accessories.htm**.

5. Click the **Refresh button** C to list the files alphabetically, then compare your screen to Figure A-22.

You added six pages to the TripSmart Web site: catalog, services, tours, newsletter, clothing, and accessories.

CREATE AND VIEW A SITE MAP

What You'll Do

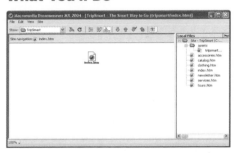

In this lesson, you will create and view a site map for the TripSmart Web site.

Creating a Site Map

As you add new Web pages to a Web site, it is easy to lose track of how they all link together. You can use the site map feature to help you keep track of the relationships between pages in a Web site. A **site map** is a graphical representation of the pages in the Web site and shows the folder structure for the Web site. You can find out details about each page by viewing the visual clues in the site map. For example, the site map uses icons to indicate pages with broken links, e-mail links, and links to external Web sites. It also indicates which pages are currently **checked out**, or being used by other team members.

Viewing a Site Map

You can view a site map using the Map view in the Files panel. You can expand the Files panel to display both the site map and the Web site file list. You can specify that the site map show a filename or a page title for each page. You can also edit page titles in the site map. Figure A-23 shows the site map and file list for the TripSmart Web site. Only the home page and pages that are linked to the home page will display in the site map. As more child pages are added, the site map will display them using a **tree structure**, or a diagram

---

DESIGNTIP **Verifying page titles**

When you view a Web page in a browser, its page title is displayed in the browser window title bar. The page title should reflect the page content and set the tone for the page. It is especially important to use words in your page title that are likely to match keywords viewers may enter when using a search engine. Search engines compare the text in page titles to the keywords typed into the search engine. When a title bar displays "Untitled Document," the designer has neglected to give the page a title. This is like giving up free "billboard space," and looks very unprofessional.

---

that visually represents the way the pages are linked to each other.

Using Site Map Images in Web Pages

It is very helpful to include a graphic of the site map in a Web site to help viewers understand the navigation structure of the site. Using Dreamweaver, you have the options of saving a site map for printing purposes or for displaying a site map on a page in a Web site. Windows users can save site maps as either a BMP (bitmapped) file or as a PNG (Portable Network Graphics) file. The BMP format is the best format to use for printing the site map or inserting it into a page layout program or slide show. The PNG format is best for inserting the site map on a Web page. Macintosh users can save site maps as PICT or JPEG file. The PICT format is the best format for printing the site map and inserting it into a page layout program or a slide show. The JPEG format is best for inserting the site map on a Web page. Though gaining in popularity, PNG files are not available on the Macintosh platform and are not supported by older versions of browsers. However, they are capable of showing millions of colors, are small in size, and compress well without losing image quality.

FIGURE A-23
TripSmart site map

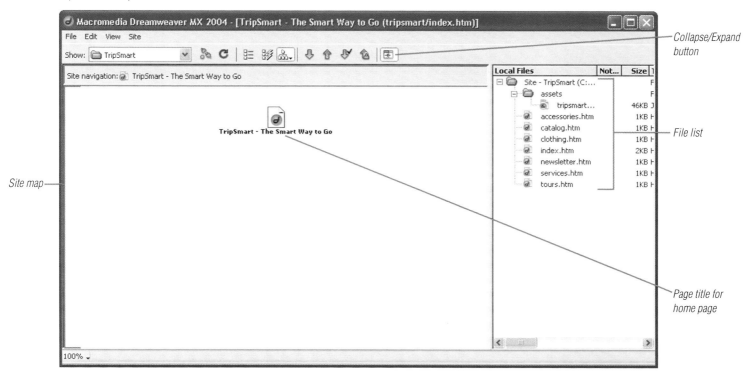

Lesson 5   *Create and View a Site Map*

Select site map options

1. Click the **Site list arrow** next to TripSmart in the Files panel, click **Manage Sites**, click **TripSmart** (if necessary), then click **Edit** to open the Site Definition dialog box.

2. Click **Site Map Layout** in the Category list.

3. Verify that index.htm is specified as the home page in the Home page text box, as shown in Figure A-24.

   TIP If the index.htm file is not specified as your home page, click the Browse for File icon next to the Home page text box, then locate and double-click index.htm.

4. Click the **Page titles option button**.

5. Click **OK**, then click **Done**.

You designated index.htm as the home page for the TripSmart Web site to create the site map. You also specified that page titles display in the site map instead of filenames.

FIGURE A-24
Options for the site map layout

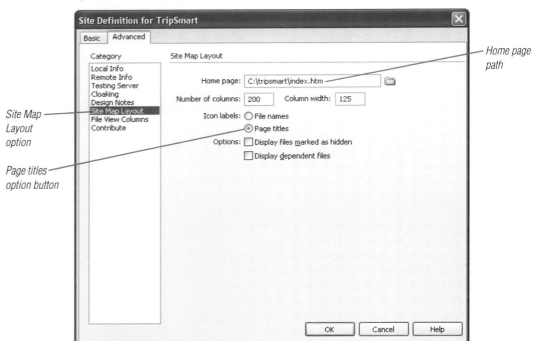

Site Map Layout option

Page titles option button

Home page path

Getting Started with Dreamweaver

FIGURE A-25
Expanding the site map

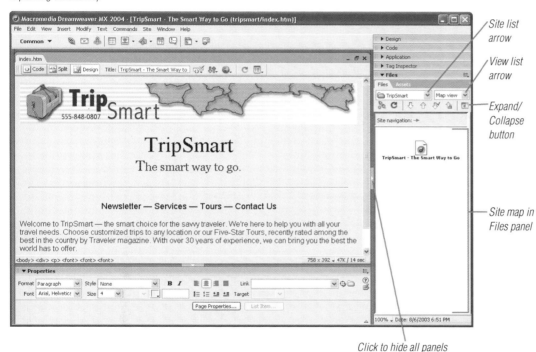

Site list arrow

View list arrow

Expand/ Collapse button

Site map in Files panel

Click to hide all panels

1. Click the **View list arrow** on the Files panel, then click **Map view**.

2. Click the **Expand/Collapse button** ⊞ on the Files panel toolbar, as shown in Figure A-25, to display the expanded site map.

   The site map shows the home page and pages that are linked to it. Because there are no pages linked to the home page, the site map shows only the home page.

   > TIP   You can drag the border between the two panes on the screen to resize them.

3. Click the **Expand/Collapse button** ⊞ on the toolbar to collapse the site map.

4. Click the **View list arrow**, then click **Local view**.

   The file list appears again in the Files panel.

5. Click **File** on the menu bar, then click **Exit** (Win) or click **Dreamweaver** on the menu bar, then click **Quit Dreamweaver** (Mac).

You opened and closed the TripSmart site map in the Files panel.

Explore the Dreamweaver workspace.

1. Start Dreamweaver.
2. Create a new HTML document.
3. Change the view to Code view.
4. Change the view to Code and Design views.
5. Change the view to Design view.
6. Expand the Application panel group.
7. View each panel in the Application panel group.
8. Collapse the Application panel group.
9. Close the page without saving it.

View a Web page and use Help.

1. Open dwa_3.htm from the folder where your Data Files are stored.
2. Locate the following page elements: a table, a banner, a graphic, and some formatted text.
3. Change the view to Code view.
4. Change the view to Design view.
5. Use the Dreamweaver Help feature to search for information on panel groups.
6. Display and read one of the topics you find.
7. Close the Help window.
8. Close the page without saving it.

Plan and define a Web site.

1. Select the drive and folder where you will store your Web site files using Windows Explorer or the Macintosh Finder.
2. Create a new root folder called **blooms**.
3. Close Windows Explorer or the Finder (Mac), then activate the Dreamweaver window.
4. Create a new site called **Blooms & Bulbs**.
5. Specify the blooms folder as the Local root folder.
6. Verify that the Refresh local file list automatically and the Enable cache check boxes are both selected.
7. Use the Remote Info category in the Site Definition dialog box to set up Web server access. (Specify None if you do not have the necessary information to set up Web server access.)
8. Click OK to close the Site Definition dialog box, then click Done.

Add a folder and pages and set the home page.

1. Create a new folder in the blooms root folder called **assets**.
2. Edit the site to set the assets folder as the default location for the Web site graphics.
3. Open dwa_4.htm from the folder where your Data Files are stored, then save this file in the blooms root folder as **index.htm**.
4. Set index.htm as the home page.
5. Select the Blooms & Bulbs banner on the page.
6. Use the Property inspector to browse for blooms.gif, then save it in the assets folder of the Blooms & Bulbs Web site.
7. Create three new pages in the Files panel, then name them: **plants.htm**, **workshops.htm**, and **tips.htm**.
8. Refresh the view to list the new files alphabetically.

Create and view a site map.

1. Use the Site Map Layout dialog box to verify that the index.htm file is shown as the home page.
2. Select Map view in the Files panel.
3. View the expanded site map for the Web site.
4. Show the page titles.
5. Compare your screen to Figure A-26.
6. Collapse the site map, return to Local view, save your work, then close index.htm.

FIGURE A-26
Completed Skills Review

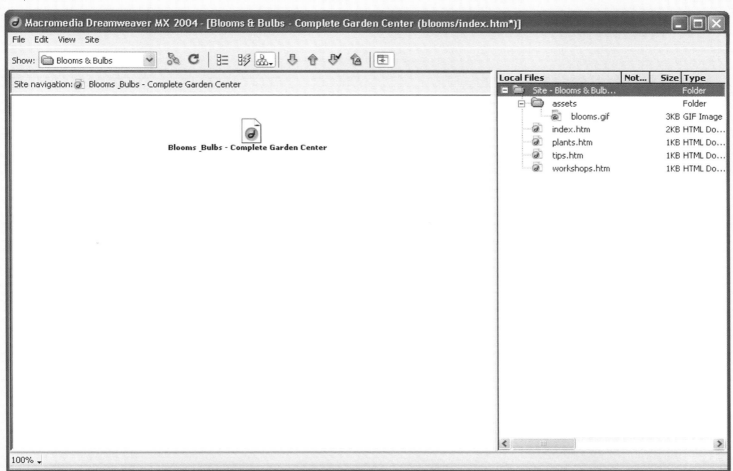

You have been hired to create a Web site for a river expedition company named Rapids Transit, located on the Buffalo River in Arkansas. In addition to renting canoes, kayaks, and rafts, they have a country store and a snack bar. If requested, river guides are available to accompany clients on float trips. The clients range from high school and college students to families to vacationing professionals. The owner, Mike Andrew, has requested a dynamic Web site that conveys the beauty of the Ozark Mountains and the Buffalo River.

1. Using the information in the paragraph above, create a storyboard for this Web site, using either a pencil and paper or a software program such as Microsoft Word. Include the home page with links to three child pages named **guides.htm**, **rentals.htm**, and **store.htm**.
2. Create a folder named **rapids** in the drive and folder where you store your Web site files.
3. Start Dreamweaver, then create a Web site with the name **Rapids Transit**.
4. Create an assets folder and set it as the default location for images.
5. Open dwa_5.htm from the location where your Data Files are stored, then save it in the rapids root folder as **index.htm**.
6. Save the rapids.jpg file in the assets folder.
7. Set index.htm as the home page.

8. Create three additional pages for the site, and name them as follows: **guides.htm**, **rentals.htm**, and **store.htm**. Use your storyboard and Figure A-27 as a guide.
9. Refresh the Files panel.
10. View the site map for the Web site.

FIGURE A-27
Completed Project Builder 1

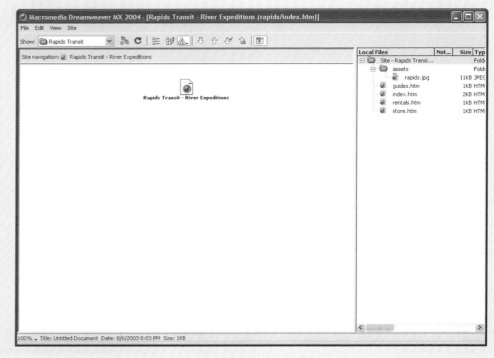

Your company has been selected to design a Web site for Jacob's, a new upscale restaurant in London that caters to business executives and theatre patrons. Jacob's has an extensive menu featuring French cuisine that includes set dinners and pre- and post-theatre dinner specials. They also like to feature some of their more popular recipes on their Web site. The chef, Jacob Richard, is famous in London for his creative cuisine and innovative culinary events.

1. Create a storyboard for this Web site that includes a home page and child pages named **directions.htm**, **menus.htm**, and **recipes.htm**.
2. Create a folder for the Web site in the drive and folder where you save your Web site files, then name it **jacobs**.
3. Create a Web site with the name **Jacob's**.
4. Create an assets folder for the Web site and set the assets folder as the default location for images.
5. Open dwa_6.htm from the folder where your Data Files are stored, then save it as **index.htm** in the jacobs folder.
6. Save the jacobs.jpg file in the assets folder.
7. Set index.htm as the home page.
8. Using Figure A-28 and your storyboard as guides, create the additional pages shown for the Web site.
9. View the site map that displays page titles.

FIGURE A-28
Completed Project Builder 2

Figure A-29 shows the Audi Web site, a past selection for the Macromedia Site of the Day. To visit the current Audi Web site connect to the Internet, go to *www.course.com*, navigate to the page for this book, click the Online Companion link, then click the link for this chapter. The current page might differ from the figure since dynamic Web sites are updated frequently to reflect current information. If you are viewing the Web page on a screen whose resolution is set to 800×600, you will see that the design fits very well. The main navigation structure is accessed through the images along the right side of the page. You can also click images in the center o the page to open new pages. The page title is Audi World Site.

Go to the Macromedia Web site at *www.macromedia.com*, click the Visit the Showcase link, then click the current Site of the Day. Explore the site and answer the following questions:

1. Do you see page titles for each page you visit?
2. Do the page titles accurately reflect the page content?
3. View the pages using more than one screen resolution, if possible. For which resolution does the site appear to be designed?

4. Is the navigation structure clear?
5. How is the navigation structure organized?

6. Why do you think this site was chosen as a Site of the Day?

FIGURE A-29
Design Project

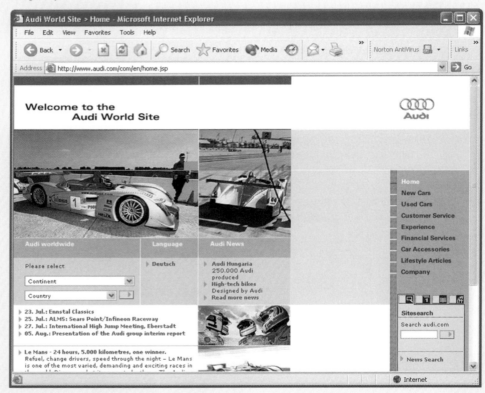

Work with a group to come up with a plan for a Web site that the group will create entirely on its own, without any data files. The focus of the Web site can be on any topic, organization, sports team, club, or company that you would like. Depending on the size of your group, you can assign individual elements of the project to group members, or work collectively to create the finished product. You will build on this Web site from chapter to chapter, so you must do each Group Project assignment in each chapter to complete your Web site.

1. Decide among your members what type of Web site you would like to create. It can be a personal Web site about you, or a business Web site that promotes a fictitious or real company, or an informational Web site that provides information about a topic, cause, or organization.

2. With the whole group participating, write a list of questions and answers about the Web site you have decided to create. Assign team members questions and have them report back to the group with answers.

3. Brainstorm as a group to construct a storyboard for your Web site to include at least four pages. The storyboard should include the home page with at least three child pages under it. Assign a team member the task of creating the storyboard.

4. Assign a team member the task of creating a root folder and an assets folder to house the Web site assets, then set it as the default location for images.

5. Create a blank page named **index.htm** as a placeholder for the home page, then set it as the home page.

6. Assign team members to collect content, such as pictures or text to use in your Web site. You can use a digital camera to take photos, scan pictures, or create your own graphics using a program such as Macromedia Fireworks. Gather the content in a central location that is accessible to the team as you develop your site.

DEVELOPING A WEB PAGE

1. Create head content and set page properties.

2. Create, import, and format text.

3. Add links to Web pages.

4. Use the History panel and edit code.

5. Modify and test Web pages.

DEVELOPING A WEB PAGE

Introduction

The process of developing a Web page requires several steps. If the page is a home page, you need to decide on the head content. The head content contains information used by search engines to help viewers find your Web site. You also need to choose the colors for the page background as well as the links. You then need to add the page content and format it attractively, and add links to other pages in the Web site or to other Web sites. To ensure that all links work correctly and are current, you need to test them regularly.

Understanding Page Layout

Before you add content to a page, consider the following guidelines for laying out pages:

Use White Space Effectively. A living room crammed with too much furniture makes it difficult to appreciate the individual pieces. The same is true of a Web page. Too many text blocks, links, and images can be distracting. Consider leaving some white space on each page. White space, which is not necessarily white, is the area on a Web page that contains no text or graphics.

Limit Multimedia Elements. Too many multimedia elements, such as graphics, video clips, or sounds, may result in a page that takes too much time to load. Viewers may leave your Web site before the entire page finishes loading. Use multimedia elements only if you have a good reason.

Keep it Simple. Often the simplest Web sites are the most appealing and are also the easiest to create and maintain. A simple Web site that works well is far superior to a complex one that contains errors.

Use an Intuitive Navigation Structure. Make sure the navigation structure is easy to use. Viewers should always know where they are in the site and be able to find their way back to the home page. If viewers get lost, they may leave the site rather than struggle to find their way around.

Apply a Consistent Theme. To help give pages in your Web site a consistent appearance, consider designing your pages using elements that relate to a common theme.

Tools You'll Use

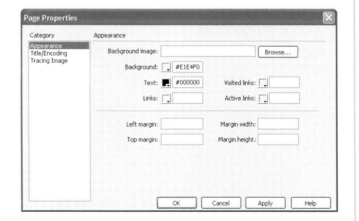

CREATE HEAD CONTENT AND SET PAGE PROPERTIES

What You'll Do

In this lesson, you will learn how to enter titles, keywords, and descriptions in the head content section of a Web page. You will also change the background color for a Web page.

Creating the Head Content

A Web page is composed of two distinct sections: the head content and the body. The **head content** includes the page title that is displayed in the title bar of the browser and some important page elements, called meta tags, that are not visible in the browser. **Meta tags** are HTML codes that include information about the page, such as keywords and descriptions.

Meta tags are also used to provide the server information such as the PICS rating for the page. PICS is the acronym for **Platform for Internet Content Selection.** This is a rating system for Web pages that is similar to rating systems used for movies. **Keywords** are words that relate to the content of the Web site. A **description** is a short paragraph that describes the content and features of the Web site. For

---

DESIGNTIP **Using Websafe colors**

Before 1994, colors appeared differently on different types of computers. For instance, if a designer chose a particular shade of red in a document created on a Windows computer, he or she could not be certain that the same shade of red would appear on a Macintosh computer. In 1994, Netscape developed the first **Websafe color palette,** a set of colors that appears consistently in all browsers and on Macintosh, Windows, and UNIX platforms. If you want your Web pages to be viewed across a wide variety of computer platforms, make sure you choose Websafe colors for all your page elements. Dreamweaver has two Websafe color palettes, Color Cubes and Continuous Tones, each of which contains 216 Websafe colors. Color Cubes is the default color palette. To choose a different color palette, click Modify on the menu bar, click Page Properties, click the Appearance category, click the Background, Text, or Links color box to open the color picker, click the color picker list arrow, then click the color palette you want.

---

instance, "travel" and "tours" would be appropriate keywords for the TripSmart Web site. It is important to include concise, useful information in the head content, because search engines find Web pages by matching the title, description, and key-words in the head content of Web pages with keywords that viewers enter in search engine text boxes. The **body** is the part of the page that appears in a browser window. It contains all the page content that is visible to viewers, such as text, graphics, and links.

Setting Web Page Properties

When you create a Web page, one of the first design decisions that you should make is choosing the **background color**, or the color that fills the entire Web page. The background color should complement the colors used for text, links, and graphics that are placed on the page. A strong contrast between the text color and the background color makes it easier for view-ers to read the text on your Web page. You can choose a light background color and a dark text color, or a dark background color and a light text color. A white background with dark text, though not terribly exciting, provides good contrast and is the easiest to read for most viewers. The next important design decision you need to make is to choose the **default font** and **default link colors**, which are the colors used by the browser to display text, links, and visited links. The default color for **unvisited links**, or links that the viewer has not clicked yet, is blue. In Dreamweaver, unvisited links are simply called **links**. The default color for **visited links**, or links that have been previ-ously clicked, is purple. You change the background color, text, and link colors using the color picker in the Page Properties dialog box. You can choose col-ors from one of the five Dreamweaver color palettes, as shown in Figure B-1.

QUICK**TIP**

Not all browsers recognize link color settings.

FIGURE B-1
Color picker showing color palettes

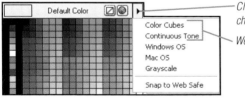

Click list arrow to choose a color palette

Websafe palettes

DESIGN**TIP**   **Making pages accessible to viewers of all abilities**

Never assume that all your viewers have perfect vision and hearing or full use of both hands. There are several techniques you can use to ensure that your Web site is accessible to individuals with disabilities. These techniques include using alternate text with graphic images, avoiding certain colors on Web pages, and supplying text as an alternate source for information that is presented in an audio file. You can test your Web site for accessibility before publishing it by submitting it to be tested by **Bobby**, a free service provided by **CAST**, the Center for Applied Special Technology. The Web site address for information about Bobby is *www.cast.org/bobby/*. Macromedia also provides a vehicle for testing Web site compliance with Section 508 accessibility guidelines. For more information, visit the Macromedia Web site at http://*www.macromedia.com/macromedia/accessibility/*.

Edit a page title

1. Click the **Site list arrow** on the Files panel, then click **TripSmart** (if necessary).

2. Double-click **index.htm** in the Files panel to open the TripSmart home page, click **View** on the menu bar, then click **Head Content**.

   The Title icon and Meta icon are now visible in the head content section, as shown in Figure B-2.

3. Click the **Title icon** in the head content section.

   The page title TripSmart - The Smart Way To Go appears in the Title text box in the Property inspector.

4. Select TripSmart - The Smart Way To Go in the Title text box in the Property inspector, type **TripSmart - Serving All Your Travel Needs**, then press **[Enter]** (Win) or **[return]** (Mac).

   Compare your screen with Figure B-3. The new title is better, because it incorporates the word "travel," a word that potential customers might use as a keyword when using a search engine.

   > TIP You can also change the page title using the Title text box on the Document toolbar.

You opened the TripSmart Web site, opened the home page in Design view, opened the head content section, and changed the page title.

FIGURE B-2
Viewing the head content

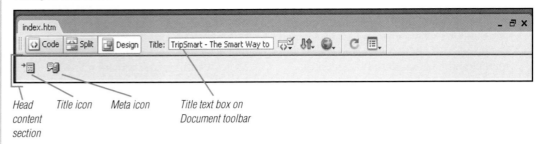

Head content section   Title icon   Meta icon   Title text box on Document toolbar

FIGURE B-3
Property inspector displaying new page title

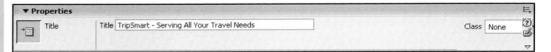

DESIGNTIP Planning the page layout

When you begin developing the content for your Web site, you need to decide what content to include and how to arrange each element on each page. You must design the content with the audience in mind. What is the age group of your audience? What reading level is appropriate? Should you use a formal or informal tone? Should the pages be simple, containing mostly text, or rich with images and multimedia files? Usually the first page that your audience will see when they visit your Web site is the home page. The home page should be designed so that viewers will feel "at home," and comfortable finding their way around the pages in your site. To ensure that viewers do not get lost in your Web site, make sure you design all the pages with a consistent look and feel. You can use templates to maintain a common look for each page. **Templates** are Web pages that contain the basic layout for each page in the site, including the location of a company logo or a menu of buttons.

Insert bar displaying the HTML category

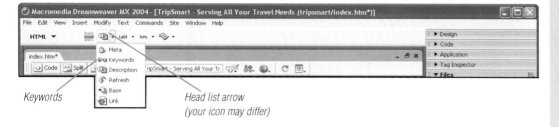

Keywords

Head list arrow
(your icon may differ)

Enter keywords

1. Click the **Insert bar list arrow**, then click **HTML**.

2. Click the **Head list arrow**, as shown in Figure B-4, then click **Keywords**.

   Some buttons on the Insert bar include a list arrow indicating that there is a menu of choices beneath the current button. The button that you select last will appear on the Insert bar until you select another.

3. Type **travel**, **traveling**, **supplies**, **trips**, **vacations** in the Keywords text box, as shown in Figure B-5, then click **OK**.

   You added keywords relating to travel to the head content of the TripSmart home page.

FIGURE B-5
Keywords dialog box

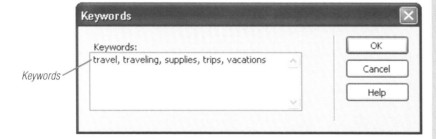

Keywords

DESIGNTIP   **Entering keywords and descriptions**

Search engines use keywords, descriptions, and titles to find pages after a user enters search terms. Therefore, it is very important to anticipate the search terms your potential customers would use and include these words in the keywords, description, or title. Many search engines display page titles and descriptions in their search results. Some search engines limit the number of keywords that they will index, so make sure you list the most important keywords first. Keep your keywords and description concise to ensure that all search engines will include your site.

Enter a description

1. Click the **Head list arrow** on the Insert bar, then click **Description**.

2. Type **TripSmart is a comprehensive travel store. We can help you plan trips, make travel arrangements, and supply you with travel gear.**

   Your screen should resemble Figure B-6.

3. Click **OK**.

4. Click the **Show Code view button**  on the Document toolbar.

   Notice the title, keywords, and description appear in the HTML code in the document window, as shown in Figure B-7.

5. Click the **Show Design view button** to return to Design view.

6. Click **View** on the menu bar, then click **Head Content** to close the head content section.

You added a description of the TripSmart company to the head content of the home page. You then viewed the home page in Code view and examined the HTML code for the head content.

FIGURE B-6
Description dialog box

Description

Description

FIGURE B-7
Head Content displayed in Code view

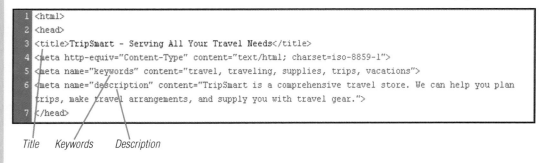

```
1 <html>
2 <head>
3 <title>TripSmart - Serving All Your Travel Needs</title>
4 <meta http-equiv="Content-Type" content="text/html; charset=iso-8859-1">
5 <meta name="keywords" content="travel, traveling, supplies, trips, vacations">
6 <meta name="description" content="TripSmart is a comprehensive travel store. We can help you plan
  trips, make travel arrangements, and supply you with travel gear.">
7 </head>
```

Title *Keywords* *Description*

Developing a Web Page

Background color box

Hexadecimal number for white

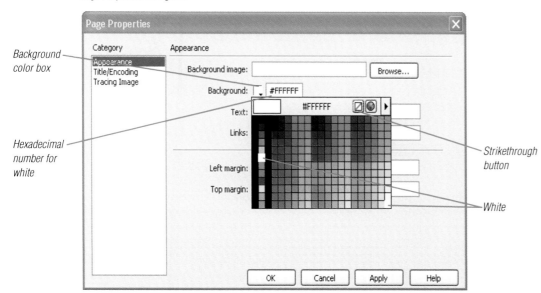

Strikethrough button

White

1. Click **Modify** on the menu bar, then click **Page Properties** to open the Page Properties dialog box.

2. Click the **Appearance category**.

3. Click the **Background color box** ☐ to open the color picker, as shown in Figure B-8.

4. Click the last color in the bottom row (white).

5. Click **Apply**, then click **OK**.

   Clicking Apply lets you see the changes you made to the Web page without closing the Page Properties dialog box.

   > TIP If you don't like the color you chose, click the Strikethrough button ☐ in the color picker to switch back to the default color.

   The background color of the Web page is now white. The black text against the white background provides a nice contrast and makes the text easy to read.

You used the Page Properties dialog box to change the background color to white.

Understanding hexadecimal values

Each color is assigned a **hexadecimal** value, a value that represents the amount of red, green, and blue present in the color. For example, white, which is made of equal parts of red, green, and blue, has a hexadecimal value of FFFFFF. Each pair of characters in the hexadecimal value represents the red, green, and blue values. The hexadecimal number system is based on 16, rather than 10 in the decimal number system. Since the hexadecimal number system includes only numbers up to 9, values after 9 use the letters of the alphabet. A represents the number 10 in the hexadecimal number system. F represents the number 15.

CREATE, IMPORT AND FORMAT TEXT

What You'll Do

In this lesson, you will apply heading styles and text styles to text on the TripSmart home page. You will also import an HTML file and set text properties for the text on the new page.

Creating and Importing Text

Most information in Web pages is presented in the form of text. You can type text directly in Dreamweaver or copy and paste it from another software program. To import text from a Microsoft Word file, you use the Import Word Document command. Not only will the formatting be preserved, but clean HTML code will be generated. When you import Word text into Dreamweaver, you have a choice of using the styles that are associated with the Word file or sticking with HTML font tags. You make this choice in the General Preferences dialog box. When you import text, it is important to keep in mind that visitors to your site must have the same fonts installed on their computers as the fonts applied to the imported text. Otherwise, the text may appear incorrectly.

Using keyboard shortcuts

When working with text, the standard Windows keyboard shortcuts for the Cut, Copy, and Paste commands are very useful. These are [Ctrl][X] (Win) or ⌘[X] (Mac) for Cut, [Ctrl][C] (Win) or ⌘[C] (Mac) for Copy, and [Ctrl][V] (Win) or ⌘[V] (Mac) for Paste. You can view all Dreamweaver keyboard shortcuts using the Keyboard Shortcuts dialog box, which lets you view existing shortcuts for menu commands, tools, or miscellaneous functions, such as copying HTML or inserting an image. You can also create your own shortcuts or assign shortcuts from other applications, such as Macromedia FreeHand or Adobe Illustrator and Photoshop. To view or modify keyboard shortcuts, click the Keyboard Shortcuts command on the Edit menu, then select the shortcut key set you want. The Keyboard Shortcuts feature is also available in Macromedia Fireworks and Flash. A printable version of all Dreamweaver keyboard shortcuts can be downloaded from the Dreamweaver Support Center at *http://www.macromedia.com/support/dreamweaver/documentation/dwmx_shortcuts/*.

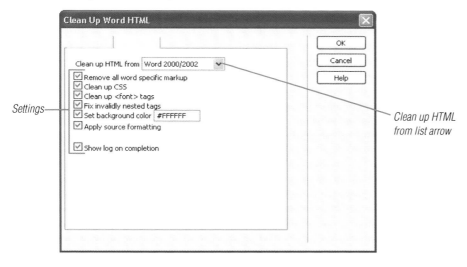

Settings

Clean up HTML from list arrow

Importing Microsoft Office documents

Macromedia has made enormous strides in providing for easy transfer of data between Microsoft Office documents and Dreamweaver MX 2004 Web pages. When importing a Word or Excel document, the formatting will be preserved as it is placed on a Web page. However, if you know in advance that you are creating a document that will later be placed on a Web page; it is still smart to format the text after you import it into Dreamweaver. This practice will save time and unnecessary frustration. It is also a good idea to use the Clean Up Word HTML command after importing a Word file. It is also very important to remove the check mark in the Use CSS instead of HTML tags check box if you do not want to import Word styles.

Import text

1. Click **Edit** (Win) or **Dreamweaver** (Mac) on the menu bar, click **Preferences**, then click the General category (if necessary).

2. Verify that the Use CSS instead of HTML tags check box is not checked, then click **OK**.

   TIP   It is very important to remove the check mark in the Use CSS instead of HTML tags check box unless you want to import Word styles from imported text into your HTML document. Leaving this option checked will also direct the Property inspector to display text sizes in points, rather than in HTML font sizes.

3. Click to the right of the Travel Tidbits graphic on the newsletter.htm page.

4. Click **File** on the menu bar, point to **Import**, click **Word Document**, navigate to the drive and folder where your Data Files are stored, double-click the **chapter_b folder** (Win) or click the **chapter_b folder** (Mac), then double-click **packing_essentials.doc**.

5. Click **Commands** on the menu bar, then click **Clean Up Word HTML**.

   TIP   If a dialog box appears stating that Dreamweaver was unable to determine the version of Word used to generate this document, click OK, click the Clean up HTML from list arrow, then choose a version of Word.

6. Make sure each check box in the Clean Up Word HTML dialog box is checked, as shown in Figure B-12, click **OK**, then click **OK** again to close the Clean Up Word HTML Results window.

7. Select the imported text, click the **Style list arrow**, then click **None**.

You imported a Word HTML file, then used the Cleanup Word HTML command.

MACROMEDIA DREAMWEAVER B-15

Set text properties

1. Click the **Insert bar list arrow**, click **Common**, then place the insertion point anywhere within the words Packing Essentials.

2. Click the **Format list arrow** in the Property inspector, then click **Heading 3**.

   The Heading 3 format is applied to the entire paragraph.

3. Click the **Align Center button** ≣ in the Property inspector to center the heading.

4. Select the words Packing Essentials, click the **Font list arrow**, then click **Arial, Helvetica, sans-serif**.

   Because setting a font is a character command, you must select all the characters you want to format before applying a font.

   TIP You can modify the font combinations in the Font list by clicking Text on the menu bar, pointing to Font, then clicking Edit Font List.

5. With the heading still selected, click the **Text Color button** ☐ in the Property inspector to open the color picker, then click the dark blue color in the third row of the first column (#000066).

   TIP You can also type #000066 in the color text box in the Property inspector to select the color in Step 5.

   (continued)

FIGURE B-13
Properties of Packing Essentials text

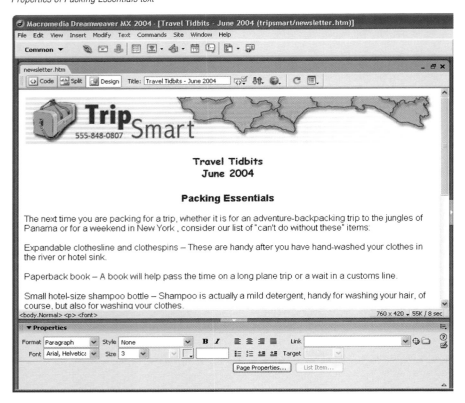

6. Click to the left of the T in The next time you are packing, press and hold **[Shift]**, scroll to the end of the text, click to place the insertion point after the end of the last sentence, then release [Shift].

7. Click the **Font list arrow** in the Property inspector, click **Arial, Helvetica, sans-serif**, click the **Size list arrow** in the Property inspector, then click **3**.

   TIP To change the size of selected text, use either the Format list arrow or the Size list arrow, but not both.

8. Click anywhere on the page to deselect the text, save your work, then compare your screen to Figure B-13.

You formatted the Packing Essentials text using the Heading 3 style and the Arial, Helvetica, sans-serif font combination. Next, you centered the heading on the page and changed the text color to a dark blue. You then selected the rest of the text on the page and changed it to the Arial, Helvetica, sans-serif font combination with a text size of 3.

DESIGNTIP Choosing fonts

There are two classifications of fonts: sans serif and serif. **Sans-serif fonts** are block-style characters that are often used for headings and subheadings. The headings in this book use a sans-serif font. Examples of sans-serif fonts include Arial, Verdana, and Helvetica. **Serif fonts** are more ornate, and contain small extra strokes at the beginning and end of the characters. Some people consider serif fonts easier to read in printed material, because the extra strokes lead your eye from one character to the next. This paragraph you are reading uses a serif font. Examples of serif fonts include Times New Roman, Times, and Georgia. Many designers feel that a sans-serif font is preferable when the content of a Web site is primarily intended to be read on the screen, but that a serif font is preferable if the content will be printed. When you choose fonts, you need to keep in mind the amount of text each page will contain and whether most viewers will read the text on-screen or print it out. A good rule of thumb is to limit each Web site to no more than three font variations. Using more than three may make your Web site look unprofessional and suggest the "ransom note effect." The phrase **ransom note effect** implies that fonts have been randomly used in a document without regard to style, similar to a ransom note made up of words cut from various sources and pasted onto a page.

ADD LINKS TO WEB PAGES

What You'll Do

In this lesson, you will open the home page and add links to the navigation bar that link to the Catalog, Services, Tours, and Newsletter pages. You will then insert an e-mail link at the bottom of the page and create page titles for the untitled pages in the site map.

Adding Links to Web Pages

Links provide the real strength for Web pages. Links make it possible for viewers to navigate through all the pages in a Web site and to connect to other pages you choose anywhere on the Web. Viewers are more likely to return to Web sites that have a user-friendly navigation structure. Viewers also enjoy Web sites that have interesting links to other Web pages or other Web sites.

To add links to a Web page, you first select the text or graphic that you want to serve as a link, then you specify a path to the page to which you want to link in the Link text box in the Property inspector. After you add all your links, you can open the site map to see a diagram of how the linked pages relate to each other.

When you create links on a Web page, it is important to avoid **broken links**, or links that cannot find their intended destinations. You can accidentally cause a broken link by typing the incorrect address for the link in the Link text box. Broken links are often caused by companies merging, going out of business, or simply moving their Web site addresses.

In addition to adding links to your pages, you should also provide a **point of contact**, or a place on a Web page that provides viewers with a means of contacting the company. A common point of contact is a **mailto: link**, which is an e-mail address that viewers with questions or problems can use to contact someone at the company's headquarters.

FIGURE B-21

TripSmart site map

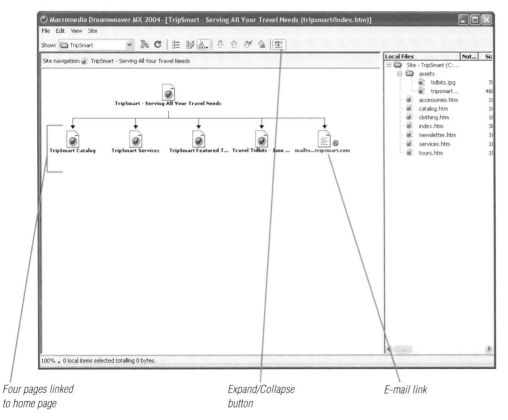

Four pages linked
to home page

Expand/Collapse
button

E-mail link

1. Click the **View list arrow** on the Files panel, then click **Map view** to view the site map.

2. Click the **Expand/Collapse button** ⊞ on the Files panel to expand the site map (Win).

   The site map shows the home page, the four pages that are linked to it, and the e-mail link on the home page.

3. Click **View** on the Files panel menu bar, then click **Show Page Titles** (Win), or click the **Files panel list arrow**, point to **View**, then click **Show Page Titles** (Mac) (if necessary).

4. Select the first Untitled Document page in the site map, click the words **Untitled Document**, type **TripSmart Catalog,** then press **[Enter]** (Win) or **[return]** (Mac).

5. Repeat Step 4 for the other two Untitled Document pages, naming them **TripSmart Services** and **TripSmart Featured Tours**, as shown in Figure B-21.

6. Click the **Expand/Collapse button** ⊞ on the toolbar to collapse the site map.

7. Click the **View list arrow** on the Files panel, then click **Local view** (Win).

You viewed the site map and added page titles to the untitled pages.

USE THE HISTORY PANEL AND EDIT CODE

What You'll Do

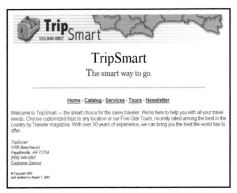

 In this lesson, you will use the History panel to undo formatting changes you make to a horizontal rule. You will then use the Code inspector to view the HTML code for the horizontal rule. You will also insert a date object and then view its code in the Code inspector.

Using the History Panel

Throughout the process of creating a Web page, it's likely that you will make mistakes along the way. Fortunately, you can use the History panel to undo your mistakes. The **History panel** records each editing and formatting task you perform and displays each one in a list in the order in which you completed them. Each task listed in the History panel is called a **step**. You can drag the **slider** on the left side of the History panel to undo or redo steps, as shown in Figure B-22. By default, the History panel records 50 steps. You can change the number of steps the History panel records in the General category of the Preferences dialog box. However, keep in mind that setting this number too high might require additional memory and could hinder the way Dreamweaver operates.

Understanding other History panel features

Dragging the slider up and down in the History panel is a quick way to undo or redo steps. However, the History panel offers much more. It has the capability to "memorize" certain tasks and consolidate them into one command. This is a useful feature for steps that are executed repetitively on Web pages. Some Dreamweaver features, such as drag and drop, cannot be recorded in the History panel and have a red x placed next to them. The History panel also does not show steps performed in the Files panel.

Viewing HTML Code in the Code Inspector

If you enjoy writing code, you occasionally might want to make changes to Web pages by entering HTML code rather than using the panels and tools in Design view. You can view HTML code in Dreamweaver using Code view, Code and Design views, or the Code inspector. The **Code inspector**, shown in Figure B-23, is a separate window that displays the current page in Code view. The advantage of using the Code inspector is that you can see a full-screen view of your page in Design view while viewing the underlying code in a floating window that you can resize and position wherever you want.

You can add advanced features, such as JavaScript functions, to Web pages by copying and pasting code from one page to another in the Code inspector. A **JavaScript** function is a block of code that adds dynamic content such as rollovers or interactive forms to a Web page. A **rollover** is a special effect that changes the appearance of an object when the mouse "rolls over" it.

QUICKTIP

If you are new to HTML, you can use the Reference panel to find answers to your HTML questions. The Reference panel is part of the Code panel group and contains many resources besides HTML help, such as JavaScript help.

FIGURE B-22
History panel

Slider   Red x indicates action cannot be undone

FIGURE B-23
Code inspector

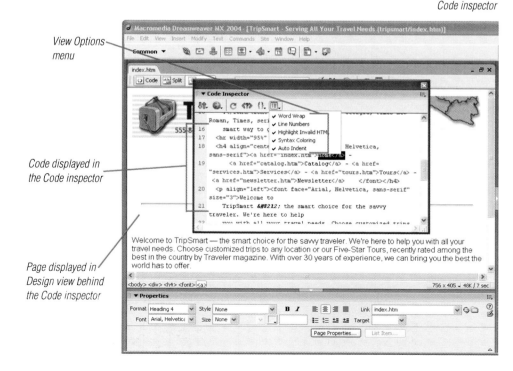

View Options menu

Code displayed in the Code inspector

Page displayed in Design view behind the Code inspector

Use the History panel

1. Click **Window** on the menu bar, then click **History**.

   The History panel opens and displays steps you have recently performed.

2. Click the **History panel list arrow**, click **Clear History**, as shown in Figure B-24, then click **Yes** to close the warning box (if necessary).

3. Select the horizontal rule on the home page.

   A **horizontal rule** is a line used to separate page elements or to organize information on a page.

4. Select the number in the W text box, type **90**, click the list arrow next to the W text box, click **%**, press **[Tab]**, then compare your screen to Figure B-25.

5. Using the Property inspector, change the width of the horizontal rule to 80%, click the **Align list arrow**, then click **Left**.

6. Drag the slider on the History panel up to Set Width: 90%, as shown in Figure B-26.

   The bottom two steps in the History panel appear gray, indicating that these steps have been undone.

7. Click the **History panel list arrow**, then click **Close panel group** to close the History panel.

You formatted the horizontal rule, made changes to it, then used the History panel to undo the changes.

FIGURE B-24

Clearing the History panel

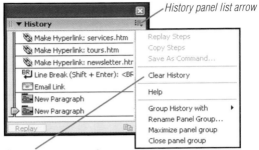

History panel list arrow

Clear History command

FIGURE B-25

Property inspector settings for horizontal rule

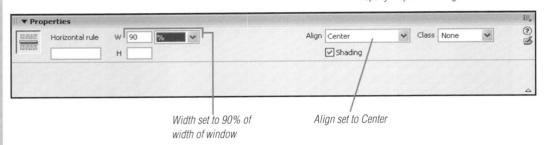

Width set to 90% of width of window

Align set to Center

FIGURE B-26

Undoing steps using the History panel

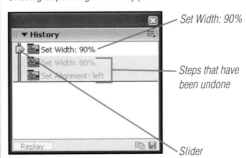

Set Width: 90%

Steps that have been undone

Slider

Developing a Web Page

Use the Code inspector

1. Click the **horizontal rule** to select it (if necessary), click **Window** on the menu bar, then click **Code Inspector**.

   The Code inspector highlights the code for the horizontal rule.

   TIP You can also press [F10] to display the Code inspector.

2. Click the **View Options list arrow** on the Code inspector toolbar to display the View Options menu, then click **Word Wrap** (if necessary), to activate Word Wrap.

   The Word Wrap feature forces text to stay within the confines of the Code inspector window, allowing you to read without scrolling sideways.

3. Click the **View Options list arrow**, then verify that the Highlight Invalid HTML, Line Numbers, Syntax Coloring, and Auto Indent menu items are checked, as shown in Figure B-27.

4. Replace the 90% horizontal rule width in the code with 80%.

5. Click **Refresh** in the Property inspector.

   After typing in the Code inspector, you must refresh your changes to see them.

You changed the width of the horizontal rule by changing the code in the Code inspector.

FIGURE B-27
Viewing the View Options menu in the Code inspector

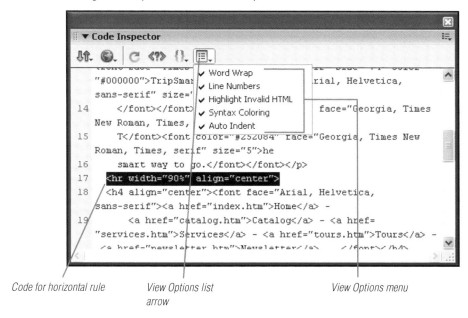

Code for horizontal rule   View Options list arrow   View Options menu

Use the Reference panel

1. Click the **Reference button** <?> on the Code inspector toolbar, as shown in Figure B-28, to open the Code panel group with the Reference panel displayed.

   > **TIP** Verify that the horizontal rule is still selected, or you will not see the horizontal rule description in the Reference panel.

2. Read the information about horizontal rules in the Reference panel, as shown in Figure B-29, then click the **Code panel group title bar** (Win) or the **collapse triangle** in the Code panel title bar (Mac) to collapse the Code panel group.

3. Close the Code inspector.

You read information about horizontal rule settings in the Reference panel.

FIGURE B-28
Reference button on the Code inspector toolbar

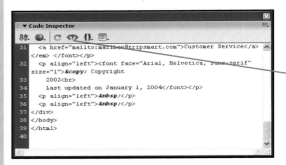

Reference button

FIGURE B-29
Viewing the Reference panel

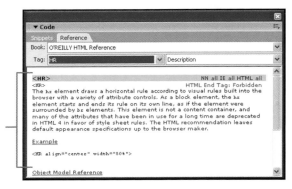

Information on the HR (horizontal rule) tag

Inserting comments

A handy Dreamweaver feature is the ability to insert comments into HTML code. Comments can provide helpful information describing portions of the code, such as a JavaScript function. You can create comments in any Dreamweaver view, but you must turn on Invisible Elements to see them in Design view. To create a comment, click the Insert bar list arrow, click Common, click the Comment button, type a comment in the Comment dialog box, then click OK. Comments are not visible in browser windows.

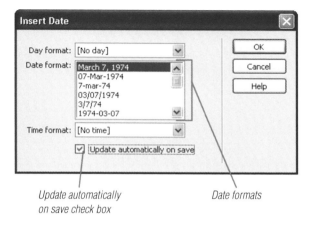

Update automatically
on save check box   Date formats

Insert a date object

1. Select January 1, 2004, then press **[Delete]** (Win) or **[delete]** (Mac).

2. Click the **Date button** 🗓 on the Insert bar, then click **March 7, 1974** in the Date format text box.

3. Click the **Update automatically on save check box**, as shown in Figure B-30, then click **OK**.

4. Click the **Show Code and Design views button** 🔲 Split .

   Notice that the code has changed to reflect the date object, as shown in Figure B-31.

5. Return to Design view.

You inserted a date object that will be updated automatically when you open and save the home page.

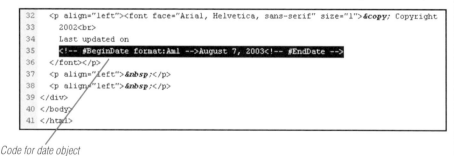

```
32  <p align="left"><font face="Arial, Helvetica, sans-serif" size="1">&copy; Copyright
33    2002<br>
34    Last updated on
35    <!-- #BeginDate format:Am1 -->August 7, 2003<!-- #EndDate -->
36  </font></p>
37  <p align="left"> </p>
38  <p align="left"> </p>
39  </div>
40  </body>
41  </html>
```

Code for date object

MODIFY AND TEST WEB PAGES

What You'll Do

 In this lesson, you will preview the home page in the browser to check for typographical errors, grammatical errors, broken links, and overall appearance. After previewing, you will make slight formatting adjustments to the page to improve its appearance.

Testing and Modifying Web Pages

Testing Web pages is a continuous process. You never really finish a Web site, as there are always additions and corrections to make. As you add and modify pages, you must test each page as part of the development process. The best way to test a Web page is to preview it in a browser window to make sure that all text and graphic elements appear the way you expect them to. You should also test your links to make sure they work properly. You also need to proofread your text to make sure it contains all the necessary information for the page and no typographical or grammatical errors. Designers typically view a page in a browser, return to Design view to make necessary changes, then view the page in a browser again. This process may be repeated many times before the page is ready for publishing. In fact, it is sometimes difficult to stop making improvements to a page and move on to another project. You need to strike a balance between quality, creativity, and productivity.

DESIGNTIP   Using "Under Construction" pages

Many people are tempted to insert an unfinished page as a placeholder for a page that will be finished later. Rather than have real content, these pages usually contain text or a graphic that indicates the page is not finished, or "under construction". You should not publish a Web page that has a link to an unfinished page. It is frustrating to click a link for a page you want to open only to find an "under construction" note or graphic displayed. You want to make the best possible impression on your viewing audience. If you cannot complete a page before publishing it, at least provide enough information on it to make it "worth the trip."

Testing a Web Page Using Different Browsers

Because users access the Internet using a wide variety of computer systems, it is important to design your pages so that all browsers and screen sizes can display them well. You should test your pages using different browsers and a wide variety of screen sizes and resolutions to ensure the best view of your page by all types of computer equipment. Although the most common screen size that designers use today is 800×600, many viewers view at 1024×768. A page that is designed for a screen resolution of 800×600 will look much better at that setting than at a higher one. Many designers place a statement such as "this Web site is best viewed at 800×600" on the home page. To view your page using different screen sizes, click the Window Size pop-up menu in the middle of the status bar (Win) or at the bottom of the document window (Mac), then choose the setting you want to use. Table B-1 lists the default Dreamweaver window screen sizes.

TABLE B-1: Dreamweaver Default Window Screen Sizes	
window size (inside dimensions of the browser window without borders)	**monitor size**
592W	
536×196	640×480, default
600×300	640×480, maximized
760×420	800×600, maximized
795×470	832×624, maximized
955×600	1024×768, maximized
544×378	Web TV

Modify a Web page

1. Click the **Restore Window button** on the index.htm title bar to decrease the size of the home page window.

2. Click the **Window Size list arrow** on the status bar, as shown in Figure B-32, then click **600 × 300 (640 × 480, Maximized)**.

   A viewer using this setting will be forced to use the horizontal scroll bar to view the entire page. This should be avoided, but very few people view at this resolution anymore.

   > TIP You cannot use the Window Size options if your document window is maximized.

3. Click the **Window Size list arrow**, click **760 × 420 (800 × 600, Maximized)**.

4. Replace the period after The smart way to go with an exclamation point.

5. Shorten the horizontal rule to 75%.

6. Select the text "The Smart way to go!" then change the text size to 5.

7. Click the **Maximize button** on the index.htm title bar to maximize the home page window.

8. Save your work.

You viewed the home page using two different window sizes and you made simple formatting changes to the page.

FIGURE B-32
Window screen sizes

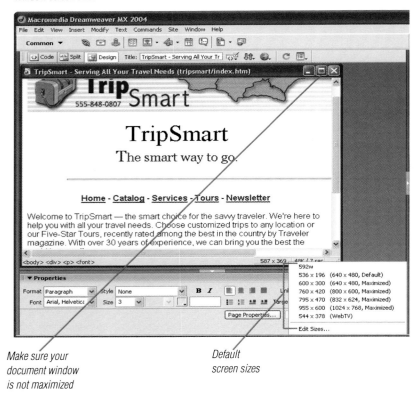

Make sure your document window is not maximized

Default screen sizes

Depending on the size of your group, you can assign individual elements of the project to group members, or work collectively to create the finished product.

In this assignment, you will continue to work on the Web site your group defined in Chapter A. In Chapter A, you created a storyboard for your Web site with at least four pages. You also created a local root folder for your Web site and an assets folder to store the Web site asset files. You set the assets folder as the default storage location for your images. You began to collect information and resources for your Web site and started working on the home page.

1. Brainstorm as a group and come up with a title and several appropriate keywords for your site. Work together to write a description for the site.
2. Add the title, keywords, and description to the head content for the home page.
3. Assign a team member the task of creating the main page content for the home page and formatting it attractively.
4. Assign a team member the task of adding the address and other contact information to the home page, including an e-mail address.
5. Consult your storyboard and assign a team member the task of designing the navigation bar and linking it to the appropriate pages.
6. Add a last updated statement to the home page with a date that will automatically update when the page is saved.
7. Edit and format the page content until the group is satisfied with the results.
8. Verify that each page has a page title by viewing the site map.
9. Verify that all links, including the e-mail link, work correctly.
10. When you are satisfied with the home page, review the check list questions shown in Figure B-39, then make any necessary changes.
11. Save your work.

FIGURE B-39
Group Project check list

Web Site Check List

1. Do all pages have a page title?
2. Does the home page have a description and keywords?
3. Does the home page contain contact information, including an e-mail address?
4. Do all completed pages in the Web site have consistent navigation links?
5. Does the home page have a last updated statement that will automatically update when the page is saved?
6. Do all pages have attractively formatted text?
7. Do all paths for links and images work correctly?
8. Does the home page view well using at least two different screen resolutions?

CHAPTER C

WORKING WITH TEXT AND GRAPHICS

1. Create unordered and ordered lists.

2. Create, apply, and edit Cascading Style Sheets.

3. Insert and align graphics.

4. Enhance an image and use alternate text.

5. Insert a background image and perform site maintenance.

CHAPTER C
WORKING WITH TEXT AND GRAPHICS

Introduction
Most Web pages contain a combination of text and graphics. Dreamweaver provides many tools for working with text and graphics that you can use to make your Web pages attractive and easy to use. Dreamweaver also has tools that help you format text quickly and ensure a consistent appearance of text elements across all your Web pages.

Formatting Text as Lists
If a Web page contains a large amount of text, it can be difficult for viewers to digest it all. You can break up the monotony of large blocks of text by creating lists. You can create four types of lists in Dreamweaver: unordered lists, ordered lists, directory lists, and menu lists.

Using Cascading Style Sheets
You can save time and ensure that all your page elements have a consistent appearance by using Cascading Style Sheets (CSS). You can use Cascading Style Sheets to define formatting attributes for page elements such as text and tables. You can then apply the formatting attributes you define to any element in a single document or to all of the pages in a Web site.

Using Graphics to Enhance Web Pages
Graphics make Web pages visually stimulating and more exciting than pages that contain only text. However, you should use graphics sparingly. If you think of text as the meat and potatoes of a Web site, the graphics would be the seasoning. You should add graphics to a page just as you would add seasoning to food. A little seasoning enhances the flavor and brings out the quality of the dish. Too much seasoning overwhelms the dish and masks the flavor of the main ingredients. Too little seasoning results in a bland dish. There are many ways to work with graphics so that they complement the content of pages in a Web site. There are specific file formats that should be used to save graphics for Web sites to ensure maximum quality with minimum file size. You should store graphics in a Web site's assets folder in an organized fashion.

Tools You'll Use

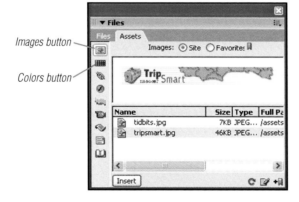

Images button

Colors button

Attach Style Sheet button   New CSS Style button

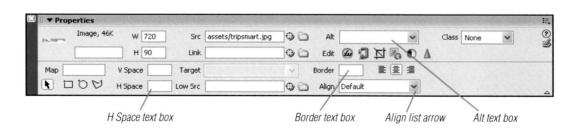

H Space text box   Border text box   Align list arrow   Alt text box

CREATE UNORDERED AND ORDERED LISTS

What You'll Do

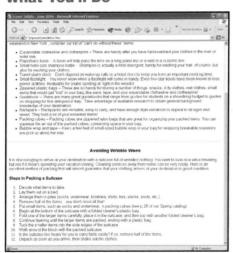

 In this lesson, you will create an unordered list of essential items to pack on the TripSmart newsletter page. You will also import text describing the steps for packing a suitcase on the newsletter page, and format it as an ordered list.

Creating Unordered Lists

Unordered lists are lists of items that do not need to be placed in a specific order. A grocery list that lists items in a random order is a good example of an unordered list. Items in unordered lists are usually preceded by a **bullet**, or a small raised dot or similar icon. Unordered lists that contain bullets are sometimes called **bulleted lists**. Though you can use paragraph indentations to create an unordered list, bullets can often make lists easier to read. To create an unordered list, you first select the text you want to format as an unordered list, then you use the Unordered List button in the Property inspector to insert bullets at the beginning of each paragraph of the selected text.

Formatting Unordered Lists

In Dreamweaver, the default bullet style is a round dot. To change the bullet style to square, you need to expand the Property inspector to its full size, as shown in Figure C-1, click List Item in the Property inspector to open the List Properties dialog box, then set the style for bulleted lists to square. Be aware, however, that not all browsers display square bullets correctly, in which case the bullets will appear as round dots. **Menu lists** and directory lists are very similar to unordered lists.

Creating Ordered Lists

Ordered lists, which are sometimes called **numbered lists**, are lists of items that are presented in a specific order and that are preceded by numbers or letters in sequence.

An ordered list is appropriate for a list in which each item must be executed according to its specified order. A list that provides numbered directions for driving from Point A to Point B or a list that provides instructions for assembling a bicycle are both examples of ordered lists.

Formatting Ordered Lists

You can format an ordered list to show different styles of numbers or letters using the List Properties dialog box, as shown in Figure C-2. You can apply numbers, Roman numerals, lowercase letters, or capital letters to an ordered list.

FIGURE C-1
Expanded Property inspector

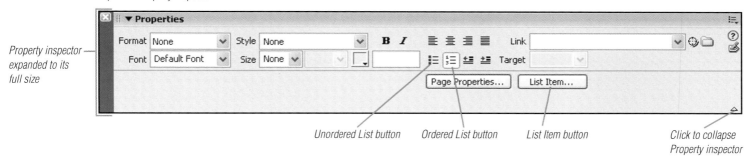

Property inspector expanded to its full size

Unordered List button   Ordered List button   List Item button   Click to collapse Property inspector

FIGURE C-2
Choosing a numbered list style in the List Properties dialog box

List type list arrow

Numbered List styles

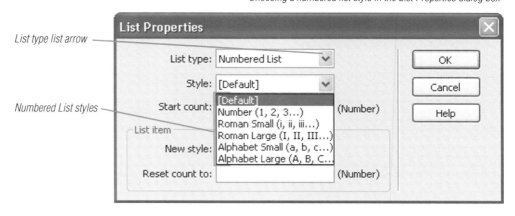

Create an unordered list

1. Open the newsletter page in the TripSmart Web site.

2. Position the insertion point to the left of Expandable clothesline and clothespins in the second paragraph, scroll to the end of the page, press and hold **[Shift]**, click to the right of the last sentence on the page, then release [Shift].

3. Click the **Unordered List button** ☰ in the Property inspector to format the selected text as an unordered list, click anywhere to deselect the text, then compare your screen to Figure C-3.

4. Click the insertion point after the last sentence on the page, then press **[Enter]** (Win) or **[return]** (Mac) twice to end the unordered list.

    TIP Pressing [Enter] (Win) or [return] (Mac) once at the end of an unordered list creates another bulleted item. To end an unordered list, press [Enter] (Win) or [return] (Mac) twice.

You opened the newsletter page in Design view and formatted the list of essential items to pack as an unordered list.

FIGURE C-3
Creating an unordered list

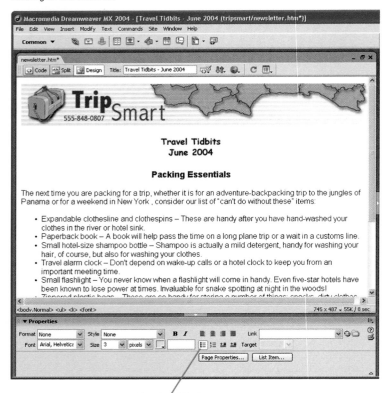

Unordered List button

FIGURE C-4
List Properties dialog box

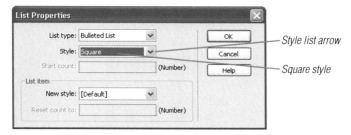

Style list arrow

Square style

FIGURE C-5
HTML tags in Code view for unordered list

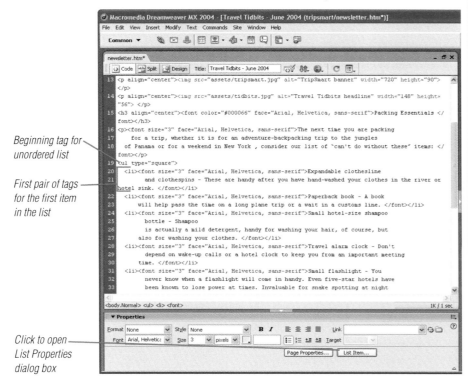

Beginning tag for unordered list

First pair of tags for the first item in the list

Click to open List Properties dialog box

Format an unordered list

1. Click any of the items in the unordered list to place the insertion point in the list.

2. Expand the Property inspector (if necessary), click **List Item** in the Property inspector to open the List Properties dialog box, click the **Style list arrow**, click **Square**, as shown in Figure C-4, then click **OK**.

   The bullets in the unordered list now have a square shape.

3. Position the insertion point to the left of the first item in the unordered list, then click the **Show Code view button** on the toolbar to view the code for the unordered list, as shown in Figure C-5.

   Notice that there is a pair of HTML codes, or tags, surrounding each type of element on the page. The first tag in each pair begins the code for a particular element, and the last tag ends the code for the element. For instance, the tags <ul></ul> surround the unordered list. The tags <li> and </li> surround each item in the list.

4. Click the **Show Design view button** on the toolbar.

You used the List Properties dialog box to apply the square bullet style to the unordered list. You then viewed the HTML code for the unordered list in Code view.

Create an ordered list

1. Place the insertion point under the unordered list.

   > TIP You may have to press Enter (Win) or [return] (Mac) twice to end the unordered list and position the insertion point.

2. Use the Import Word Document command to import how_to_pack.doc from the chapter_c folder where your Data Files are stored.

   > TIP Remember to remove the check mark in the Use CSS instead of HTML tags check box in the General section of the Preferences dialog box before importing Word text.

3. Click the **Insert bar list arrow**, click **HTML**, place the insertion point to the left of Avoiding Wrinkle Woes, then click the **Horizontal Rule button** ▦ on the Insert bar.

   A horizontal rule appears and helps to separate the unordered list from the text you just pasted.

4. Select the text beginning with "Decide what items to take" and ending with the last sentence on the page.

5. Click the **Ordered List button** ≔ in the Property inspector to format the selected text as an ordered list.

6. Deselect the text, then compare your screen to Figure C-6.

You imported text onto the newsletter page. You also added a horizontal rule to help organize the page. Finally, you formatted selected text as an ordered list.

FIGURE C-6
Creating an ordered list

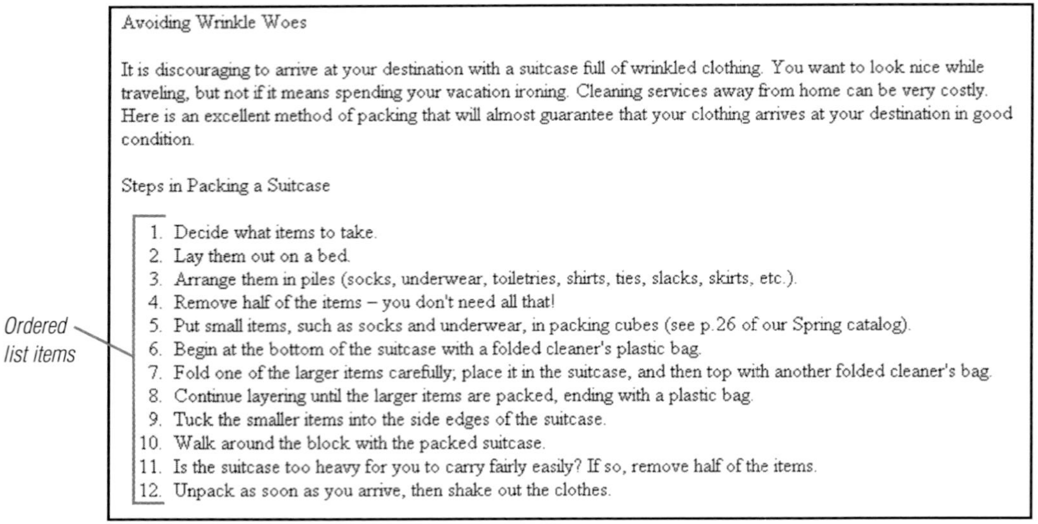

Avoiding Wrinkle Woes

It is discouraging to arrive at your destination with a suitcase full of wrinkled clothing. You want to look nice while traveling, but not if it means spending your vacation ironing. Cleaning services away from home can be very costly. Here is an excellent method of packing that will almost guarantee that your clothing arrives at your destination in good condition.

Steps in Packing a Suitcase

Ordered list items

1. Decide what items to take.
2. Lay them out on a bed.
3. Arrange them in piles (socks, underwear, toiletries, shirts, ties, slacks, skirts, etc.).
4. Remove half of the items — you don't need all that!
5. Put small items, such as socks and underwear, in packing cubes (see p.26 of our Spring catalog).
6. Begin at the bottom of the suitcase with a folded cleaner's plastic bag.
7. Fold one of the larger items carefully; place it in the suitcase, and then top with another folded cleaner's bag.
8. Continue layering until the larger items are packed, ending with a plastic bag.
9. Tuck the smaller items into the side edges of the suitcase.
10. Walk around the block with the packed suitcase.
11. Is the suitcase too heavy for you to carry fairly easily? If so, remove half of the items.
12. Unpack as soon as you arrive, then shake out the clothes.

FIGURE C-7

Newsletter page with ordered list

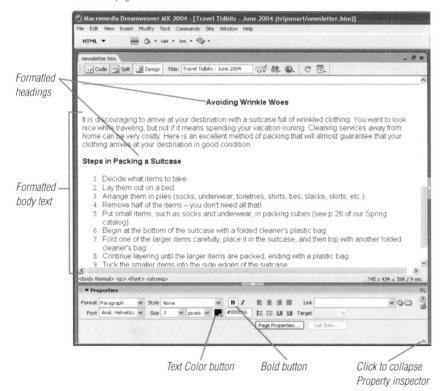

Formatted headings

Formatted body text

Text Color button   Bold button   Click to collapse Property inspector

1. Select all the text below the horizontal rule, then change the font to Arial, Helvetica, sans-serif, size 3.

2. Select the heading Steps in Packing a Suitcase, then click the **Bold button** **B** in the Property inspector.

3. Click the **Text Color button** in the Property inspector to open the color picker, then click the first square in the third row, color #000066.

4. Format the Avoiding Wrinkle Woes heading to match the Packing Essentials heading, center the heading, then compare your screen to Figure C-7.

   TIP   If you want to see more of your Web page in the document window, you can collapse the Property inspector.

5. Save your work.

You applied a new font and font size to the ordered list. You also formatted the Avoiding Wrinkle Woes heading to match the Packing Essentials heading.

CREATE, APPLY AND EDIT CASCADING STYLE SHEETS

What You'll Do

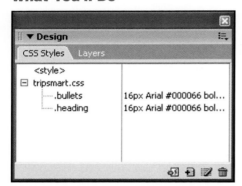

In this lesson, you will create a Cascading Style Sheet file for the TripSmart Web site. You also will create styles called bullets and heading and apply them to the newsletter page.

Using Cascading Style Sheets

When you want to apply the same formatting attributes to page elements such as text, objects, and tables, you can save a significant amount of time by using Cascading Style Sheets. A **Cascading Style Sheet** (CSS) is made up of sets of formatting attributes that are either saved with a descriptive name or that redefine the appearance of an HTML tag. CSS style sheets are saved as individual files with the .css extension and stored in the directory structure of a Web site, as shown in Figure C-8. CSS style sheets contain **styles**, which are formatting attributes that can be applied to page elements.

You use the buttons on the CSS Styles panel to create, edit, and apply styles. To add a style, you use the New CSS Style dialog box to name the style and specify whether to add it to a new or existing style sheet. You then use the CSS Style Definition dialog box to set the formatting attributes for the style. Once you add a new style to a style sheet, it appears in a list in the CSS Styles panel. To apply a

style, you select the text to which you want to apply the style, then choose a style from the Style list in the Property inspector. You can apply CSS styles to any element on a Web page or to all of the pages in a Web site. When you make a change to a style, all page elements formatted with that style are automatically updated. Once you create a CSS style sheet you can attach it to other pages in your Web site.

The CSS panel in the Tag inspector is another screen resource for managing styles. If you select a style in the CSS Styles panel, the properties are displayed in the Tag inspector. A drop-down list can be accessed next to each property value to enable you to make quick changes, such as increasing the font size.

You can use CSS Styles to save an enormous amount of time. Being able to define a style and then apply it to page elements on all the pages of your Web site means that you can make hundreds of formatting changes in a few minutes. Be aware, however, that not all browsers can read CSS

Styles. Versions of Internet Explorer that are 4.0 or lower do not support CSS styles. Only Netscape Navigator version 6.0 or higher supports CSS styles.

QUICKTIP

You can also use CSS styles to format other page content such as backgrounds, borders, lists, and boxes.

Understanding CSS Style Sheet Settings

If you open a style sheet file, you will see the code for the CSS styles. A CSS style consists of two parts: the selector and the declaration. The **selector** is the name or the tag to which the style declarations have been assigned. The **declaration** consists of the property and the value. For example, Figure C-9 shows the code for the tripsmart.css style sheet. In this example, the first property listed for the bullets style is font-family. The value for this property is Arial, Helvetica, sans-serif. When you create a new Cascading Style Sheet, you will see it as an open document in the Dreamweaver document window. Save this file as you make changes to it.

FIGURE C-8
Cascading Style Sheet file listed in tripsmart root folder

FIGURE C-9
tripsmart.css style file

New Cascading Style Sheet file

```
1   .bullets {
2       font-family: Arial, Helvetica, sans-serif;
3       font-size: 16px;
4       font-style: normal;
5       font-weight: bold;
6       color: #000066;
7   }
8   .heading {
9       font-family: Arial, Helvetica, sans-serif;
10      font-size: 16px;
11      font-style: normal;
12      font-weight: bold;
13      color: #000066;
14      text-align: center;
15  }
16
```

Create a Cascading Style Sheet and a style

1. Expand the Design panel group, then select the CSS Styles panel tab (if necessary).

2. Click the **New CSS Style button** ![button] in the CSS Styles panel to open the New CSS Style dialog box, verify that the Class option button is selected, then type **bullets** in the Name text box.

   TIP Class names are preceded by a period. If you don't enter a period when you type the name, Dreamweaver will add the period for you.

3. Click the **Define in list arrow**, click **(New Style Sheet File)**, compare your screen with Figure C-10, then click **OK**.

4. Type **tripsmart** in the File name text box (Win) or the Save As text box (Mac), then click **Save** to open the CSS Style Definition for .bullets in tripsmart.css dialog box.

   The bullets style will be stored within the tripsmart.css file.

5. Verify that Type is selected in the Category list, set the Font to Arial, Helvetica, sans-serif, set the Size to 12 pixels, set the Weight to bold, set the Color to #000066, set the Style to normal, compare your screen to Figure C-11, then click **OK**.

6. Click the **plus sign** (Win) or the **expander arrow** (Mac) next to tripsmart.css in the CSS Styles panel to list the bullets style.

   The CSS style named bullets appears in the CSS Styles panel, as shown in Figure C-12.

You created a Cascading Style Sheet file named tripsmart.css and a style called .bullets.

FIGURE C-10
New CSS Style dialog box

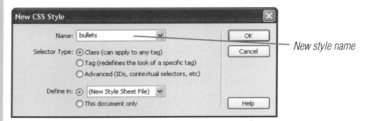

New style name

FIGURE C-11
CSS Style Definition for .bullets in tripsmart.css dialog box

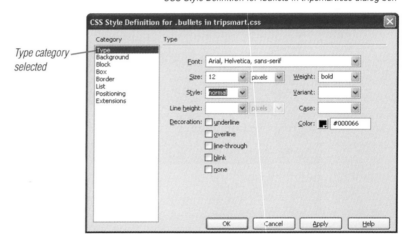

Type category selected

FIGURE C-12
CSS Styles panel with bullets style added

New bullets style

FIGURE C-13

Applying a CSS style to selected text

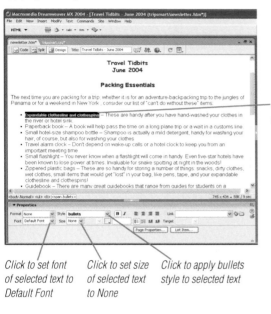

Selected
text

Click to set font
of selected text to
Default Font

Click to set size
of selected text
to None

Click to apply bullets
style to selected text

Bullets style
applied to each
item in list

FIGURE C-14

Unordered list with bullets style applied

1. Select the text Expandable clothesline and clothespins, as shown in Figure C-13, then use the Property inspector to set the Font to Default Font, the Size to None, and the Style to bullets.

   > **TIP** Before you apply a style to selected text you need to remove all formatting attributes such as font and color from it, or the style will not be applied correctly.

2. Repeat Step 1 to apply the bullets style to each of the nine remaining items in the unordered list, then compare your screen to Figure C-14.

You applied the bullets style to each item in the Packing Essentials list.

Attaching a style sheet file to another document

When you have several pages in a Web site, you will probably want to use the same CSS style sheet for each page to ensure that all your elements have a consistent appearance. To attach a style sheet to another document, click the Attach Style Sheet button 🔗 on the CSS Styles panel to open the Attach External Style Sheet dialog box, make sure the Add as Link option is selected, browse to locate the file you want to attach, then click OK. The styles contained in the attached style sheet will appear in the CSS Styles panel, and you can use them to apply styles to any text on the page.

Edit a Cascading Style Sheet

1. Click **bullets** in the CSS Styles panel.

   TIP Click the plus sign (Win) or expander arrow (Mac) to the left of tripsmart.css in the CSS Styles panel if you do not see bullets. Click the plus sign (Win) or expander arrow (Mac) to the left of <style> if you do not see tripsmart.css.

2. Expand the Tag inspector, click the Attributes tab, (if necessary), then click the **Show list view button** in the CSS Properties panel (if necessary).

   The style name is displayed in the Tag inspector, along with the style's properties and values, as shown in Figure C-15. You can also click the **Edit Style Sheet button** in the CSS Styles panel to open the CSS Style Definition dialog box.

3. Click **12px** in the CSS Properties panel, click the **font-size list arrow**, click **16**, then compare your screen to Figure C-16.

   The bullet text is now much bigger than before, reflecting the changes you made to the bullets style.

   TIP If you position the insertion point in text that has a CSS style applied to it, that style is highlighted in the Tag inspector listed on the Property inspector.

You edited the bullet style to change the font size to 16 pixels. You then viewed the results of the edited style in the unordered list.

FIGURE C-15
Editing a CSS Style

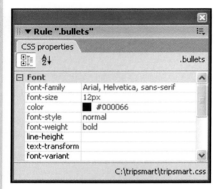

FIGURE C-16
Viewing the changes made to the bullets style

- **Expandable clothesline and clothespins** – These are handy after you have hand-washed your clothes in the river or hotel sink.
- **Paperback book** – A book will help pass the time on a long plane trip or a wait in a customs line.
- **Small hotel-size shampoo bottle** – Shampoo is actually a mild detergent, handy for washing your hair, of course, but also for washing your clothes.
- **Travel alarm clock** – Don't depend on wake-up calls or a hotel clock to keep you from an important meeting time.
- **Small flashlight** – You never know when a flashlight will come in handy. Even five-star hotels have been known to lose power at times. Invaluable for snake spotting at night in the woods!
- **Zippered plastic bags** – These are so handy for storing a number of things: snacks, dirty clothes, wet clothes, small items that would get "lost" in your bag, like pens, tape, and your expandable clothesline and clothespins!
- **Guidebook** – There are many great guidebooks that range from guides for students on a shoestring budget to guides on shopping for fine antiques in Italy . Take advantage of available research to obtain general background knowledge of your destination.
- **Backpack** – Backpacks are versatile, easy to carry, and have enough style variations to appeal to all ages and sexes. They hold a lot of your essential items!
- **Packing cubes** – Packing cubes are zippered nylon bags that are great for organizing your packed items. You can squeeze the air out of the packed cubes, conserving space in your bag.
- **Bubble wrap and tape** – Keep a few feet of small-sized bubble wrap in your bag for wrapping breakable souvenirs you pick up along the way.

Text that has bullets style applied to it is now larger

FIGURE C-17
Adding a style to a CSS style sheet

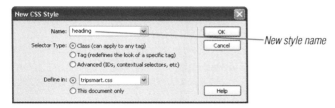

New style name

FIGURE C-18
Formatting options for heading style

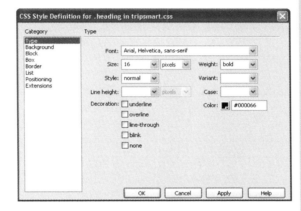

FIGURE C-19
Setting text alignment for heading style

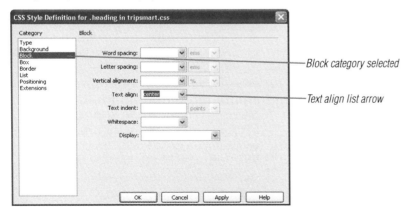

Block category selected

Text align list arrow

Lesson 2   Create, Apply, and Edit Cascading Style Sheets

Add a style to a Cascading Style Sheet

1. Click the **New CSS Style button** ⊞ in the CSS Styles Panel.

2. Type **heading** in the Name Text box, as shown in Figure C-17, then click **OK**.

3. Set the Font to Arial, Helvetica, sans-serif, set the Size to 16, set the Style to normal, set the Weight to bold, set the Color to #000066, then compare your screen to Figure C-18.

4. Click the **Block category** in the New CSS Style Definition for .heading in tripsmart.css dialog box, click the **Text align list arrow**, click **center**, as shown in Figure C-19, then click **OK**.

5. Select the heading Packing Essentials, then use the Property inspector to set the Format to None and the Font to Default Font.

6. With the heading still selected, click the **Text Color button** ☐ to open the color picker, then click the **Strikethrough button** ☑.

7. Click the **heading style** in the Style list in the Property inspector to apply it to the Packing Essentials heading.

8. Repeat Steps 5 through 7 to apply the heading style to the text Avoiding Wrinkle Woes, collapse the Design panel group, then save your work.

> TIP You must save the open tripsmart.css file after editing it, or you will lose your changes.

You added a new style called heading to the tripsmart.css file. You then applied the heading style to selected text.

INSERT AND ALIGN GRAPHICS

What You'll Do

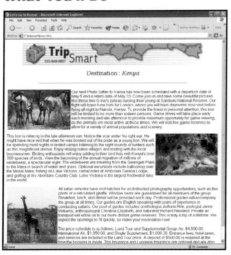

 In this lesson, you will insert three graphics on the tours page in the TripSmart Web site. You will then stagger the alignment of the images on the page to make the page more visually appealing.

Understanding Graphic File Formats

When you add graphics to a Web page, it's important to choose the appropriate graphic file format. The three primary graphic file formats used in Web pages are GIF (Graphics Interchange Format), JPEG (Joint Photographic Experts Group), and PNG (Portable Network Graphics). GIF files download very quickly, making them ideal to use on Web pages. Though limited in the number of colors they can represent, GIF files have the ability to show transparent areas. JPEG files can display many colors. Because they often contain many shades of the same color, photographs are often saved in JPEG format. Files saved with the PNG format share advantages of both GIFs and JPEGs, but are not universally recognized by older browsers.

QUICKTIP

The status bar displays the download time for the page. Each time you add a new graphic to the page, you can see how much additional time is added to the total download time.

Understanding the Assets Panel

When you add a graphic to a Web site, it is added automatically to the Assets panel. The **Assets panel,** located in the Files panel group, displays all the assets in a Web site. The Assets panel contains nine category buttons that you use to view your assets by category. These include Images, Colors, URLs, Flash, Shockwave, Movies, Scripts, Templates, and Library. To view a particular type of asset, click the appropriate category button. The Assets panel is split into two panes. When you click the Images button, as shown in Figure C-20, the lower pane displays a list of all the images in your site and contains four columns. The top pane displays a thumbnail of the selected image in the list. You can view assets in each category in two ways. You can use the Site option button to view all the assets in a Web site, or you can use the Favorites option button to view those assets that you have designated as **favorites,** or assets that you expect to use repeatedly while you work on the site.

You might need to resize the Assets panel to see all four columns when it is docked. To resize the Assets panel, undock the Files panel group and drag the window borders as needed or drag the left border of the panel.

Aligning Images

When you insert an image on a Web page, you need to position it in relation to other elements on the page. Positioning an image is referred to as **aligning** an image. By default, when you insert an image in a paragraph, its bottom edge aligns with the baseline of the first line of text or any other element in the same paragraph. When you select an image, the Align text box in the Property inspector displays the alignment setting for the image. You can change the alignment setting using the options in the Align menu in the Property inspector.

The Align menu options function differently than the Align buttons in the Property inspector. You use the Align buttons to center, left-align, or right-align an element without regard to how the element is aligned in relation to other elements.

FIGURE C-20
Assets panel

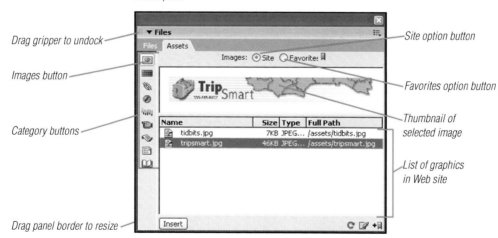

Drag gripper to undock

Images button

Category buttons

Drag panel border to resize

Site option button

Favorites option button

Thumbnail of selected image

List of graphics in Web site

Insert a graphic

1. Open dwc_1.htm from the chapter_c folder where your Data Files are stored, then save it as **tours.htm** in the tripsmart root folder.

2. Click **Yes** to overwrite the existing file, click **Yes** to update links, then set the path for the TripSmart banner as assets/tripsmart.jpg.

3. Position the insertion point in front of Our in the first paragraph, click the **Insert bar list arrow**, click **Common**, click the **Images list arrow**, then click **Image** to open the Select Image Source dialog box, navigate to the chapter_c assets folder, double-click **zebra_mothers.jpg** to insert this image on the page, then verify that the file was copied to your assets folder in the tripsmart root folder.

   Compare your screen to Figure C-21.

4. Click the **Assets panel tab** in the Files panel group, click the **Images button** on the Assets panel (if necessary), then click the **Refresh Site List button** at the bottom of the Assets panel to update the list of images in the TripSmart Web site.

   The Assets panel displays a list of all the images in the TripSmart Web site, as shown in Figure C-22. A thumbnail of the zebra image appears above the list.

   (continued)

FIGURE C-21
TripSmart tours page with inserted image

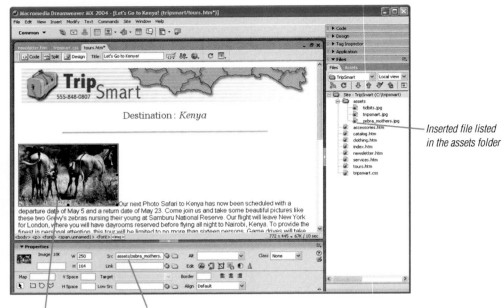

Inserted file listed in the assets folder

zebra_mothers.jpg file inserted

Path should begin with the word "assets"

FIGURE C-22
Image files for TripSmart Web site listed in Assets panel

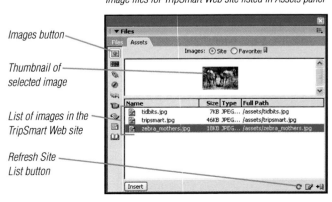

Images button

Thumbnail of selected image

List of images in the TripSmart Web site

Refresh Site List button

FIGURE C-23

Assets panel with five images

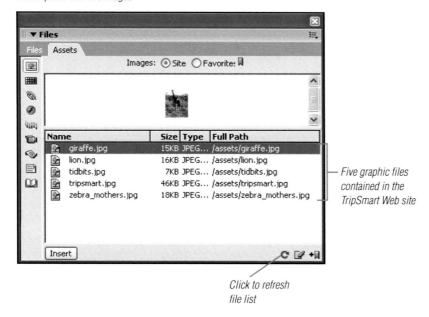

Five graphic files
contained in the
TripSmart Web site

Click to refresh
file list

5. Insert lion.jpg to the left of "This" at the beginning of the second paragraph, then refresh the Assets panel to verify that the lion.jpg file was copied to the assets folder of the TripSmart Web site.

> TIP   The file lion.jpg is located in the assets folder in the chapter_c folder where your Data Files are stored.

6. Insert giraffe.jpg to the left of All safari vehicles at the beginning of the third paragraph, then refresh the Assets panel to verify that the file was copied to the Web site.

Your Assets panel should resemble Figure C-23.

You inserted three images on the tours page and copied each image to the assets folder of the TripSmart Web site.

Align a graphic

1. Scroll to the top of the page, click the **zebra image**, then expand the Property inspector (if necessary).

   Because an image is selected, the Property inspector displays tools you can use to set the properties of an image.

2. Click the **Align list arrow** in the Property inspector, then click **Left**.

   The zebra photo is now left-aligned and the paragraph text flows around its right edge, as shown in Figure C-24.

   (continued)

(continued)

FIGURE C-24
Left-aligned zebra image

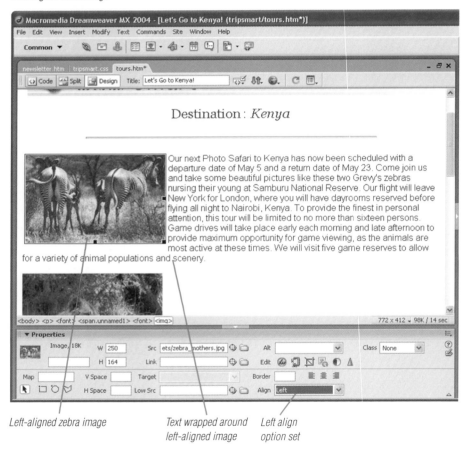

Left-aligned zebra image

Text wrapped around left-aligned image

Left align option set

Working with Text and Graphics

FIGURE C-25

Aligned images on the tours page

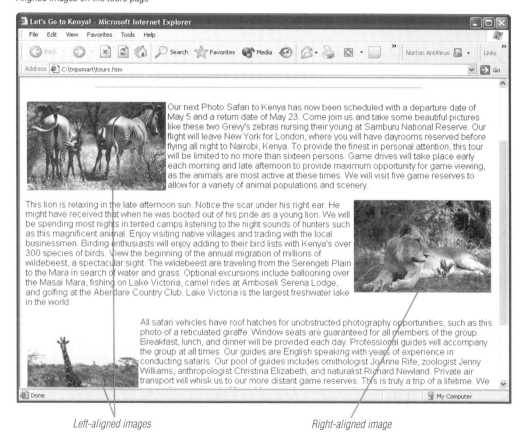

Left-aligned images   *Right-aligned image*

3. Select the lion image, click the **Align list arrow** in the Property inspector, then click **Right**.

4. Align the giraffe image, using the Left Align option.

5. Save your work.

6. Preview the Web page in your browser, compare your screen to Figure C-25, then close your browser.

You used the Property inspector to set the alignment for the zebra, giraffe, and lion images. You then previewed the page in your browser.

ENHANCE AN IMAGE AND USE ALTERNATE TEXT

What You'll Do

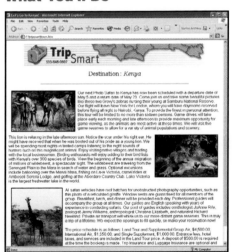

 In this lesson, you will add borders around the images on the tours page, adjust the horizontal space around the images to set them apart from the text, and then add alternate text to describe each image on the page.

Enhancing an Image

After you place an image on a Web page, you have several options for **enhancing** it, or improving its appearance. To make changes to the image itself, such as removing scratches from it, or making it lighter or darker, you need to use an image editor such as Macromedia Fireworks or Adobe Photoshop. However, you can use Dreamweaver to enhance certain aspects of how images appear on a page. For example, you can add borders around an image or add horizontal and vertical space. **Borders** are frames that surround an image. Horizontal and vertical space is blank space above, below, and on the sides of an image that separates the image from text or other elements on the page. Adding horizontal or vertical space, which is the same as adding white space, helps images

DESIGNTIP Resizing graphics using an external editor

Each image on a Web page takes a specific number of seconds to download, depending on the size of the file. Larger files (in kilobytes, not width and height) take longer to download than smaller files. It's important to figure out the smallest acceptable size for an image on your Web page. Then, if you need to resize an image to reduce the file size, use an external image editor to do so, *instead* of resizing it in Dreamweaver. Although you can adjust the width and height settings of an image in the Property inspector to change the size of the image as it appears on your screen, these settings do not affect the file size. Decreasing the size of an image using the H (height) and W (width) settings in the Property inspector does *not* reduce the time it will take the file to download. Ideally you should use graphics that have the smallest file size and the highest quality possible, so that each page downloads in eight seconds or less.

stand out on a page. In the Web page shown in Figure C-26, the horizontal and vertical space around the images in the center column helps make these images more prominent. Adding horizontal or vertical space does not affect the width or height of the image.

QUICKTIP

Because some linked images are displayed with borders, viewers might mistake an image that contains a border with a hyperlink. For this reason, you should use borders sparingly.

Using Alternate Text

One of the easiest ways to make your Web page viewer-friendly and handicapped-accessible is to use alternate text. **Alternate text** is descriptive text that appears in place of an image while the image is downloading or when the mouse pointer is placed over it. You can program some browsers to display only alternate text and to download images manually. Alternate text can be "read" by a **screen reader**, a device used by the visually impaired to convert written text on a computer monitor to spoken words. Screen readers and alternate text make it possible for visually impaired viewers to have an image described to them in detail. You can also set up Dreamweaver to prompt you to enter alternate text whenever you insert an image on a page.

FIGURE C-26
Lands' End Web site

Add a border

1. Select the zebra image, then expand the Property inspector (if necessary).

2. Type **2** in the Border text box, then press **[Tab]** to apply the border to the zebra image, as shown in Figure C-27.

3. Repeat Step 2 to add borders to the lion and giraffe images.

You added a 2-pixel border to each image on the tours page.

Add horizontal space

1. Select the zebra image, type **10** in the H Space text box in the Property inspector, press **[Tab]**, then compare your screen to Figure C-28.

   The text is more evenly wrapped around the image and is easier to read, since it is not so close to the edge of the image.

2. Repeat Step 1 to set the H Space to 10 for the lion and giraffe images.

   The spacing under each picture differs because of the difference in the lengths of the paragraphs.

You added horizontal spacing around each image on the tours page.

FIGURE C-27

Using the Property inspector to add a border

Selected image with 2-pixel border applied

Border text box

FIGURE C-28

Using the Property inspector to add horizontal space

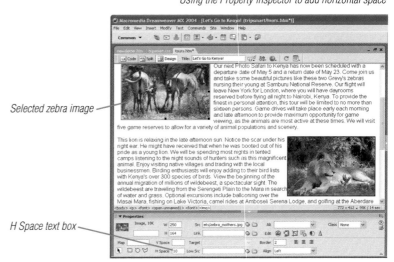

Selected zebra image

H Space text box

FIGURE C-29

Brightness and contrast settings for the lion image

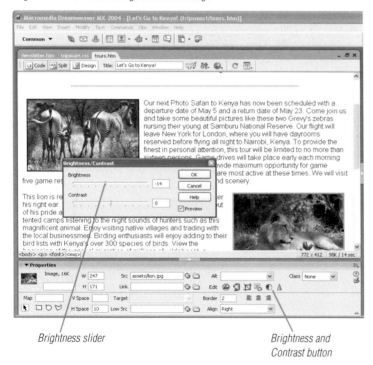

Brightness slider

Brightness and
Contrast button

Apply the Brightness/Contrast feature to graphics

1. Select the lion image.

2. Click the **Brightness and Contrast button** in the Property inspector, then click **OK** to close the warning dialog box and open the Brightness/Contrast dialog box.

3. Drag the **Brightness slider** slightly to the left to darken the image, as shown in Figure C-29.

4. Repeat Step 3 for the giraffe image, if desired, then click **OK**.

You used the Brightness/Contrast dialog box to darken an image.

Use alternate text

1. Select the zebra image, type **Two zebra mothers with their babies** in the Alt text box in the Property inspector, as shown in Figure C-30, then press **[Enter]** (Win) or **[return]** (Mac).

2. Save your work, preview the page in your browser, then point to the **zebra image** until the alternate text appears, as shown in Figure C-31.

3. Close your browser.

4. Select the lion image, type **Lion relaxing in the Kenyan sun** in the Alt text box in the Property inspector, then press **[Enter]** (Win) or **[return]** (Mac).

5. Select the giraffe image, type **Reticulated giraffe posed among acacia trees and brush** in the Alt text box in the Property inspector, then press **[Enter]** (Win) or **[return]** (Mac).

6. Save your work.

7. Preview the page in your browser, view the alternate text for each image, then close your browser.

You added alternate text to three images on the page, then you viewed the alternate text in your browser.

FIGURE C-30

Alternate text setting in the Property inspector

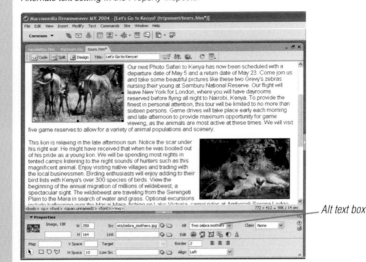

Alt text box

FIGURE C-31

Alternate text displayed in browser

Alternate text displayed on top of image

Working with Text and Graphics

FIGURE C-32

Preferences dialog box with Accessibility category selected

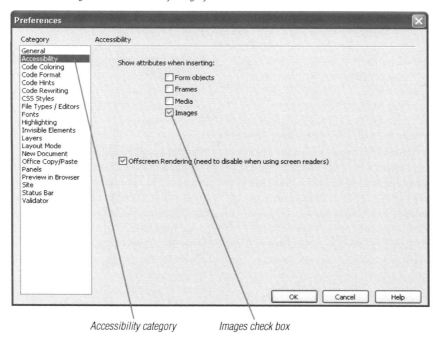

Accessibility category   Images check box

1. Click **Edit** (Win) or **Dreamweaver** (Mac) on the menu bar, click **Preferences** to open the Preferences dialog box, then click the **Accessibility** category.

2. Click the **Images check box**, as shown in Figure C-32, then click **OK**.

   TIP   Once you set the Accessibility preferences, they will be in effect for all Web sites that you develop, not just the one that's open when you set them.

You set the Accessibility preferences to prompt you to enter alternate text each time you insert a graphic on a Web page.

INSERT A BACKGROUND IMAGE AND PERFORM SITE MAINTENANCE

What You'll Do

 In this lesson, you will insert a tiled image and then a seamless image. You will then use the Assets panel to delete them both from the Web site. You will also check for Non-Websafe colors in the Assets panel and delete one that you locate on the home page.

Inserting a Background Image

You can insert a background image on a Web page to provide depth and visual interest to the page, or to communicate a message or mood. **Background images** are graphic files used in place of background colors. Although you can use background images to create a dramatic effect, you should avoid inserting them on Web pages that have lots of text and other elements. Even though they might seem too plain, standard white backgrounds are usually the best choice for Web pages. If you choose to use a background image on a Web page, it should be small in file size, and preferably in GIF format. You can insert either a tiled image or a seamless image as a background. A **tiled image** is a small graphic that repeats across and down a Web page, appearing as individual squares or rectangles. A **seamless image** is a tiled image that is blurred at the edges so it appears to be one image. When you create a Web page, you should use either a background color or a background image, but not both, unless you have a need for

the background color to be displayed while the background image finishes downloading. The background in the Web page shown in Figure C-33 contains several images arranged in a table format.

Managing Graphics

As you work on a Web site, you might find that you accumulate files in your assets folder that are not used in the site. To avoid accumulating unnecessary files, it's a good idea to look at a graphic on a page first, before you copy it to the assets folder. If you inadvertently copy an unwanted file to the assets folder, you should delete it or move it to another location. This is a good Web-site management practice that will prevent the assets folder from filling up with unwanted graphics.

Removing a graphic from a Web page does not remove it from the assets folder in the local root folder of the Web site. To remove an asset from a Web site, you first locate the file you want to remove in the Assets panel. You then use the Locate in Site command to open the Files panel with the unwanted file selected. You then use the Delete command to remove the file from the site.

QUICKTIP

You cannot use the Assets panel to delete a file. You must use the Files panel to delete files and perform all file-management tasks.

Removing Colors from a Web Site

You can use the Assets panel to locate Non-Websafe colors in a Web site. **Non-Websafe** colors are colors that may not be displayed uniformly across computer platforms. After you remove colors from a Web site, you should use the Refresh Site List button on the Assets panel to verify that these colors have been removed. Sometimes it's necessary to press [Ctrl] (Win) or ⌘ (Mac)

while you click the Refresh Site List button. If refreshing the Assets panel does not work, try recreating the site cache, then refreshing the Assets panel again

QUICKTIP

To recreate the site cache, click Site on the menu bar, point to Advanced, then click Recreate Site Cache.

FIGURE C-33
Mansion on Turtle Creek

Insert a background image

1. Click **Modify** on the menu bar, then click **Page Properties** to open the Page Properties dialog box.

2. Click the **Appearance category**.

3. Click **Browse** next to the Background image text box, navigate to the chapter_c assets folder, then double-click **tile_bak.gif**.

   The tile_bak.gif file is automatically copied to the TripSmart assets folder.

4. Click **OK** to close the Page Properties dialog box, then click the **Refresh Site List button** C to refresh the file list in the Assets panel.

   A blue tiled background made up of individual squares replaces the white background, as shown in Figure C-34.

5. Repeat Steps 1 through 4 to replace the tile_bak.gif background image with seamless_bak.gif, located in the chapter_c assets folder.

   As shown in Figure C-35, the seamless background makes it hard to tell where one square stops and the other begins.

You applied a tiled background to the tours page. Then you replaced the tiled background with a seamless background.

FIGURE C-34
Tours page with a tiled background

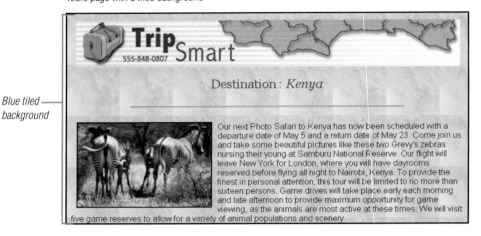

Blue tiled background

FIGURE C-35
Tours page with a seamless background

Seamless background

Working with Text and Graphics

FIGURE C-36

Removing a background image

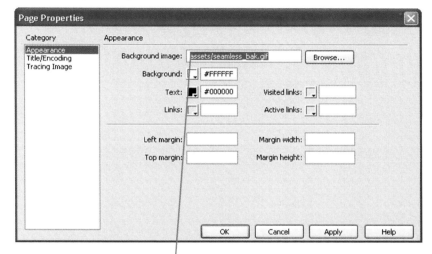

Selected filename

1. Click **Modify** on the menu bar, click **Page Properties**, then click **Appearance**.

2. Select the text in the Background image text box, as shown in Figure C-36, press **[Delete]**, then click **OK**.

   The background of the tours page is white again.

You deleted the link to the background image file to change the tours page background back to white.

Delete files from a Web site

1. Click the **Assets panel tab** (if necessary).

2. Right-click (Win) or [control] click (Mac) **seamless_bak.gif** in the Assets panel, click **Locate in Site** to open the Files panel, select **seamless_bak.gif** in the Files panel (if necessary), press **[Delete]**, then click **Yes** in the dialog box that appears.

3. Repeat Step 2 to remove tile_bak.gif from the Web site, open the Assets panel, then refresh the Assets panel.

   Your Assets panel should resemble Figure C-37.

You removed two image files from the TripSmart Web site, then refreshed the Assets panel.

FIGURE C-37
Images listed in Assets panel

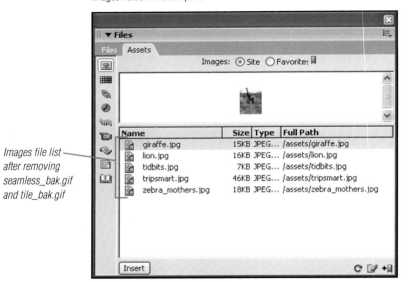

Images file list after removing seamless_bak.gif and tile_bak.gif

Managing graphic files

It is a good idea to store copies of your original Web site graphic files in a separate folder, outside the assets folder of your Web site. If you edit the original files, save them again using different names. Doing this ensures that you will be able to find a file in its original, unaltered state. You might have no need for certain files now, but you might need them later. Storing currently unused files also helps to keep your assets folder free of clutter. Storing copies of original Web site graphic files in a separate location also ensures that you have back-up copies in the event that you accidentally delete a file from the Web site that you need later.

FIGURE C-38
Colors listed in Assets panel

Non-Websafe
color

Drag this border to the left
to expand panel width

FIGURE C-39
Non-Websafe color removed from Assets panel

All colors
are now
Websafe

Remove Non-Websafe colors from a Web site

1. Click the **Colors button** ▦ in the Assets panel to display the colors used in the Web site, then drag the left border of the Assets panel (if necessary) to display the second column.

   The Assets panel shows that color 252084 is Non-Websafe, as shown in Figure C-38. This color appears in a heading on the home page.

2. Click the **Files panel tab**.

3. Double-click **index.htm** to open the home page.

4. Select The smart way to go!, click the **Text Color button** ☐ in the Property inspector to open the color picker, click the **Strikethough button** ☑, type **#003399** in the Color text box, then press **[Tab]**.

   The heading text is now the Websafe color #003399.

5. Click the **Assets panel tab**, press and hold **[Ctrl]** (Win) or ⌘ (Mac), click the **Refresh Site List button** ↻, then compare your screen to Figure C-39.

   TIP If the list does not refresh, press and hold [ctrl] (Win) or ⌘ (Mac), then click the Refresh Site List button again, or recreate the site cache.

6. Save your work, preview the page in your browser, close your browser, then close all open files.

You removed one Non-Websafe color from the Web site, then refreshed the Assets panel.

Create unordered and ordered lists.

1. Open the Blooms & Bulbs Web site.
2. Open the tips page.
3. Select the four lines of text below the Seasonal Gardening Checklist heading and format them as an unordered list.
4. Select the lines of text below the Basic Gardening Tips heading and format them as an ordered list.
5. Save your work.

Create, apply, and edit Cascading Style Sheets.

1. Create a new CSS Style named **.seasons**, making sure the Class selector type and the New Style Sheet File option buttons are both selected in the New CSS Style dialog box.
2. Name the style sheet file **blooms** in the Save Style Sheet File As dialog box.
3. Choose the following settings for the seasons style: Font = Arial, Helvetica, sans-serif, Size = 12 pixels, Style = normal, Weight = bold, and Color = #006633.
4. Change the Font setting to Default Font and the Size setting to None for the following text in the Seasonal Gardening Checklist: Fall, Winter, Spring, and Summer. Then, apply the seasons style to Fall, Winter, Spring, and Summer.

5. Edit the seasons style by changing the font size to 16 pixels.
6. Add an additional style called **headings** and define this style choosing the following type settings: Font = Arial, Helvetica, sans-serif, Size = 18 pixels, Style = normal, Weight = bold, and Color = #006633.
7. Apply the heading style to the two subheadings on the page: Seasonal Gardening Checklist and Basic Gardening Tips. (Make sure you remove any manual formatting before applying the style.)
8. Click File on the menu bar, click Save All, then view the page in the browser.
9. Close the browser and the tips page.

Insert and align graphics.

1. Open dwc_3.htm from the chapter_c Data Files folder, save it as **plants.htm** in the Blooms & Bulbs Web site, overwriting the existing plants.htm file, and update all links.
2. Verify that the path of the Blooms & Bulbs banner is set correctly to the assets folder in the blooms root folder.
3. Set the Accessibility preferences to prompt you to add alternate text to images, (if necessary).
4. Insert the iris.jpg file from the assets folder located in the chapter_c Data Files folder to the left of the words Beautiful spring iris and add **Purple iris** as alternate text.

5. Insert the tulips.jpg file from the chapter_c assets folder file in front of the words Dramatic masses and add **Red and yellow tulips** as alternate text.
6. Insert the pansies.jpg file from the chapter_c assets folder in front of the words Pretty pansies and add **Deep violet pansies** as alternate text.
7. Refresh the Files panel to verify that all three images were copied to the assets folder.
8. Left-align the iris image.
9. Left-align the tulips image.
10. Left-align the pansies image.
11. Save your work.

Enhance an image and use alternate text.

1. Apply a 2-pixel border and horizontal spacing of 5 pixels around the iris image.
2. Apply a 2-pixel border and horizontal spacing of 5 pixels around the tulips image.
3. Apply a 2-pixel border and horizontal spacing of 5 pixels around the pansies image.
4. Add the text **Blooms & Bulbs banner** as alternate text for the banner.
5. Add appropriate alternate text to the banner on the index and tips pages.
6. Save your work and close the index and tips pages.

In this assignment, you continue to work on the group Web site that you started in Chapter A. Depending on the size of your group, you can assign individual elements of the project to group members, or work collectively to create the finished product. There will be no data files supplied. You are building this Web site from chapter to chapter, so you must do each Group Project assignment in each chapter to complete your Web site.

You will continue building your Web site by designing and completing a page that contains a list, headings, body text, graphics, and a background. During this process, you will develop a style sheet and add several styles to it. You will insert appropriate graphics on your page and enhance them for maximum effect. You will also check for Non-Websafe colors and remove any that you find.

1. Consult your storyboard and brainstorm as a group to decide which page to create and develop for this chapter.
2. As a team, plan the page content for the page and make a sketch of the layout. You might want to create your sketch on a large piece of paper taped to the wall. Your sketch should include at least one ordered or unordered list, appropriate headings, body text, several graphics, and a background. Your sketch should also show where the

body text and headings should be placed on the page and what styles should be used for each type of text. You should plan on creating at least two styles.
3. Assign a team member the task of creating this page and adding the text content to it.
4. Assign a team member the task of creating a Cascading Style Sheet for the Web site and adding to it the styles you decided to use. Assign the same team member the task of applying the styles to the appropriate content.
5. Access the graphics you gathered in Chapter A and assign a team member the task of placing the graphics on the page so that the page matches the sketch you created in Step 2. This team member should also add a background image and appropriate alternate text for each graphic.

6. Assign a team member the task of checking for and removing any Non-Websafe colors.
7. Assign a team member the task of identifying any files in the Assets panel that are currently not used in the Web site. Decide as a group which of these assets should be removed, then assign a team member to delete these files.
8. As a team, preview the new page in a browser, then check for page layout problems and broken links. Make any necessary fixes in Dreamweaver, then preview the page again in a browser. Repeat this process until the group is satisfied with the way the page looks in the browser.
9. Use Figure C-46 to check all the pages of your site.
10. Close the browser, save your changes to the page, then close the page.

FIGURE C-46
Group Project check list

Web Site Check List

1. Does each page have a page title?
2. Does the home page have a description and keywords?
3. Does the home page contain contact information?
4. Does every page in the Web site have consistent navigation links?
5. Does the home page have a last updated statement that will automatically update when the page is saved?
6. Do all paths for links and images work correctly?
7. Do all images have alternate text?
8. Are all colors Websafe?
9. Are there any unnecessary files you can delete from the assets folder?
10. Is there a style sheet with at least two styles?
11. Did you apply the styles to page content?
12. Do all pages view well using at least two different browser settings?

CHAPTER D

WORKING WITH LINKS

1. Create external and internal links.

2. Create internal links to named anchors.

3. Insert Flash text.

4. Create, modify, and copy a navigation bar.

5. Manage Web site links.

CHAPTER D
WORKING WITH LINKS

Introduction

What makes Web sites so powerful are the links that connect one page to another within a Web site or to any page on the Web. Though you can add graphics, animations, movies, and other enhancements to a Web site to make it visually attractive, the links you include are often the most essential components of a Web site. Links that connect the pages within a Web site are always very important because they help viewers navigate between the pages of the site. However, if one of your goals is to keep viewers from leaving your Web site, you might want to avoid including links to other Web sites. For example, most e-commerce sites include only links to other pages in the site to discourage shoppers from leaving the site. In this chapter you will create links to other pages in the TripSmart Web site and to other sites on the Web. You will also insert a navigation bar that contains graphics instead of text, and check the links in the TripSmart Web site to make sure they all work.

Understanding Internal and External Links

Web pages contain two types of links: internal links and external links. **Internal links** are links to Web pages in the same Web site, and **external links** are links to Web pages in other Web sites or to e-mail addresses. Both internal and external links have two important parts that work together. The first part of a link is the element that viewers see and click on a Web page, for example, text, a graphic, or a button. The second part of a link is the **path**, or the name and location of the Web page or file that will open when the element is clicked. Setting and maintaining the correct paths for all your links is essential to avoid having broken links in your site.

Tools You'll Use

Named Anchor button

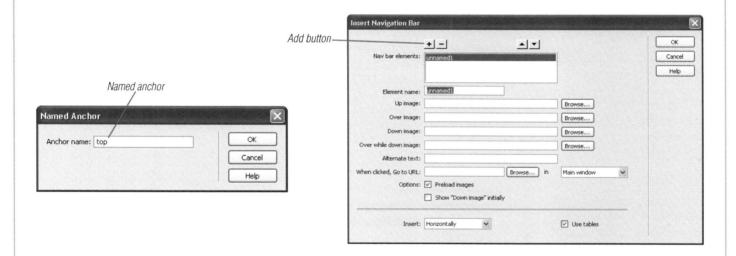

Add button

Named anchor

CREATE EXTERNAL AND INTERNAL LINKS

What You'll Do

In this lesson, you will create external links on the TripSmart services page that link to several Web sites related to travel. You will also create internal links to other pages within the TripSmart Web site.

Creating External Links

A good Web page usually includes a variety of external links to other related Web sites so that viewers can get more information on a particular topic. To create an external link, you first select the text or object that you want to serve as a link, then you type the absolute path to the destination Web page in the Link text box in the Property inspector. An **absolute path** is a path used for external links that includes the complete address for the destination page, including the protocol (such as http://) and the complete **URL** (Uniform Resource Locator), or address, of the destination page. When necessary, the Web page filename and folder hierarchy are also part of an absolute path. Figure D-1 shows an example of an absolute path showing the protocol, URL, and filename. After you enter external links on a Web page, you can view them in the site map.

FIGURE D-1
An example of an absolute path

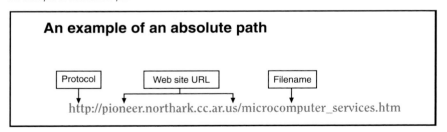

An example of an absolute path

| Protocol | Web site URL | Filename |

http://pioneer.northark.cc.ar.us/microcomputer_services.htm

Creating Internal Links

Each page in a Web site usually focuses on an individual category or topic. You should make sure that the home page provides links to each page in the site, and that all pages in the site contain numerous internal links so that viewers can move easily from page to page. To create an internal link, you first select the text element or graphic object that you want to make a link, then you use the Browse for File icon next to the Link text box in the Property inspector to specify the relative path to the destination page. A **relative path** is a type of path used to reference Web pages and graphic files within the same Web site. Relative paths include the filename and folder location of a file. Figure D-2 shows an example of a relative path. Table D-1 describes absolute paths and relative paths. Relative paths can either be site root relative or document relative.

You should take great care in managing your internal links to make sure they work correctly and are timely and relevant to the page content. You should design the navigation structure of your Web site so that viewers are never more than three or four clicks away from the page they are seeking.

An example of a relative path

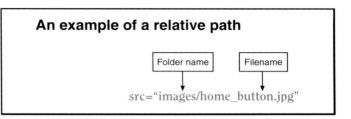

TABLE D-1: Description of absolute and relative paths

type of path	description	examples
Absolute path	Used for external links and specifies protocol, URL, and filename of destination page	*http://www.yahoo.com/recreation*
Relative path	Used for internal links and specifies location of file relative to the current page	services.htm or assets/tripsmart.gif
Root-relative path	Used for internal links when publishing to a server that contains many Web sites or where the Web site is so large it requires more than one server	/tripsmart/services.htm
Document-relative path	Used in most cases for internal links and specifies the location of file relative to current page	services.htm or assets/tripsmart.gif

Create an external link

1. Open the TripSmart Web site that you completed in Chapter C, open dwd_1.htm from the chapter_d folder where your Data Files are stored, then save it as **services.htm** in the tripsmart root folder, overwriting the existing services page, then update links.

2. Set the path for the TripSmart banner to the assets folder of the Web site.

3. Scroll down, then select CNN Travel Channel under the heading Travel Information Sites.

4. Click in the Link text box in the Property inspector, type **http://www.cnn.com/TRAVEL**, press [**Enter**] (Win) or [**return**] (Mac), then compare your screen to Figure D-3.

5. Repeat Steps 3 and 4 to create links for the following Web sites listed on the services page:

   US Department of State:
   http://travel.state.gov

   Yahoo!: **http://www.yahoo.com/ Recreation/Travel**

   MapQuest: **http://www.mapquest.com**

   Rand McNally: **http://www.randmcnally.com**

   AccuWeather: **http://www.accuweather.com**

   The Weather Channel:
   http://www.weather.com

6. Save your work, preview the page in your browser, test all the links to make sure they work, then close your browser.

   TIP You must have an active Internet connection to test the links. If clicking a link does not open a page, make sure you typed the URL correctly in the Link text box.

You opened the TripSmart Web site, replaced the existing services page, then added seven external links to other travel Web sites on the page. You also tested each link in your browser.

FIGURE D-3

Creating an external link to the CNN Travel Channel Web site

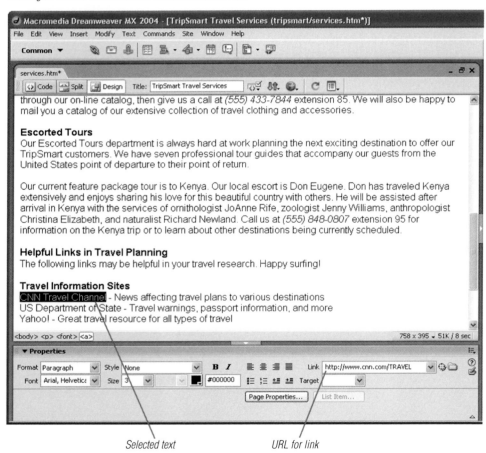

Selected text   URL for link

1. Display the Files panel, (if necessary).

2. Click the **View list arrow** on the Files panel, click **Map view**, then click the **Expand/Collapse button** 🔲 to expand the Files panel.

   TIP   If you want to view or hide page titles in the site map, click View on the menu bar, then click Show Page Titles (Win) or click the Options button in the Files panel group title bar, point to View, then click Show Page Titles (Mac).

3. Click the **plus sign** to the left of the services page icon in the site map (if necessary) to view a list of the seven external links you created, as shown in Figure D-4.

   The TripSmart e-mail link also appears in the list.

4. Click the **minus sign** to the left of the services page icon in the site map to collapse the list of links.

5. Click the **Expand/Collapse button** 🔲 on the toolbar, click the **View list arrow** on the Files panel, then click **Local view**.

You viewed the TripSmart site map and expanded the view of the services page to display the seven external links you added.

FIGURE D-4

Site map displaying external links on the services page

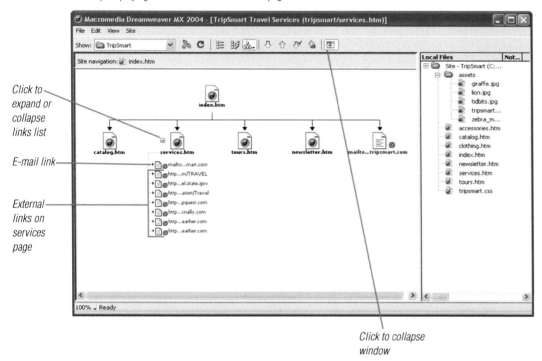

Click to expand or collapse links list

E-mail link

External links on services page

Click to collapse window

Create an internal link

1. Select on-line catalog in the paragraph under the Travel Outfitters heading.

2. Click the **Browse for File icon** in the Property inspector, then double-click **catalog.htm** in the Select File dialog box to set the relative path to the catalog page.

   Notice that catalog.htm appears in the Link text box in the Property inspector, as shown in Figure D-5.

   TIP To collapse all open panels below the document window, such as the Link Checker or the Property inspector, click the expander arrow in the center of the bottom border of the Document window. Pressing [F4] will hide all panels, including the ones on the right side of the screen.

3. Scroll down as necessary, then select Kenya in the second paragraph under the Escorted Tours heading.

4. Click the **Browse for File icon** next to the Link text box in the Property inspector, then double-click **tours.htm** in the Select File dialog box to specify the relative path to the tours page.

   The word Kenya is now a link to the tours page.

5. Save your work, preview the page in your browser to verify that the internal links work correctly, then close your browser.

You created two internal links on the services page, and then tested the links in your browser.

FIGURE D-5

Creating an internal link on the services page

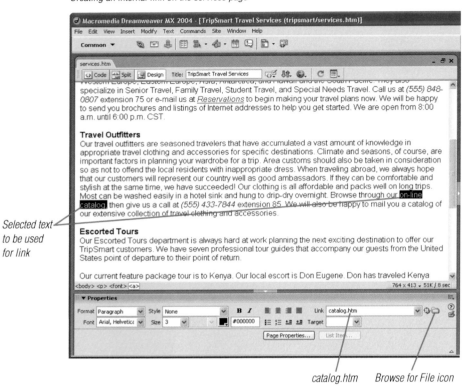

Selected text to be used for link

catalog.htm   Browse for File icon

Typing URLs

Typing URLs in the Link text box in the Property inspector can be very tedious. When you need to type a long and complex URL, it is easy to make mistakes and create a broken link. You can avoid such mistakes by copying and pasting the URL from the Address text box (Internet Explorer) or Location text box (Netscape Navigator and Communicator) to the Link text box in the Property inspector. Copying and pasting a URL ensures that the URL is entered correctly.

FIGURE D-6

Site map displaying external and internal links on the services page

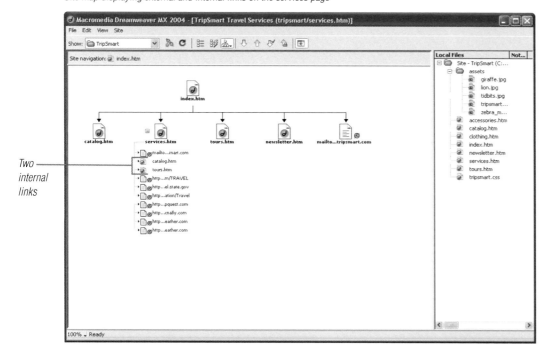

Two internal links

View internal links in the site map

1. Click the **View list arrow** on the Files panel, click **Map view**, then click the **Expand/Collapse button** 🔲.

2. Click the **plus sign** to the left of the services page icon.

   A list of 10 links appears below the services page icon, as shown in Figure D-6. One is an e-mail link, seven are external links, and two are internal links.

   > TIP If your links do not display correctly, recreate the site cache. To recreate the site cache, click Site on the menu bar, point to Advanced, then click Recreate Site Cache.

3. Click the **Expand/Collapse button** 🔲, click the **View list arrow** on the Files panel, then click **Local view**.

   You viewed the links on the services page in the site map.

CREATE INTERNAL LINKS
TO NAMED ANCHORS

What You'll Do

In this lesson, you will insert five named anchors on the services page: one for the top of the page and four for each heading. You will then create internal links to each named anchor.

Inserting Named Anchors

Some Web pages have so much content that viewers must scroll repeatedly to get to the bottom of the page and then back up to the top of the page. To make it easier for viewers to navigate to specific areas of a page without scrolling, you can use a combination of internal links and named anchors. A **named anchor** is a specific location on a Web page that has a descriptive name. Named anchors act as targets for internal links and make it easy for viewers to jump to a particular place on the same page quickly. A **target** is the location on a Web page that a browser displays when an internal link is clicked. For example, you can insert a named anchor called "top" at the top of a Web page, then create a link to

it at the bottom of the page. You can also insert named anchors in strategic places on a Web page, such as at the beginning of paragraph headings.

You insert a named anchor using the Named Anchor button on the Common category of the Insert bar, as shown in Figure D-7. You then enter the name of the Anchor in the Named Anchor dialog box. You should choose short names that describe the named anchor location on the page. Named anchors are represented by yellow anchor icons on a Web page. You can show or hide named anchor icons by clicking View on the menu bar, pointing to Visual Aids, then clicking Invisible Elements.

Notice that when you click the Escorted Tours and Helpful Links in Travel Planning in the browser, their associated named anchors appear in the middle of the page instead of at the top. This happens because the services page is not long enough to position these named anchors at the top of the page.

4. Close your browser.

You created internal links to the named anchors next to the department headings on the services page. You then previewed the page in your browser and tested each link.

FIGURE D-11
Services page in Internet Explorer with internal links to named anchors

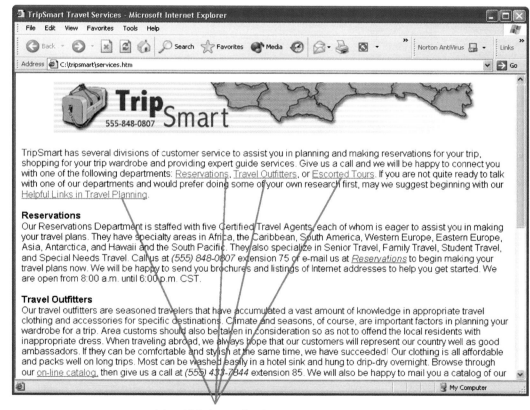

Internal links to named anchors

INSERT FLASH TEXT

What You'll Do

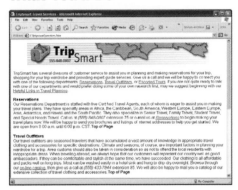

In this lesson, you will use the Insert Flash Text dialog box to create a button that links to the top named anchor on the services page. You will copy this button to several locations on the services page, and then change the alignment of each button.

Understanding Flash Text

Flash is a Macromedia software program that you can use to create vector-based graphics and animations. **Vector-based graphics** are graphics that are based on mathematical formulas, as opposed to other types of graphic files such as JPG and BMP, which are based on pixels. Vector-based graphics have a smoother look and are smaller in file size than pixel-based graphics. Because they download quickly, vector-based graphics are ideal for Web sites. **Flash text** is a vector-based graphic file that contains text. You can insert Flash text to add visual interest to an otherwise dull Web page or to help deliver or reinforce a message. You can use Flash text to create internal or external links. Flash text files are saved with the .swf filename extension.

QUICK**TIP**

In order to view Flash animations, you must have the Flash player installed on your computer. The Flash player is free software that lets you view movies created with Macromedia software.

Inserting Flash Text on a Web Page

You can create Flash text in Dreamweaver without opening the Flash program. To insert Flash text on a Web page, you choose Common from the Insert bar, click the Media list arrow, then click Flash Text, as shown in Figure D-12. Clicking this button opens the Insert Flash Text dialog box, which you use to specify the settings for the Flash text. You first need to specify the text you want to create as Flash text by typing it in the Text text box. You can then specify the font, size, and color of the Flash text, apply bold or italic styles to it, and align it using left, center, or right alignment options. You can also specify a **rollover color**, or the color in which the text will appear when the mouse pointer is placed on it. You also need to enter the path for the destination link in the Link text box. The destination link can be an internal link to another page in the site or to a named anchor on the same page, or an external link

to a page on another Web site. You then use the Target list to specify how to open the destination page. The four options are described in Table D-2.

QUICKTIP

Notice that the _parent option in the table specifies to display the page in the parent frameset. A **frameset** is a group of Web pages displayed using more than one **frame** or window.

Before you close the Insert Flash Text dialog box, you need to type a descriptive name for your Flash text file in the Save as text box. Flash text files must be saved in the same folder as the page that contains the Flash text. For this reason, you should save your Flash text files in the root folder of the Web site.

FIGURE D-12
Media menu on the Insert bar

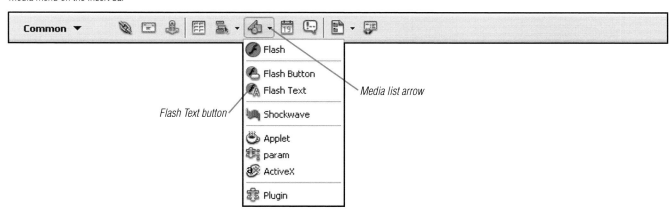

Flash Text button

Media list arrow

TABLE D-2: Options in the Target list	
target	**result**
_blank	Displays the destination page in a separate browser window
_parent	Displays the destination page in the parent frameset (replaces the frameset)
_self	Displays the destination page in the same frame or window
_top	Displays the destination page in the whole browser window

Create Flash text

1. Click after the last word on the services page, then press **[Enter]** (Win) or **[return]** (Mac).

2. Click the **Insert bar list arrow**, click **Common**, click the **Media list arrow** then click **Flash Text** to open the Insert Flash Text dialog box.

3. Type **Top of Page** in the Text text box, set the Font to Arial, set the Size to 16, set the Color to #000066, set the Rollover color to #66CCFF, type **services.htm#top** in the Link text box, use the Target list arrow to set the Target to _top, type **top.swf** in the Save as text box, as shown in Figure D-13, then click **OK**.

   The Top of Page Flash text now appears as a button at the bottom of the page. When a viewer clicks this button, the browser will display the top of the page.

4. Click **Assets** in the Files panel group to open the Assets panel, click the **Flash button** ● on the Assets panel, as shown in Figure D-14, then click the **Refresh Site List button** ⟳.

5. Drag **top.swf** from the Assets panel to the end of the Reservations, Travel Outfitters, and Escorted Tours paragraphs to insert three more links to the top of the page.

   | TIP   Drag top.swf directly after the period in each section.

6. Click the **Files panel tab**, then refresh the Files panel (if necessary).

(continued)

FIGURE D-13
Insert Flash Text dialog box

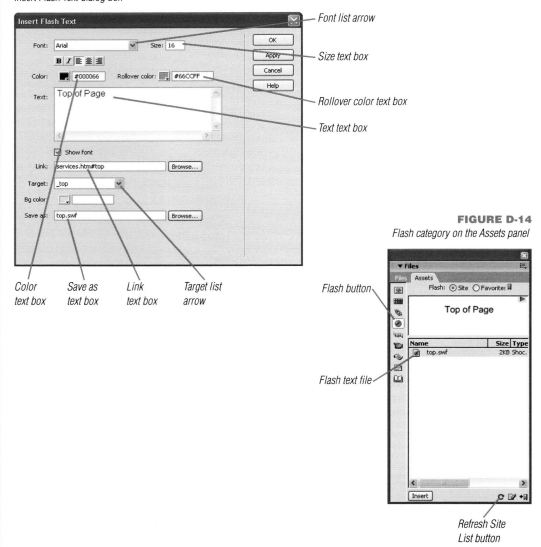

Font list arrow

Size text box

Rollover color text box

Text text box

Color text box

Save as text box

Link text box

Target list arrow

FIGURE D-14
Flash category on the Assets panel

Flash button

Flash text file

Refresh Site List button

FIGURE D-15

Flash text aligned to top

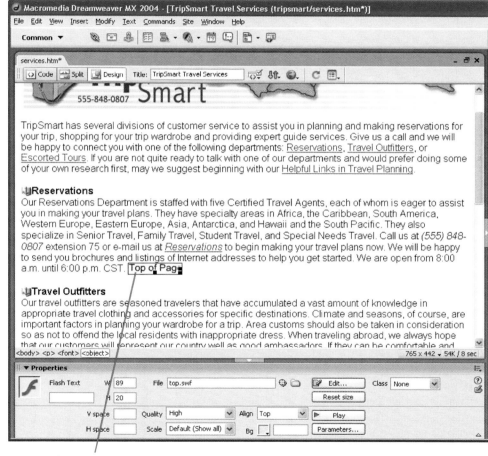

Flash text aligned with top of paragraph text line

7. Save your work, preview the services page in your browser, test each Top of Page link, then close your browser.

   TIP   If the top of the page is already displayed, the window will not move when you click the Flash text.

You used the Insert Flash Text dialog box to create a Top of Page button that links to the top named anchor on the services page. You also inserted the Top of Page button at the end of each department paragraph, so viewers will be able to go quickly to the top of the page without scrolling.

Change the alignment of Flash text

1. Click the **Top of Page button** at the end of the Reservations paragraph, expand the Property inspector, click the **Align list arrow** in the Property inspector, then click **Top**.

   The Top of Page button is now aligned with the top of the line of text, as shown in Figure D-15.

2. Apply the Top alignment setting to the Top of Page button located at the end of the Travel Outfitters and Escorted Tours paragraphs.

3. Collapse the Property inspector, turn off Invisible Elements, then save your work.

4. Preview the services page in your browser, test each Top of Page button, then close your browser.

You aligned the Flash text to improve its appearance on the page.

CREATE, MODIFY, AND COPY A NAVIGATION BAR

What You'll Do

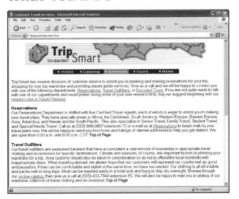

 In this lesson, you will create a navigation bar that can be used to link to each major page in the Web site. The navigation bar will have five elements: home, catalog, services, tours, and newsletter. You will also copy the new navigation bar to the index, newsletter, and tours pages. On each page you will modify the appropriate element state to reflect the current page.

Creating a Navigation Bar Using Images

To make your Web site more visually appealing, you can create a navigation bar with graphics rather than text. Any graphics you use in a navigation bar must be created in a graphics software program, such as Macromedia Fireworks or Adobe Illustrator. In order for a browser to display a navigation bar correctly, all graphic links in the navigation bar must be exactly the same size. You insert a navigation bar using the Navigation Bar button on the Insert bar or the Navigation Bar command found in the Image Objects command in the Insert menu to open the Insert Navigation Bar dialog box. You use this dialog box to specify the appearance of each graphic link, called an **element**, in each of four possible states. A **state** is the condition of the element in relation to the mouse pointer. The four states are as follows: **Up image** (the state when the mouse pointer is not on top of the element), **Over image** (the state when the

mouse pointer is positioned on top of the element), **Down image** (the state when you click the element), and **Over while down image** (the state when you click the element and continue pressing and holding the mouse button). You can create a rollover effect by using different colors or images to represent each element state. You can add many special effects to navigation bars or to links on a Web page. For instance, the Web site shown in Figure D-16 contains a navigation bar that uses rollovers and also contains images that link to featured items in the Web site.

QUICKTIP

You can place only one navigation bar on a Web page using the Insert Navigation Bar dialog box.

Copying and Modifying a Navigation Bar

After you create a navigation bar, you can copy and paste it to the other main pages in your site to save time. Make sure you place the navigation bar in the same position on each page. This practice ensures that the navigation bar will look the same on each page, making it much easier for viewers to navigate to all the pages in a Web site.

You can then use the Modify Navigation Bar dialog box to customize the appearance of the copied navigation bar on each page. For example, you can change the appearance of the services navigation bar element on the services page so that it appears in a different color. Highlighting the navigation element for the current page provides a visual reminder so that viewers can quickly tell which page they are viewing. This process ensures that the navigation bar will look consistent across all pages, but will be customized for each page.

FIGURE D-16
Ohio Historical Society Web site

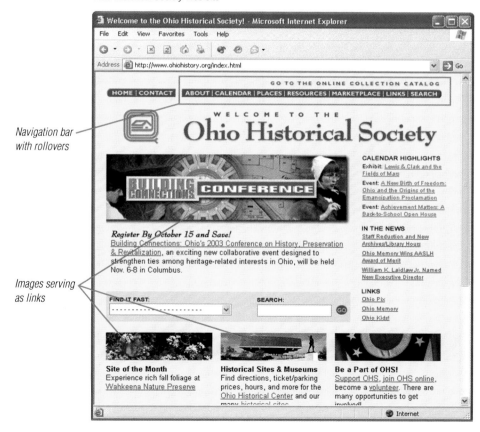

Navigation bar with rollovers

Images serving as links

Create a navigation bar using images

1. Position the insertion point to the right of the TripSmart banner on the services page, then press **[Enter]** (Win) or **[return]** (Mac).

   The insertion point is now positioned between the TripSmart banner and the first paragraph of text.

2. Click the **Insert bar list arrow**, click **Common**, click the **Images list arrow**, then click **Navigation Bar**.

3. Type **home** in the Element name text box, click the **Insert list arrow** in the dialog box, click **Horizontally** (if necessary), to specify that the navigation bar be placed horizontally on the page, then remove the check mark in the Use tables check box.

4. Click **Browse** next to the Up image text box, navigate to the drive and folder where your Data Files are stored, double-click the **chapter_d folder**, double-click the **assets folder**, then double-click **nav_home_up.jpg**.

   The path to the file nav_home_up.jpg appears in the Up image text box, as shown in Figure D-17.

5. Click **Browse** next to the Over image text box to specify a path to the file nav_home_down.jpg located in the chapter_d assets folder.

   (continued)

FIGURE D-17
Insert Navigation Bar dialog box

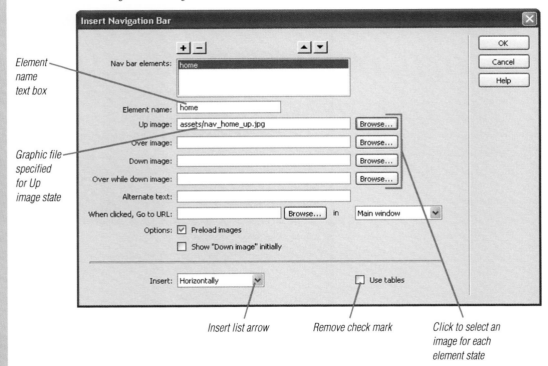

Element name text box

Graphic file specified for Up image state

Insert list arrow

Remove check mark

Click to select an image for each element state

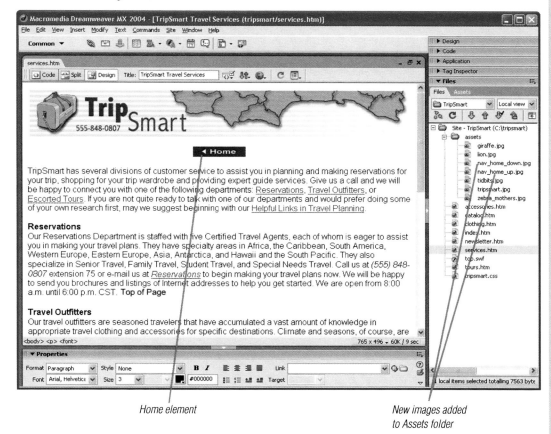

Home element

New images added
to Assets folder

6. Click **Browse** next to the Down image text box to specify a path to the file nav_home_down.jpg located in the chapter_d assets folder, overwriting the existing file.

> TIP Instead of clicking Browse in Steps 6 and 7, you could copy the path of the nav_home_down.jpg file in the Over image text box and paste it to the Down image and Over while down image text boxes. You could also reference the nav_home_down.jpg file in the TripSmart assets folder once it is copied there in Step 5.

7. Click **Browse** next to the Over while down image text box to specify a path to the file nav_home_down.jpg located in the chapter_d assets folder, overwriting the existing file.

   By specifying one graphic for the Up image state, and another graphic for the Over image, Down image, and Over while down image states, you will create a rollover effect.

8. Type **Navigation bar element linking to home page** in the Alternate text text box, click **Browse** next to the When clicked, Go to URL text box, then double-click **index.htm** in the tripsmart root folder.

9. Click **OK**, refresh the Files panel to view the new images you added to the TripSmart assets folder, deselect the button, compare your screen to Figure D-18, then save your work.

You used the Insert Navigation Bar dialog box to create a navigation bar for the services page and added the home element to it. You used two images for each state, one for the Up image state and one for the other three states.

Add elements to a navigation bar

1. Click **Modify** on the menu bar, then click **Navigation Bar**.

2. Click the **Add button** ➕ in the Modify Navigation Bar dialog box, type **catalog** in the Element name text box, then compare your screen with Figure D-19.

   TIP You use the Add button ➕ to add a new navigation element to the navigation bar, and the Delete button ➖ to delete a navigation element from the navigation bar.

3. Click **Browse** next to the Up image text box, navigate to the chapter_d assets folder, click **nav_catalog_up.jpg**, then click **OK** (Win) or **Choose** (Mac).

   TIP If a dialog box appears asking if you would like to copy the file to the root folder, click Yes, then click Save (Mac).

4. Click **Browse** next to the Over image text box to specify a path to the file nav_catalog_down.jpg located in the chapter_d assets folder.

5. Click **Browse** next to the Down image text box to specify a path to the file nav_catalog_down.jpg located in the chapter_d assets folder, overwriting the existing file.

6. Click **Browse** next to the Over while down image text box to specify a path to the file nav_catalog_down.jpg located in the chapter_d assets folder, overwriting the existing file.

(continued)

FIGURE D-19

Adding navigation bar elements

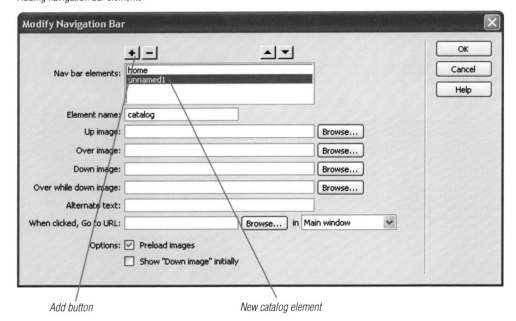

Add button   New catalog element

FIGURE D-20

Navigation bar with all elements added

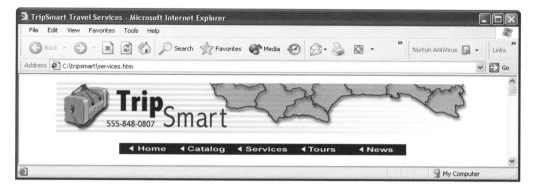

TABLE D-3: Settings to use in the Modify Navigation Bar dialog box for each new element

dialog box item	services element	tours element	newsletter element
Up image file	nav_services_up.jpg	nav_tours_up.jpg	nav_news_up.jpg
Over image file	nav_services_down.jpg	nav_tours_down.jpg	nav_news_down.jpg
Down image file	nav_services_down.jpg	nav_tours_down.jpg	nav_news_down.jpg
Over while down image file	nav_services_down.jpg	nav_tours_down.jpg	nav_news_down.jpg
Alternate text	Navigation bar element linking to services page	Navigation bar element linking to tours page	Navigation bar element linking to newsletter page
When clicked, Go to URL	services.htm	tours.htm	newsletter.htm

Lesson 4   Create, Modify, and Copy a Navigation Bar

7. Type **Navigation bar element linking to catalog page** in the Alternate text text box, click **Browse** next to the When clicked, Go to URL text box, then double-click **catalog.htm**.

8. Using the information provided in Table D-3, add three more navigation bar elements in the Modify Navigation Bar dialog box called **services**, **tours**, and **newsletter**.

   TIP   All files listed in the table are located in the assets folder of the chapter_d folder where your Data Files are stored.

9. Click **OK** to close the Modify Navigation Bar dialog box, then compare your screen to Figure D-20.

10. Save your work, preview the page in your browser, check each link to verify that each element works correctly, then close your browser.

You completed the TripSmart navigation bar by adding four more elements to it, each of which contain links to the other four pages in the site. All images added to the navigation bar are now stored in the assets folder of the TripSmart Web site.

Copy and paste a navigation bar

1. Place the insertion point to the left of the navigation bar, press and hold **[Shift]**, then click to the right of the navigation bar.

2. Click **Edit** on the menu bar, then click **Copy**.

3. Double-click **newsletter.htm** in the Files panel to open the newsletter page.

4. Click to the right of the TripSmart banner, then press **[Enter]** (Win) or **[return]** (Mac).

5. Click **Edit** on the menu bar, click **Paste**, then compare your screen to Figure D-21.

You copied the navigation bar from the services page and pasted it on the newsletter page.

Customize a navigation bar

1. Click **Modify** on the menu bar, then click **Navigation Bar** to open the Modify Navigation Bar dialog box.

2. Click **newsletter** in the Nav bar elements text box, then click the **Show "Down image" initially check box**, as shown in Figure D-22.

   An asterisk appears next to newsletter in the Nav bar elements text box, indicating that this element will be displayed in the Down image state initially. The light blue newsletter navigation element normally used for the Down image state of the newsletter navigation bar element will remind viewers that they are on the newsletter page.

   (continued)

Navigation bar copied to the newsletter page

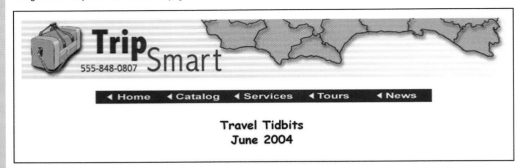

Travel Tidbits
June 2004

FIGURE D-22
Changing settings for the newsletter element

Show "Down image" initially is selected

Working with Links

FIGURE D-23

Tours page with the modified navigation bar

◄ Home ◄ Catalog ◄ Services ◄ Tours ◄ News

Destination : *Kenya*

Our next Photo Safari to Kenya has now been scheduled with a departure date of May 5 and a return date of May 23. Come join us and take some beautiful pictures like these two Grevy's zebras nursing their young at Samburu National Reserve. Our flight will leave New York for London, where you will have dayrooms reserved before flying all night to Nairobi, Kenya. To provide the finest in personal attention, this tour will be limited to no more than sixteen persons. Game drives will take place early each morning and late afternoon to provide maximum opportunity for game viewing, as the animals are most active at these times. We will visit five game reserves to allow for a variety of animal populations and scenery.

Creating an image map

Another way to create navigation links for Web pages is to create an image map. An **image map** is a graphic that has one or more hotspots placed on top of it. A **hotspot** is an area on a graphic that, when clicked, links to a different location on the page or to another Web page. For example, a map of the United States could have a hotspot placed on each state so that viewers could click a state to link to information about that state. To create a hotspot on an image, select the image on which you want to place the hotspot, then create the hotspot using one of the hotspot tools in the Property inspector.

3. Click **OK** to save the new settings and close the Modify Navigation Bar dialog box, then save and close the newsletter page.

4. Repeat Steps 1 through 3 to modify the navigation bar on the services page to show the Down image initially for the services element, then save and close the services page.

> TIP The Show "Down image" initially check box should only be checked for the element that links to the current page.

5. Open the home page, paste the navigation bar under the TripSmart banner, then modify the navigation bar to show the Down image initially for the home element.

6. Delete the original navigation bar and the horizontal line on the home page, then save and close the home page.

7. Open the Tours page, paste the navigation bar under the TripSmart banner, then use the Modify Navigation Bar dialog box to specify that the Down image be displayed initially for the tours element.

8. Delete the horizontal line on the page, then compare your screen to Figure D-23.

9. Save your work, preview the current page in your browser, test the navigation bar on the home, newsletter, services, and tours pages, then close your browser.

You modified the navigation bar on the newsletter page to show the newsletter element in the Down state initially. You then copied the navigation bar to two additional pages in the TripSmart Web site, modifying the navigation bar elements each time to show the down image state initially.

MANAGE WEB SITE LINKS

What You'll Do

In this lesson, you will use some of Dreamweaver's reporting features to check the TripSmart Web site for broken links and orphaned files.

Managing Web Site Links

Because the World Wide Web changes constantly, Web sites may be up one day and down the next. To avoid having broken links on your Web site, you need to check external links frequently. If a Web site changes server locations or goes down due to technical difficulties or a power failure, the links to it become broken. An external link can also become broken when an Internet connection fails to work properly. Broken links, like misspelled words on a Web page, indicate that a Web site is not being maintained diligently.

Checking links to make sure they work is an ongoing and crucial task you need to perform on a regular basis. You must check external links manually by reviewing your Web site in a browser and clicking each link to make sure it works correctly. The Check Links Sitewide feature is a helpful tool for managing your internal links. You can use it to check your entire Web site for the total number of links and the number of links that are OK, external, or broken, and then view the results of the link check in the Link Checker panel. The Link Checker panel also provides a list of all of the files used in a Web site, including those that are **orphaned files**, or files that are not linked to any pages in the Web site.

DESIGNTIP **Considering navigation design issues**

As you work on the navigation structure for a Web site, you should try to limit the number of links on each page to no more than is necessary. Too many links may confuse visitors to your Web site. You should also design links so that viewers can reach the information they want within three or four clicks. If finding information takes more than three or four clicks, the viewer may become discouraged or lost in the site. It's a good idea to provide visual clues on each page to let viewers know where they are, much like a "You are here" marker on a store directory at the mall.

FIGURE D-24
Link Checker panel displaying external links

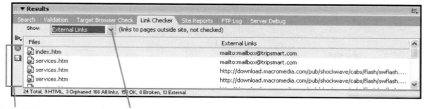

External links
displayed   Show list arrow

1. Click **Site** on the menu bar, point to **Advanced**, then click **Recreate Site Cache**.

2. Click **Site** on the menu bar, then click **Check Links Sitewide**.

   The Results panel group opens with the Link Checker panel displayed. By default the Link Checker panel initially displays any broken internal links found in the Web site. The TripSmart Web site has no broken links.

3. Click the **Show list arrow** in the Link Checker panel, click **External Links**, then compare your screen to Figure D-24.

   Some external links are listed more than once because the Link Checker displays each instance of an external link.

4. Click the **Show list arrow**, then click **Orphaned Files** to view the orphaned files in the Link Checker panel, as shown in Figure D-25.

5. Click the **Options button** in the Results panel group title bar, then click **Close panel group**.

6. Display the Assets panel (if necessary), then click the **URLs button** in the Assets panel to display the list of links in the Web site.

   The Assets panel displays the external links used in the Web site, as shown in Figure D-26.

7. Save your work, then close all open pages.

You used the Link Checker panel to check for broken links, external links, and orphaned files in the TripSmart Web site.

FIGURE D-25
Link Checker panel displaying orphaned files

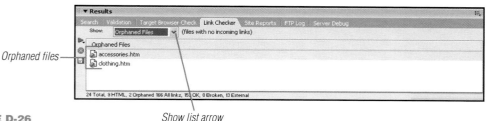

Orphaned files   Show list arrow

FIGURE D-26
Assets panel displaying links

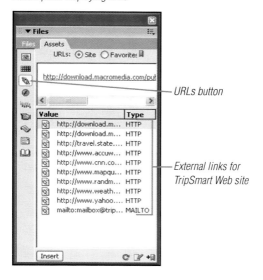

URLs button

External links for
TripSmart Web site

Lesson 5   Manage Web Site Links

Create external and internal links.

1. Open the Blooms & Bulbs Web site.
2. Open dwd_2.htm from the chapter_d Data Files folder, then save it as **master_ gardener.htm** in the Blooms & Bulbs Web site.
3. Verify that the banner path is set correctly to the assets folder in the Web site, and correct it if it is not.
4. Scroll to the bottom of the page, then link the National Gardening Association text to *http://www.garden.org.*
5. Link the Better Homes and Gardens Gardening Home Page text to *http://bhg.com/gardening.*
6. Link the Southern Living text to *http://www.southernliving.com.*
7. Save the file, then preview the page in your browser, verifying that each link works correctly.
8. Close your browser, then return to the master_gardener page in Dreamweaver.
9. Scroll to the paragraph about gardening issues, select the gardening tips text in the last sentence, then link the selected text to the tips.htm file in the blooms root folder.
10. Save the file, test the links in your browser, then close your browser.

Create internal links to named anchors.

1. Show Invisible Elements (if necessary).
2. Click the Insert bar list arrow, then click Common.

3. Insert a named anchor in front of the Grass heading named **grass**.
4. Insert a named anchor in front of the Plants heading named **plants**.
5. Insert a named anchor in front of the Trees heading named **trees**.
6. Insert a named anchor at the top of the page named **top**.
7. Click the Point to File icon in the Property inspector to create a link from the word grass in the Gardening Issues paragraph to the grass named anchor.
8. Create a link from the word trees in the Gardening Issues paragraph to the trees named anchor.
9. Create a link from the word plants in the Gardening Issues paragraph to the plants named anchor.
10. Save your work, view the page in your browser, test all the links to make sure they work, then close your browser.

Insert Flash text.

1. Insert Flash text at the bottom of the page that will take you to the top of the page. Use the following settings: Font: Arial, Size: 16, Color: #006600, Rollover color: #009933, Link: master_gardener.htm#top, Target: _top.
2. Save the Flash text file as **top.swf**.
3. Save the file, view the page in your browser, test the Flash text link, then close your browser.

Create, modify, and copy a navigation bar.

1. Using the Common category of the Insert bar, insert a horizontal navigation bar at the top of the master_gardener page below the banner.
2. Type **home** as the first element name, then use the blooms_home_up.gif file for the Up image state. This file is in the assets folder of the chapter_d Data Files folder.
3. Specify the file blooms_home_down.gif file for the three remaining states. This file is in the assets folder of the chapter_d Data Files folder.
4. Enter **Navigation element linking to the home page** as the alternate text, then set the index.htm file as the link for the home element.
5. Create a new element named **plants**, and use the blooms_plants_up.gif file for the Up image state and the blooms_plants_down.gif file for the remaining three states. These files are located in the assets folder of the chapter_d Data Files folder.
6. Enter **Navigation element linking to the plants page** as the alternate text, then set the plants.htm file as the link for the plants element.
7. Create a new element named **workshops**, and use the blooms_workshops_up.gif file for the Up image state and the blooms_ workshops_down.gif file for the remaining three states. These files are located in the assets folder of the chapter_d Data Files folder.

8. Enter **Navigation element linking to the workshops page** as the alternate text, then set the workshops.htm file as the link for the workshops element.

9. Create a new element named **tips**, and use the blooms_tips_up.gif file for the Up image state and the blooms_tips_down.gif file for the remaining three states. These files are in the assets folder of the chapter_d Data Files folder.

10. Enter **Navigation element linking to the tips page** as the alternate text, then set the tips.htm file as the link for the tips element.

11. Create a new element named **ask**, then use the blooms_ask_up.gif file for the Up image state and the blooms_ask_down.gif file for the remaining three states. These files are in the assets folder of the chapter_d Data Files folder.

12. Enter the alternate text **Navigation element linking to the master gardener page**, then set the master_gardener.htm file as the link for the ask element.

13. Center the navigation bar (if necessary), then save the page and test the links in your browser.

14. Select and copy the navigation bar, then open the home page.

15. Delete the current navigation bar on the home page, then paste the new navigation bar in its place.

16. Modify the home element on the navigation bar to show the Down image state initially.

17. Save the page, test the links in your browser, then close the browser and the page.

18. Modify the navigation bar on the master_gardener page so the Down image is shown initially for the ask element, then save and close the master_gardener page.

19. Paste the navigation bar to the plants.htm page and the tips.htm page, making the necessary modifications so that the Down image is shown initially for each element.

20. Save your work, preview all the pages in your browser, test all the links, then close your browser.

Manage Web site links.

1. Use the Link Checker panel to view broken links, external links, and orphaned files in the Blooms & Bulbs Web site.

2. If you see broken links or orphaned files, refresh the Files panel to remove them. If this does not remove the broken links, recreate the site cache. If you still see broken links, check for typing errors in the Link text box for any broken links to correct them.

3. View the external links in the Assets panel.

4. Save your work, then close all open pages.

FIGURE D-27
Completed Skills Review

Use Figure D-28 as a guide to continue your work on the Rapids Transit Web site that you began in Project Builder 1 in Chapter A. Mike Andrew, the owner, has asked you to create a new page for the Web site that lists helpful links for his customers. Also, because he no longer wants Equipment Rentals as an element in the navigation bar, he asked you to replace the existing navigation bar with a new one that contains the following elements: Home, Before You Go, Our Guides, and Country Store.

1. Open the Rapids Transit Web site.
2. Open dwd_3.htm from the chapter_d Data Files folder, then save it as **before.htm** in the Rapids Transit Web site root folder.
3. Save the buffalo_fall.gif file on the page in the assets folder of the Rapids Transit Web site, then set the path for the banner to the assets folder.
4. Create the following links:
   Buffalo National River: **http://www.ozarkmtns.com/buffalo**
   Map of the Buffalo National River: **http://www.ozarkmtns.com/buffalo/buffmap.html**

Arkansas, the Natural State: **http://www.arkansas.com**
5. Design a navigation bar using either text or graphics, then place it on each completed page of the Web site. If you decide to use graphics for the navigation bar, you will have to create your own graphic files using a graphics program. There are no data files for you to use. (*Hint*: if you create your own graphic files, be sure to create two graphic files for each element: one for the Up image state and one for the Down image state.) To design a navigation bar using text, you simply type the text for each navigation bar

element, format the text appropriately, and insert links to each text element as you did in Chapter B. The navigation bar should contain the following elements: Home, Before You Go, Our Guides, and Country Store.

6. Save each page, then check for broken links and orphaned files. You should see one orphaned file, rentals.htm, which has no links to other pages yet. You will link this page to the country store page later.

7. Test all links in your browser, close your browser, then close all open pages.

FIGURE D-28
Sample Project Builder 1

Use Figure D-29 as a guide to continue your work on the Jacob's Web site that you started in Project Builder 2 in Chapter A. Chef Jacob has sent you a copy of this month's featured pre-theatre dinner menu to place on the Web site. He has also included some links to London theatre reviews. He has asked you to add this information to the Web site. He has also asked you to insert a new navigation bar on each page of the Web site to help viewers navigate through the site easily.

1. Open the Jacob's Web site.
2. Open dwd_4.htm from the chapter_d Data Files folder, save it as **menus.htm** in the root folder of the Jacob's Web site, overwriting the existing file, then update all links.
3. Change the path of the Jacob's banner so that it is set to the jacobs.jpg file in the assets folder of the Web site.
4. Select the text post-theatre dessert specials in the first paragraph, then link it to the after_theatre.htm page.
5. Select The London Theatre Guide - Online text, and link it to **http://www.londontheatre.co.uk/**
6. Select the London Theatre Guide from the Society of London Theatre text, and link it to **http://www.officiallondontheatre.co.uk/**
7. Select the London Theatre Tickets text, and link it to **http://www.londontheatrebookings.com/**
8. Design a new navigation bar using either text or graphics, then place it at the top of the menus page. The navigation bar should contain the following elements: Home, Menus, Recipes, and Directions and Hours.

9. Copy the navigation bar, then paste it to the after_theatre.htm and index.htm pages of the site. Delete the old navigation bar on any of the pages where it appears.

10. Insert a named anchor at the top of the menus page, then create Flash text at the bottom of the page to link to it.

11. Save all the pages, then check for broken links and orphaned files.

12. Preview all the pages in your browser, check to make sure the links work correctly, close your browser, then close all open pages.

FIGURE D-29
Sample Project Builder 2

Grace Keiko is a talented young water-color artist who specializes in botanical works. She wants to develop a Web site to advertise her work, but isn't sure what she would like to include in a Web site, or how to tie the pages together. She decides to spend several hours looking at other artists' Web sites to help her get started.

1. Connect to the Internet, navigate to the Online Companion, and review the links for this chapter.
2. Spend some time looking at several of the artist Web sites that you find to familiarize yourself with the types of content that each contains.
3. What categories of page content would you include on your Web site if you were Grace?
4. What external links would you consider including?
5. Describe how you would place external links on the pages, and list examples of ones you would use.
6. Would you use text or graphics for your navigation bar?
7. Would you include rollover effects on the navigation bar elements? If so, describe how they might look.

8. How could you incorporate named anchors on any of the pages?
9. Sketch a Web site plan for Grace, including the pages that you would use as links from the home page.

FIGURE D-30
Source for Design Project

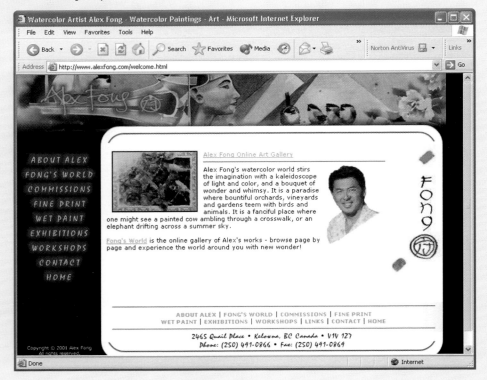

10. Refer to your Web site sketch, then create a home page for Grace that includes a navigation bar, a short introductory paragraph about her art, and a few external links.

In this assignment, you will continue to work on the group Web site that you started in Chapter A and developed in Chapters B and C. Depending on the size of your group, you can assign individual elements of the project to group members, or work collectively to create the finished product.

You will continue building your Web site by designing and completing a page with a navigation bar. After creating the navigation bar, you will copy it to each completed page in the Web site. In addition to the navigation bar, you will add several external links and several internal links to other pages as well as to named anchors. You will also link Flash text to a named anchor. After you complete this work, you will check for broken links and orphaned files.

1. Consult your storyboard and brainstorm as a team to decide which page or pages you would like to develop in this chapter. Decide how to design and where to place the navigation bar, named anchors, Flash text, and any additional page elements you decide to use. Decide which reports should be run on the Web site to check for accuracy.

2. Assign everyone on the team the task of researching Web sites that could be included on one or more of your pages as external links of interest to your viewers. Reconvene as a group to discuss your findings, then create a list of the external links you want to use. Using your storyboard as a guide, decide as a group where each external link should be placed in the site.

3. Assign a team member the task of adding external links to existing pages or creating any additional pages that contain external links.

4. Assign a team member the task of creating named anchors for key locations on the page, such as the top of the page, then linking appropriate text on the page to them.

5. Insert at least one Flash text object that links to either a named anchor or an internal link.

6. Brainstorm as a team to decide on a design for a navigation bar that will be used on all pages of the Web site.

7. Assign a team member the task of creating the navigation bar and copying it to all finished pages on the Web site. If you decided to use graphics for the navigation bar, assign a team member the task of creating the graphics that will be used.

8. Assign a team member the task of using the Link Checker panel to check for broken links and orphaned files.

9. Use the check list in Figure D-31 to make sure your Web site is complete, save your work, then close all open pages.

FIGURE D-31
Group Project check list

Web Site Check List
1. Do all pages have a page title?
2. Does the home page have a description and keywords?
3. Does the home page contain contact information?
4. Does every page in the Web site have consistent navigation links?
5. Does the home page have a last updated statement that will automatically update when the page is saved?
6. Do all paths for links and images work correctly?
7. Do all images have alternate text?
8. Do all pages have page titles?
9. Are all colors Websafe?
10. Are there any unnecessary files that you can delete from the assets folder?
11. Is there a style sheet with at least two styles?
12. Did you apply the style sheet to page content?
13. Does at least one page contain links to one or more named anchors?
14. Does at least one page contain Flash text that links to either a named anchor or an internal link?
15. Do all pages view well using at least two different browser settings?

CHAPTER 5

WORKING WITH TABLES

1. Create a table.

2. Resize, split, and merge cells.

3. Insert and align graphics in table cells.

4. Insert text and format cell content.

5. Perform Web site maintenance.

CHAPTER 5
WORKING WITH TABLES

Introduction

You have learned how to place and align elements on a page and enhance them using various formatting options. However, page layout options are fairly limited without the use of tables. Tables offer another solution for organizing text and graphics on a page. **Tables** are placeholders made up of small boxes called **cells**, into which you can insert text and graphics. Cells in a table are arranged horizontally in **rows**, and vertically in **columns**. Using tables on a Web page gives you total control over the placement of each object on the page. In this chapter, you will learn how to create and format tables, work with table rows and columns, and format the contents of table cells. You will also learn how to select and format table cells using table tags on the tag selector. Clicking a table tag on the tag selector selects the table element associated with that tag.

Inserting Graphics and Text in Tables

Once you insert a table on a Web page, it becomes very easy to place text and graphics exactly where you want them on the page. You can use a table to control both the placement of elements in relation to each other and the amount of space between each page element. Before you insert a table, however, you should always plan how your table will look with all the text and graphics in it. Even a rough sketch before you begin will save you time as you add content to the page.

Maintaining a Web Site

You already know how to check for broken links and Non-Websafe colors in your Web site. Dreamweaver also provides many other management tools to help you identify other problems. For instance, you can run a report to check for pages that have no page titles, or to search for images that are missing alternate text. It's a good idea to set up a schedule to run these and other reports on a regular basis.

Tools You'll Use

Table properties

Row properties

Cell properties

CREATE A TABLE

What You'll Do

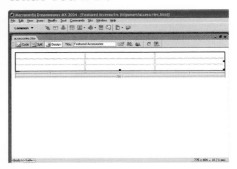

In this lesson, you will create a table for the accessories page in the TripSmart Web site to showcase several items in the TripSmart online catalog. This page, along with the clothing page, will be linked from the catalog page in the Web site.

Understanding Table Modes

There are two ways to create a table in Dreamweaver. Each method requires working in Design view. The first method is to click the Table button on the Insert bar. The Table button is available in the Common category of the Insert bar and in the Layout category of the Insert bar, whenever the Standard mode button is enabled. The second method is to click the Insert bar, click Layout, click the Layout mode button on the Insert bar, then click the Layout Table button or the Draw Layout Cell button. You can choose Standard mode, Expanded Tables mode, or Layout mode by clicking the appropriate button on the Insert bar, when the Layout category of the Insert bar is displayed.

Creating a Table in Standard Mode

Creating a table in Standard mode is useful when you want to create a table with a specific number of columns and rows. To create a table in Standard mode, click the Table button on the Insert bar to open the Table dialog box. You then enter values for the number of rows and columns, the border thickness, table width, cell padding, and cell spacing. The **border** is the outline or frame around the table and the individual cells and is measured in pixels. The table width, which can be specified in pixels or as a percentage, refers to the width of the table. When the table width is specified as a percentage, the table width will adjust to the width of the browser window. When the table width is specified in pixels, the table width stays the same, regardless of the size of the browser window. **Cell padding** is the distance between the cell content and the **cell walls**, the lines inside the cell borders. **Cell spacing** is the distance between cells.

Setting Table Accessibility Preferences for Tables

You can make a table more accessible to visually handicapped viewers by adding a table caption and a table summary that can be read by screen readers. The table caption appears on the screen. The table summary does not. These features are especially useful for tables that are used for tabular data.

Drawing a Table in Layout Mode

You use Layout mode when you want to draw your own table. Drawing a table is a good idea for those situations where you want to place page elements on a Web page, and have no need for a specific number of rows and columns. You can use the Draw Layout Cell button or the Layout Table button in the Layout category of the Insert bar to draw a cell or a table. After you draw the first cell, Dreamweaver plots a table for you automatically.

Planning a Table

Before you create a table, you should sketch a plan for it that shows its location on the Web page and the placement of text and graphics in its cells. You should also decide whether to include borders around the tables and cells. Setting the border value to zero causes the table to appear invisible, so that viewers will not realize that you used a table for the page layout unless they looked at the code. Figure E-1 shows a sketch of the table you will create on the TripSmart accessories page to organize graphics and text.

FIGURE E-1
Sketch of table on the accessories page

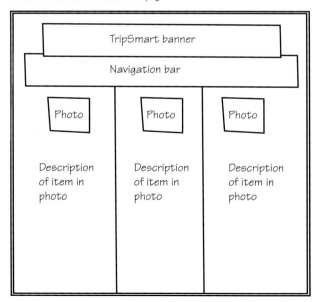

Create a table

1. Open the TripSmart Web site that you completed in Chapter D.

2. Double-click **accessories.htm** in the Files panel to open the accessories page in Design view.

   The accessories page is blank.

3. Select **Untitled Document** in the Title text box on the Document toolbar, type **Featured Accessories**, then press **[Enter]** (Win) or **[return]** (Mac) to enter a title for the table.

4. Click the **Insert bar list arrow**, click **Layout**, click the **Standard mode button** Standard, then click the **Table button** ⊞.

5. Type **3** in the Rows text box, type **3** in the Columns text box, type **750** in the Table width text box, click the **Table width list arrow**, click **pixels**, then type **0** in the Border thickness text box, as shown in Figure E-2.

   (continued)

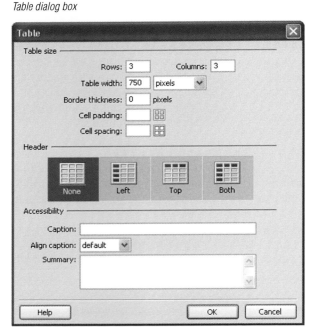

Expanded Tables mode

Expanded Tables mode is a feature that allows you to change to a table view with expanded table borders and temporary cell padding and cell spacing. This mode makes it much easier to actually see how many rows and columns you have in your table. Many times, especially after splitting empty cells, it is difficult to place the insertion point precisely in a table cell. The Expanded Tables mode allows you to see each cell clearly. However, most of the time you will want to work in Standard mode to maintain the WYSIWYG environment. **WYSIWYG** is the acronym for What You See Is What You Get. This means that your Web page should look the same in the browser as it does in the Web editor. You can toggle between Expanded Tables mode and Standard mode by pressing [F6].

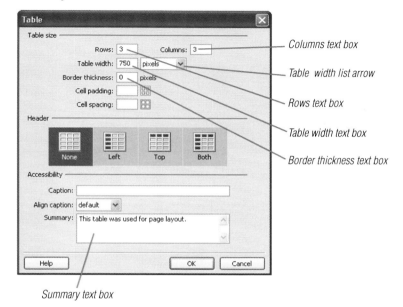

Columns text box

Table width list arrow

Rows text box

Table width text box

Border thickness text box

Summary text box

6. Type **This table was used for page layout.** in the Summary text box, then compare your screen to Figure E-3.

7. Click **OK**.

The table appears on the page, but the table summary is not visible. The summary will not appear in the browser, but will be read by screen readers.

   TIP To edit accessibility preferences for a table, you can view the page in Code view to edit the code directly.

8. Click the **Expanded Tables mode button** Expanded to view the table in Expanded Tables mode, as shown in Figure E-4.

The Expanded Tables mode makes it easier to select and edit tables.

9. Click **OK** to close the Getting Started in Expanded Tables Mode dialog box (if necessary).

10. Click the **Standard mode button** Standard to return to Standard mode.

   TIP You can also return to Standard mode by clicking [exit] at the top of the table.

You opened the accessories page in the TripSmart Web site and added a page title. You then created a table containing three rows and three columns and set the width to 750 pixels so it will appear in the same size regardless of the browser window size. Finally, you entered a table summary that will be read by screen readers.

FIGURE E-4
Expanded Tables mode

Click to exit Expanded Tables mode

Expanded Tables mode displays more space between cells for easier editing

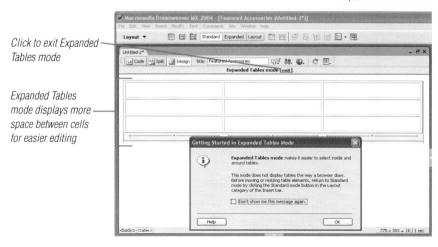

Set table properties

1. Move the pointer slowly to the edge of the table until you see the pointer change to a table pointer ⊞, then click the table border to select the table.

   TIP You can also select a table by (1) clicking the insertion point in the table, then clicking Modify, Table, Select Table; (2) selecting a cell in the table, then clicking Edit, Select All; or (3) clicking the table tag <table> on the tag selector.

2. Expand the Property inspector (if necessary) to display the current properties of the new table.

   TIP The Property inspector will only display information about the table if the table is selected.

3. Click the **Align list arrow** on the Property inspector, then click **Center** to center the table on the page, as shown in Figure E-5.

   The center alignment formatting ensures that the table will be centered in all browser windows, regardless of the screen size.

You selected and center-aligned the table.

Property inspector showing properties of selected table

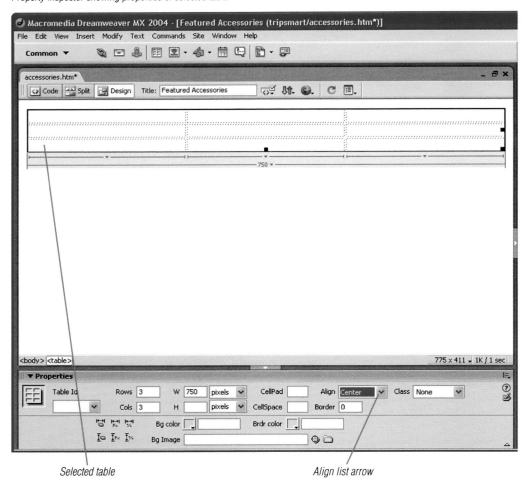

Selected table   Align list arrow

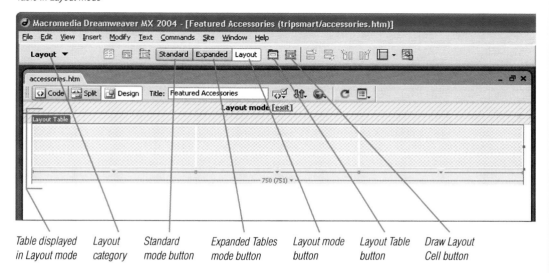

Table displayed   Layout   Standard   Expanded Tables   Layout mode   Layout Table   Draw Layout
in Layout mode   category   mode button   mode button   button   button   Cell button

View the table in Layout mode

1. Click the **Layout mode button** `Layout` on the Insert bar.

The table appears in Layout mode, as shown in Figure E-6.

> TIP The Getting Started in Layout Mode dialog box might open, providing instructions on creating and editing a table in Layout mode.

2. Click **OK** (if necessary) to close the Getting Started in Layout Mode dialog box.

3. Click the **Standard mode button** `Standard` to return to Standard mode.

4. Click the **Insert bar list arrow**, then click **Common**.

You viewed the table in Layout mode, then returned to Standard mode.

DESIGNTIP **Setting table and cell widths**

If you use a table to place all the text and graphics contained on a Web page, it is wise to set the width of the table in pixels. This ensures that the table will not resize itself proportionally if the browser window size is changed. If you set the width of a table using pixels, the table will remain one size, regardless of the browser window size. For instance, if the width of a table is set to slightly less than 800, the table will stretch across the whole width of a browser window set at a resolution of 800×600. The same table would be the same size on a screen set at 1024×768 and therefore would not stretch across the entire screen. Most designers design to a resolution of 800×600. Be aware, however, that if you set the width of your table at 800 pixels, your table will be too wide to print the entire width of the page, and part of the right side of the page will be cut off. If you are designing a table layout for a page that is likely to be printed by the viewer, you should make your table narrower to fit on a printed page. If you set a table width as a percentage, however, the table would resize itself proportionally in any browser window, regardless of the resolution. You can also set each cell width as either a percentage of the table or as fixed pixels.

RESIZE, SPLIT, AND MERGE CELLS

What You'll Do

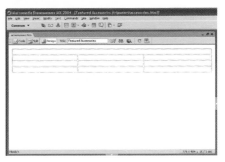

In this lesson, you will set the width of the table cells to be split evenly across the table. You will then split each of the three cells. You will also merge some cells to provide space for the banner.

Resizing Table Elements

You can resize the rows or columns of a table manually. To resize a table, row, or column, you must first select the table, then drag one of the table's three selection handles. To change all the columns in a table so that they are the same size, drag the middle-right selection handle. To resize the height of all rows simultaneously, drag the middle-bottom selection handle. To resize the entire table, drag the right-corner selection handle.

To resize a row or column individually, drag the interior cell borders up, down, to the left, or to the right. You can also resize selected columns, rows, or individual cells by entering specific measurements in the W and H text boxes in the Property inspector specified either in pixels or as a percentage. Cells whose width or height is specified as a percentage will maintain that percentage in relation to the width or height of the entire table if the table is resized.

Resetting table widths and heights

After resizing columns and rows in a table, you might want to change the sizes of the columns and rows back to their previous sizes. To reset columns and rows to their previous widths and heights, click Modify on the menu bar, point to Table, then click Clear Cell Heights or Clear Cell Widths. Using the Clear Cell Heights command also forces the cell border to snap to the bottom of any inserted graphics, so you can also use this command to tighten up extra white space in a cell.

Splitting and Merging Cells

Using the Table button creates a new table with evenly spaced columns and rows. Sometimes you might want to adjust the cells in a table by splitting or merging them. To **split** a cell means to divide it into multiple rows or columns. To **merge** cells means to combine multiple cells into one cell. Using split and merged cells gives you more flexibility and control in placing page elements on a page and can help you create a more visually exciting layout. When you merge cells, the HTML tag used to describe the merged cell changes from a width size tag to a column span or row span tag. For example, <td colspan="2"> is the code for two cells that have been merged into one cell that spans two columns.

QUICKTIP

You can split merged cells and merge split cells.

DESIGNTIP **Using nested tables**

You can insert a nested table in a table. A nested table is a table inside a table. To create a nested table, you place the insertion point in the cell where you want to insert the nested table, then click the Table button on the Insert bar. The nested table is a separate table that can be formatted differently from the table in which it is placed. Nested tables are useful when you want part of your table data to have visible borders and part to have invisible borders. For example, you can nest a table with red borders inside a table with invisible borders. You need to plan carefully when you insert nested tables. It is easy to get carried away and insert too many nested tables, which makes it more difficult to apply formatting and rearrange table elements. Before you insert a nested table, consider whether you could achieve the same result by adding rows and columns or by splitting cells.

Resize columns

1. Click inside the first cell in the bottom row, then click the **cell tag <td>** on the tag selector, as shown in Figure E-7.

   Clicking the cell tag (the HTML tag for that cell) selects the corresponding cell in the table.

   | TIP To select the entire table, click the table tag on the tag selector.

2. Type **33%** in the W text box in the Property inspector to change the width of the cell to 33 percent of the table width.

   | TIP You need to type the % sign next to the number you type in the W text box. Otherwise, the width will be expressed in pixels.

3. Repeat Steps 1 and 2 for the next two cells in the last row, using **33%** for the middle cell and **34%** for the last cell.

   The combined widths of the three cells now add up to 100 percent. As you add content to the table, the first two columns will remain 33 percent of the width of the table, and the third column will remain 34 percent.

   | TIP Changing the width of a single cell changes the width of the entire column.

You set the width of each of the three cells in the bottom row to ensure that the width of all three cells is equal.

FIGURE E-7
Selecting a cell

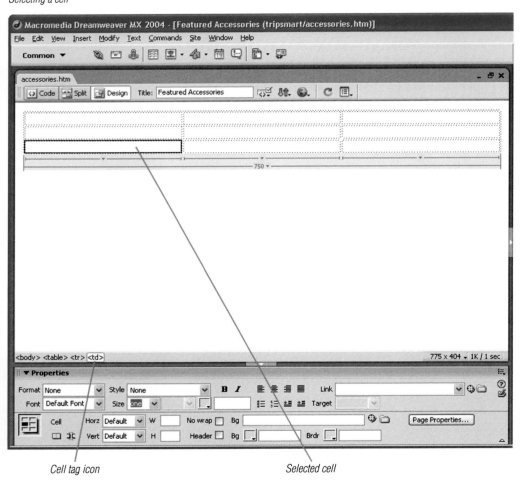

Cell tag icon   Selected cell

FIGURE E-8
Resizing the height of a row

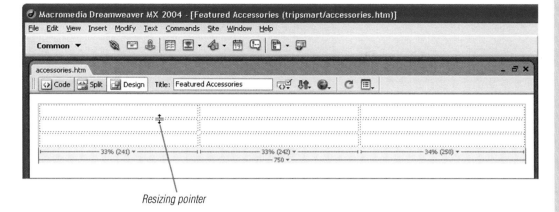

Resizing pointer

1. Place the pointer over the bottom border of the first row until it changes to a resizing pointer ↕, as shown in Figure E-8, then click and drag down about ¼ of an inch to increase the height of the row.

   The border turns darker when you select and drag it.

2. Click **Window** on the menu bar, click **History**, then drag the slider in the History panel up one line to return the row to its original height.

3. Close the History panel group.

You changed the height of the top row, then used the History panel to change it back it to its original height.

HTML table tags

When formatting a table, it is important to understand the basic HTML table tags. The tags used for creating a table are <table> </table>. The tags used to create table rows are <tr></tr>. The tags used to create table cells are <td></td>. Dreamweaver places the   code into each empty table cell at the time it is created. The   code represents a non-breaking space, or a space that a browser will display on the page. Some browsers will collapse an empty cell, which can ruin the look of a table. The non-breaking space will hold the cell until content is placed in it, at which time it will be automatically removed.

Split cells

1. Click inside the first cell in the bottom row, then click the **cell tag <td>** in the tag selector.

2. Click the **Splits cell into rows or columns button** ⬚⬚ in the Property inspector.

3. Click the **Split cell into Rows option button** (if necessary), type **2** in the Number of rows text box (if necessary), as shown in Figure E-9, then click **OK**.

4. Repeat Steps 1 through 3 to split the other two cells in the bottom row to two rows each.

   TIP To create a new row identical to the one above it, place the insertion point in the last cell of a table, then press [Tab].

You split the three cells in the bottom row into two rows, creating a new row of cells.

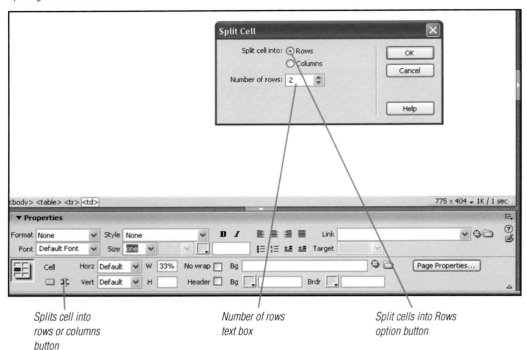

Splits cell into rows or columns button

Number of rows text box

Split cells into Rows option button

Adding or deleting a row

As you add new content to your table, you might find that you have too many or too few rows or columns. You can add or delete one row or column at a time or several at once. You use commands on the Modify menu to add and delete table rows and columns. When you add a new column or row, you must first select the existing column or row to which the new column or row will be adjacent. The Insert Rows or Columns dialog box lets you choose how many rows or columns you want to insert or delete, and where you want them placed in relationship to the selected row or column. The new column or row will have the same formatting and number of cells as the selected column or row.

FIGURE E-10
Merging selected cells into one cell

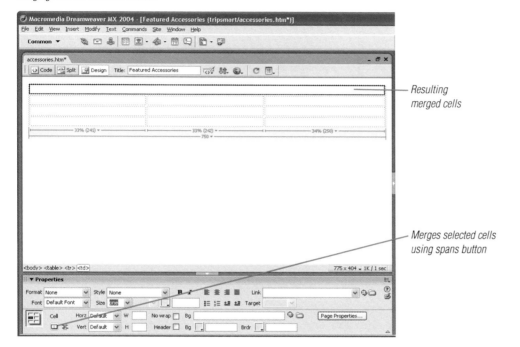

Resulting
merged cells

Merges selected cells
using spans button

FIGURE E-11
Code view for merged cells

colspan tag

Merge cells

1. Click the insertion point in the first cell in the top row, then click and drag to the right to select the second and third cells in the top row.

2. Click the **Merges selected cells using spans button** ⬚ in the Property inspector.

   The three cells are merged into one cell, as shown in Figure E-10. Merged cells are good placeholders for banners or page headings.

   TIP You can only merge cells that are adjacent to each other.

3. Click the **Show Code view button** ⟨⟩ Code , then view the code for the merged cells, as shown in Figure E-11.

   Notice the table tags denoting the column span (td colspan="3") and the non-breaking spaces ( ) inserted in the empty cells.

4. Click the **Show Design view button** 🖳 Design then save your work.

You merged three cells in the first row to make room for the TripSmart banner.

INSERT AND ALIGN GRAPHICS IN TABLE CELLS

What You'll Do

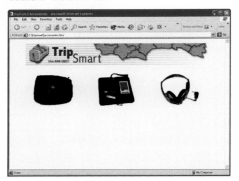

 In this lesson, you will insert the TripSmart banner in the top row of the table. You will then insert three graphics showing three TripSmart catalog items. After placing the three graphics, you will center them within their cells.

Inserting Graphics in Table Cells

You can insert graphics in the cells of a table using the Image command in the Images menu on the Insert bar. If you already have graphics saved in your Web site that you would like to insert in a table, you can drag them from the Assets panel into the table cells. When you add a large graphic to a cell, the cell expands to accommodate the inserted graphic. If you select the Show attributes when inserting

Images check box in the Accessibility preferences dialog box, the Image Tag Accessibility Attributes dialog box will open after you insert a graphic, prompting you to enter alternate text. Figure E-12 shows the John Deere Web site, which uses a table for page layout and contains several images in its table cells. Notice that some images appear in cells by themselves, and some appear in cells containing text or other graphics.

Aligning Graphics in Table Cells

You can align graphics both horizontally and vertically within a cell. You can align a graphic horizontally using the Align Left, Align Right, and Align Center buttons in the Property inspector. You can also align a graphic vertically by the top, middle, bottom, or baseline of a cell. To align a graphic vertically within a cell, use the Align list arrow in the Property inspector, then choose an alignment option, as shown in Figure E-13.

FIGURE E-12
John Deere Web site (courtesy of Deere & Company)

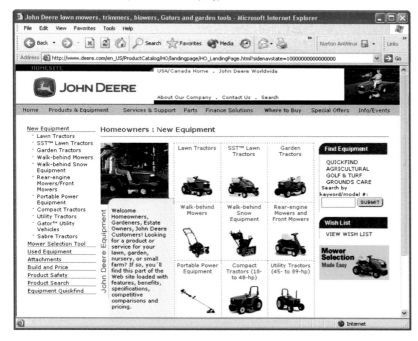

FIGURE E-13
Vertically aligning cell contents

Vertical alignment options

Insert graphics in table cells

1. Show the Assets panel (if necessary), click the **Images button** 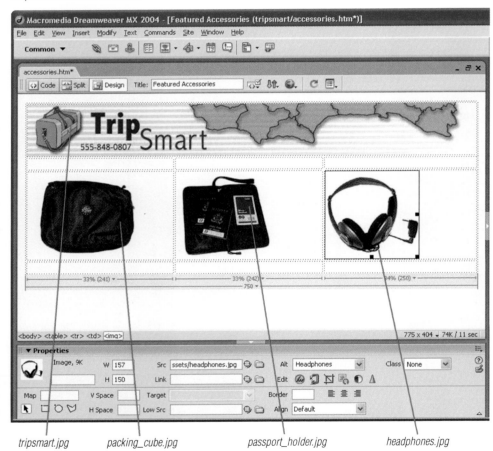 on the Assets panel (if necessary), then drag the tripsmart.jpg graphic from the Assets panel to the top row of the table.

    The Image Tag Accessibility Attributes dialog box opens.

2. Type **TripSmart banner** as alternate text for the TripSmart banner, (if necessary), then click **OK**.

3. Click in the first cell in the third row, insert packing_cube.jpg from the chapter_e assets folder, then enter **Packing Cube** for the alternate text.

4. Repeat Step 3 to insert passport_holder.jpg and headphones.jpg in the next two cells, using **Passport Holder** and **Headphones** for the alternate text, then compare your screen to Figure E-14.

    TIP Press [Tab] to move your insertion point to the next cell in a row. Press [Shift][Tab] to move your insertion point to the previous cell.

5. Refresh the Assets panel to verify that the three new graphics were copied to the TripSmart Web site assets folder.

6. Save your work, then preview the page in your browser.

    Notice that the page would look better if each graphic were evenly distributed across the page.

7. Close your browser.

You inserted images into four cells of the table on the accessories page.

FIGURE E-14

Graphics inserted into table cells

tripsmart.jpg   packing_cube.jpg   passport_holder.jpg   headphones.jpg

1. Click the **TripSmart banner**, then click the **Align Center button** ☰ in the Property inspector.

2. Center-align the packing cube, passport holder, and headphones images, as shown in Figure E-15.

3. Save your work.

4. Preview the page in your browser, view the centered images, then close your browser.

You center-aligned the TripSmart banner and the three graphics within their respective cells.

FIGURE E-15
Centering images in cells

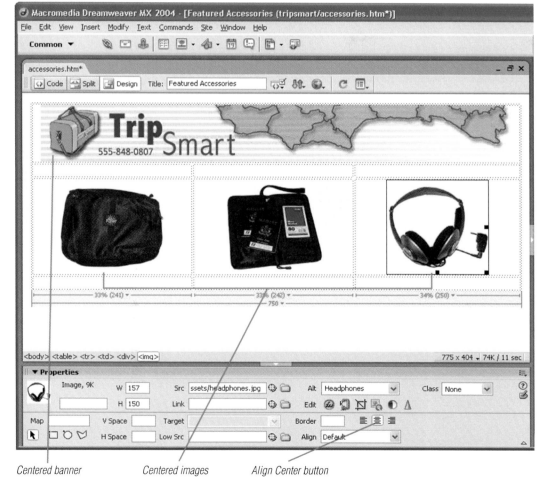

Centered banner   *Centered images*   *Align Center button*

INSERT TEXT AND FORMAT CELL CONTENT

What You'll Do

 In this lesson, you will type a heading for the accessories page and copy and paste descriptive text for each item on the page. You will then format the text to enhance its appearance on the page. Last, you will add descriptive names for each item and then format the text you added.

Inserting Text in a Table

You can enter text in a table either by typing it in a cell, copying it from another source and pasting it into a cell, or importing it from another program. Once you place text in a table cell, you can format it to make it more readable and more visually appealing on the page.

Formatting Cell Content

Making modifications and formatting changes to a table and its contents is easier to do in Standard mode than in Layout mode. To format the contents of a cell in Standard mode, you select the contents in the cell, and then apply formatting to it. If a cell contains multiple objects of the same type, such as text, you can either format each item individually or select the entire cell and apply formatting that will be applied identically to all items. You can tell whether you have selected the cell contents or the cell by looking to see what options are showing in the Property inspector. Figure E-16 shows a selected graphic in a cell. Notice that the Property inspector displays options for formatting the object, rather than options for formatting the cell.

Formatting Cells

Formatting cells is different than formatting cell contents. Formatting a cell can include setting properties that visually enhance the cell appearance, such as setting a cell width, assigning a background color, or setting global alignment properties for the cell content. To format a cell, you need to either select the cell or place the insertion point inside the cell you want to format, then choose the cell formatting options you want in the Property inspector. For example, to choose a fill color for a selected cell, you click the Background Color button in the Property inspector, then choose a color from the color picker.

In order to format a cell, you must expand the Property inspector to display the cell formatting options. In Figure E-17, notice that the insertion point is positioned in the passport holder cell, but the passport holder graphic is not selected. The Property inspector displays the formatting options for cells.

FIGURE E-16
Property inspector showing options for formatting cell contents

Property inspector shows properties for selected graphic

Graphic cell contents selected

FIGURE E-17
Property inspector showing options for formatting a cell

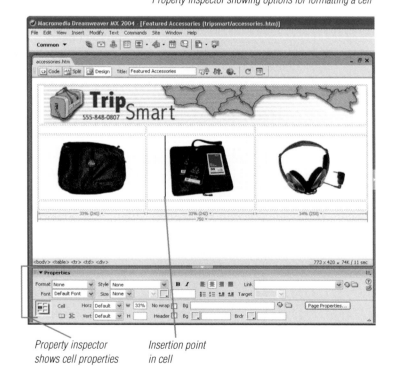

Property inspector shows cell properties

Insertion point in cell

Insert text

1. Click to the right of the TripSmart banner to place the insertion point, press **[Enter]** (Win) or **[return]** (Mac), then type **Featured Catalog Accessories**.

2. Open packing_cube.htm from the chapter_e Data Files folder, click **Edit** on the menu bar, click **Select All**, click **Edit** on the menu bar, click **Copy**, then close packing_cube.htm.

3. Click in the cell under the packing cube image, click **Edit** on the menu bar, then click **Paste**.

4. Repeat Steps 2 and 3 to paste all the text contained in the passport_holder.htm and headphones.htm files in the cells below their respective images.

5. Click in the cell above the packing cube image, type **Packing Cubes**, press **[Tab]**, type **Passport Holder**, press **[Tab]**, then type **Headphones**, as shown in Figure E-18.

You typed headings into four cells and copied and pasted descriptive text in the three cells under the three images.

Copying and pasting text into cells

Passport Holder heading

Packing Cubes heading

Packing Cubes description

Table tag

Page heading

Headphones heading

Headphones description

Passport Holder description

Importing and exporting data from tables

You can import and export tabular data into and out of Dreamweaver. Tabular data is data that is arranged in columns and rows and separated by a **delimiter**: a comma, tab, colon, semicolon, or similar character. **Importing** means to bring data created in another software program into Dreamweaver, and **exporting** means to save data created in Dreamweaver in a special file format that can be inserted into other programs. Files that are imported into Dreamweaver must be saved as delimited files. **Delimited files** are database or spreadsheet files that have been saved as text files with delimiters such as tabs or commas separating the data. Programs such as Microsoft Access and Microsoft Excel offer many file formats for saving files. To import a delimited file, you click File on the menu bar, point to Import, then click Tabular Data. The Import Tabular Data dialog box opens, offering you formatting options for the imported table. To export a table that you created in Dreamweaver, you click File on the menu bar, point to Export, then click Table. The Export Table dialog box opens, letting you choose the type of delimiter you want for the delimited file.

FIGURE E-19

Formatting text using the Property inspector and Assets panel

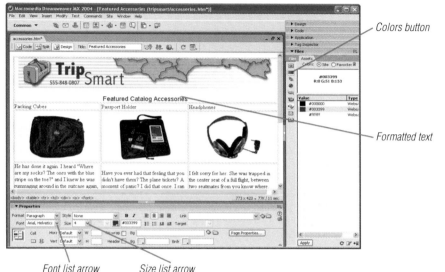

Colors button

Formatted text

Font list arrow   Size list arrow

FIGURE E-20

Formatting catalog item descriptions

Three descriptions
with uniform look

Format cell content

1. Select the Featured Catalog Accessories text, click the **Font list arrow** in the Property inspector, click **Arial, Helvetica, sans-serif**, click the **Size list arrow**, then click **4**.

   TIP   If you do not see numeric sizes in the Size menu, remove the check mark in the Use CSS instead of HTML tags check box in the General Preferences dialog box.

2. Make sure that Featured Catalog Accessories is still selected, click the **Colors button** 🔳 on the Assets panel, click and drag color # 003399 onto the selected text, then deselect the text.

   Compare your screen to Figure E-19.

3. Click in the cell below the packing cube image, then use the Property inspector to set the horizontal alignment to Left and the vertical alignment to Top.

4. Select all of the text in the same cell, then change the font to Arial, Helvetica, sans serif, size 2.

5. Repeat Steps 3 and 4 to format the description text in the cells below the passport holder and headphones graphics, using the same formatting applied to the packing cubes description text.

   Your screen should resemble Figure E-20.

You formatted text in table cells.

Format cells

1. Click the **table tag** on the tag selector to select the entire table.

2. Type **12** in the CellSpace text box in the Property inspector, then press **[Enter]**(Win) or **[return]**(Mac) to add 12 pixels of space between the cells, as shown in Figure E-21.

   The descriptions are easier to read now because you inserted a little white space between the columns.

3. Click in the cell with the Packing Cubes heading.

4. Click the **Background Color (Bg) button** in the Property inspector, then click the second color in the fourth row (#003399).

5. Repeat Step 4 to apply the background color #003399 to the next two cells containing the text Passport Holder and Headphones, then compare your screen to Figure E-22.

   The headings are no longer visible against the blue background.

You formatted table cells by adding cell spacing. You set the background color for three cells to blue.

FIGURE E-21
Changing the CellSpace amount

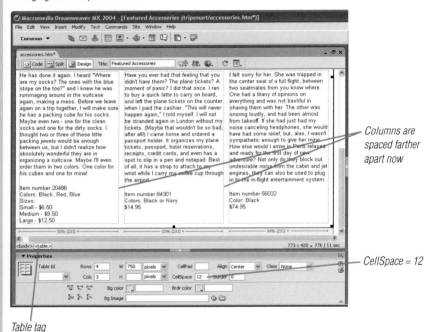

Columns are spaced farther apart now

CellSpace = 12

Table tag

FIGURE E-22
Formatted backgrounds

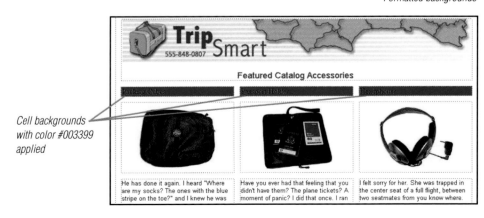

Cell backgrounds with color #003399 applied

Working with Tables

FIGURE E-23
Formatted text labels

Formatted text labels

He has done it again. I heard "Where are my socks? The ones with the blue stripe on the toe?" and I knew he was rummaging around in the suitcase

Have you ever had that feeling that you didn't have them? The plane tickets? A moment of panic? I did that once. I ran to buy a quick latte to carry on board,

I felt sorry for her. She was trapped in the center seat of a full flight, between two seatmates from you know where. One had a litany of opinions on

1. Select the Packing Cubes text label in the cell above the packing cube image, use the Property inspector to format the text as Arial, Helvetica, sans-serif, size 4, center-aligned, white (#FFFFFF), then deselect the text.

    Compare your screen with Figure E-23.

2. Repeat Step 1 to format the Passport Holder and Headphones text labels.

3. Scroll to the bottom of the page, select Item number 20486, then click the **Bold button B** in the Property inspector.

4. Apply bold formatting to the item numbers in the next two cells, as shown in Figure E-24.

5. Save your work, preview the accessories page in your browser, then close your browser.

You formatted the text headings and the item numbers on the accessories page.

FIGURE E-24
Formatted item numbers

Item numbers with bold formatting applied

He has done it again. I heard "Where are my socks? The ones with the blue stripe on the toe?" and I knew he was rummaging around in the suitcase again, making a mess. Before we leave again on a trip together, I will make sure he has a packing cube for his socks. Maybe even two - one for the clean socks and one for the dirty socks. I thought two or three of these little packing jewels would be enough between us, but I didn't realize how absolutely wonderful they are in organizing a suitcase. Maybe I'll even order them in two colors. One color for his cubes and one for mine!

Item number 20486
Colors: Black, Red, Blue
Sizes:
Small - $6.50
Medium - $9.50
Large - $12.50

Have you ever had that feeling that you didn't have them? The plane tickets? A moment of panic? I did that once. I ran to buy a quick latte to carry on board, and left the plane tickets on the counter when I paid the cashier. "This will never happen again," I told myself. I will not be stranded again in London without my tickets. (Maybe that wouldn't be so bad, after all!) I came home and ordered a passport holder. It organizes my plane tickets, passport, hotel reservations, receipts, credit cards, and even has a spot to slip in a pen and notepad. Best of all, it has a strap to attach to my wrist while I carry my coffee cup through the airport.

Item number 84301
Colors: Black or Navy
$14.95

I felt sorry for her. She was trapped in the center seat of a full flight, between two seatmates from you know where. One had a litany of opinions on everything and was not bashful in sharing them with her. The other was snoring loudly, and had been almost from takeoff. If she had just had my noise canceling headphones, she would have had some relief, but, alas, I wasn't sympathetic enough to give her mine. How else would I arrive in Paris relaxed and ready for the first day of new adventure? Not only do they block out undesirable noise from the cabin and jet engines, they can also be used to plug in to the in-flight entertainment system.

Item number 56032
Color: Black
$74.95

33% (231) ▼   33% (231) ▼   34% (231) ▼

PERFORM WEB SITE MAINTENANCE

What You'll Do

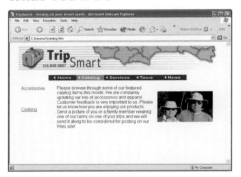

 In this lesson, you will use some of Dreamweaver's site maintenance tools to check for broken links, orphaned files, and missing alternate text. You will also verify that all colors are Websafe. You will then correct any problems that you find.

Maintaining a Web Site

As you add pages, links, and content to a Web site, it can quickly become difficult to manage. It's important to perform maintenance tasks frequently to make sure your Web site operates smoothly. To keep a Web site "clean," you should use Dreamweaver site maintenance tools frequently. You have already learned about some of the tools described in the paragraphs below. While it is important to use them as you create and modify your pages, it is also important to run them at periodic intervals after publishing your Web site to make sure your Web site is always error-free.

Checking Links Sitewide

Before and after you publish your Web site, you should use the Link Checker panel to make sure all internal links are working. If the Link Checker panel displays any broken links, you should repair them. If the Link Checker panel displays any orphaned files, you should evaluate whether to delete them or link them to existing pages.

Using the Assets Panel

You should also use the Assets panel to check the list of images and colors used in your Web site. If you see images listed that are not being used, you should move them to a storage folder outside the Web site until you need them. You should also check the Colors list to make sure that all colors in the site are Websafe. If there are Non-Websafe colors in the list, locate the elements to which these colors are applied and apply Websafe colors to them.

Using Site Reports

You can use the Reports command in the Site menu to generate six different HTML reports that can help you maintain your Web site. You choose the type of report you want to run in the Reports dialog box, shown in Figure E-25. You can specify whether to generate the report for the entire current local site, selected files in the site, or a selected folder. You can also generate Workflow reports to see files that have been checked out by others or recently modified or to view the Design Notes attached to files.

Using the Site Map

You can use the site map to check your navigation structure. Does the navigation structure shown in the site map reflect a logically organized flowchart? Is each page three or four clicks from the home page? If the answer is no to either of these questions, you can make adjustments to improve the navigation structure.

Testing Pages

Finally, you should test your Web site using many different types and versions of browsers, platforms, and screen resolutions. You should test all links to make sure they connect to valid, active Web sites. Pages that download slowly should be trimmed in size to improve performance. You should analyze all feedback on the Web site objectively, saving both positive and negative comments for future reference to help you make improvements to the site.

FIGURE E-25
Reports dialog box

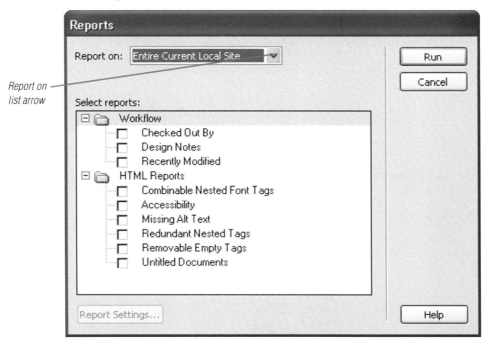

Report on list arrow

Check for broken links

1. Show the Files panel (if necessary).
2. Click **Site** on the menu bar, point to **Advanced**, then click **Recreate Site Cache**.
3. Click **Site** on the menu bar, then click **Check Links Sitewide**.

   No broken links are listed in the Link Checker, as shown in Figure E-26.

You verified that there are no broken links in the Web site.

FIGURE E-26

Link Checker panel displaying no broken links

Your total number of files and links may differ   *No broken links*

Check for orphaned files

1. Click the **Show list arrow**, then click **Orphaned Files**.

   As Figure E-27 shows, the accessories page and the clothing page appear as orphaned files. You will link the catalog page to these pages later.

   TIP   If you have more than two orphaned files, click Site on the menu bar, point to Advanced, click Recreate Site Cache, then check for orphaned files again.

2. Close the Results panel group.

You used the Link Checker to find two orphaned files in the Web site.

FIGURE E-27
Link Checker panel displaying orphaned files

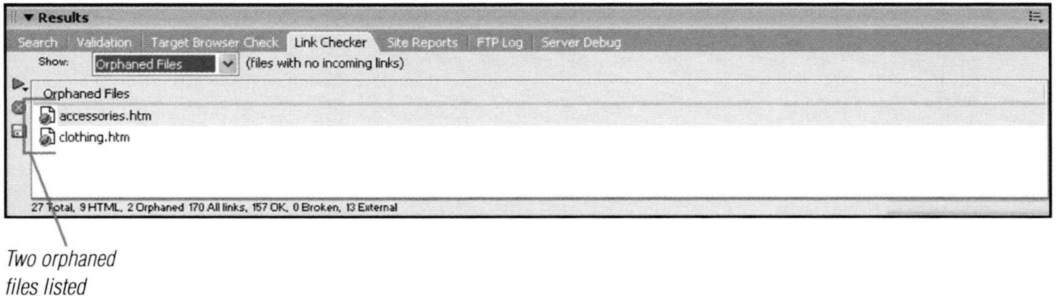

Two orphaned files listed

Remove orphaned files

1. Open dwe_1.htm from the chapter_e Data Files folder, then save it in the Web site as **clothing.htm**, overwriting the existing file.

2. Copy hat.jpg, vest.jpg, and pants.jpg on the clothing page to the assets folder in the Web site.

3. Change the path of the TripSmart banner path to the tripsmart.jpg image in the assets folder in the TripSmart Web site, then save and close the clothing page.

4. Open dwe_2.htm from the chapter_e Data Files folder, then save it in the TripSmart Web site as **catalog.htm**, overwriting the existing file.

5. Copy hats_on_the_amazon.jpg to the assets folder in the Web site.

6. Check all internal links and images to verify that all paths are set correctly, then save and close the catalog page.

   TIP Use the Modify Navigation Bar dialog box to change the paths of the navigation bar images and links to appropriate files in the TripSmart Web site.

7. Direct your attention to the accessories page.

8. Place the insertion point in the last cell in the table, press **[Tab]** to insert a new row, then type **Back to catalog page**.

9. Format the Back to catalog page text as Arial, Helvetica, sans serif, size 3, then link the Back to catalog page text to catalog.htm.

   Compare your screen to Figure E-28.

(continued)

Link to catalog page on accessories page

are my socks? The ones with the blue stripe on the toe?" and I knew he was rummaging around in the suitcase again, making a mess. Before we leave again on a trip together, I will make sure he has a packing cube for his socks. Maybe even two - one for the clean socks and one for the dirty socks. I thought two or three of these little packing jewels would be enough between us, but I didn't realize how absolutely wonderful they are in organizing a suitcase. Maybe I'll even order them in two colors. One color for his cubes and one for mine!

Item number 20486
Colors: Black, Red, Blue
Sizes:
Small - $6.50
Medium - $9.50
Large - $12.50

didn't have them? The plane tickets? A moment of panic? I did that once. I ran to buy a quick latte to carry on board, and left the plane tickets on the counter when I paid the cashier. "This will never happen again," I told myself. I will not be stranded again in London without my tickets. (Maybe that wouldn't be so bad, after all!) I came home and ordered a passport holder. It organizes my plane tickets, passport, hotel reservations, receipts, credit cards, and even has a spot to slip in a pen and notepad. Best of all, it has a strap to attach to my wrist while I carry my coffee cup through the airport.

Item number 84301
Colors: Black or Navy
$14.95

the center seat of a full flight, between two seatmates from you know where. One had a litany of opinions on everything and was not bashful in sharing them with her. The other was snoring loudly, and had been almost from takeoff. If she had just had my noise canceling headphones, she would have had some relief, but, alas, I wasn't sympathetic enough to give her mine. How else would I arrive in Paris relaxed and ready for the first day of new adventure? Not only do they block out undesirable noise from the cabin and jet engines, they can also be used to plug in to the in-flight entertainment system.

Item number 56032
Color: Black
$74.95

Back to catalog page.

Inserted row   *Text link*

10. Save and close the accessories page, then open the clothing page.

11. Repeat Steps 8 and 9 to create a Back to catalog page text link at the bottom of the clothing page, then compare your screen with Figure E-29.

12. Recreate the site cache, click the **Refresh button** C on the Files panel, then run the Check Links Sitewide report again to verify that there are no orphaned files.

> TIP If the Link Checker panel shows orphaned files, recreate the site cache. If orphaned files still appear in the report, locate them in the Web site, then correct the paths that contain errors. If you still have orphaned files after performing these steps, record the names of the orphaned files, determine which page(s) should have links to them, then open those pages and correct the links.

13. Save and close the clothing page.

You corrected the two orphaned files by linking the accessories and clothing pages from the catalog page.

FIGURE E-29

Link to catalog page on clothing page

Link to catalog page

Verify that all colors are Websafe

1. Click the **Colors button** 🎨 on the Assets panel to view the Web site colors, as shown in Figure E-30.

   The Assets panel shows that all colors used in the Web site are Websafe.

   > TIP If you type a color name in the color picker, include the # sign as part of the name.

You verified that the Web site contains all Websafe colors.

Check for untitled documents

1. Click **Site** on the menu bar, then click **Reports** to open the Reports dialog box.

2. Click the **Untitled Documents check box**, click the **Report on list arrow**, click **Entire Current Local Site**, as shown in Figure E-31, then click **Run**.

   The Site Reports panel opens and shows no files, indicating that all documents in the Web site contain titles.

3. Close the Results panel group.

You verified that the Web site contains no untitled documents.

FIGURE E-30
Assets panel displaying Websafe colors

— All colors are Websafe

FIGURE E-31
Reports dialog box with Untitled Documents option selected

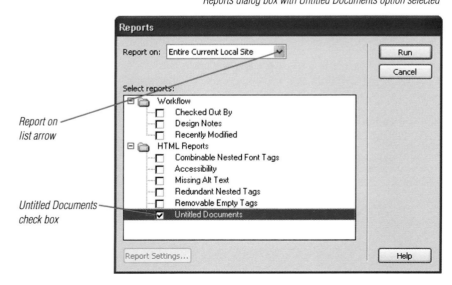

Report on list arrow

Untitled Documents check box

Reports dialog box with Missing Alt Text option selected

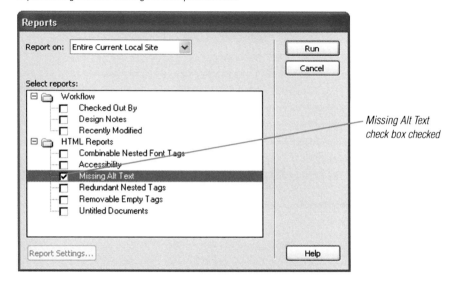

Missing Alt Text
check box checked

Check for missing alternate text

1. Using Figure E-32 as a guide, run another report that checks the entire current local site for missing alternate text.

   Two pages contain images that are missing alternate text, as shown in Figure E-33.

2. Open the catalog page, then find the image that is missing alternate text.

3. Add appropriate alternate text to the image.

4. Repeat Steps 2 and 3 to locate the image on the home page that is missing alternate text, then add alternate text to it.

5. Save your work, then run the report again to check the entire site for missing alternate text.

   No files should appear in the Site Reports panel.

6. Close the Results panel group, then close all open pages.

You ran a report to check for missing alternate text in the entire site. You then added alternate text to two images, and ran the report again.

FIGURE E-33
Site Reports panel displaying missing "alt" tags

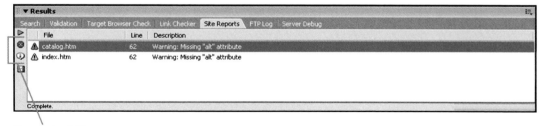

Two missing "alt"
tags found

Create a table.

1. Open the Blooms & Bulbs Web site.
2. Open workshops.htm from the Web site.
3. Insert a table on the page with the following settings: Rows: 5, Columns: 3, Table width: 750 pixels, Border thickness: 0.
4. Enter the text **This table is used for page layout.** in the Summary text box.
5. Center the table on the page, then use Figure E-34 as a guide for completing this exercise.
6. Save your work.

Resize, split, and merge cells.

1. Select the first cell in the first row, then set the cell width to 35%.
2. Select the second cell in the first row, then set the cell width to 35%.
3. Select the third cell in the first row, then set the cell width to 30%.
4. Merge the third cell in the third row with the third cell in the fourth row.
5. Split the first cell in the third row into two rows.
6. Split the second cell in the third row into two rows.
7. Merge the three cells in the first row.
8. Merge the three cells in the second row.
9. Save your work.

Insert and align graphics in table cells.

1. Use the Assets panel to insert the Blooms & Bulbs banner in the first row and enter appropriate alternate text when prompted.
2. Center the banner.
3. Copy the navigation bar from the home page, paste it in the second row of the table, then center the navigation bar using the Property inspector.
4. Modify the navigation bar to show the workshops element in the Down image state and the home element in the Up image state.
5. Use the Insert bar to insert texas_rose.jpg in the third cell of the third row (the merged cell) directly below the navigation bar. You can find the texas_rose.jpg file in the in the chapter_e assets folder where your Data Files are stored. Add the alternate text **Texas Rose Festival logo** to the texas_rose.jpg when prompted, then center the image in the cell.
6. Use the tag selector to select the cell containing the texas_rose.jpg image, then set the vertical alignment to Top.
7. Use the Insert bar to insert the yellow_rose.jpg file from the chapter_e assets folder in the second cell in the fifth row. Add the alternate text **Yellow roses** to the yellow_rose.jpg when prompted.
8. Use the Align list arrow to set the alignment of the yellow_rose.jpg to Left.
9. Select the cell containing the yellow_rose.jpg, then set the vertical alignment of the selected cell to Top.
10. Insert tearoom.jpg from the chapter_e assets folder in the second cell of the last row, adding the alternate text **Rose arrangement in antique pitcher** when prompted.
11. Center the tearoom.jpg image.
12. Set the vertical alignment of the cell containing the tearoom.jpg image to Top.
13. Save your work.

Insert text and format cell content.

1. Type **Texas Rose Festival** in the second cell in the fourth row, insert a line break, then type **Tyler, Texas**.
2. Type **Agenda** in the first cell in the fourth row.
3. Open the file agenda.htm from the chapter_e Data Files folder, copy all the text in this file, close agenda.htm, then paste the text into the first cell in the fifth row.
4. Open nursery.htm from the chapter_e Data Files folder, copy all the text from this file, paste it into the cell containing the yellow_rose.jpg image to the right of the image, then close the file.
5. Open tearoom.htm from the chapter_e Data Files folder, copy all the text from this file, close tearoom.htm, then paste the text in the first cell in the last row.
6. Open exhibition.htm from the chapter_e Data Files folder, copy all the text from this file, close exhibition.htm, then paste the text in the last cell in the last row.

Working with Tables

CHAPTER F

COLLECTING DATA WITH FORMS

1. Plan and create a form.

2. Format a form.

3. Work with form objects.

4. Create a jump menu.

CHAPTER F
COLLECTING DATA WITH FORMS

Introduction

Many Web sites have pages designed to collect information from viewers. You've likely seen such pages when ordering books online from Barnes and Noble or purchasing airline tickets from an airline Web site. Adding a form to a Web page provides interactivity between your viewers and your business. To collect information from viewers, you add forms for them to fill out and send to a Web server to be processed. Forms on a Web page are no different from forms in everyday life. Your checks are simple forms that ask for six pieces of information every time you fill them out: the date, the amount in digits, the amount written out, the name of the check's recipient, a comment/memo about the check, and your signature. A form on a Web page consists of **form objects** such as text boxes or radio buttons into which viewers type information or from which they make selections.

In this chapter you will begin working with a new Web site for Northwest Warehouse, a leading retailer of portable computer devices that also offers technical training and consulting services. You will add a form to a page on this Web site that asks viewers to provide information about themselves and their interests.

Using Forms to Collect Information

Forms are just one of the many different tools that Web developers use to collect information from viewers. They can range from the simple to the complex. A simple form can consist of one form object and a button that submits information to a Web server, for example, a search text box that you fill out, and a button that you click to start the search. More complex forms can collect contact information, or even allow students to take exams online and receive grades after a short wait. You can use forms to insert information into databases, or to find a specific record in a database. The range of uses for forms is limited only by your imagination.

All forms need to be connected to an application that will process the information that the form collects. This application can store the form data in a database, or simply send it to you in an e-mail message. You need to specify how you want the information used, stored, and processed.

Tools You'll Use

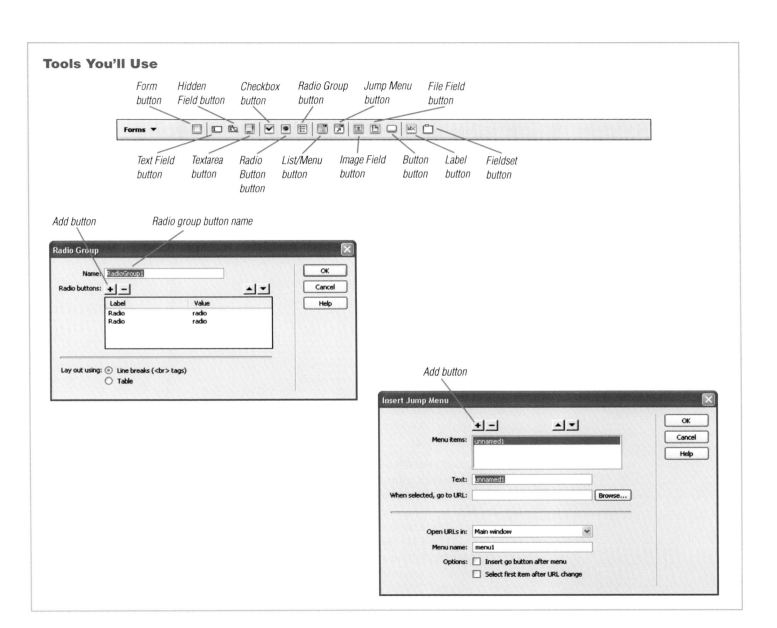

PLAN AND CREATE A FORM

What You'll Do

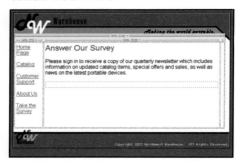

In this lesson, you will add a new form to the survey.htm page in the Northwest Warehouse Web site.

Planning a Form

Before you use Dreamweaver to create a form, it's a good idea to write down the information you want to collect and the order in which you want to collect it. It's also a good idea to make a sketch of the form. Planning your form content at the beginning saves you from spending time organizing the information when you create the form in Dreamweaver. The survey page of the Northwest Warehouse Web site will contain a form that asks viewers to fill in their contact information and sign up for a quarterly newsletter. Figure F-1 shows a sketch of the form that you will create in this chapter.

When planning your form content, you should organize the information in a logical order that will make sense to viewers. For instance, no one will expect to fill in their address before their name, simply because it isn't typically done that way. Almost all forms, from your birth certificate to your IRS tax forms, request your name before your address, so you should

follow this standard. Placing information in an unusual order will only confuse your viewers.

QUICKTIP

People on the Internet are notoriously hurried and will often provide only information that is required or that is located on the top half of the form. Therefore, it's a good idea to put the most important information at the top of your form.

Creating Forms

Once you have finished planning your form content, you are ready to create the form in Dreamweaver. To create a form on a Web page, you use the Form button in the Forms category of the Insert bar. Clicking the Form button will insert a dashed red outline around the area of the form. In order to make your form function correctly, you then need to configure the form so that it "talks" to the scripts or e-mail server, and processes the information submitted by the viewer. By itself, a form can do nothing. It has to have some type of script or program running behind it that will process the information to be used in a certain way.

There are two methods used to process the information your form collects: server-side scripting and client-side scripting. **Server-side scripting** uses applications that reside on the Web server and interact with the information collected in the form. The most common types of server-side applications are **Common Gateway Interface (CGI)** scripts, **Cold Fusion** programs, and **Active Server Pages (ASP)** applications. **Client-side scripting** means that the form is processed on the user's computer. The script resides on the Web page, rather than on the server. An example of this is a mortgage calculator that allows you to estimate mortgage payments. The data is processed on the user's computer. The most common types of scripts stored on a Web page are created with a scripting language called **JavaScript**, or **Jscript** if you are using a Microsoft Web browser. Server-side applications and scripts collect the information from the form, process the information, and react to the information the form contains.

You can process form information in a variety of ways. The easiest and most common way is to collect the information from the form and e-mail it to the owner of the Web site. You can also specify that form data be stored in a database for the Web site owner to use at a later date. You can even specify that the application do both: collect the form data in a database, as well as send it in an e-mail message. You can also specify that the form data be processed instead of stored. For instance, you can create a form that totals the various prices and provides a total price to the site viewer on the order page, without recording any subtotals in a database or e-mail message. In this example, only the final total of the order would be stored in the database or sent in an e-mail message.

FIGURE F-1

Sketch of Web form you will add to survey page

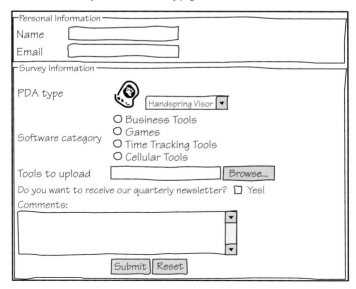

You can also create forms that make changes to your Web page based on information entered by viewers. For example, you could create a form that asks viewers to select a background color for a Web page. In this type of form, the information could be collected and sent to the processor. The processor could then compare the selected background color to the current background color, and change the color if it is different from the viewer's selection.

Setting Form Properties

After you insert a form, you use the Property inspector to specify the application that will process the form information, and to specify how the information will be sent to the processing application. The **Action property** in the Property inspector specifies the application or script that will process the form data. Most of the time the Action property is the name and location of a CGI script, such as

/cgi-bin/myscript.cgi; a Cold Fusion page, such as mypage.cfm; or an Active Server Page, such as mypage.asp. Figure F-2 shows the properties of a selected form with the Action property set to a CGI script.

FIGURE F-2
Form controls in the Property inspector

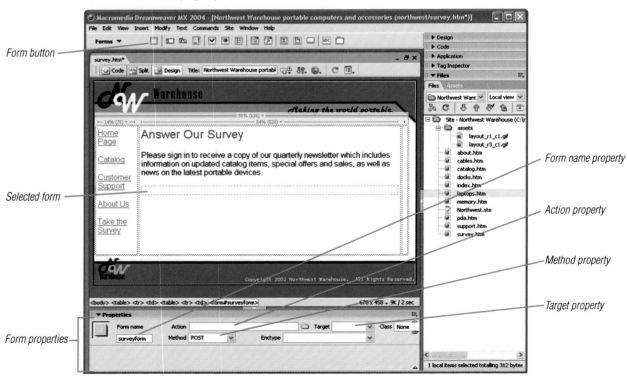

The **Method property** specifies the HyperText Transfer Protocol (HTTP) method used to send the form data to the Web server. The **GET method** specifies that ASCII data collected in the form will be sent to the server appended to the URL or file included in the Action property. For instance, if the Action property is set to /cgi-bin/myscript.cgi, then the data will be sent as a string of characters after the address, as follows: /cgi-bin/ myscript.cgi?a+collection+of+data+ collected+by+the+form. Data sent with the GET method is usually limited to 8K or less, depending on the Web browser. The **POST method** specifies that the form data be sent to the processing script as a binary or encrypted file, allowing you to send data securely. When you specify the POST method, there is no limit to the amount of information that can be collected in the form, and the information is secure.

The **Form name property** specifies a unique name for the form. The name can be a string of any alphanumeric characters and cannot include spaces. The **Target property** lets you specify the window in which you want the form data to be processed.

Understanding CGI Scripts

CGI is one of the most popular tools used to collect form data. CGI allows a Web browser to work directly with the programs that are running on the server and also makes it possible for a Web site to change in response to user input. CGI programs can be written in Perl or in C, depending

on the type of server that is hosting your Web site. When a CGI script collects data from a Web form, it passes the data to a program running on a Web server, which in turn passes the data back to your Web browser, which then makes changes to the Web site in response to the form data. The

resulting data is then stored in a database or sent to an e-mail server, which then sends the information in an e-mail message to a designated recipient. Figure F-3 illustrates how a CGI script processes information collected by a form.

FIGURE F-3
Illustration of CGI process on Web server

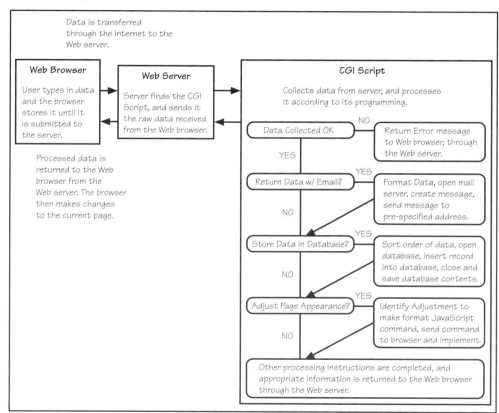

Create the Northwest Warehouse Web site (Win)

1. Open Windows Explorer, then navigate to the chapter_f Data Files folder, so that the contents of the chapter_f Data Files folder appear in the right pane.

2. Press and hold **[Ctrl]**, then drag the **northwest folder** from the chapter_f folder in the right pane to the drive and folder in the left pane where you want to store the Northwest Warehouse Web site, as shown in Figure F-4.

3. Close Windows Explorer, then start Dreamweaver.

4. Click **Site** on the menu bar, click **Manage Sites**, then click **Import**.

   The Import Site dialog box opens.

5. Click the **Look in list arrow** to navigate to the northwest folder located in the chapter_f Data Files folder, click **Northwest.ste**, as shown in Figure F-5, click **Open**.

   (continued)

FIGURE F-4

Dragging the northwest folder to another folder or drive

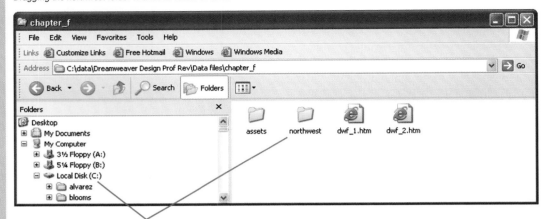

Drag the northwest folder from the right pane to the folder in the left pane where you want to store the Web site files

FIGURE F-5

Import Site dialog box

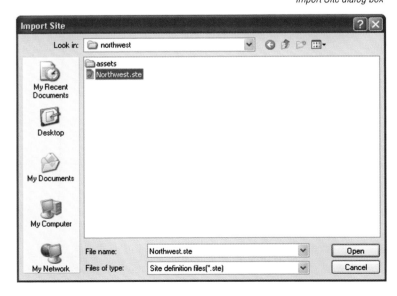

FIGURE F-6

Site Definition for Northwest Warehouse dialog box (Win)

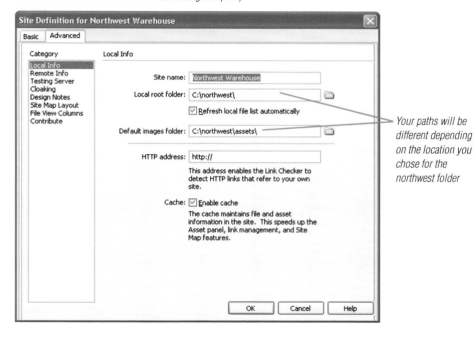

Your paths will be different depending on the location you chose for the northwest folder

6. Verify that the Northwest Warehouse site is selected in the Manage Sites dialog box, then click **Edit**.

7. Verify that the northwest folder is the root folder for the Web site and the assets folder under the northwest folder is the default location for images, as shown in Figure F-6.

   TIP If you receive a warning that the selected folder does not contain the current site's home page, return to the Site Definition dialog box, click Site Map Layout in the Category column, click the Browse for File button 📁 next to the Home page text box, then double-click index.htm in the northwest root folder.

8. Click **OK**, then click **Done**.

   The Northwest Warehouse Web site is now visible in the Files panel. Because you used the Import command to import the Northwest Warehouse site, all the links that were created in this site are preserved in the northwest folder that you copied.

   TIP If you do not see the Northwest Warehouse site in the Files panel, expand the Files panel to view its contents.

You copied the northwest folder from the chapter_f Data Files folder to a different folder on your computer or external drive. You then imported the Northwest Warehouse site and verified that the root folder was set to the northwest folder that you copied. You also set the default images folder to the assets folder of the northwest folder.

Create the Northwest Warehouse Web site (Mac)

1. Open Finder, then navigate to the folder on your computer or external drive where you want to store the Northwest Warehouse Web site.

2. Click **File** on the menu bar, then click **New Finder Window** to open another version of Finder, then open the chapter_f Data Files folder.

3. Drag the northwest folder from the chapter_f folder to the drive and folder where you want to store the Northwest Warehouse Web site, as shown in Figure F-7.

4. Close the Finder windows, start Dreamweaver (if necessary), click **Site** on the menu bar, click **Manage Sites**, then click **Import**.

   The Import Site dialog box opens.

5. Click **Northwest.ste** in the northwest folder that you moved in Step 3, then click **Open**.

   The Choose Local Root Folder for Site Northwest Warehouse opens.

   (continued)

FIGURE F-7

Dragging the northwest folder to a new location (Mac)

Adding Labels to Form Objects

When you create a form, you need to include form field labels so that viewers know what information you want them to enter in each field of the form. Because labels play such an important part in identifying the information that the form collects, you need to make sure to use labels that make sense to your viewers. For example, First Name and Last Name are good form field labels, because viewers understand clearly what information they should enter. However, a label such as Top 6 Directory Names might confuse viewers and cause them to leave the field blank or enter incorrect information. When you create a form field label, you should use a simple name that makes it obvious what information viewers should enter in the form field. If creating a simple and obvious label is not possible, then include a short paragraph that describes the information that should be entered into the form field. Figure F-12 shows very clearly marked labels for both the form fields and the groups of related information.

You can add labels to a form using one of two methods. You can simply type a label in the appropriate table cell of your form, or use the Label button on the Forms group of the Insert bar to link the label to the form object.

FIGURE F-11

Web site that uses a table to lay out a form

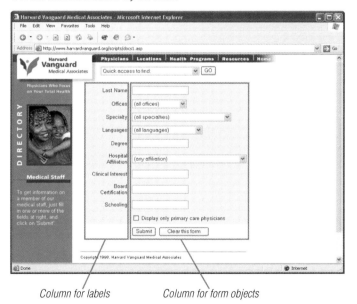

Column for labels   *Column for form objects*

FIGURE F-12

Web site that uses clearly marked labels for form fields and groups of related information

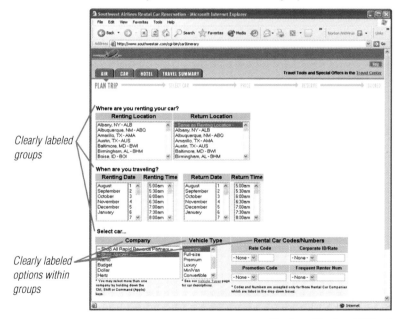

Clearly labeled groups

Clearly labeled options within groups

(Courtesy of Southwest Airlines)

Create fieldsets

1. Place the insertion point inside the dashed red outline of the form (if necessary).

2. Click the **Insert bar list arrow**, click **Forms**, then click the **Fieldset button** 🔲 to open the Fieldset dialog box.

   Notice that the view changes to Code and Design view.

3. Type **Personal Information** in the Label text box of the Fieldset dialog box.

4. Compare your screen to Figure F-13, then click **OK**.

   Notice the insertion point is in the Code view pane.

5. Click to the right of the closing </fieldset> tag in the Code view pane, press **[Enter]** (Win) or **[return]** (Mac), then click **Refresh** in the Property inspector.

   The fieldset label Personal Information appears in the form outline in the Design view pane, and new code appears in the Code view pane, as shown in Figure F-14.

6. Click the **Fieldset button** 🔲 on the Insert bar to open the Fieldset dialog box, type **Survey Information**, click **OK**, then click anywhere in the Design view pane.

   The Survey Information fieldset appears below the Personal Information fieldset in the Design view pane.

You created two fieldsets with the labels Personal Information and Survey Information that will organize form elements into two separate areas on the form.

FIGURE F-13
Fieldset dialog box

FIGURE F-14
Code for Personal Information fieldset

Fieldset button —

Fieldset code —

Visible fieldset label —

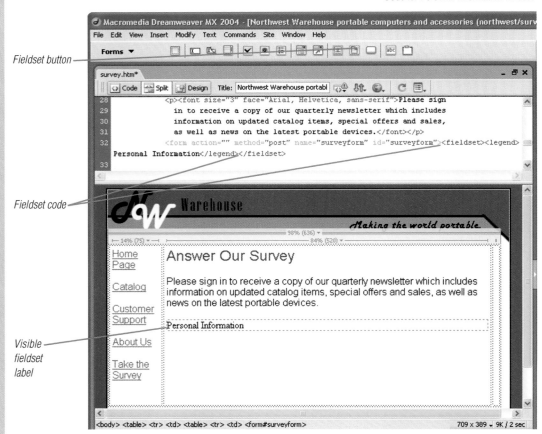

FIGURE F-15

Adding a table within a fieldset

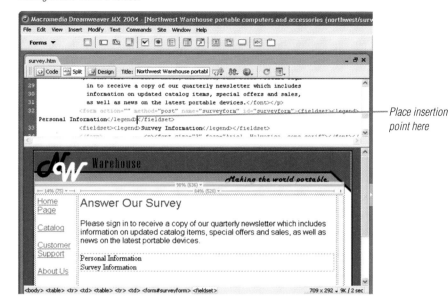

Place insertion
point here

FIGURE F-16

Table dialog box

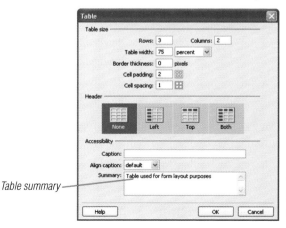

Table summary

1. Click to place the insertion point between the </legend> and </fieldset> tags for the Personal Information fieldset in the Code view pane, as shown in Figure F-15.

2. Click the **Insert bar list arrow**, click **Common**, then click the **Table button** 🗐.

3. In the Table dialog box, set the Rows to 3, Columns to 2, Table width to 75 percent, Border thickness to 0, Cell padding to 2, and Cell spacing to 1.

4. Type **Table used for form layout purposes** in the Summary text box, compare your screen to Figure F-16, then click **OK**.

   You might have to scroll up in the Code view pane to see the table inserted between the Personal Information and Survey Information fieldset tags. The table dimension information may be on top of your fieldset label in Design view. To see the label, click to place the insertion point on the page outside the table boundaries.

5. Place the insertion point between the </legend> and </fieldset> tags for the Survey Information fieldset in the Code view pane.

   TIP If you have trouble finding these tags, select the Survey Information fieldset in the Design view pane.

6. Click the **Table button** 🗐 on the Insert bar.

   TIP Click away from the table to be able to see the fieldset label.

   (continued)

Lesson 2   Format a Form

7. In the Table dialog box, set the Rows to 6, Columns to 2, Table width to 75 percent, Border thickness to 0, Cell padding to 2, Cell spacing to 1, add appropriate text to the Summary text box, then click **OK**.

8. Click the **Show Design view button** ![Design] on the Document toolbar to view the entire form with the two tables added, as shown in Figure F-17.

You added two tables to each fieldset of the form on the survey page.

Add form labels to table cells

1. Click in the upper-left cell of the Personal Information table to set the insertion point.

2. Type **First Name**, then press [↓].

3. Type **Last Name**, then press [↓].

4. Type **Email**.

5. Click in the upper-left cell of the Survey Information table to set the insertion point.

6. Type **PDA type**, press [↓], type **Software category**, press [↓], then type **Tools to upload**.

7. Format each label you typed in Steps 2 through 6 in Arial, Helvetica, sans-serif, size 2.

8. Format the fieldset labels as Arial, Helvetica, sans-serif, size 2, bold, then compare your screen to Figure F-18.

You added six form labels to table cells in the form and formatted them in Arial, Helvetica, sans-serif, size 2. You added two fieldset labels and formatted them as Arial, Helvetica, sans-serif, size 2, bold.

FIGURE F-17
Tables inserted in fieldsets in Design view

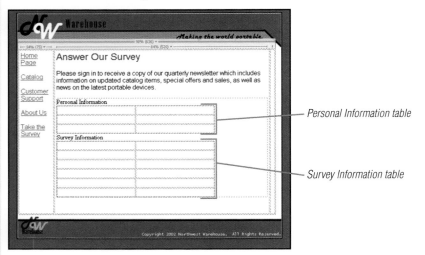

Personal Information table

Survey Information table

FIGURE F-18
Typing and formatting labels in table cells

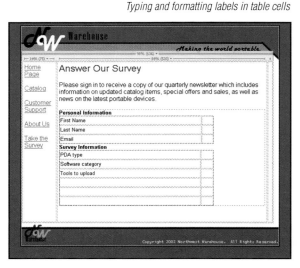

FIGURE F-19

Adding a label to a form using the Label button

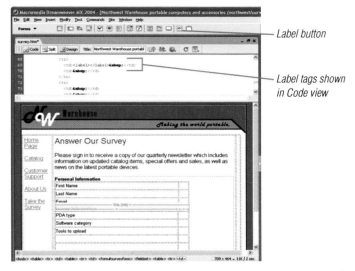

Label button

Label tags shown
in Code view

FIGURE F-20

New labels added using the Label button in Code and Design view

Label button

Label tags shown
in Code view

New labels

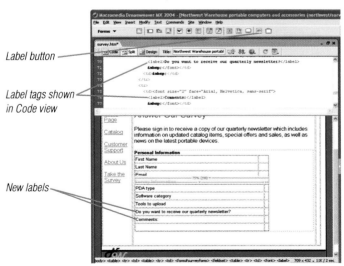

1. Click in the cell below the Tools to upload label.

2. Click the **Insert bar list arrow**, click **Forms**, then click the **Label button** abc.

   The view changes to Code and Design view, as shown in Figure F-19. The insertion point is positioned in the Code view pane between the tags <label> and </label> which were added when you clicked the Label button.

3. Type **Do you want to receive our quarterly newsletter?**, then click anywhere in the Design view pane.

   The label appears in the table cell in the Design view pane.

4. Click in the cell below Do you want to receive our quarterly newsletter?.

5. Click the **Label button** abc on the Insert bar, then type **Comments:**.

6. Click **Refresh** in the Property inspector to refresh the page in Design view.

   | TIP You can also press [F5] to refresh the page in Design view.

7. Format the new labels using Arial, Helvetica, sans-serif, size 2, then compare your screen to Figure F-20.

8. Click the **Show Design view button** [Design], then save your work.

You added two new labels to the form on the survey page using the Label button, and formatted them as Arial, Helvetica, sans-serif, size 2.

WORK WITH FORM OBJECTS

What You'll Do

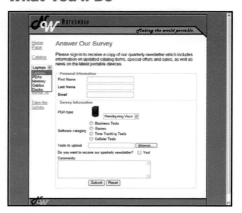

In this lesson, you will add form objects to the form on the survey page.

Understanding Form Objects

A form provides a structure in which you can place form objects. Form objects—which are also called **form elements**, **form controls**, or **fields**—are the components of a form such as check boxes, text boxes, and radio buttons that allow viewers to provide information and interact with the Web site. You can use form objects in any combination to collect the information you require. Figure F-21 shows a form that contains a wide range of form objects.

Text fields are the most common type of form object and are used for collecting a string of characters, such as a name, address, password, or e-mail address. For some text fields, such as those collecting dollar amounts, you might want to set an initial value of 0. Use the Text Field button on the Insert bar to insert a text field.

A **text area field** is a text field that can store several lines of text. You can use

text area fields to collect descriptions of problems, answers to long questions, comments, or even a résumé. Use the Textarea button on the Insert bar to insert a text area.

You can use **check boxes** to create a list of options from which a viewer can make multiple selections. For instance, you could add a series of check boxes listing hobbies and ask the viewer to select the ones that interest him/her. You could also use a check box to answer a yes or no question.

You can use **radio buttons** to provide a list of options from which only one selection can be made. A group of radio buttons is called a **radio group**. Each radio group you create allows only one selection from within that group. You could use radio groups to ask viewers to select their annual salary range, their age group, or the t-shirt color they want to order. Use

Collecting Data with Forms

the Radio Group button on the Insert bar to insert a radio group.

You can insert a **menu** or **list** on a form using the List/Menu button on the Insert bar. You use menus when you want a viewer to select a single option from a list of choices. You use lists when you want a viewer to select one or more options from a list of choices. Menus are often used to provide navigation on a Web site, while lists are commonly used in order forms to let viewers choose from a list of possibilities.

Menus must be opened to see all of the options they contain, whereas lists display some of their options all of the time. When you create a list, you need to specify the number of lines that will be visible on the screen by setting a value for the Height property in the Property inspector.

Using **hidden fields** makes it possible to provide information to the Web server and form processing script without the viewer knowing that the information is being sent. For instance, you could add a hidden field

that tells the server who should receive an e-mail message and what the subject of the message should be. You can also use hidden fields to collect information from a viewer without his/her knowledge. For instance, you can use a hidden field to send you the viewer's browser type or their IP address.

You can insert an **image field** into a form using the Image Field button on the Insert bar. You can use the Image Field button to create buttons that contain custom graphics.

FIGURE F-21

Web site displaying several form objects

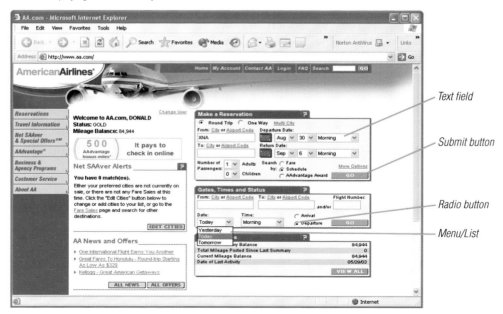

Text field

Submit button

Radio button

Menu/List

If you want your viewers to upload files to your Web server, you can insert a **file field**. You could insert a file field to let your viewers upload sample files to your Web site, or to post photos to your Web site's photo gallery.

All forms must include a Submit button, which a viewer clicks to transfer their form data to the Web server. You can also insert a Reset button, which lets viewers clear data from a form and reset it to its default values. You can also insert a plain button to trigger an action on the page that you specify. You can insert a Submit, Reset, or plain button using the Button button on the Insert bar.

Jump menus are navigational menus that let viewers go quickly to different pages in your site or to different sites on the Internet. You can create jump menus quickly and easily by using the Jump Menu button.

Figure F-22 shows the Insert bar with all of the form object buttons labeled. When you insert a form object in a form, you use the Property inspector to specify a unique name for it. You can also use the Property inspector to set other appropriate properties for the object, such as the number of lines or characters you wish the object to display.

QUICKTIP

To obtain form controls designed for creating specific types of forms, such as online tests and surveys, you can visit the Macromedia Dreamweaver Exchange and search available extensions (http://www.macromedia.com/exchange/dreamweaver).

FIGURE F-22
Insert bar showing form object buttons

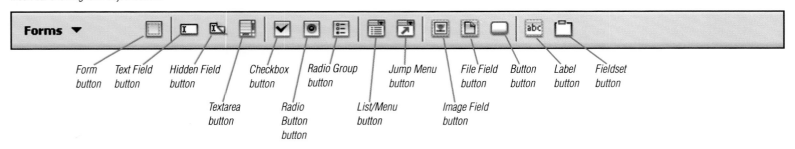

FIGURE F-23

Property inspector showing properties of selected text field

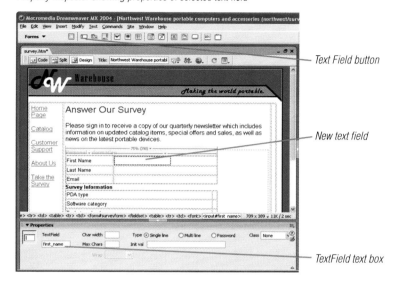

Text Field button

New text field

TextField text box

FIGURE F-24

Form with single-line text fields added

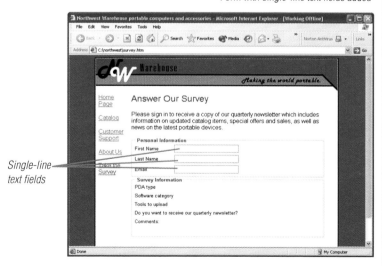

Single-line
text fields

1. Place the insertion point in the empty table cell to the right of the First Name label in the form.

2. Click the **Text Field button** 🔲 on the Insert bar.

3. Select textfield in the TextField text box in the Property inspector, then type **first_name**, as shown in Figure F-23.

4. Click the **Single line option button** in the Property inspector (if necessary).

5. Type **25** in the Char width text box in the Property inspector.

    This specifies that 25 characters will be visible inside this text field when displayed in a browser.

6. Type **100** in the Max chars text box in the Property inspector.

    This specifies that a user can type no more than 100 characters in this field.

7. Repeat Steps 2 through 6 to create another single-line text field to the right of the Last Name label, using last_name for the TextField name, and specifying 25 for Char width and 100 for Max chars.

8. Repeat Steps 2 through 6 to create another single-line text field to the right of the Email label, using email for the TextField name, and specifying 25 for Char width and 100 for Max chars.

9. Preview the page in your browser, compare your screen to Figure F-24, then close your browser.

You added three single-line text fields to the form and previewed the page in your browser.

Insert a multiple-line text field

1. Click to the right of the Comments: label, then press **[Shift] [Enter]** (Win) or **[Shift] [return]** (Mac) to insert a line break.

   Be sure to click in the same cell as the Comments: label (and not in the cell to the right of it).

2. Click the **Textarea button** 🔲 on the Insert bar.

3. Select **textarea** in the TextField text box in the Property inspector, then type **comments**.

4. Click the **Multi line option button** in the Property inspector (if necessary).

5. Type **40** in the Char width text box in the Property inspector.

   This specifies that 40 characters will be visible inside this text field when the page is displayed in a browser.

6. Type **4** in the Num Lines text box in the Property inspector, as shown in Figure F-25.

   This specifies that the text box will display four lines of text.

You added a multi-line text field to the form.

Insert a check box

1. Place the insertion point in the empty table cell to the right of Do you wish to receive our quarterly newsletter?

   (continued)

FIGURE F-25

Property inspector with properties of selected text area displayed

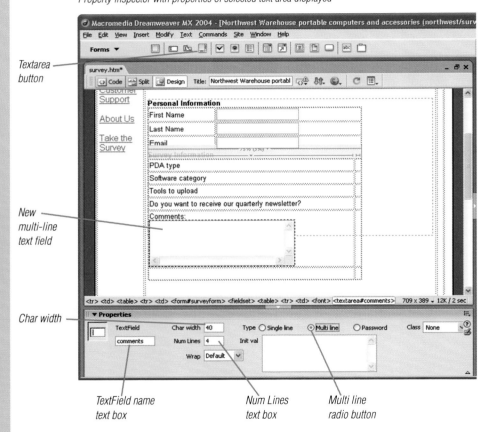

Textarea button

New multi-line text field

Char width

TextField name text box

Num Lines text box

Multi line radio button

Property inspector with check box properties displayed

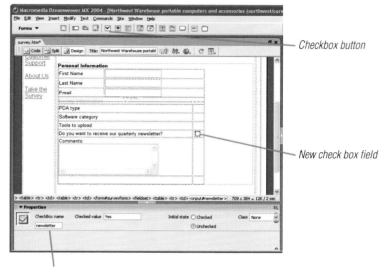

Checkbox button

New check box field

CheckBox name
text box

FIGURE F-27

Survey page in Internet Explorer with check box added to the form

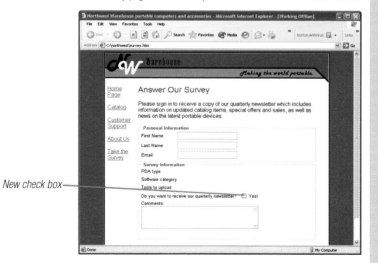

New check box

2. Click the **Checkbox button** ☑ on the Insert bar to insert a check box in the form.

3. Type **newsletter** in the CheckBox name text box in the Property inspector.

4. Type **Yes** in the Checked value text box in the Property inspector.

   This is the value that will be sent to your script or program when the form is processed.

5. Click the **Initial state Unchecked option button** in the Property inspector (if necessary), as shown in Figure F-26.

   Selecting the Checked option button would make a check mark appear in the check box by default.

6. Click to the right of the check box, type **Yes!**, then format the Yes! text in Arial, Helvetica, sans-serif, size 2.

   TIP If the Yes! label appears on the line below the check box, make the table wider by dragging the right table border so that the label appears to the right of the check box.

7. Merge the cell that contains Do you want to receive our quarterly newsletter? with the cell next to it that contains the check box.

8. Merge the Comments cell with the cell next to it, preview the page in your Web browser, compare your screen to Figure F-27, then close your browser.

   TIP Always save changes before previewing.

You added a check box to the form that will let viewers subscribe to the Northwest Warehouse newsletter, and merged two rows of cells in the table.

Add radio groups to a form

1. Click in the empty table cell to the right of Software category.

2. Click the **Radio Group button** 🖽 on the Insert bar to open the Radio Group dialog box.

3. Type **Category** in the Name text box.

4. Click the first instance of Radio in the Label column of the Radio Group dialog box to select it, then type **Business Tools**.

5. Click the first instance of radio in the Value column to select it, then type **business**.

   You specified that the first radio button will be named Business Tools and set business as the value that will be sent to your script or program when the form is processed.

6. Verify that the Lay out using Line breaks option button is selected.

   TIP If Lay out using Table is selected, then the radio buttons will appear in a separate table within the currently selected table.

7. Repeat Steps 2 through 6 to add another radio button named **Games** with a value of **games**.

8. Click the **Add button** ➕ , then add two more radio buttons named **Time Tracking Tools** and **Cellular Tools**, using the values of **time** and **cellular**.

9. Compare your screen with Figure F-28, then click **OK** to close the Radio Group dialog box.

   TIP If the radio buttons appear on more than four lines, make the table wider.

(continued)

FIGURE F-28
Radio Group dialog box

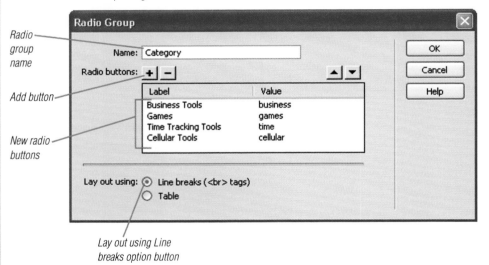

Radio group name

Add button

New radio buttons

Lay out using Line breaks option button

FIGURE F-36

New Submit and Reset buttons added to form

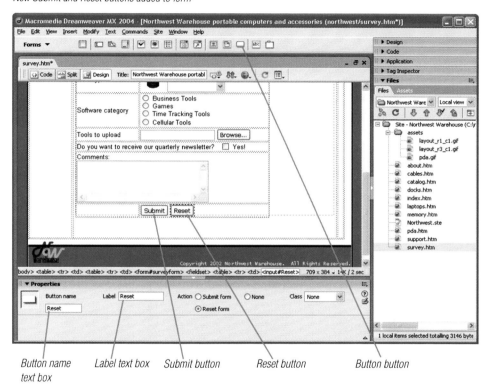

Button name   Label text box   Submit button   Reset button   Button button
text box

1. Click in the second cell of the last row of the Survey Information table.

2. Click the **Button button** ▢ on the Insert bar.

3. Verify that the Submit form option button is selected in the Property inspector.

   When a viewer clicks this Submit button, the information in the form will be sent to the processing script.

4. Verify that Submit is entered in the Button name text box and the Label text box in the Property inspector.

   The name Submit is automatically set when you select the Submit form option in the Property inspector.

5. Click the **Button button** ▢ on the Insert bar, click the **Reset form option button** in the Property inspector, name the new button **Reset**, verify that the Label text box is set to Reset, then compare your screen to Figure F-36.

   When a viewer clicks this Reset button, the form will remove any information typed by the viewer.

6. Save your work.

You added a Submit button and a Reset button to the form.

CREATE A JUMP MENU

What You'll Do

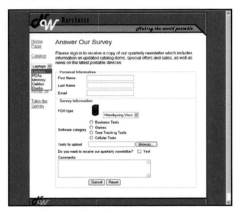

 In this lesson you will add a jump menu to the survey page of the Northwest Warehouse Web site.

Understanding Jump Menus

If your Web site contains a large number of pages, you can add a jump menu to make it easier for viewers to navigate through the site. Jump menus are menus that let viewers go directly from the current Web page to another page in the site with a single click. You can also use jump menus to provide links to other Web sites. You can create jump menus using the Jump Menu on the Insert bar to open the Insert Jump Menu dialog box. Figure F-37 shows an example of a jump menu on the Wallowa County Chamber of Commerce Web site.

Creating a jump menu is faster and easier than creating a navigation bar. When you create a navigation bar that contains images, you need to spend significant time creating two or three images for each link, each of which takes up a certain amount of precious space on the page. Jump menus are more compact and can fit on a single line. Jump menus only take up additional space when you open the menu. Even then, a jump menu won't disrupt the layout of your pages, because the menu opens on top of your existing page layout.

DESIGNTIP   **Adding a Go button to a jump menu**

If you want, you can add a Go button to a jump menu that viewers must click in order to jump to the selected page on the menu. Adding a Go button is optional. Many designers choose not to use Go buttons because they require viewers to make one more click to navigate to the page they want, and the goal of the jump menu is to minimize the number of clicks. To add a Go button to a jump menu, check the Insert go button after menu check box in the Insert Jump Menu dialog box.

Updating Jump Menus

As you add pages to your Web site, you will probably want to add additional links to your jump menu. Fortunately, updating and modifying a jump menu is easy in Dreamweaver. To add or remove links to a jump menu, select the jump menu, then click List Values in the Property inspector to open the List Values dialog box. You use this dialog box to add or delete a jump menu item.

Testing Jump Menus

Clicking broken links in a Web site can frustrate and irritate viewers. To prevent them from experiencing this frustration you must test, test, test, and test again until you are sure that there are no misplaced or broken links in your jump menu. The easiest way to test your jump menu is to preview the page in your browser and click each link. When an option in your menu is selected, the page it represents will automatically open, unless the menu contains a Go button. If there is a Go button, you must click Go in order to open the selected page.

FIGURE F-37

Jump menu on Wallowa County Chamber of Commerce Web site

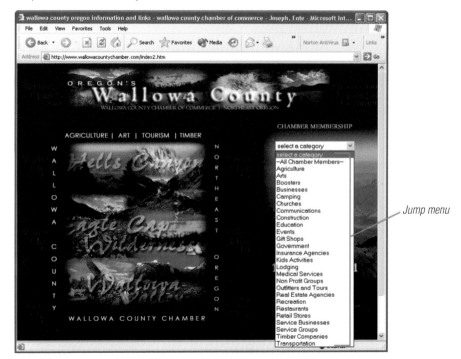

Jump menu

Insert a jump menu

1. Click to the right of the word Catalog on the left side of the page, then press **[Enter]** (Win) or **[return]** (Mac).

2. Click the **Jump Menu button** 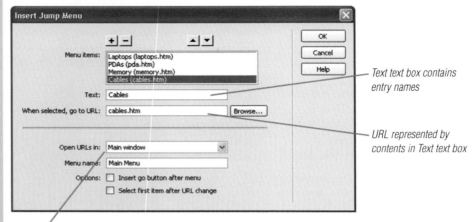 on the Insert bar to open the Insert Jump Menu dialog box.

3. Type **Laptops** in the Text text box.

4. Click **Browse** next to the When selected, go to URL: text box, click **laptops.htm** in the northwest root folder, then click **OK** (Win) or **Choose** (Mac).

5. Click the **Add button** **+** in the Insert Jump Button dialog box, type **PDAs** in the Text text box, click **Browse**, click **pda.htm**, then click **OK** (Win) or **Choose** (Mac).

6. Repeat Step 5 to add the following menu items and corresponding URLs: **Memory / memory.htm**, and **Cables / cables.htm**.

7. Click the **Open URLS in list arrow**, then click **Main window** (if necessary).

8. Type **Main Menu** in the Menu name text box, then compare your screen to Figure F-38.

9. Click **OK**, preview the page in your browser, test the menu links, compare your screen to Figure F-39, then close your browser.

You inserted a jump menu on the survey page.

FIGURE F-38
Insert Jump Menu dialog box

Text text box contains entry names

URL represented by contents in Text text box

Target where menu items will open

FIGURE F-39
Completed jump menu on services page in Internet Explorer

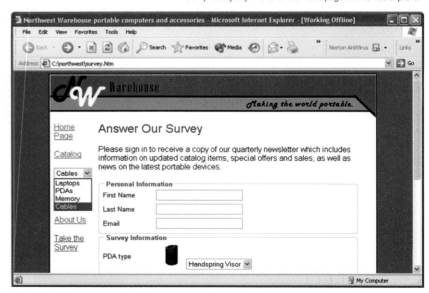

In this project, you will continue to work on the group project that you have been developing since Chapter A. Depending on the size of your group, you can assign individual elements of the project to group members, or work collectively to create the finished product.

You will continue building your Web site by designing and completing a page that contains a form to collect visitor information as it relates to the topic of your site.

1. Meet as a group to review your storyboard. Choose a page to develop that will use a form to collect information. Choose another page that you already developed, on which you will place a jump menu.

2. Plan the content for the new page by making a list of the information that you will collect and the types of form objects you will use to collect that information. Plan to include at least one of every type of form object you learned about in the chapter. Be sure to specify whether you will organize the form into fieldsets and how you will use a table to structure the form.

3. Assign team members the task of creating the form, its labels, and its contents.

4. Assign another group of team members the task of creating the jump menu.

5. After the assigned members complete the page containing the form and the page containing the jump menu, assign another team member the task of running a report that checks for broken links in the Web site. The team member should also correct any broken links that appear in the report.

6. Assign a team member the task of testing the form by previewing it in a browser, entering information into it, and submitting it. The team member should then check to make sure the information gets to its specified location, whether that is a database or an e-mail address.

7. As a group, preview all the pages in a browser, then test all menus and links. Evaluate the pages for both content and layout.

8. Review the check list shown in Figure F-46. Assign team members the task of making any modifications necessary to improve the form, the jump menu, or the page containing the form.

9. Close all open pages.

FIGURE F-46
Group Project check list

> **Web Site Check List**
> 1. Do all navigation links work?
> 2. Do all images appear?
> 3. Are all colors Websafe?
> 4. Do all form objects align correctly with their labels?
> 5. Do any extra items appear on the form that need to be removed?
> 6. Does the order of form fields make sense?
> 7. Does the most important information appear at the top of the form?
> 8. Did you test the pages in at least two different browsers?
> 9. Do your pages look good in at least two different screen resolutions?

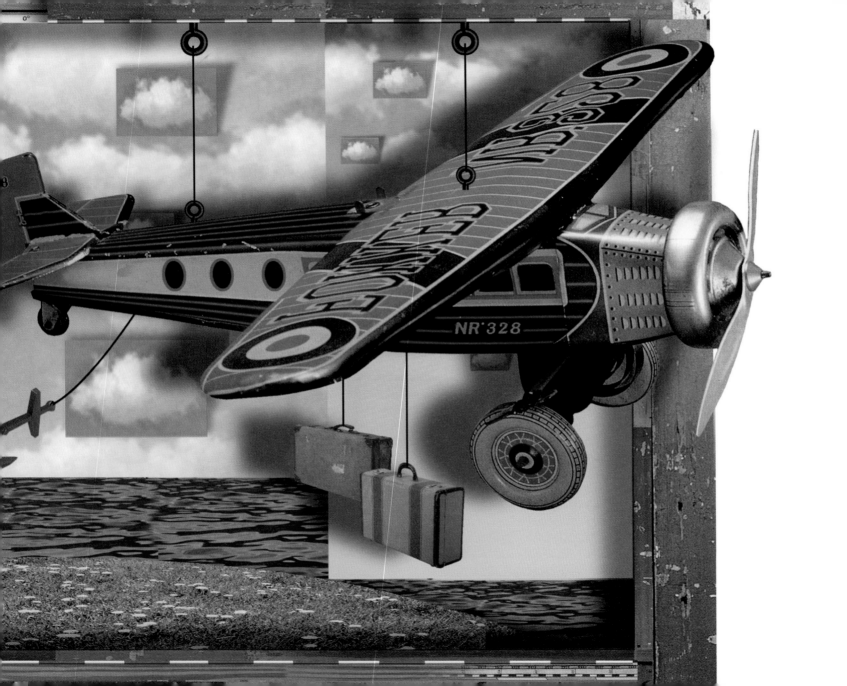

CHAPTER G

POSITIONING OBJECTS WITH LAYERS

1. Create a layer.

2. Set the position and size of a layer.

3. Use the Layers panel.

4. Configure layer preferences.

5. Convert layers to tables and tables to layers.

POSITIONING OBJECTS WITH LAYERS

Introduction

If you want to control the position of text and graphic elements with precision on your Web pages, you can use layers. **Layers** are containers in which you place text and graphics and which you use to position elements on a Web page according to specific pixel coordinates. Using layers, you can position elements next to each other as well as on top of each other in a stack. In this chapter you will use layers to place text and graphics on a page.

Using Layers versus Tables for Page Layout

Like tables, layers let you control the appearance of your Web page. But unlike tables, layers allow you to stack your information in a vertical pile, allowing for just one piece of information to be visible at a time. Tables are static, which makes it difficult to change them on the fly. Layers, on the other hand, are treated as their own documents, so that you can easily change their contents. Dreamweaver even includes the JavaScript behavior to do so. **Behaviors** in Dreamweaver are simple action scripts that allow you to perform common tasks quickly, either on a Web page while it is being viewed in a browser, or to a Web page while you are creating it in Dreamweaver.

The biggest factor you should consider when deciding between layers or tables for page layout is the browsers that will be used to view the pages. If you think a high percentage of Netscape Navigator 4.0 users will view your site, then you should use tables for laying out your pages. Netscape Navigator 4.0 and earlier versions do not support all of the formatting and options available with layers in Dreamweaver. All versions of Internet Explorer 4 and later fully support Dreamweaver's layers.

Tools You'll Use

Draw Layer button

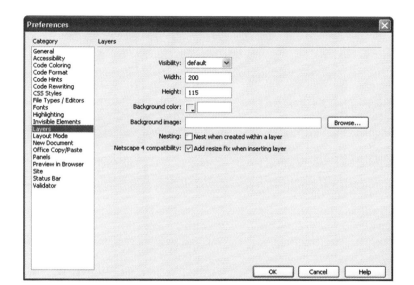

Z-Index

Background image

Layer ID

Overflow setting

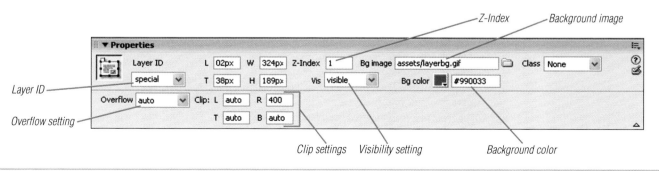

Clip settings

Visibility setting

Background color

CREATE A LAYER

What You'll Do

In this lesson, you will draw a layer on the Northwest Warehouse home page and set its properties using the Property inspector. You will also insert a background image in the layer and set its background color. You will also add text to the layer and format it. Finally, you will add an image to the layer.

Understanding Layers

Layers are one of the newer developments in the world of Web page layout and design. Using layers, you can stack elements on top of each other and specify that only certain elements be visible at certain times or in specified conditions. Layers can be used to create special effects on a Web page. For instance, you can use layers to build a whole image from individual pieces. You can also use them to create a jigsaw puzzle that allows you to slide the pieces into their positions one at a time. You can also use layers to create dynamic pages that contain moving parts or objects that become visible or invisible based on a selection made by the Web site viewer.

Using layers to lay out a Web page is like working with a stack of transparency sheets that you can stack on top of each other. Figure G-1 illustrates how to use layers to stack graphical elements on top of each other to create the single image of a flower.

To insert a layer, you can use the Draw Layer button on the Insert bar and drag a rectangular shaped layer anywhere on your page, as shown in Figure G-2. You can also insert a layer using the Insert Layer command. Specify the exact dimensions, color, and other specifications of a new layer by changing the layer settings in the Preferences dialog box.

Using HTML Tags to Create Layers

You can create layers in Dreamweaver using one of two HTML tags: <div> or <span>. Both tags support all types of images, backgrounds, and advanced formatting options for layers. The default tag in Dreamweaver is the <div> tag because it is supported by all browsers, including the early versions of Netscape Navigator. Netscape Navigator browsers prior to version 4.5 do not support the <span> tag.

Understanding Layer Content

A layer is like a separate document within a Web page. It can contain the same types of elements that a page can, such as background colors, images, links, tables, and text. You can also make the contents of a layer work directly with a specified Dreamweaver behavior to make the page interact with a viewer in a certain way.

Using Advanced Layer Formatting

You should be careful not to add too much content to a layer. If a layer contains more information than it can readily display, you will need to use the advanced layer formatting controls to format the content so that it appears the way you want it to. You can control the appearance of a selected layer by making changes to the Clip, Visibility, and Overflow properties in the Property inspector.

The **Clip property** identifies the portion of a layer's content that is visible when displayed in a Web browser. By default, the clipping region matches the outside borders of the layer, but you can change the amount that is visible by clipping one or all sides of the layer. For instance, if you set the L (left) Clip property to 10 pixels, then everything from the eleventh pixel to the right will be displayed in the browser. If you clip off 10 pixels from the right side, you will need to subtract 10 from the total width of the layer and then type this value in the Clip R text box in the Property inspector. The clip setting can only be applied to layers that have an Overflow attribute set to a value other than visible.

The **Vis (visible) property** lets you control whether the selected layer is visible. You can set the Vis property to default, visible, hidden, or **inherit**, which means that the visibility of the layer is automatically inherited from its parent layer or page.

The **Overflow property** specifies how to treat excess content that does not fit inside a layer. You can choose to make the content visible, specify that scroll bars appear on the layer, hide the content, or let the current layer automatically deal with the extra content in the same manner as its parent layer or page.

FIGURE G-1
Using layers to create a single image

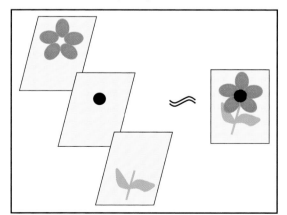

FIGURE G-2
Inserting a layer using the Draw Layer button

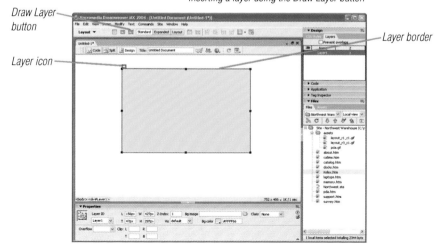

Draw a layer

1. Open the home page of the Northwest Warehouse Web site that you imported and developed in Chapter F.

2. Click the **Insert bar list arrow**, click **Layout**, then click the **Draw Layer button** 🖹.

3. Using Figure G-3 as a guide, drag a rectangle in the upper-right corner of the home page that is approximately 4 inches wide and 2 inches tall.

   A new layer appears on the page, but it is not selected. A Layer icon appears above the upper-left corner of the layer.

   > TIP   You can also insert a layer by clicking Insert on the menu bar, pointing to Layout Objects, then clicking Layer.

4. Click the **Layer icon** 🔲 above the layer to select it.

   > TIP   You can also select a layer by clicking one of its borders.

You drew a layer on the home page, then selected it.

FIGURE G-3
New layer added to the homepage

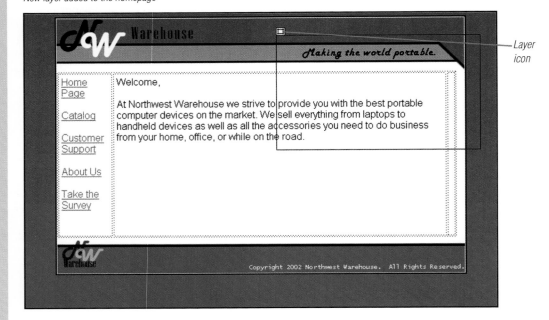

Layer icon

FIGURE G-4
Property inspector showing properties of selected layer

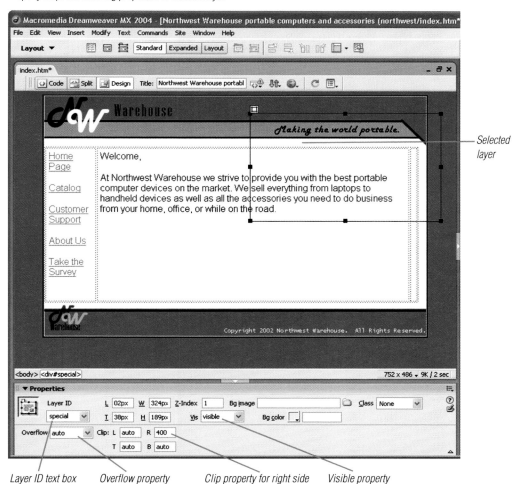

Selected layer

Layer ID text box   Overflow property   Clip property for right side   Visible property

1. With the layer selected, select Layer1 in the Layer ID text box in the Property inspector, type **special**, then press **[Enter]** (Win) or **[return]** (Mac).

2. Verify that <div#special> is selected in the Tag selector.

3. Click the **Overflow list arrow** in the Property inspector, then click **auto**.

4. Click the **Vis list arrow**, then click **visible**.

5. Type **400** in the Clip R text box in the Property inspector, then press **[Enter]** (Win) or **[return]** (Mac).

   When you specify the clip measurement of one side, measurements for the other three clip fields fill in automatically.

6. Compare your screen to Figure G-4.

   The L, T, W, and H settings in the Property inspector specify the position and size of the layer. Your settings will probably differ from those shown in the figure because you probably drew your layer with slightly different measurements.

You specified a name and other HTML properties for the selected layer.

Set a background image

1. Click the **Browse for File icon** 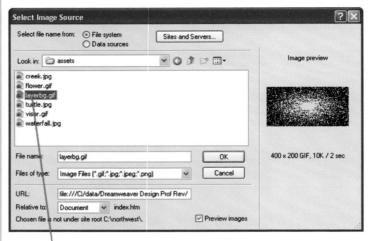 next to the Bg image text box in the Property inspector to open the Select Image Source dialog box.

2. Navigate to the chapter_g assets folder, then click **layerbg.gif** as shown in Figure G-5.

3. Click **OK** (Win) or **Choose** (Mac), then compare your screen to Figure G-6.

   > TIP If a dialog box opens asking if you want to copy this file to your site, click Yes to open the Copy File As dialog box, navigate to the assets folder of the Northwest Warehouse Web site, then Click Save.

   Your screen might look different than the figure, depending on the size of the layer that you drew.

4. Refresh the Files panel to verify that layerbg.gif was copied to the assets folder of the Web site.

You added a background image to the special layer.

FIGURE G-5
Select Image Source dialog box

Background image for layer

FIGURE G-6
Layer containing a background image

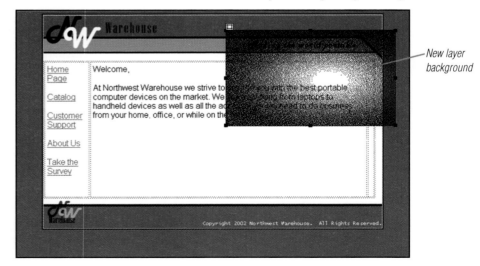

New layer background

FIGURE G-7
Color picker with new background color selected

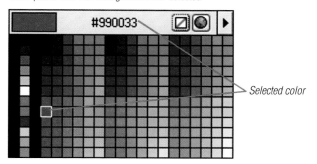

Selected color

Set a background color

1. With the layer selected, click the **Bg color button** ⬚ in the Property inspector to open the color picker.

2. Click the dark maroon color in the first column that has the hex value #990033, as shown in Figure G-7.

   The transparent area of the image is now filled with the maroon background color you selected, as shown in Figure G-8.

You added a background color to the layer.

FIGURE G-8
Maroon color applied to layer background image

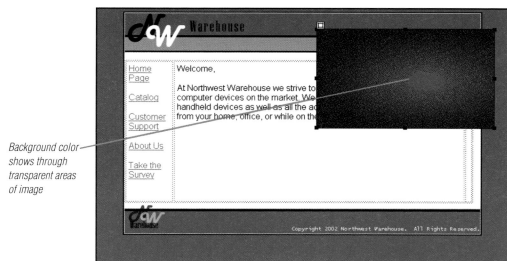

Background color shows through transparent areas of image

Add text to a layer

1. Click inside the layer to set the insertion point.

2. Type **Special Sale**.

3. Format Special Sale using the following attributes: Font: Arial, Helvetica, sans-serif, Size: 4, Color: white, and Alignment: Align Center.

4. Click to the right of Special Sale, press and hold **[Shift]**, then press **[Enter]** (Win) or **[return]** (Mac) to insert a line break.

5. Type **TODAY ONLY!!**

   The same formatting you applied to the first line of text is automatically applied to this new line of text.

6. Press **[Enter]** (Win) or **[return]** (Mac), type **Handspring Visor Deluxe only $129.00 + shipping**, then change the text size to 2.

7. Save your work, preview the page in your Web browser, compare your screen with Figure G-9, then close your browser.

You added text to the layer and formatted it.

FIGURE G-9

Home page in Internet Explorer showing text added to layer

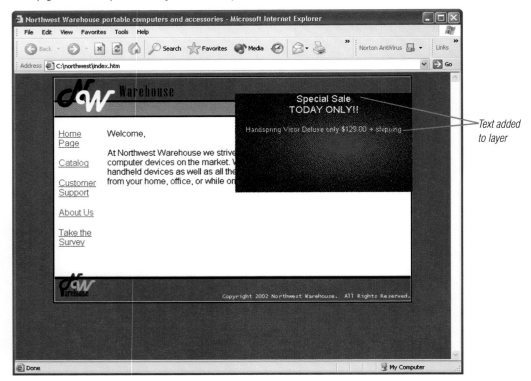

Text added to layer

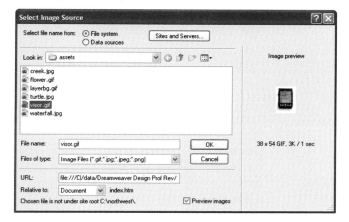

Add an image to a layer

1. Click to the right of the TODAY ONLY!! text to set the insertion point, then press **[Enter]** (Win) or **[return]** (Mac).

2. Click the **Insert bar list arrow**, click **Common**, Click the **Images list arrow**, then click **Image**.

3. Navigate to the chapter_g assets folder, then double-click **visor.gif**, as shown in Figure G-10.

4. Type appropriate alternate text in the Image Tag Accessibility Attributes dialog box, then click **OK**.

   TIP If the Image Tag Accessibility Attributes dialog box does not appear, type appropriate alternate text in the Alt text box in the Property inspector.

5. Save your work, preview the page in your Web browser, then compare your screen to Figure G-11.

You added an image to the layer, then added alternate text to it.

FIGURE G-11

Image added to layer

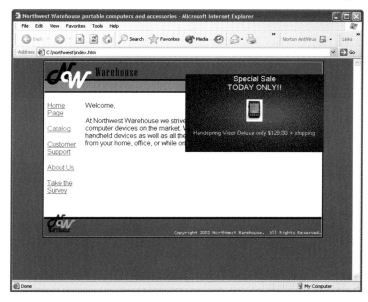

SET THE POSITION AND SIZE OF A LAYER

What You'll Do

In this lesson, you will use the Property inspector to position and size layers on the home page of the Northwest Warehouse Web site.

Understanding Absolute Positioning

One of the greatest benefits of using layers to lay out a page is that you can position them precisely using a practice called **absolute positioning**. A layer is positioned absolutely by specifying the distance between the upper-left corner of the layer and the upper-left corner of the page or layer in which it is contained. Figure G-12 illustrates how an absolutely positioned layer keeps its relative position on a page when the page is scrolled. Because Dreamweaver treats layers as if they are separate documents contained within a page, layers do not interrupt the flow of content on the page or layer in which they are contained. This means that layers placed on top of a page will hide the contents of the page.

Absolutely positioned layers have no impact on the location of other layers. In other words, if you position a layer using absolute positioning, the remaining page elements that follow it within the code will continue along with the flow of the page, ignoring the presence of the absolutely positioned layer. This means you can create overlapping layers. You can create dynamic effects with overlapping layers on a Web page by using JavaScript or CGI programs to change the attributes associated with each layer in response to actions by the viewer. For instance, a layer could move or change its size when a viewer clicks or moves the mouse over a link on the page or in the layer.

Setting Positioning Attributes

You can control the absolute positioning of layers by setting five primary attributes, four of which are available in the Property inspector. These attributes work together to create a layer that will hold its position on a page.

The **Position property** plays the most important role in turning a standard <div> or <span> tag into your positioned layer. Use this property to define how an object is positioned on the page. Standard HTML allows for fixed, absolute, relative, static, or floating positioned objects, but Dreamweaver only uses the absolute value.

Positioning Objects with Layers

When configuring your layers in Dreamweaver, you do not need to set this property. It is automatically set to absolute when you create a layer.

The **Left property (L)** in the Property inspector specifies the distance between the left edge of your layer and the left edge of the page or layer that contains it. The **Top property (T)** in the Property inspector specifies the distance between the top edge of your layer and the top edge of the page or layer that contains it.

The **Width (W)** and **Height (H) properties** specify the dimensions of the layer, most often in pixels, although it can be specified as a percentage of your screen dimension. For instance, you can specify that your layer be 250 pixels by 250 pixels, or you can set it to 25% by 25%, which will create a layer that is roughly 200 by 150 on a fully expanded Web browser in an 800×600 resolution monitor.

Use the **Z-Index property** in the Property inspector to specify the vertical stacking order of layers on a page. If you think of the page itself as layer 0, then any number higher than that will appear on top of the page. For instance, if you have three layers with the Z-Index values of 1, 2, and 3, then 1 will appear below 2 and 3, while 3 will always appear above 1 and 2. You can create a dynamic Web site by adjusting the Z-Index settings on the fly using Dreamweaver's built-in JavaScript behaviors within the Web page you are creating.

QUICKTIP
You cannot set Z-Index values below zero.

FIGURE G-12
Scrolling a page containing an absolutely positioned layer

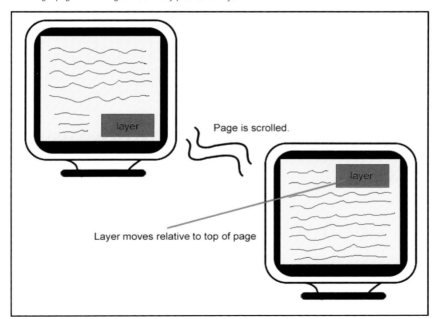

Page is scrolled.

Layer moves relative to top of page

Set the left and top position of a layer

1. Click the **layer border** to select the layer.
2. Type **375px** in the L text box, then press **[Enter]** (Win) or **[return]** (Mac).

   The layer moves automatically to the position you specified.
3. Type **260px** in the T text box, then press **[Enter]** (Win) or **[return]** (Mac).
4. Save your work, preview the page in your browser, compare your screen to Figure G-13, then close your browser.

You adjusted the upper-left corner position of the layer.

Set layer height and width

1. Click the **layer border** to select the layer (if necessary).
2. Type **375px** in the W text box, then press **[Tab]**.

   The layer automatically adjusts its width to the dimension you specified.
3. Type **175px** in the H text box, then press **[Tab]**.

   The layer automatically adjusts to the height you specified. Notice that the upper-left corner stays in the same position.
4. Save your work, preview the page in your Web browser, compare your screen with Figure G-14, then close your browser.

You adjusted the height and width of the layer.

FIGURE G-13

Layer moved down and to the left on the page

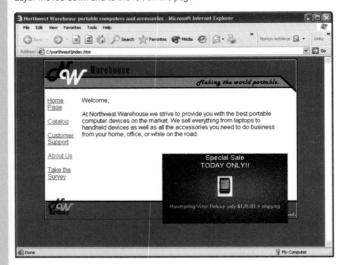

FIGURE G-14

Home page in Internet Explorer showing layer with height and width adjusted

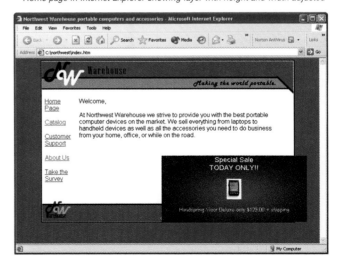

FIGURE G-15
New layer obscuring special layer

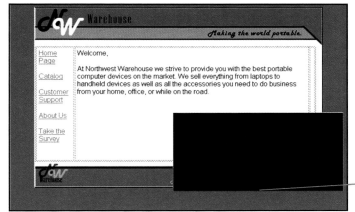

Images layer on
top of special layer

FIGURE G-16
Special layer moved on top of images layer

Special layer positioned
on top of images layer
with Z-Index value
changed to 2

Click red border
of image

Z-Index value

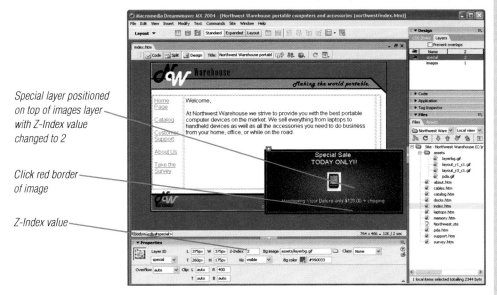

1. Create another layer anywhere on the page, select it, then name it **images**.

2. Select the **images layer** (if necessary), then adjust its size and position by setting the following properties in the Property inspector: L: 370px, T: 255px, W: 385px, and H: 185px.

   The new layer is now positioned on top of the special layer.

3. Change the background color of the images layer to black, then compare your screen with Figure G-15.

4. Change the Z-Index value of the images layer to 1 in the Property inspector.

5. Click the **special layer** to select it.

   | TIP Be careful to click the red border of the special layer rather than the outside border of the images layer.

6. Click the **layer icon** for the special layer to select it.

7. Change the Z-Index value of the special layer to 2 in the Property inspector.

   The images layer is now positioned behind the special layer, as shown in Figure G-16.

8. Save your work, preview the page in your browser, then close your browser.

You added a new layer named images to the home page, and specified its dimensions and position on the page using the Property inspector. You changed the background color of the images layer, then adjusted the vertical stacking order of the two layers.

USE THE LAYERS PANEL

What You'll Do

In this lesson, you will use the Layers panel to change the name of a layer, view and hide a layer, and work with nested layers.

Controlling Layers

You can use the **Layers panel** to control the visibility, name, and Z-Index order of all the layers on a Web page. You can also use the Layers panel to see how a layer is nested within the page structure, and to change the nesting status of a layer. **Nested layers** are layers whose HTML code is included within another layer's code. A nested layer does not affect the way a layer appears to the page viewer; it establishes a relationship of how it appears in relation to its parent layer. To change the nesting status of a layer, drag the nested layer to a new location in the Layers panel. Figure G-17 shows the Layers panel with a nested layer.

You can open the Layers panel using the Window menu. The Layers panel is very handy when you are trying to select a layer on the bottom of a stack of layers. Clicking the layer name selects the layer on the page. You can access the same information that is available in the Layers panel by selecting the layer and viewing its settings in the Property inspector.

Using the Layers panel is the easiest way to change a series of layer names, control layer visibility while testing a site, and control the visible stacking order of layers. The Layers panel also keeps track of all the layers on a page, making it easy to review the settings for each.

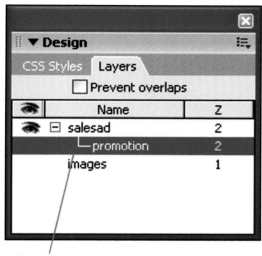

Nested layers are
indented under
their parent layer

Layer names ——

—— Z-Index values

Change the name of a layer

1. Click **Window** on the menu bar, then click **Layers**.

   The Design panel group opens with the Layers panel displayed, as shown in Figure G-18.

2. Click **special** on the Layers panel to select the special layer.

3. Double-click **special** on the Layers panel to edit its name.

4. Type **salesad**, then press **[Enter]** (Win) or **[return]** (Mac).

   The name of the layer is now salesad.

You used the Layers panel to change the name of one of the layers on the home page.

Controlling layer visibility

1. Click the **Eye icon column** for the images layer in the Layers panel, then compare your screen with Figure G-19.

   The Closed eye icon appears indicating that the images layer no longer appears in the document window.

2. Click the **Closed eye icon** 👁 on the images layer.

   Clicking the Closed eye icon makes the layer visible, as shown in Figure G-20. The Eye icon appears in the Layers panel.

3. Click the **Eye icon** 👁 on the images layer.

   Clicking the Eye icon makes the layer inherit the visibility status of its parent objects. In this case, the parent object of the images layer is the home page. Because the home page is visible, the images layer is visible too.

You used the Layers panel to change the visibility status of the images layer.

FIGURE G-19
Using the Layers panel to hide the images layer

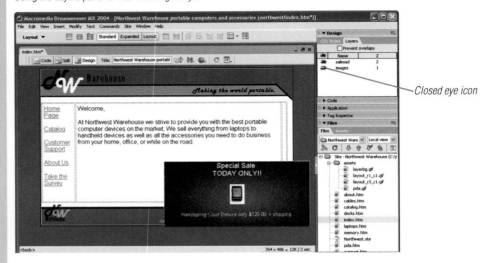

Closed eye icon

FIGURE G-20
Using the Layers panel to make the images layer visible

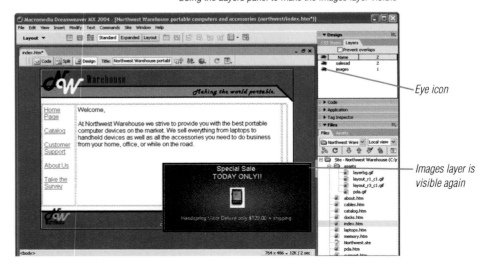

Eye icon

Images layer is visible again

FIGURE G-21
Formatted nested layer

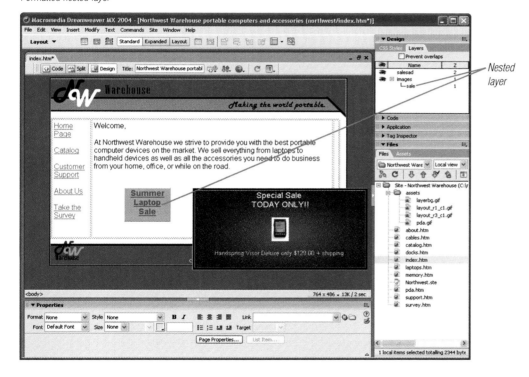

Nested
layer

1. Click the **images layer** in the Layers panel, then click in the images layer in the document window to place the insertion point.

2. Click **Insert** on the menu bar, point to **Layout Objects**, then click **Layer**.

   A new layer is inserted as a nested layer of the images layer.

3. Use the Layers panel to select this new nested layer, then name this new layer **sale**.

4. Type **–150px** in the L text box, then type **0px** in the T text box.

5. Type **100px** in the W text box, then type **75px** in the H text box.

   These dimensions specify the position and size of the nested layer in relation to the upper-left corner of the images layer.

6. Set the background color to #CC9999.

7. Click in the sale layer to place the insertion point, type **Summer Laptop Sale**, format this text using the following attributes: Font: Arial, Helvetica, sans-serif, Size: 4, Style: Bold, and Alignment: Align Center.

8. Insert a link from this text to the laptops.htm page, deselect the text, then compare your screen to Figure G-21.

9. Save your work.

You created a nested layer within the images layer.

CONFIGURE LAYER PREFERENCES

What You'll Do

 In this lesson, you will configure the default preferences for layers.

Setting Layer Preferences

If you know that you want all new layers to have a consistent appearance, you can save time by using the Preferences dialog box to set default specifications for new layers. Once you set layer preferences, you can then use the Insert Layer command to insert a layer that has the size and color settings you specified. When you draw a new layer using the Draw Layer button, the background color and image options specified in the Preferences dialog box are applied to the new layer. Figure G-22 shows an example of a page that contains four different layers. One of the layers was inserted based on settings in the Preferences dialog box. The other three were customized with different colors and dimensions.

Fixing the Netscape Resize Problem

Netscape Navigator 4 was one of the first browsers that had support for layers, but it had a problem. It did not adjust the position of layers based on changes in the screen size. As you can imagine, this created oddly formatted pages after the screen size was altered, or whenever adjustments were made to the page appearance during the processing of any scripts contained on the page.

To fix this problem, you can use the Preferences dialog box to specify that a special JavaScript function automatically be added to the code of any page that contains layers. This code is shown in Figure G-23.

QUICKTIP

If you convert tables to layers on a Web page, the code for the Netscape Resize Fix is not automatically added to the code for your page. To add the code, you need to add one additional layer to the page, which can be removed after adding the code. Before you remove the layer, however, switch to Code view and make sure that the code has been added.

Default layer

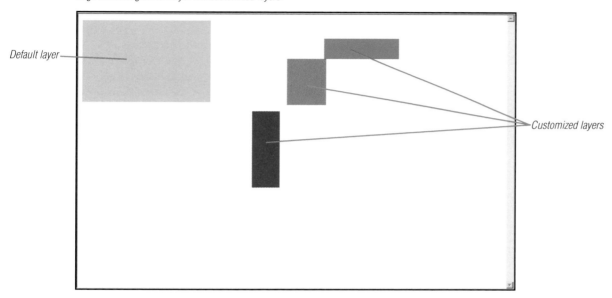

Customized layers

New code to handle Netscape resize problem

```
1  <html>
2  <head>
3  <title>Northwest Warehouse portable computers and accessories</title>
4  <meta http-equiv="Content-Type" content="text/html; charset=iso-8859-1">
5  <script language="JavaScript" type="text/JavaScript">
6  <!--
7  function MM_reloadPage(init) {  //reloads the window if Nav4 resized
8    if (init==true) with (navigator) {if ((appName=="Netscape")&&(parseInt(appVersion)==4)) {
9      document.MM_pgW=innerWidth; document.MM_pgH=innerHeight; onresize=MM_reloadPage; }}
10   else if (innerWidth!=document.MM_pgW || innerHeight!=document.MM_pgH) location.reload();
11 }
12 MM_reloadPage(true);
13 //-->
14 </script>
15 </head>
```

Control the appearance of a layer

1. Click **Edit** (Win) or **Dreamweaver** (Mac) on the menu bar, then click **Preferences** to open the Preferences dialog box.

2. Click **Layers** in the Category list.

3. Click the **Visibility list arrow** then click **visible**.

4. Type **300** in the Width text box, then type **200** in the Height text box.

5. Set the Background color to **#CCCCCC**.

   TIP If you want all layers to have a default background image, you can specify an image file in the Background image text box.

6. Compare your settings to Figure G-24, then click **OK**.

7. Click **Insert** on the menu bar, point to **Layout Objects**, click **Layer**, then compare your screen with Figure G-25.

   A new layer appears on the page that has a gray background and is 300px wide by 200px high, as you specified in your preferences.

8. Click **Edit** on the menu bar, then click **Undo Insert** to remove this layer.

You used the Preferences dialog box to adjust the default appearance of new layers.

FIGURE G-24

Preferences dialog box with new default settings for layers

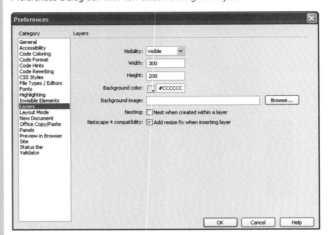

FIGURE G-25

New layer with new default layer settings applied

New layer with modified default settings (yours may appear in a different location)

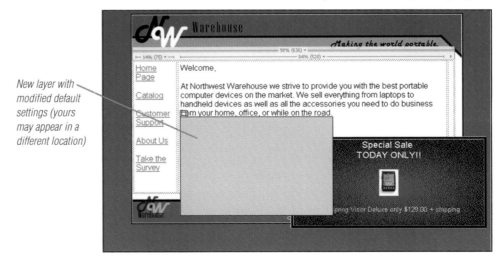

FIGURE G-26

Reload page function for the Netscape Resize Fix error

New code added to deal with Netscape resize problem

```
1   <html>
2   <head>
3   <title>Northwest Warehouse portable computers and accessories</title>
4   <meta http-equiv="Content-Type" content="text/html; charset=iso-8859-1">
5   <script language="JavaScript" type="text/JavaScript">
6   <!--
7   function MM_reloadPage(init) {  //reloads the window if Nav4 resized
8     if (init==true) with (navigator) {if ((appName=="Netscape")&&(parseInt(appVersion)==4)) {
9       document.MM_pgW=innerWidth; document.MM_pgH=innerHeight; onresize=MM_reloadPage; }}
10    else if (innerWidth!=document.MM_pgW || innerHeight!=document.MM_pgH) location.reload();
11  }
12  MM_reloadPage(true);
13  //-->
14  </script>
15  </head>
16  <body bgcolor="#990033" text="#000000" link="#990033" vlink="#0000FF" alink="#990066" leftmargin="5"
    topmargin="5" marginwidth="5">
```

Adjust for Netscape resize problems

1. Click **Edit** (Win) or **Dreamweaver** (Mac) on the menu bar, then click **Preferences**.

2. Click **Layers** in the Category list (if necessary).

3. Verify that the Netscape 4 compatibility check box is checked, then click **OK**.

4. Click the **Show Code view button** [◁▷ Code] on the Document toolbar.

5. Scroll to the top of the page.

6. Verify that the MM_reloadPage function has been added to the code for the page, as shown in Figure G-26.

7. Click the **Show Design view button** [◰ Design] on the Document toolbar.

8. Save your work.

You set up Dreamweaver to deal with the Netscape layer resize problem.

CONVERT LAYERS TO TABLES AND TABLES TO LAYERS

What You'll Do

In this lesson, you will learn about converting tables to layers and layers to a table.

Using Layers and Tables for Page Layout

Layers and tables are the two most common formats that Web designers use to lay out Web pages. The ability to convert easily between these two different layout styles is one of Dreamweaver's most powerful features.

Of course, like anything else, there are pros and cons to using each type of layout. The primary reason to use tables over layers is that all versions of Web browsers prior to Internet Explorer 4.0 and Netscape Navigator 4.5 are unable to read layers. All versions of browsers, however, are able to read tables.

For this reason, you will probably find the Convert Layers to Tables a useful tool. Pages designed with layers can be converted to allow all browsers to display the information properly. These commands are designed to work with pages that are designed either entirely in tables or entirely in layers.

Converting Layers to Tables

When you convert layers to tables, you need to keep a few important rules in mind. First, you cannot convert overlapping layers. Therefore, you must adjust the positioning of overlapping layers prior to converting them to a table. This sometimes forces you to make changes to the layout of your page. Second, you cannot convert nested layers into tables, which means that you need to remove any code related to nested layers. This might require you to change the nesting of your layers in the layers pane by dragging your layer to a new location. You can convert the layers on a page to a table by clicking Modify on the menu bar, pointing to Convert, then clicking Layers to Table.

Adding Links to Frames in the Frameset

Once you choose the layout of your frameset, you then need to create new pages or choose existing pages to place in the frames in the frameset. In most cases, a top frame will display a page that contains a logo or a series of navigational images or buttons. Most left-hand frames display a page containing a list of links or navigational images. Bottom frames are most commonly used for displaying a series of text links and copyright statements that protect the rights of the site owner. Though right-hand frames are rare, they can be used to display secondary information to accentuate the contents of the frame that contains the primary body information.

Saving a Frameset and Frames

When you create a frames-based page, you need to ensure that you save both the frameset and all of the individual pages that are stored in each frame. The first document you must save is the frameset. To save a frameset, use the Save Frameset command in the File menu. You can save each individual frame by selecting a frame and clicking Save Frame from the File menu, or you can select Save All from the File menu to save all the frames in the frameset.

QUICKTIP

You can also create a frameset page by clicking Framesets in the Create from Samples column in the Macromedia Dreamweaver MX 2004 start screen.

Frameset layout

Frames list arrow on the Insert bar

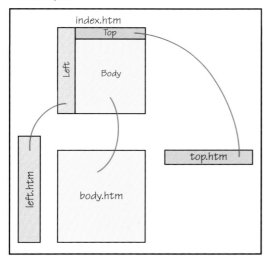

Layout category

Frames list arrow

DESIGNTIP   Setting the number of frames in a frameset

If you have decided to create a frameset, consider limiting the number of frames to two or three. Using more than two or three may be confusing or distracting to viewers. Viewing too many frames in a frameset can be compared to watching television with multiple channels being displayed simultaneously on one screen. Some people find it difficult to view two screens at once. Even when they are only concentrating on one screen at a time, they find the other distracting. The same may be true for viewers of multiple frames.

When you lay out a Web page using frames, you will always be working with one more file than is visible in the frameset. For instance, imagine that you created a frameset that contains three frames. One frame displays a navigation bar at the top of every page, another frame displays a copyright statement at the bottom of every page, and a third frame displays text. In this example you would need to have a minimum of four files. The first would be the frameset file that contains the information for laying out the frames themselves. The second would be the page containing the navigation bar. The third would be the page containing the copyright statement. The fourth would be the page that will appear in the middle frame of the frameset. Any additional documents that you want to load using the links in the frames would typically appear in the middle frame.

It is quite easy to tell the difference between a frame and a frameset by examining the code for both. The HTML code used for a file in a frame is the same as that for any individual Web page. It contains opening and closing HTML tags, heading tags, title tags, and body tags. The HTML code for a frameset is quite different from the code used for a frame. It has opening and closing HTML tags, heading tags, and title tags, but uses opening and closing frameset tags rather than body tags for the frameset code. Inside the frameset tags are short instructions for the way the individual frames should appear inside the frameset. The code for a frameset is quite short compared to the code for a frames page, as shown in Figure H-3.

FIGURE H-3
Code for frameset and frame

```
1  <!DOCTYPE HTML PUBLIC "-//W3C//DTD HTML 4.01 Frameset//EN" "http://www.w3.org/TR/html4/frameset.dtd">
2  <html>
3  <head>
4  <title>Northwest Warehouse Catalog</title>
5  <meta http-equiv="Content-Type" content="text/html; charset=iso-8859-1">
6  </head>
7
8  <frameset rows="151,*" cols="*" frameborder="NO" border="0" framespacing="0">
9    <frame src="top_frame.htm" name="logo_frame" frameborder="no" scrolling="NO" noresize marginwidth="0" marginheight="0" id="logo_frame" >
10   <frameset rows="*" cols="142,*" framespacing="0" frameborder="NO" border="0">
11     <frame src="left_frame.htm" name="main_links" frameborder="yes" scrolling="NO" noresize marginwidth="0" marginheight="0" bordercolor="#000000" id="main_links">
12     <frame src="laptops.htm" name="content_frame" marginwidth="10" marginheight="10" id="content_frame">
13   </frameset>
14 </frameset>
15 <noframes><body>
16 </body></noframes>
17 </html>
18
```

Code for frameset

```
1  <html>
2  <head>
3  <title>Northwest Warehouse portable computers and accessories</title>
4  <meta http-equiv="Content-Type" content="text/html; charset=iso-8859-1">
5  <link href="northwest.css" rel="stylesheet" type="text/css">
6  </head>
7  <body bgcolor="#990033" text="#000000" link="#990033" vlink="#0000FF" alink="#990066" leftmargin="5" topmargin="5" marginwidth="5">
8  <table width="126" border="2" align="left" cellpadding="0" cellspacing="0" bordercolor="#000000" bgcolor="#FFFFFF">
9    <tr>
10     <td bordercolor="#FFFFFF"><p class="currentpage"><font size="3" face="Arial, Helvetica, sans-serif">Home
11       Page</font>
12     <p class="currentpage"><font size="3" face="Arial, Helvetica, sans-serif">Catalog</font>
13     <p class="currentpage"><font size="3" face="Arial, Helvetica, sans-serif">Customer<br>
14   Support</font>
15     <p class="currentpage"><font size="3" face="Arial, Helvetica, sans-serif">About
16       Us</font>
17     <p class="currentpage"><font size="3" face="Arial, Helvetica, sans-serif">Take
18       the Survey</font>
19     <p class="currentpage">
20     <p class="currentpage">
21     <p class="currentpage"> </td>
22   </tr>
23 </table>
24 </body>
25 </html>
26
```

Code for frame

FIGURE H-4

Choosing Top and Nested Left Frames

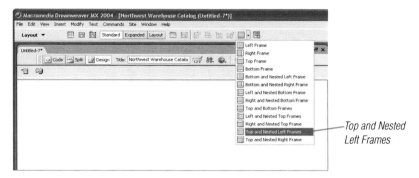

Top and Nested
Left Frames

FIGURE H-5

New page with Top and Nested Left Frames layout applied

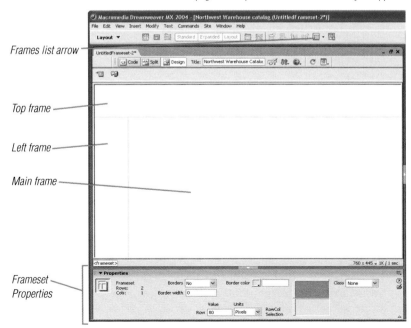

Frames list arrow

Top frame

Left frame

Main frame

Frameset
Properties

Create a frameset

1. Open the Northwest Warehouse Web site that you imported and developed in Chapters F and G.

2. Create a new HTML page in the Northwest Web site, then type **Northwest Warehouse Catalog** in the Title text box on the Document toolbar.

3. Click the **Insert bar list arrow**, click **Layout**, click the **Frames list arrow**, then click **Top and Nested Left Frames**, as shown in Figure H-4.

   The frames appear in the document window, as shown in Figure H-5.

You created a new blank page, titled it Northwest Warehouse Catalog, and applied a predefined frameset to it.

Save a frameset

1. Click **File** on the menu bar, then click **Save Frameset** to open the Save As dialog box.

   The contents of the northwest folder appear in the dialog box.

2. Type **catalog.htm** in the File name text box, then click **Save**, replacing the existing file.

You saved the new page as a frameset.

CONFIGURE FRAMES

What You'll Do

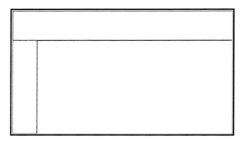

 In this lesson, you will name the three frames contained in the catalog frameset. You will also adjust the size of one frame in the frameset and set the border and scroll properties for each frame. Finally, you will set the margin height and width for each frame.

Understanding Frames Configuration

After you create a frameset, you will need to configure each of the frames it contains. Configuring frames is relatively simple and consists of three tasks. First, you need to name each frame. Second, you need to specify frame sizes. Finally, you need to set the border and scroll bar properties for each frame.

Selecting Frames

In order to configure a frame, you must first select it using the Frames panel. The Frames panel is a panel that shows a visual representation of the frameset. To select a frame, click the frame you want in the Frames panel. To open the Frames panel click Window on the menu bar, then click Frames.

Naming Frames

Simply put, all frames must have a name. The name is used to control the destination of links within pages contained in the frame and the frameset. The name of the frame will go into the target property of any link that you want to open in a location other than the frame in which the link itself is located.

For instance, if you create a frame named body, the name body must be referenced in the target property of every link (within other frames) that you wish to open inside the body frame. Figure H-6 illustrates how this works.

Frame names are also used to automate the loading of pages into a Web browser using JavaScript. Using JavaScript, you can write a program that will alter the contents of the frame by loading content with a script, or by using the script to load a new page. A script will also allow you to change images and other objects on the page by simply referencing the name of the object within the named frame.

Setting Frame Size

If you choose a predefined frameset, the size of each frame is automatically set. However, you can make frames larger or smaller by dragging the frame borders. You can also adjust the size of a frame by manipulating its dimensions in the <frameset> tags on the frameset page.

You can format frames using a specific set of dimensions, such as 100 pixels or 1 inch. You can also specify frame size as a percentage of the screen size. For instance, you can size a frame so that it takes up just a few more pixels of space than an image in the frame, or you can size a frame so that a specific percentage of screen space is taken up no matter how large the screen is. Figure H-7 shows frames formatted with percentage dimensions that change based on the screen size (resolution), as well as frames formatted with exact dimensions whose size stays the same no matter what the screen size.

Unlike tables, frames will not resize themselves to adjust to larger and smaller amounts of information. This means that when you set the size of your frames, you need to know the dimensions of any images that will be displayed within that frame. For instance, if you want to display the banner for your company in the top frame, make sure the top frame is as large as the banner. If the frame is only 50 pixels tall, and the banner is 75 pixels tall, then the bottom 25 pixels of the banner will not be visible, and viewers will need to scroll to see it.

Controlling Frame Borders and Scroll Bars

You can specify the use of scroll bars and borders in the frames in your Web site. You can control the presence of scroll bars for a selected frame by adjusting the Scroll property in the Property inspector. You can use different scroll settings for each frame in a frameset. For instance, you can specify the use of scroll bars on the body frame, but not on the top and bottom frames. You can also specify whether to show borders around a frame by setting the Borders property in the Property inspector. You can also use the Property inspector to specify a border color. Adding borders around frames can help separate them in a browser, and improve the appearance of your site. Setting the Scroll property to Yes also creates visible borders around a frame.

FIGURE H-6
Understanding frames and links

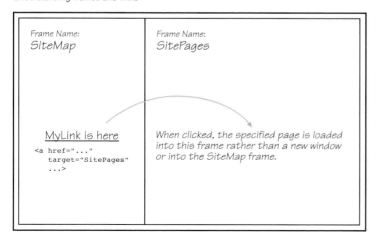

FIGURE H-7
Setting frame sizes in different resolutions using pixels and percentages

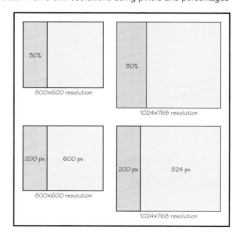

Set frame names

1. Click **Window** on the menu bar, then click **Frames** to display the Frames panel.

2. Click **topFrame** in the Frames panel to select it.

   A dotted outline surrounds the top frame on the page, indicating that it is selected.

3. Type **logo_frame** in the Frame name text box in the Property inspector, press **[Enter]** (Win) or **[return]** (Mac), then compare your screen to Figure H-8.

   TIP If you do not see the frame borders, deselect the frame, click View on the menu bar, point to Visual Aids, then click Frame Borders to turn them on.

4. Click **mainFrame** in the Frames panel to select it.

5. Type **content_frame** in the Frame name text box in the Property inspector, then press **[Enter]** (Win) or **[return]** (Mac).

6. Click **leftFrame** in the Frames panel to select it.

7. Type **main_links** in the Frame name text box in the Property inspector, then press **[Enter]** (Win) or **[return]** (Mac).

8. Click **File** on the menu bar, then click **Save Frameset**.

   TIP You can also select a frameset by clicking the outside border in the Frames panel.

You named the three frames in the catalog frameset.

FIGURE H-8
Selected frame in document window

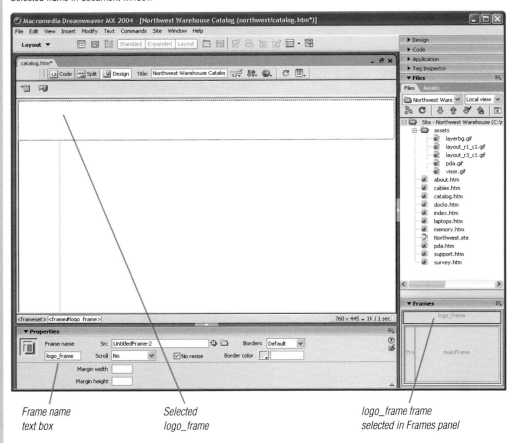

Frame name text box

Selected logo_frame

logo_frame frame selected in Frames panel

FIGURE H-9

Adjusting frame sizes

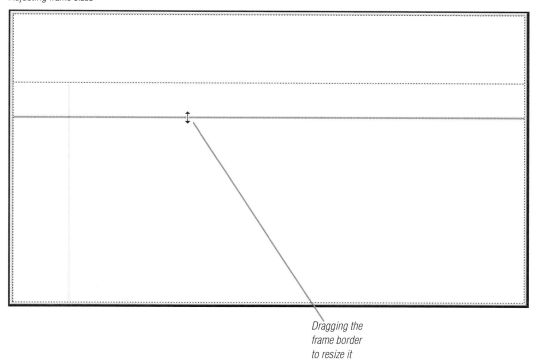

Dragging the
frame border
to resize it

1. Position the mouse pointer on the bottom border of the top frame until the pointer turns into a vertical double arrow.

2. Drag the **border** down about half an inch, as shown in Figure H-9.

3. Click **logo_frame** in the Frames panel to select it (if necessary).

4. Verify that the No resize check box is checked in the Property inspector.

   This prevents viewers from resizing the frame to ensure that it will keep the same dimensions.

5. Click **main_links** in the Frames panel.

6. Verify that the No resize check box is checked in the Property inspector.

You changed the size of the top frame in the frameset and specified that the top and bottom frames cannot be resized.

Set frame borders and border colors

1. Click **logo_frame** in the Frames panel.

2. Click the **Borders list arrow** in the Property inspector, then click **No**.

3. Click **main_links** in the Frames panel.

4. Click the **Borders list arrow** in the Property inspector, then click **Yes**.

5. Change the border color to #000000, then compare your screen to Figure H-10.

6. Select the **frameset** by clicking the outermost border around the three frames in the Frames panel, then save the frameset.

You specified that the border not appear for the top frame and that the border appear for the left frame. You also set the border color to black for the left frame.

FIGURE H-10
Inserting a layer using the Draw Layer button

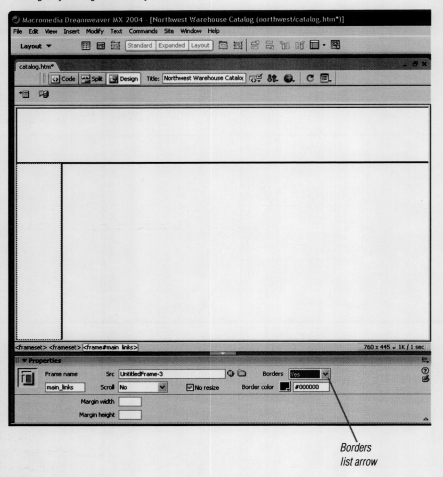

Borders
list arrow

Scroll bars added to the content_frame

Scroll list arrow

Setting page margins for frames

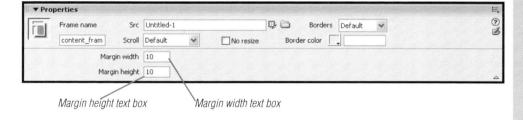

Margin height text box   Margin width text box

Configure frame scrollbars

1. Click **content_frame** in the Frames panel, click the **Scroll list arrow** in the Property inspector, click **Default**, then compare your screen to Figure H-11.

2. Click **main_links** in the Frames panel, click the **Scroll list arrow** in the Property inspector, then click **No**.

3. Click **logo_frame** in the Frames panel, click the **Scroll list arrow** in the Property inspector, then click **No**.

You set the Scroll property to Default for the content_frame. This means that scroll bars will appear when the page content is too large for the frame, allowing viewers to scroll through the entire content. You set the scroll bars to not appear on the main_links and logo_frame frames.

Control page margins

1. Click **logo_frame** in the Frames panel.

2. Type **0** in the Margin width text box in the Property inspector, then press **[Enter]** (Win) or **[return]** (Mac).

3. Type **0** in the Margin height text box in the Property inspector, then press **[Enter]** (Win) or **[return]** (Mac).

4. Click **content_frame** in the Frames panel, set the Margin width and the Margin height to **10**, as shown in Figure H-12.

5. Select **main_links** in the Frames panel, then set the Margin width and the Margin height to **0**.

6. Save the frameset.

You set the page margins for the three frames in the frameset.

ADD CONTENT TO FRAMES

What You'll Do

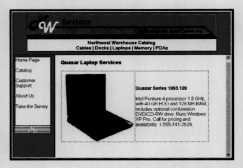

In this lesson, you will specify source files to appear in the logo_frame frame and the main_links frame, then you will create content in the content_frame frame.

Understanding How to Add Content to a Frame

After you create a frameset, you need to add content to the frames it contains. There are two ways you can do this. You can either load existing documents into each frame, or you can create new pages from scratch in each frame. The frameset shown in Figure H-13 contains three frames, two of which contain loaded documents. The middle frame contains no content.

Loading Existing Pages in a Frame

The easiest way to add content to a frame is to load an existing page or file into the frame. This works well when you want to convert a site from a non-frames layout to a frames layout, because you already have existing pages that were created in the previous version of the site. To do this, select the frame, then specify the name of the file you want to load in the Src text box in the Property inspector.

When you load an existing page into a frame, you can then make modifications to the page, just as you would if it were not in the frame. By loading documents into the frames of a frameset, you are simply specifying that multiple Web pages appear in a Web browser at the same time.

Creating Content from Scratch

If you want to create a completely new page that will be displayed in a frame, you can do so from within the frame itself. Creating a new page in a frame is just as simple as creating a page outside of a frame. You simply place the insertion point in the frame and start typing. You can then apply fonts or formatting attributes to the text, or add images or tables, just as if you were creating a new page from scratch outside of a frame.

Catalog frameset showing two frames with loaded documents and one empty frame

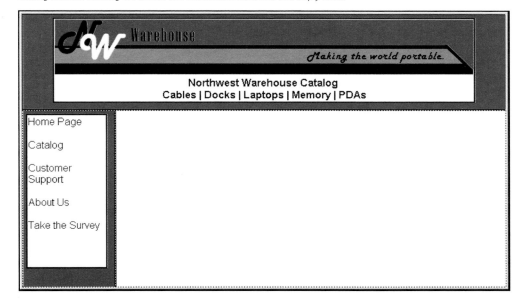

Specify a source file to display in a frame

1. Open dwh_1.htm from the chapter_h Data Files folder, save it as **top_frame** in the Northwest Warehouse Web site, then update the links.

2. Copy topbanner.png at the top of the page to the site's assets folder, then save.

3. Open dwh_2.htm from the chapter_h Data Files folder, save it as **left_frame** in the Northwest Warehouse Web site, then update the links.

4. Click the **catalog.htm name tab** in the upper-left corner of the document window, as shown in Figure H-14, to activate the catalog page.

   TIP   If you do not see the name tabs in the upper-left corner of the documents window, maximize at least one of the open Dreamweaver documents.

5. Click **logo_frame** in the Frames panel, click the **Browse for File icon** 📁 next to the Src text box in the Property inspector.

6. Select **top_frame.htm** from the file list, then click **OK** (Win) or **Choose** (Mac).

7. Click the **main_links** in the Frames panel, then click the **Browse for File icon** 📁 next to the Src text box in the Property inspector.

8. Select **left_frame.htm** from the file list, then click **OK** (Win) or **Choose** (Mac).

9. Drag the bottom border of the logo_frame frame and the right border of the main_links frame if you do not see all of the contents in those frames, then compare your screen to Figure H-15.

You set the source file for two frames. You then resized the frame borders to make room for each frame's content.

FIGURE H-14
Three open files shown by three tabs

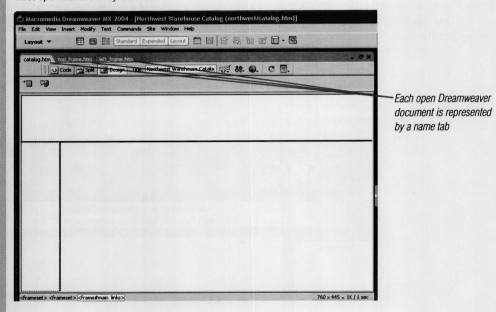

Each open Dreamweaver document is represented by a name tab

FIGURE H-15
Frameset with top and left frames loaded

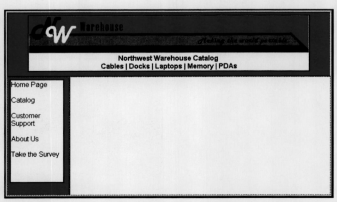

FIGURE H-16

Table added to the content_frame

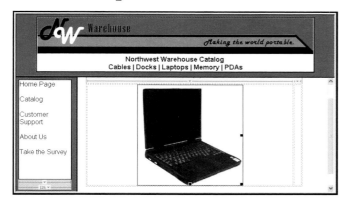

FIGURE H-17

content_frame with all content added

1. Click inside content_frame in the document window to place the insertion point, then type **Quasar Laptop Services**.

2. Type **Laptops** in the Title text box on the Document toolbar.

3. Click **File** on the menu bar, click **Save Frame As**, then save the frame as **laptops.htm**, replacing the existing file.

4. Format the text using the following attributes: Font: Arial, Helvetica, sans-serif, Size: 4, Style: Bold, and Color: 660033.

5. Deselect the text, press **[Enter]** (Win) or **[return]** (Mac), then insert a table that has the following attributes: Rows: 1, Columns: 2, Table width: 90%, and Border thickness: 0 pixels.

6. Insert laptop.jpg from the chapter_h assets folder in the left cell of the table, add appropriate text, center it, then compare your screen to Figure H-16.

7. Type **Quasar Series 1993.109** in the right cell of the table.

8. Format the text using the following attributes: Font: Arial, Helvetica, sans-serif, Size: 3, Style: Bold, deselect the text, then press **[Enter]** (Win) or **[return]** (Mac).

9. Type **Intel Pentium 4 processor 1.8 GHz, with 40 GB HDD and 128 MB RAM. Includes optional combination DVD/CD-RW drive. Runs Windows XP Pro. Call for pricing and availability. 1-555-741-2629.** Then format the text attractively, as shown in Figure H-17.

10. Click **File** on the menu bar, then click **Save All**.

You inserted a table into the content_frame, saved it as laptops.htm, then added content to it.

LESSON 4

LINK FRAMES

What You'll Do

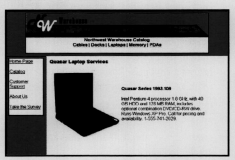

In this lesson, you will set targets and links for the links in the logo_frame and the main_links frames.

Understanding Linking Relationships

The purpose of creating a frameset is to be able to display multiple frames simultaneously in a browser window. One of the frames usually remains unchanged while another one changes depending on what the user clicks. The main frame, which is usually the largest frame, contains changing content. The smaller frame contains navigation links that control the main frame. To link frames together, each link must have a target. A target is the frame that will open when users click the link. When you assign a target to a link, you use the name given to the frame in the Property inspector. The target locations are shown in Table H-1.

TABLE H-1: Target locations

target	description
_blank	Opens the linked document in a separate browser window
_parent	Opens the linked document in the parent frameset
_self	Opens the linked document in the same frame
_top	Opens the linked document in the whole browser window, replacing the original frameset

FIGURE H-18

Link established from the logo_frame to the content_frame

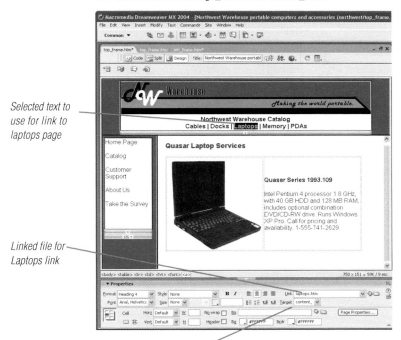

Selected text to use for link to laptops page

Linked file for Laptops link

Target set to content_frame

Link frames

1. Close the left_frame and the top_frame pages.

2. Select the word Laptops in the logo_frame, click the **Browse for File icon** 🗀 next to the Link text box in the Property inspector, then double-click **laptops.htm** in the Web site root folder.

3. Click the **Target list arrow** in the Property inspector, then click **content_frame**, as shown in Figure H-18.

   This will cause the laptops page to display in the main content frame of the frameset when the link is clicked.

4. Repeat Steps 2 and 3 to set the links for the rest of the catalog items in the logo_frame.

5. Select the words Home Page in the main_links frame, click the **Browse for File icon** 🗀 next to the Link text box in the Property inspector, then double-click **index.htm** in the Web site root folder.

6. Click the **Target list arrow**, then click **_top**.

   This will cause the links to the main Web site pages to open in a full window, rather than a frameset.

7. Repeat Steps 5 and 6 to set the links for each item in the main_links frame to their respective pages in the Web site.

8. Click **File** on the menu bar, click **Save All**, view the page in the browser, then test each link.

You set targets and links for the links in the logo_frame and the main_links frames.

CREATE NOFRAMES CONTENT

What You'll Do

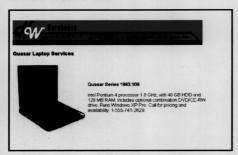

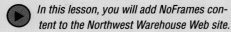

▶ *In this lesson, you will add NoFrames content to the Northwest Warehouse Web site.*

Understanding NoFrames Content

For different reasons, some viewers might not be able to view content that is contained in frames. For instance, some viewers turn off support for frames in their browser, and others might be using an older version of a browser that does not support frames. However, all viewers will still be able to view your site's content if you provide NoFrames content for every frameset in your site. **NoFrames content** is alternate content that can be viewed without frames. NoFrames content is added only to the frameset page. It is not added to any of the other pages that are viewed within one of the frames, so you only have to create one set of NoFrames content for each frameset in your site.

Adding NoFrames Content

NoFrames content provides viewers with a way to view a frames-based site without using frames. They view a special set of data provided at the end of the main frameset page which appears like any other Web page.

To add NoFrames content to a frameset document, click Modify on the menu bar, point to Frameset, then click Edit NoFrames Content to open a new page in the document window. You use this new page, which is part of the frameset document file, to lay out the NoFrames content. To do this, copy the images and text from all of the pages displayed in each frame and lay them out just as you would on a standard non-frames page. When you finish laying out the NoFrames content, you then need to change the links so that they point to other non-frames-based pages with the same content. It doesn't do any good to load NoFrames content on one page, only to reload the frames again on the next page. Providing full NoFrames content essentially means that you are creating a copy of your Web site that doesn't use frames at all. Figure H-19 shows the NoFrames content of the catalog frameset. Figure H-20 shows the same content in the frameset.

FIGURE H-19
NoFrames content of catalog frameset

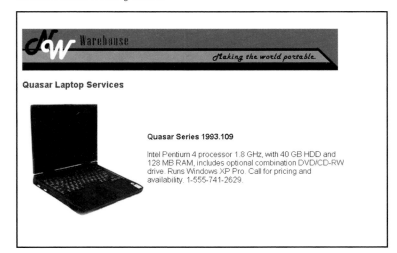

FIGURE H-20
Catalog frameset with content loaded in frames

Add NoFrames content to a Web page

1. Click in the content_frame in the document window to set the insertion point, click **Edit** on the menu bar, then click **Select All**.

2. Click **Edit** on the menu bar, then click **Copy**.

3. Click **Modify** on the menu bar, point to **Frameset**, then click **Edit NoFrames Content**.

   The NoFrames Content window appears. You will use this to create the content for the non-frames version of the Web page.

4. Verify that your insertion point is in the upper-left corner of the document window.

5. Click **Edit** on the menu bar, then click **Paste**.

   The content from the content_frame frame is pasted in the NoFrames Content window, as shown in Figure H-21.

   (continued)

FIGURE H-21

NoFrames Content window containing pasted content from the content_frame frame

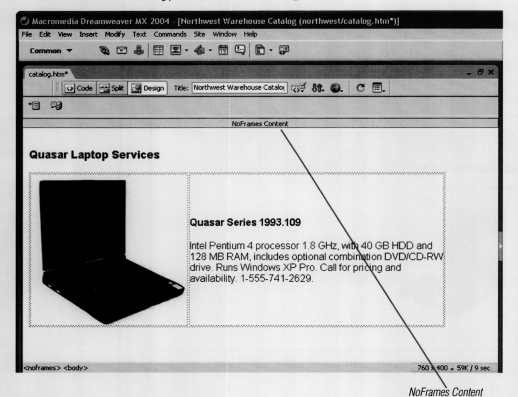

NoFrames Content

Tools You'll Use

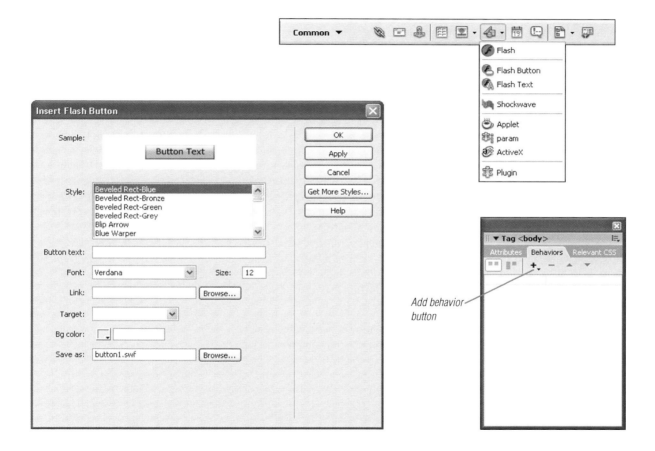

Add behavior button

ADD MACROMEDIA FLASH OBJECTS

What You'll Do

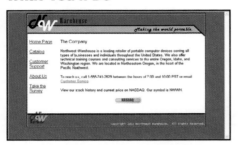

 In this lesson, you will insert a Flash button on the about page of the Northwest Warehouse Web site. You will also insert a Flash movie on the support page and then play the movie both in Dreamweaver and in a browser.

Understanding Macromedia Flash

Macromedia Flash is a software program that allows you to create low-bandwidth animations and interactive elements that can be placed on your Web pages. These animations use a series of vector-based graphics that load quickly and merge with other graphics and sounds to create short movies. Figure I-1 shows a Web page that contains several Flash objects. Figure I-2 shows the Macromedia Flash program used to create Flash objects.

Once these short movies are created, you can place them directly on your Web pages.

In order to view Flash movies, you need the Macromedia Flash Player, a software program that is embedded in the latest versions of both Internet Explorer and Netscape Navigator. If you are using an older browser that does not support the version of Flash used to create your movie, you can download the latest Flash player from the Macromedia Web site, located at *http://www.macromedia.com*. At this point, roughly 96% of Web viewers can view Flash 3, 4, and 5 movies, and about 70% of viewers are able to view Flash 6 files.

Collecting Flash objects

Macromedia and their devoted product users provide you with a variety of downloadable Flash buttons which are available on the Macromedia Exchange Web site, located at *http://www.macromedia.com/exchange/*. At this site you can find collections of different buttons, such as space and planet theme sets, and just about anything else you might want. If you can't find a movie or button that interests you, you can download a demo version of Macromedia Flash to create your own Flash objects.

Because Flash buttons and Flash text created in Dreamweaver are based on Flash 6 technology, nearly all viewers will be able to see them no matter what browser they are using.

Inserting Flash Buttons and Movies

A **Flash button** is a button made from a small, predefined Flash movie that can be inserted on a Web page to provide navigation on your Web site. Like all Flash objects, Flash buttons are saved with the .swf file extension. Using Dreamweaver, you can insert customized Flash buttons on your Web pages without having Macromedia

Flash installed. To do this, use the Flash Button command in the Media menu on the Insert bar when the Common category is displayed. This will open the Insert Flash Button dialog box, where you can choose from 44 different styles of buttons. You also use this dialog box to specify the button text, formatting, an internal or external page to which to link the button, a background color, and a filename for the button.

If the button styles provided in the Insert Flash Button dialog box do not fit your needs, you can download additional styles, use Flash to create your own buttons, or have someone else create custom-made buttons for you.

Using Macromedia Flash, you can create Flash movies that include a variety of multimedia elements, such as audio files (both music and voice-overs), animated objects, scripted objects, clickable links, and just about any other animated or clickable object imaginable. Flash movies can be used to add presentations to your existing Web site or to create an entire Web site. To add a Flash movie to a Web page, click Flash from the Media menu on the Insert bar to open the Select File dialog box, then choose the Flash movie you want to insert.

FIGURE I-1
Web site containing Flash objects

FIGURE I-2
Macromedia Flash MX 2004 window

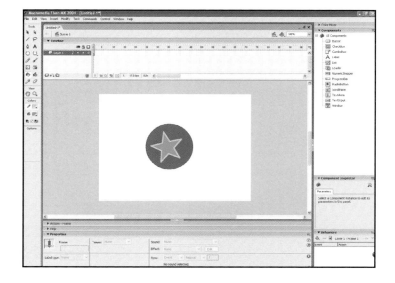

Insert Flash buttons

1. Open the Northwest Warehouse Web site that you completed in Chapter H, then open the about page.

2. Click at the end of the last paragraph to set the insertion point, press **[Enter]** (Win) or **[return]** (Mac), then type **View our stock history and current price on NASDAQ. Our symbol is NWWH.**

3. Press **[Enter]** (Win) or **[return]** (Mac), then click the **Align Center** ≣ button in the Property inspector.

4. Click the **Insert bar list arrow**, click **Common**, click the **Media list arrow**, then click **Flash Button** to open the Insert Flash Button dialog box, as shown in Figure I-3.

5. Select **Soft-Raspberry** from the Style list.

6. Type **NASDAQ** in the Button text text box.

7. Click the **Font list arrow**, click **Impact**, then type **14** in the Size text box.

(continued)

FIGURE I-3
Insert Flash Button dialog box

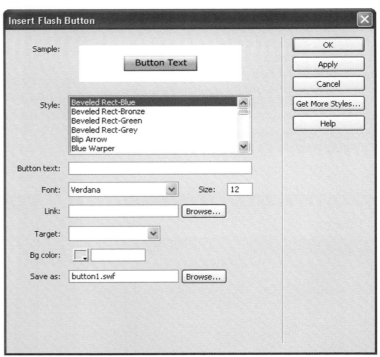

FIGURE I-4

Flash button added to the about page

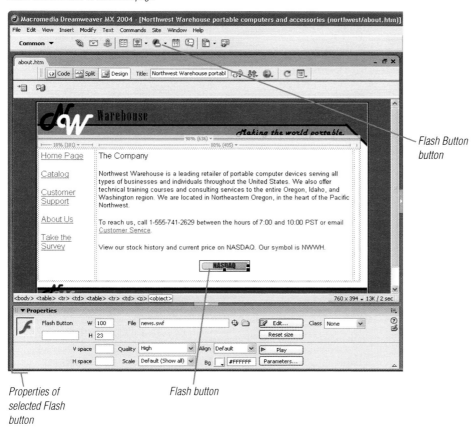

Flash Button
button

Properties of
selected Flash
button

Flash button

8. Type ***http://www.nasdaq.com*** in the Link text box.

9. Set the target to _blank.

 The _blank setting ensures that the NASDAQ Web site will open in a new window, keeping the Northwest Warehouse Web site open, also.

10. Click the **Bg color button** ☐, then click **#FFFFFF** (white).

11. Type **news** in the Save as text box, then click **OK**.

12. Compare your screen to Figure I-4.

 TIP   You may see a Flash button placeholder on the page in Dreamweaver. When you preview the page in a browser, you will see the actual Flash button you created.

13. Save your work, preview the page in your browser, test the Flash button, then close the browser.

14. Close the about page.

You added a Flash button to the about page of the Northwest Warehouse Web site.

Insert Flash movies

1. Open the support page of the Northwest Warehouse Web site.

   TIP If you are using a Macintosh computer, click the Browse for File icon next to the Src text box in the Property inspector, navigate to the assets folder in the Northwest Web site root folder, then select layout_r1_c1.gif for the top banner and layout_r3_c1.gif for the copyright footer.

2. Click to the right of the Customer Support heading, press **[spacebar]**, type **is our number one priority!**, then press **[Enter]** (Win) or **[return]** (Mac).

3. Format the paragraph using the following attributes: Font: Arial, Helvetica, sans-serif, and Size: 3.

4. Click the **Media list arrow** on the Insert bar, then click **Flash**.

5. Navigate to the chapter_i assets folder, click **cservice.swf**, click **OK** (Win) or **Choose** (Mac), then save the movie in the root folder of the Web site.

   A Flash movie placeholder appears on the page, as shown in Figure I-5.

You inserted a Flash movie on the support page of the Northwest Warehouse Web site.

FIGURE I-5

Flash movie placeholder on the support page

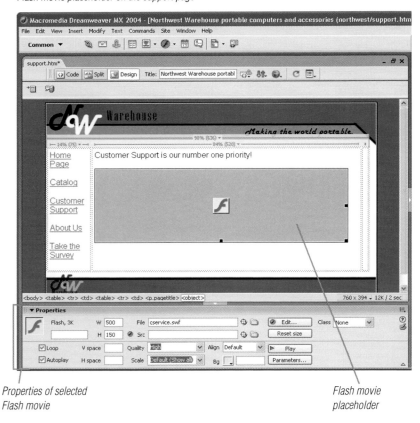

Properties of selected Flash movie

Flash movie placeholder

FIGURE I-6

Flash movie playing in Dreamweaver

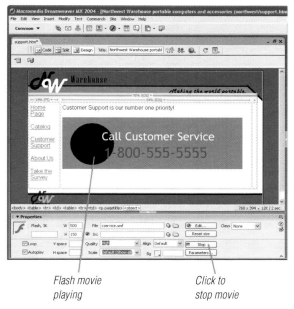

Flash movie
playing

Click to
stop movie

1. Click **Play** in the Property inspector to view the cservice.swf movie, as shown in Figure I-6, then click **Stop**.

2. Save your work, preview the page in your browser, compare your screen to Figure I-7, then close your browser.

   TIP To play Flash movies in Dreamweaver and in your browser, you must have Shockwave Player installed on your computer. If Shockwave Player is not installed, you can download it at the Macromedia Web site (*www.macromedia.com*).

3. Close the support page.

You played a Flash movie on the support page in the Northwest Warehouse Web site in Dreamweaver and in your browser.

FIGURE I-7

Flash movie playing in Internet Explorer

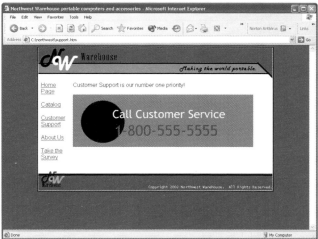

ADD ROLLOVER IMAGES

What You'll Do

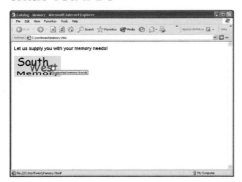

In this lesson, you will add a rollover image to the memory page of the Northwest Warehouse Web site.

Understanding Rollover Images

A **rollover image** is an image that changes its appearance when the mouse pointer is placed over it in a browser. A rollover image actually consists of two images. The first image is the one that appears when the mouse pointer is not positioned over it, and the second image is the one that appears when the mouse pointer is positioned over it. Rollover images are often used to help create a feeling of action and excitement on a Web page. For instance, suppose you are creating a Web site that promotes a series of dance classes. You could create a rollover image using two images of a dancer in two different poses. When a viewer places the mouse pointer over the image of the dancer in the first pose, the image would change to show the dancer in a different pose, creating a feeling of movement and action.

QUICKTIP

You can also add a link to a rollover image, so that the image will change only when the image is clicked.

Adding Shockwave movies

Macromedia Shockwave is part of the Macromedia Director Shockwave Studio, a software suite used to create full-blown interactive, multimedia presentations that combine text, graphics, video, animations, and sound. Adding Shockwave files to your Web pages can add excitement, sizzle, and interactivity to engage your users. To add a Shockwave movie to a Web page in Dreamweaver, select Shockwave from the Media menu on the Insert bar, open the Select File dialog box, select the file you want, then click OK. Shockwave files have a .dcr file extension.

Adding Rollover Images

You add rollover images to a Web page using the Rollover Image command in the Images menu on the Insert bar shown in Figure I-8. You specify both the original image and the rollover image in the Insert Rollover Image dialog box. The rollover image is the image that is swapped when the mouse rolls over the original image.

QUICKTIP

It's a good idea to click the Preload rollover image check box in the Insert Rollover Image dialog box to ensure that the rollover image appears without a delay.

Rollover images can also be used to display an image associated with a text link. For instance, suppose you are creating a Web site for an upcoming election. You could create a Web page that contains a list of candidates for the election, and add a rollover image for each candidate's name that would cause a photograph of the candidate to appear when the mouse is placed over his or her name. You can also use this effect to make appropriate images appear when you point to different menu options. For instance, Figure I-9 shows the Nurses Anytime Web site, which uses rollover images to highlight each menu option on its home page.

FIGURE I-8

Images menu on the Insert bar

FIGURE I-9

Nurses Anytime Web site with rollover image

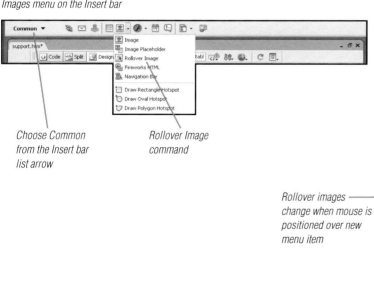

Choose Common
from the Insert bar
list arrow

Rollover Image
command

Rollover images
change when mouse is
positioned over new
menu item

Add a rollover image

1. Open the memory page of the Northwest Warehouse Web site.

2. Replace the current placeholder text with **Let us supply you with your memory needs!**, then format the text using the following attributes: Font: Arial, Helvetica, sans-serif, and Size: 4.

3. Click to the right of the new paragraph, then press **[Enter]** (Win) or **[return]** (Mac).

4. Click the **Insert bar list arrow**, click **Common**, click the **Images list arrow**, then click **Rollover Image**.

5. Type **Memory** in the Image name text box, then compare your screen to Figure I-10.

6. Click **Browse** next to the Original image text box, navigate to the chapter_i assets folder, click **nwmemory.png**, then click **OK** (Win) or **Choose** (Mac).

(continued)

FIGURE I-10

Insert Rollover Image dialog box

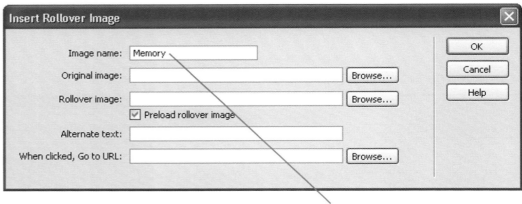

Name of image

FIGURE I-11

Memory page with rollover image in Internet Explorer

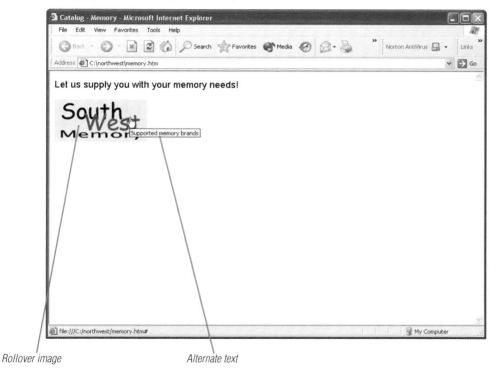

Rollover image   Alternate text

7. Click **Browse** next to the Rollover image text box, navigate to the chapter_i assets folder, click **swmemory.png**, then click **OK** (Win) or **Choose** (Mac).

8. Check the **Preload rollover image check box** to select it (if necessary).

9. Type **Supported memory brands** in the Alternate text text box, then click **OK**.

10. Save your work, preview the page in your browser, place the mouse pointer over the image to see the rollover effect, compare your screen to Figure I-11, then close your browser.

You added a rollover image to the memory page of the Northwest Warehouse Web site.

ADD SOUNDS AND POPUP MESSAGES

What You'll Do

In this lesson, you will add a sound effect and a popup message to the memory page of the Northwest Warehouse Web site.

Adding Interactive Elements

You can make your Web pages come alive by adding interactive elements such as sounds to them. For instance, if you are creating a Web page about your favorite animals, you could attach the sound of a dog barking to a photograph of a dog so that the barking sound would play when the viewer clicked the photograph. You can add sound and other multimedia actions to elements by attaching behaviors to them. **Behaviors** are sets of instructions that you can attach to page elements that tell the page element to respond in a specific way when an event occurs, such as when the mouse pointer is positioned over the element. When you attach a behavior to an element, JavaScript code for the behavior is automatically generated and inserted into the code for your page.

Using the Behaviors Panel

You can use the Behaviors panel located in the Tag panel group to insert a variety of JavaScript-based behaviors on a page. For instance, using the Behaviors panel you can automate tasks, respond to visitor selections and mouse movements, add sounds, create games, or add automatic dynamic effects to a Web page. To insert a behavior, click the Add behavior button on the Behaviors panel to open the Actions menu, as shown in Figure I-12, then click a behavior from the menu.

Inserting Sound Effects

Sound effects can add a new dimension to any Web site. You can use sounds to enhance the effect of positioning the mouse on a rollover image, clicking a link, or even loading or closing a page. By adding sounds, you can make your pages cheep, chirp, click, or squawk.

To apply a sound effect, select the link or object to which you want the sound effect added, and then select the Play Sound behavior located in the Actions menu of the Behaviors panel.

Inserting Popup Messages and Alert Boxes

Popup messages and **alert boxes** are messages that open in a browser to either clarify information, alert viewers of an action that is being taken, or even say "goodbye and thank you for visiting the Web site." You can add popup messages using the Behaviors panel.

Popup messages can be quite annoying to Web site viewers, so be judicious when adding them to your pages. Typically, you should only use them when it is imperative to confirm an action or provide viewers with more information about the site they are visiting or leaving, or about the information they are submitting in a form.

Understanding Actions and Events

Actions are triggered by events. For instance, if you want your viewer to hear a sound when an image is clicked, you would attach the Play Sound action using the onClick event to trigger the action. Other examples of events are onMouseOver and onLoad. The onMouseOver event will trigger an action when the mouse is placed over an object. The onLoad event will trigger an action when the page is first loaded in the browser window.

FIGURE I-12

Behaviors panel with the Actions menu displayed

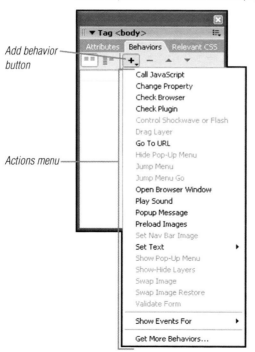

Add behavior button

Actions menu

Add sound effects

1. Select the rollover image on the memory page, click **Window** on the menu bar, then click **Behaviors** to open the Behaviors panel.

2. Click the **Add behavior button** ⊞ on the Behaviors panel toolbar to open the Actions menu, then click **Play Sound** to open the Play Sound dialog box, as shown in Figure I-13.

3. Click **Browse**, navigate to the chapter_i assets folder, click **chord.wav**, then click **OK** (Win) or **Choose** (Mac).

   TIP If a dialog box opens asking if you want to copy the chord.wav file to the Web site, click Yes, navigate to the root folder of the Web site, then click Save.

4. Click **OK** to close the Play Sound dialog box.

   Notice that Swap Image and Play Sound appear as actions in the Behaviors panel. This means that the Play Sound behavior will be triggered when the mouse is positioned over the specified object.

5. Click the left column of the Play Sound action in the Behaviors panel to display the events list arrow, then click **onMouseOver**.

6. Save your work, preview the page in your browser, test the sound effect, then close your browser.

You added a sound effect to an image on the memory page of the Northwest Warehouse Web site.

FIGURE I-13
Play Sound dialog box

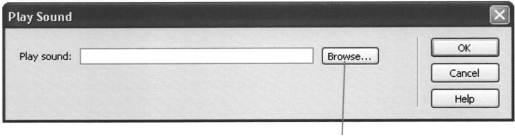

Click to select sound file

CHAPTER J
CREATING AND USING TEMPLATES

1. Create templates with editable and optional regions.

2. Enhance and nest templates.

3. Use templates to create pages.

4. Use templates to update a site.

CHAPTER J
CREATING AND USING TEMPLATES

Introduction

When you create a Web site, it's important to make sure that each page has a unified look so that viewers know they are in your site no matter what page they are viewing. For instance, you should make sure that common elements such as the navigation bar and company banner appear in the same place on every page and that every page has the same background color. One way to make sure that every page in your site has a consistent appearance is through the use of templates. A **template** is a special kind of page that contains both **locked regions**, which are areas on the page that cannot be modified by users of the template, as well as other types of regions that users can change or edit. For instance, an **optional region** is an area in the template that users can choose to show or hide, and an **editable region** is an area where users can add or change content.

Using templates not only ensures a consistent appearance throughout a Web site, but also saves considerable development time.

Templates are especially helpful if different people will be creating pages in your site. In this chapter, you will create a template from an existing page in the Super Bug Zapper Web site, and define editable and optional regions in it. You will also create a nested template, add a repeating table to a template, and create editable attributes for various elements in a template.

Understanding How to Use Templates

The ideal process for using templates is for one person (the template author) to create a template that has a locked region containing the design elements common to every page in the site, as well as regions where content can be added or changed. Once the template is fully developed, other team members can use it to create each page of the site, adding appropriate content to the editable regions of each page. If the template author makes changes to the template, all pages to which the template is attached can be automatically updated to reflect those changes.

Tools You'll Use

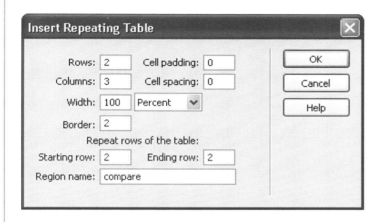

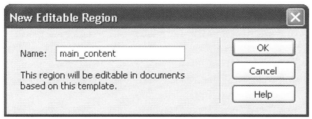

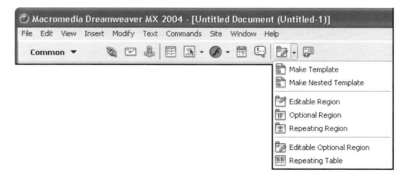

CREATE TEMPLATES WITH EDITABLE AND OPTIONAL REGIONS

What You'll Do

 In this lesson, you will create a template based on the index page of the Super Bug Zapper Web site. You will then define editable regions, optional regions, and editable optional regions in the template.

Creating a Template from an Existing Page

If you have already created and designed a page that you think looks great, and you want to use the layout and design for other pages in your site, you can save the page as a template using the Save as Template command. Templates are saved with a .dwt extension, and are stored in the Templates folder in the root folder of your Web site. If your site does not have a Templates folder, one will automatically be created for you the first time you save a template. To view a list of templates in your site, open the Templates folder in the Files panel. To preview a template before opening it, open the Assets panel, click the Templates button on the Assets panel toolbar, then click a template in the list. The template appears in the preview window above the templates list, as shown in Figure J-1.

Defining Editable Regions

By default, when you save a template, all content on the page will be locked, which

means that no one else will be able to add content or modify any part of the template to create new pages. If your template is going to be used effectively, you need to have at least one editable region in it so that other users can add content. You can specify a name for the region using the New Editable Region dialog box. Editable regions are outlined in blue on the template page, and the names of the editable regions appear in blue shaded boxes, as shown in Figure J-2.

Defining Optional Regions

In addition to editable regions, you can also add optional regions to a template. An **optional region** is an area in a template that users can choose to either show or hide. For instance, you could make a graphic an optional region, so that users of the template can decide whether or not to show it on the page they are creating. An optional region's visibility is controlled by the conditional statement **if**. You can specify a page element as an optional region using the New Optional Region dialog box. You can name the region and specify whether to show or hide it by default. The Editable and Optional Region dialog boxes are both accessed by clicking the Templates list arrow on the Insert bar when the Common category is displayed.

Defining Editable Optional Regions

If you want to give users the ability to show or hide a page element, as well as make modifications to it, then you can define the element as an **editable optional region**. For instance, you might want to make an advertisement an editable optional region so that users of the template could change its text and specify whether to show or hide it. Using the New Optional Region dialog box, you can name the region and specify whether to show or hide it by default.

FIGURE J-1
Templates in the Assets panel

FIGURE J-2
Template with locked and editable regions

Assets panel

Preview of selected template

List of templates available in this site

Templates button

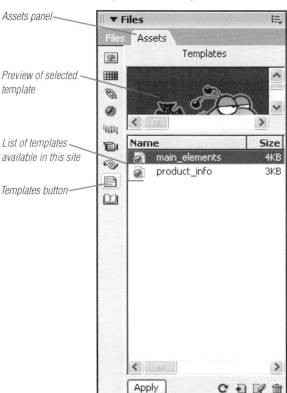

Editable Region command

Optional Region command

Blue outline of editable region

Editable region labels

Placeholder text that template users can customize

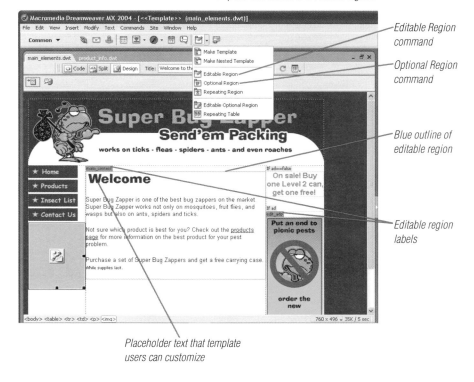

Create the Super Bug Zapper Web site (Win)

1. Open Windows Explorer, then navigate to the chapter_j Data Files folder so that the contents appear in the right pane, as shown in Figure J-3.

2. Copy the bugzapper folder in the chapter_j Data Files folder, then paste it to the drive and folder in the left pane where you want to store the Super Bug Zapper Web site.

3. Close Windows Explorer, start Dreamweaver, click **Site** menu bar, click **Manage Sites**, click **New**, then click **Site** to open the Site Definition for Unnamed Site 1 dialog box.

4. Click the **Advanced tab** (if necessary), type **Super Bug Zapper** in the Site name text box, then set the Local root folder to the bugzapper folder that you pasted in Step 2.

5. Set the Default images folder to the assets folder located in the bugzapper folder that you pasted in Step 2, compare your screen to Figure J-4, click **OK**, then click **Done**.

   The files for the Super Bug Zapper Web site are now displayed in the Files panel.

6. Open the index page, the contact_us page, the products page, and the insects page to familiarize yourself with the site.

7. Close all open pages.

You copied the bugzapper folder from the chapter_j Data Files folder to the drive and folder where you want to store the Web site files. You also used the Site Definition dialog box to name the site, set the location of the root folder, and specify the folder for storing images.

FIGURE J-3

Viewing the bugzapper folder in Windows Explorer

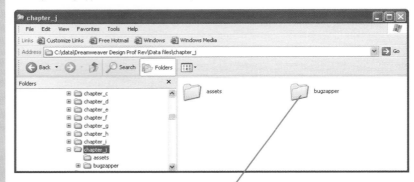

Copy this folder to the folder where you want to store Super Bug Zapper Web site files

FIGURE J-4

Site Definition dialog box with settings for the Super Bug Zapper Web site

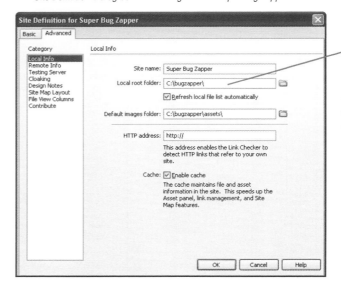

Specify the folder where you want to store Super Bug Zapper Web site (your path may differ)

FIGURE J-5

Copying the bugzapper folder using Finder

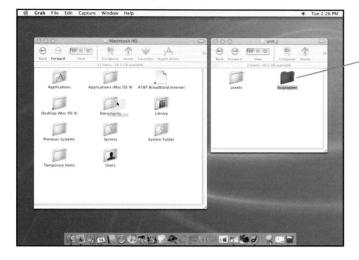

Copy this folder to the folder where you want to store Super Bug Zapper Web site files

FIGURE J-6

Site Definition dialog box with settings for Super Bug Zapper Web site

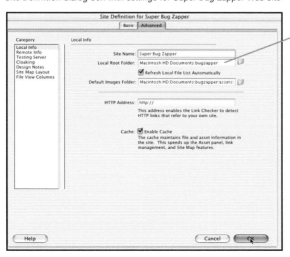

Specify folder where you want to store Super Bug Zapper Web site (your folder may be different)

Create the Super Bug Zapper Web site (Mac)

1. Open Finder, then navigate to the folder on your computer where you want to store the Super Bug Zapper Web site.

2. Open another version of Finder, then open the chapter_j Data Files folder.

3. Drag the bugzapper folder from the chapter_j folder to the drive and folder where you want to store the Super Bug Zapper Web site, as shown in Figure J-5.

4. Close the Finder windows, start Dreamweaver, click **Site** on the menu bar, click **Manage Sites** to open the Manage Sites dialog box, click **New**, then click **Site** to open the Site Definition for Unnamed Site1 dialog box.

5. Click the **Advanced tab**, type **Super Bug Zapper** in the Site name text box, then set the Local root folder to the bugzapper folder that you dragged in Step 3.

6. Set the Default images folder to the assets folder located in the bugzapper folder that you dragged in Step 3, compare your screen to Figure J-6, click **OK**, then click **Done**.

7. Open the index page, the contact_us page, the products page, and the insects page of the Super Bug Zapper Web site to familiarize yourself with the site, then close all open pages.

You copied the bugzapper folder to a different drive and folder. You then named the site and set the root and default images folders.

Create a template from an existing page

1. Open the index page.

2. Click **File** on the menu bar, then click **Save as Template** to open the Save As Template dialog box.

3. Type **main_elements** in the Save as text box, compare your screen to Figure J-7, click **Save**, update the links, then click the **Refresh button** 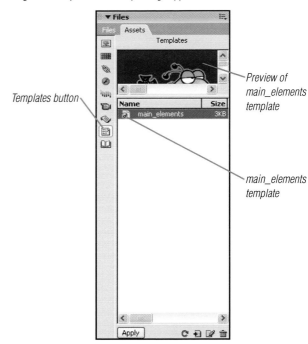 on the Files panel toolbar.

   Notice that the Templates folder, which contains the main_elements template, appears in the Files panel.

4. Display the Assets panel, click the **Templates button** to view the list of templates in the site, click the **main_elements template** in the list (if necessary), then compare your Assets panel to Figure J-8.

   > TIP   To create a template from scratch, click File on the menu bar, click New to open the New Document dialog box, click the General tab, click Template page in the Category list, then click Create.

You created a template from the home page of the Super Bug Zapper Web site.

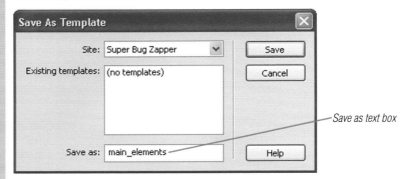

Save as text box

Templates button

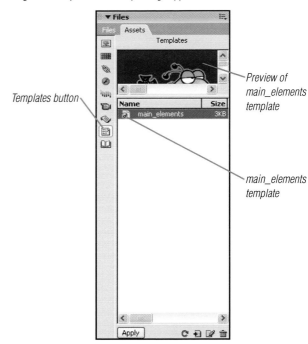

Preview of main_elements template

main_elements template

FIGURE J-9

main_elements template with editable region added

Templates
list arrow

Editable region
label

Editable region
marked by blue
outline

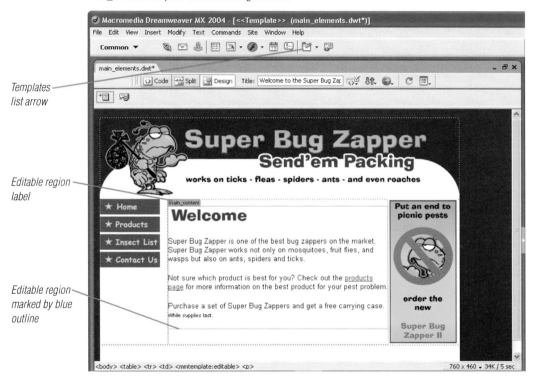

1. Click the **Welcome heading**, press and hold **[Shift]**, then click to the right of While supplies last at the bottom of the cell to select all of the content in that cell.

2. Click the **Insert bar list arrow**, then click **Common**.

3. Click the **Templates list arrow** on the Insert bar, then click **Editable Region** to open the New Editable Region dialog box.

   TIP   You can also press [Ctrl][Alt][V] (Win) or ⌘ [option][V] (Mac) to open the New Editable Region dialog box.

4. Type **main_content** in the Name text box, click **OK**, click anywhere to deselect the text.

   As shown in Figure J-9, a blue shaded box containing main_content appears above the Welcome heading.

   TIP   To remove an editable region from a template, select the editable region in the document window, click Modify on the menu bar, point to Templates, then click Remove Template Markup.

You created an editable region in the main_elements template.

Create an optional region

1. Select the orange rectangle that contains the bug image on the right side of the page, press [←] to place the insertion point to the left of the orange rectangle, then press **[Enter]** (Win) or **[return]** (Mac).

   There is now space above the graphic where you can type text for an ad.

2. Press [↑] to move the insertion point to the blank line at the top of the cell, then type **On sale! Buy one Level 2 can, get one free!**

3. Format the text using the following attributes: Font: Arial, Helvetica, sans-serif, Size: 3, Alignment: Align Center, Bold, and Color: #FF6600.

4. Select the text you typed in Step 2 (if necessary), click the **Templates list arrow**, then click **Optional Region** to open the New Optional Region dialog box.

5. Make sure the Basic tab is displayed, type **sale** in the Name text box, verify that the Show by default check box is checked, compare your screen to Figure J-10, then click **OK**.

   A blue shaded box including If sale appears above the ad text, as shown in Figure J-11.

You added and formatted text to create an ad in the main_elements template. You then defined this ad as a new optional region named sale, so that users of the template can choose whether to show or hide this element.

FIGURE J-10
New Optional Region dialog box with settings for sale optional region

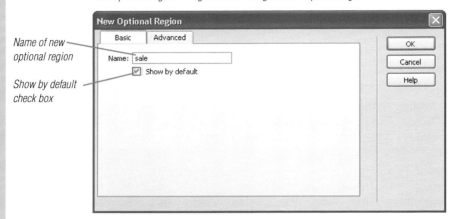

Name of new optional region

Show by default check box

FIGURE J-11
main_elements template with new optional region added

Sale optional region label

Formatted text in sale optional region label

main_elements template with new editable optional region added

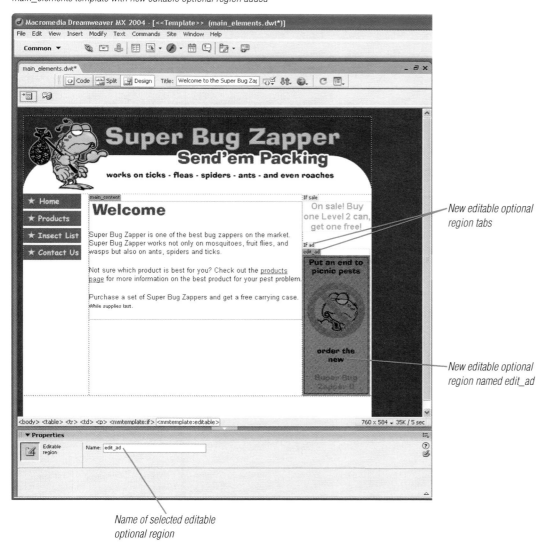

New editable optional region tabs

New editable optional region named edit_ad

Name of selected editable optional region

Create an editable optional region

1. Select the orange rectangle that contains the bug graphic.

2. Click the **Templates list arrow**, then click **Editable Optional Region** to open the New Optional Region dialog box.

3. Type **ad** in the Name text box, then click **OK**.

   Two blue shaded boxes containing If ad and EditRegion4 appear above the orange rectangle. (EditRegion4 may appear below.)

4. Select the orange rectangle that contains the bug graphic, then slowly drag it inside the small rectangle directly below the EditRegion4 label to ensure that the rectangle is inside the editable area.

5. Click the blue shaded box containing EditRegion4, use the Property inspector to change its name to **edit_ad,** press **[Enter]** (Win) or **[return]** (Mac), then compare your screen to Figure J-12.

6. Save your work.

You specified that the orange rectangle be an editable optional region in the main_elements template.

ENHANCE AND NEST TEMPLATES

What You'll Do

In this lesson, you will specify that the sale optional region appear when the ad region is not showing. You will then create another template that is nested in the main_elements template, and insert a repeating table in it. You will define the cell background color in the table as an editable attribute. Finally, you will insert an image in the template and specify that its Source property be editable.

Setting Parameters for Optional Regions

If your template will be used by many people, it might be a good idea to include several optional regions in it so that users of the template can pick and choose from a wide range of content elements. You might also want to set parameters for optional regions, specifying that they are displayed or hidden based on specific conditions. For instance, let's say you have two optional regions named red and blue, respectively. You could set the blue optional region parameter to red so that the blue optional region would appear only when the red optional region is showing, and would be hidden only when the red optional region is hidden. Use the Advanced settings in the New Optional Region dialog box to set the parameters of an optional region. You can also write a conditional expression based on JavaScript. For instance, you could write the expression *red == false* to specify that the blue optional region appear only when the red

optional region is hidden, similar to the example shown in Figure J-13.

Nesting Templates

If you are working on a complex Web site that has many different pages used by different people or departments, you might need to create **nested templates**, which are templates that are based on another template. Nested templates are helpful when you want to define a page or parts of a page in greater detail. An advantage of using nested templates is that any changes made to the original template can be automatically updated in the nested template.

To create a nested template, create a new page based on the original template, then use the Save as Template command to save the page as a nested template. You can then make changes to the nested template by adding or deleting content and defining new editable regions. Note that editable regions in the original template are passed on as editable regions to the nested template. However, if you add a new editable or optional region to an editable region that was passed on from the original template, the original editable region changes to a locked region in the nested template.

Creating Repeating Regions and Repeating Tables

Many Web sites contain elements whose format is repeated over and over again. For instance, a site that sells products uses the same format to list catalog items. In a template, you can define these areas as **repeating regions**, and you can define the areas within these regions as either locked or editable. You can also insert repeating tables in a template. A **repeating table** is a table in a template that has a predefined structure, making it very easy for template users to add content. To add a repeating table, set the insertion point where you want the table to be placed, then use the Repeating Table command in the Templates menu on the Insert bar, as shown in Figure J-14. This opens the Insert Repeating Table dialog box, which allows you to set the number of rows and columns, and other properties for the table, and also specify the number of editable rows the table will have. When a user creates a page based on a template containing a repeating table, the top row will be locked, and the rows below will be editable.

FIGURE J-13
Advanced settings in the New Optional Region dialog box

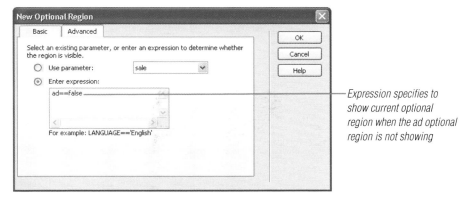

Expression specifies to show current optional region when the ad optional region is not showing

FIGURE J-14
Templates menu

Repeating Table command

Creating Editable Attributes

There might be times when you want users of your template to be able to change certain attributes of an element in a locked region. For instance, perhaps you want to give users the ability to change the cell background color of the top row in a repeating table, or change the source file for an image in a locked area of the template. You can use the Editable Tag Attributes dialog box, shown in Figure J-15, to specify that certain attributes of locked regions be editable. To do this, choose an attribute of a selected element, specify to make it editable, assign it a label, and specify its type and its default setting. When you define editable attributes of elements in locked regions, template users can make changes to the element's attributes using the Template Properties dialog box.

FIGURE J-15
Editable Attributes dialog box

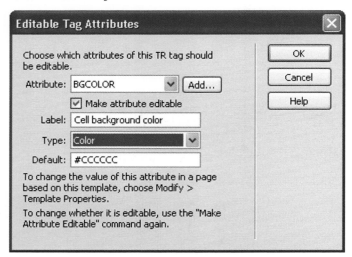

Advanced settings in the New Optional Region dialog box with expression entered

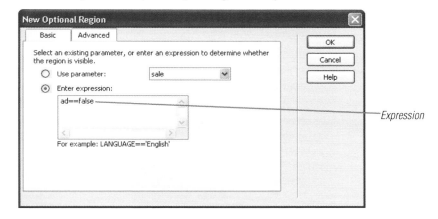

Expression

main_elements template with expression added to optional region

Label shows expression

Adjust advanced settings

1. Click the **If sale optional region label** above the text On sale! Buy one Level 2 can, get one free!

    Clicking the label selects the sale optional region.

2. Click **Edit** in the Property inspector to open the New Optional Region dialog box, then click the **Advanced tab**.

3. Click the **Enter expression radio button**, then select **sale** in the Enter expression text box.

4. Type **ad==false** in the Enter expression text box, then compare your screen to Figure J-16.

    This expression specifies that the sale optional region will be shown only if the ad optional region (the orange rectangle) is not showing.

5. Click **OK**, deselect the text, then compare your screen to Figure J-17.

    The expression that you wrote now appears above the sale optional region.

6. Save your work, then close the main_elements template.

You wrote an expression that specifies the sale optional region be shown if the ad region is not showing.

Nest a template in another template

1. Click **File** on the menu bar, then click **New** to open the New Document dialog box.

2. Click the **Templates tab**, click **Site "Super Bug Zapper"** in the Templates for column, click **main_elements** in the middle column, compare your screen to Figure J-18, then click **Create**.

3. Click **File** on the menu bar, then click **Save as Template** to open the Save As Template dialog box.

   A dialog box might open, warning that users of this template will not be able to create new paragraphs in this region.

4. Click **OK** (if necessary) to close the dialog box and open the Save As Template dialog box, type **product_info** in the Save as text box, then click **Save**.

   The product_info template appears in the Assets panel.

You created a new page based on the main_elements template, then saved it as a template named product_info.

Insert a repeating table

1. Click below the last line of text in the main_content editable region, click the **Templates list arrow**, then click **Repeating Table**.

   The Insert Repeating Table dialog box opens.

   (continued)

New from Template dialog box

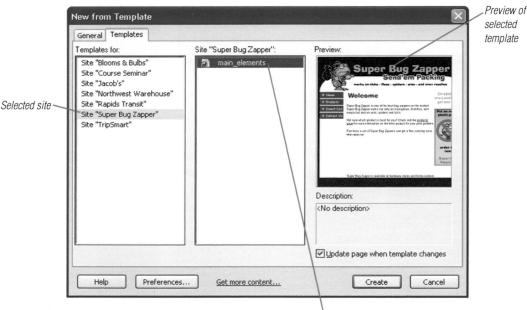

Preview of selected template

Selected site

Available templates in Super Bug Zapper site

Creating and Using Templates

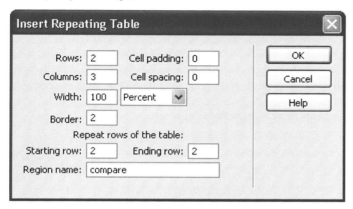

2. Type **2** in the Rows text box, type **3** in the Columns text box, set the Width to 100 Percent, set the Border to 2, type **2** in the Starting row text box, type **2** in the Ending row text box, type **compare** in the Region name text box, compare your screen to Figure J-19, then click **OK**.

The table is added below the paragraph text. Notice that the main_content editable region label is now yellow, indicating that this region is now locked.

3. Type **Feature** in the first cell in the first row, type **Super Bug Zapper** in the second cell of the first row, type **Brand X** in the third cell in the first row.

   TIP You won't be able to see the word "Feature" as you type it in the first cell because the Repeat: compare blue shaded box obscures it.

4. Click in the EditRegion2 cell, type **Enter product feature**, click in the EditRegion3 cell, type **X**, click in the EditRegion4 cell, then type **X**.

5. Format all of the table text using the following attributes: Font: Arial, Helvetica, sans-serif and Size: 2.

   TIP To format text in an editable region, you must select the table cell.

6. Apply bold formatting to the text in the top row of the table, center-align the text in the second and third columns, then compare your screen to Figure J-20.

You inserted a repeating table in the main_content editable region in the product_info template. You then entered column headings and placeholder text in the table and formatted the text.

FIGURE J-20
Repeating table object with formatted text added

Repeating table —

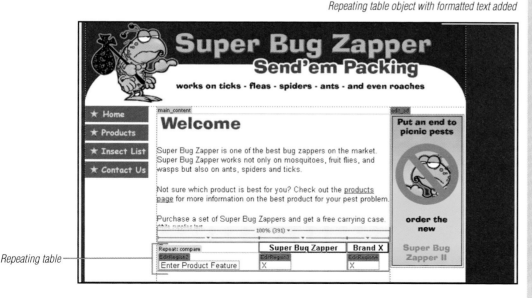

Modify a template

1. Delete the Welcome heading, then delete the three paragraphs below it.

2. Select the repeating table, press [←] to set the insertion point to the left of the table, then insert a new editable region named **product_content**, then click **OK**.

3. Delete the text "product content" that appears in the new editable region, click **Insert** on the menu bar, then click **Table** to open the Table dialog box.

4. Format the table using the following attributes: Rows: 1, Columns: 2, Table width: 100 percent, Border thickness: 0 pixels, Cell padding: 0, and Cell spacing: 0, then click **OK**.

5. Insert can_yellow.gif from the assets folder of the Web site in the first cell of the table, type **Product Level 1 can** in the Alt text box in the Property inspector, then center-align it.

6. Type **Insert product text** in the second cell of the table, then format the text using the following attributes: Font: Arial, Helvetica, sans-serif, Size: 3, and Alignment: Align Left.

7. Drag the middle border of the table so that the two cells are approximately the same size, then compare your screen to Figure J-21.

You deleted content from the product_info template, then added a new editable region to it. You inserted a table in the editable region, then added a text placeholder in the table.

product_info template with content added to the new editable region

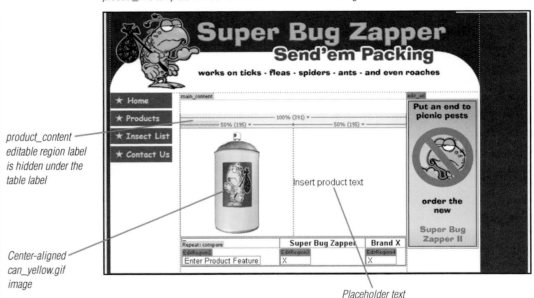

product_content
editable region label
is hidden under the
table label

Center-aligned
can_yellow.gif
image

Insert product text

Placeholder text

FIGURE J-22

Editable Tag Attributes dialog box with settings for color attribute

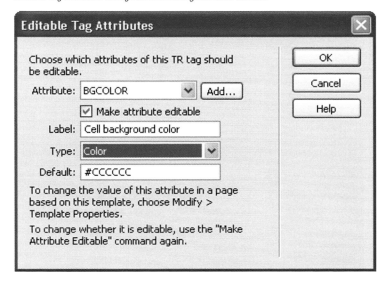

1. Select the three cells in the top row of the repeating table.

2. Click the **Background color button** in the Property inspector to open the color picker, then click the light gray color box (#CCCCCC).

3. Click **Modify** on the menu bar, point to **Templates**, then click **Make Attribute Editable** to open the Editable Tag Attributes dialog box.

4. Verify that BGCOLOR is selected in the Attribute list box, then click the **Make attribute editable check box**.

5. Type **Cell background color** in the Label text box, click the **Type list arrow**, then click **Color**.

   The Default color is automatically set to #CCCCCC, the color that is currently applied.

6. Compare your screen to Figure J-22, then click **OK**.

   Notice that the top row of the table is now white, instead of gray. It changed to white because the color of these cells is now an editable attribute.

7. Save your changes, then close the product_info template.

   > TIP If a dialog box opens telling you that you have inserted a repeating region inside a <P> tag, click OK to close the dialog box.

You specified that the color attribute of the top row of the repeating table be editable, so that users of the template can change its color.

Create editable attributes for a URL

1. Open the main_elements template.

2. Click just below the Contact Us navigation button on the left side of the page to set the insertion point, insert side_ad_1.gif from the chapter_j assets folder, then add appropriate alternate text.

   TIP If a dialog box opens, informing you that the image file is outside the root folder, be sure to save the file to the assets folder of the Web site.

3. Select the side_ad_1.gif graphic (if necessary), click **Modify** on the menu bar, point to **Templates**, then click **Make Attribute Editable** to open the Editable Tag Attributes dialog box.

   SRC appears in the Attribute text box.

4. Click the **Make attribute editable check box** to make the source file an editable attribute, type **left side ads** in the Label text box, click the **Type list arrow**, click **URL**, compare your screen to Figure J-23, then click **OK**.

   The side_ad_1.gif image is replaced with a gray box placeholder, as shown in Figure J-24, because you made the source file an editable attribute.

You inserted an image in a locked region of the main_elements template. You then made the image's SRC attribute editable, so that template users will be able to specify that a different image appear.

FIGURE J-23

Editable Tag Attributes dialog box with settings for URL attribute

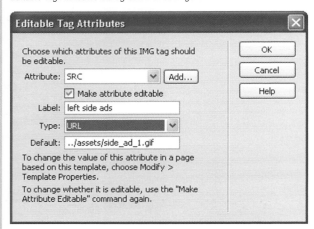

FIGURE J-24

main_elements template after making URL attribute editable

Gray placeholder indicates that the URL attribute for left side ads is now editable

FIGURE J-25

Update Template Files dialog box

Save a template and update nested templates

1. Click **File** on the menu bar, then click **Save** to open the Update Template Files dialog box, as shown in Figure J-25.

2. Click **Update** to open the Update Pages dialog box.

   The Status area indicates that one file was examined and one file was updated.

3. Click **Close** to close the Update Pages dialog box.

   You don't need to update any pages because at this point, no pages in the site are based on the main_elements template.

4. Open the product_info template.

   Notice that the sale_ad_1.gif image now appears below the Contact Us button, indicating that the changes you made to the main_elements template were updated in this template.

5. Close both templates.

You saved the main_elements template and then updated the product_info template to incorporate the saved changes.

USE TEMPLATES TO CREATE PAGES

What You'll Do

In this lesson, you will use the product_info template to create a new page in the Super Bug Zapper Web site. You will add content to the editable regions, make changes to selected objects, and add content to a repeated table. You will also insert a link on the page and apply the main_elements template to the contact_us page.

Creating Pages with Templates

There are many advantages to using a template to create a page. First, it saves a lot of time, because part of the content and format of your page is already set. Second, it ensures that the page you create matches the look and format of other pages in the site. You can create a page based on a template using many different methods. One way is to click File on the menu bar, click New to open the New Document dialog box, click the Templates tab, select the template you want to use, then click Create.

QUICKTIP

You can also create a new page based on a template by right-clicking (Win) or [control]-clicking (Mac) a template in the Assets panel, then clicking New from Template.

Modifying Editable Regions

When you create a new page that is based on a template, certain areas of the new page will be locked. You can tell which areas are locked by the appearance of the mouse pointer. When positioned over a locked region, the mouse pointer will appear in the shape of a circle with a line cutting through it, as shown in Figure J-26. Editable regions are outlined in blue and marked with a blue shaded label.

Editing, deleting, or adding content in editable regions of a template-based page works just like it does on any other page. Simply select the element you want to modify and make your changes, or click in the editable region and insert the new content.

FIGURE J-31

Template Properties dialog box with ad value set to false

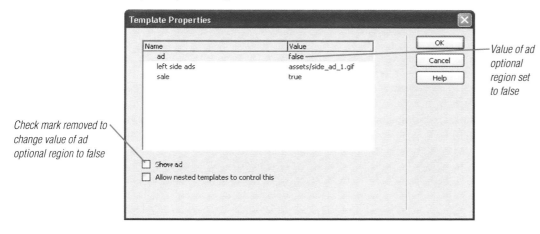

Value of ad optional region set to false

Check mark removed to change value of ad optional region to false

FIGURE J-32

Insects page with value of ad optional region set to false

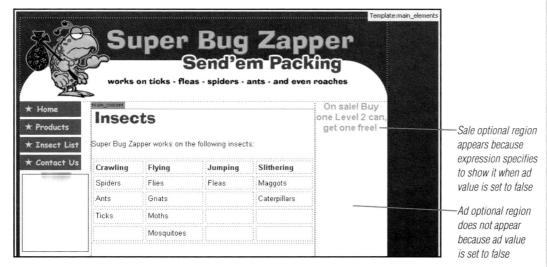

Sale optional region appears because expression specifies to show it when ad value is set to false

Ad optional region does not appear because ad value is set to false

Modify object attributes

1. Click **Modify** on the menu bar, then click **Template Properties** to open the Template Properties dialog box.

2. Click **ad** in the Name list, click the **Show ad check box** to remove the check mark, then compare your screen to Figure J-31.

   The value of the ad property changes to false.

3. Click **OK**, then compare your screen to Figure J-32.

   The orange ad no longer appears on the page, and the text contained in the sale optional region now appears.

4. Save your changes, then close the insects page.

You used the Template Properties dialog box to change the ad property to a value of false so that the ad is now hidden and the sale optional region appears.

Add links to template-based pages

1. Create a new page based on the product_info template, then save the page as **product_level_1.htm**.

2. Open the products page, then copy all the content in the cell to the right of the yellow can image.

3. Click in the cell below $5.99, type **Click here for more information.**, select the text you just typed, drag the **Point to File icon** next to the Link text box in the Property inspector to product_level_1.htm in the Files panel, then save and close the products page.

4. Switch to the product_level_1.htm page, select Insert product text in the cell next to the yellow can, paste the content you copied from the products page, then drag the right border of the cell containing the yellow spray can so that both columns are roughly the same width.

5. Select the orange rectangle containing the ad for Super Bug Zapper II, then drag the **Point to File icon** next to the Link text box to contact_us.htm in the Files panel, as shown in Figure J-33.

6. Save changes, test links for both pages in your browser, then close your browser.

7. Create another page based on the product_info template, then save it as **product_level_2.htm**.

(continued)

MACROMEDIA DREAMWEAVER J-28

FIGURE J-33

Dragging the Point to File icon to the contact_us page in the Files panel

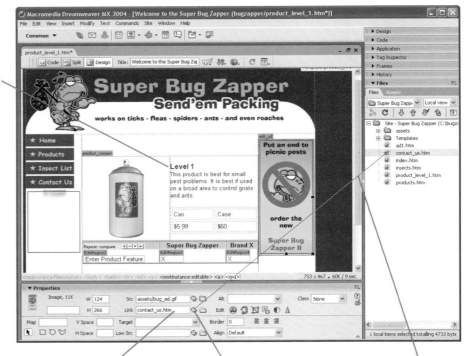

Pasted text from products page

Link text box containing link to contact_us page

Point to File icon

Path of Point to File icon being dragged to contact_us.htm

FIGURE J-34
Changing the source file on the product_level_2.htm page

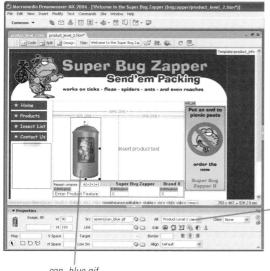

Alternate text for can_blue.gif

can_blue.gif

FIGURE J-35
product_level_3.htm page

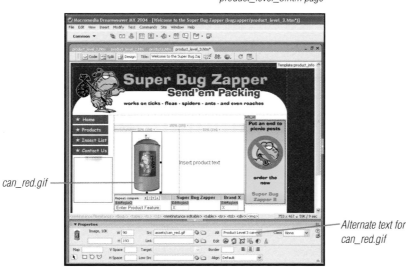

can_red.gif

Alternate text for can_red.gif

8. Change the source of the spray can graphic to can_blue.gif, then modify the alternate text, as shown in Figure J-34.

9. Open the products page, copy the Level 2 information in the cell to the right of the Level 2 can, then paste it on the product_level_2 page to the right of the blue can.

10. Link the ad for Super Bug Zapper II to the contact_us.htm page, then save your work.

11. Create another page based on the product_info template, then save it as **product_level_3.htm**.

12. Change the source of the spray can graphic to can_red.gif, then modify the alternate text, as shown in Figure J-35.

13. Switch to the products page, copy the Level 3 information in the cell to the right of the Level 3 can, then paste it on the product_level_3 page to the right of the red can.

14. Link the ad for Super Bug Zapper II to the contact_us.htm page, then save your work.

15. Switch to the products page, copy the Click here for more information link, paste it under each of the tables in the Product Level 2 and Product Level 3 sections, then use the Point to File icon 🔅 to point to the product_level_2 and product_level_3 pages.

16. Save your work, check the links in your browser, close your browser, then close all open pages.

You created three template-based pages, then modified the editable regions.

Use repeating tables

1. Open the product_level_1 page, select Enter product feature in the first cell of the second row of the repeating table, then type **Waterproof**.

2. Click the **Plus button** ✚ in the top row of the table to add a new row, type **3 Month Control** in the first cell in the third row, then delete the X in the third cell of the third row.

3. Click **Modify** on the menu bar, then click **Template Properties** to open the Template Properties dialog box.

4. Click **Cell background color** in the list, change the Cell background color to **#FFFF33**, compare your screen to Figure J-36, then click **OK**.

   The cells in the top row of the table now have a yellow background.

5. Save your changes, preview the page in your browser, compare your screen to Figure J-37, close your browser, then close the product_level_1 page.

(continued)

FIGURE J-36

Template Properties dialog box with changes made to Cell background color

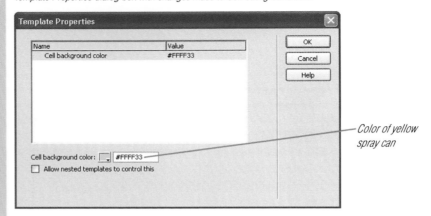

Color of yellow spray can

FIGURE J-37

product_level_1.htm page with changes made to table

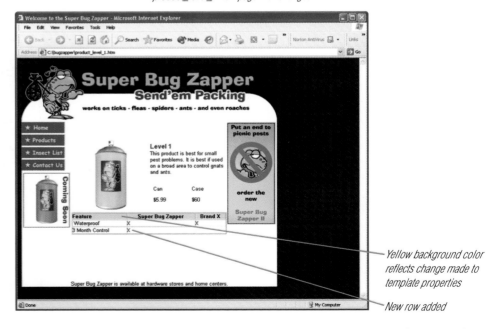

Yellow background color reflects change made to template properties

New row added

Creating and Using Templates

FIGURE J-38

Making changes to the product_level_2.htm page

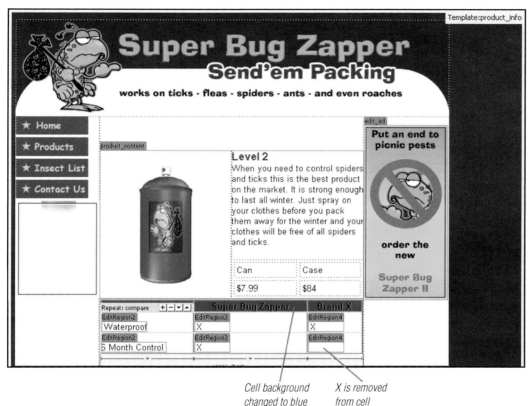

Cell background
changed to blue

X is removed
from cell

6. Open the product_level_2.htm page.

7. Replace the text in the first cell of the second row of the repeating table with the word **Waterproof**, add a new row, type **6 Month Control** in the first cell, then delete the X in the third cell of the third row.

8. Modify the template properties of the Cell background color, then change the color to blue (#0066FF), as shown in Figure J-38.

9. Save and close the product_level_2.htm page.

10. Open the product_level_3.htm page.

11. Replace the text in the first cell of the second row of the repeating table with the word **Waterproof**, add a new row, type **1 Year Control** in the first cell, then delete the X in the third cell of the third row.

12. Modify the template properties of the Cell background color, then change the color to red (#CC3300).

13. Save and close the product_level_3.htm page.

14. Open the products.htm page, preview it in your browser, then test the links to each of the individual products pages.

15. Close your browser, then close all open pages.

You added text and a new row to the repeating table on each of the three new pages. You also used the Template Properties dialog box to change the cell background colors of the top rows of the tables to match each of the cans.

Convert an existing page to a template-based page

1. Open the contact_us.htm page.

2. Copy the contact information text in the middle of the page, then close the contact_us.htm page.

3. Create a new HTML page based on the main_elements template.

4. Replace the three paragraphs of text in the template with the text you copied from the contact_us.htm page, as shown in Figure J-39.

(continued)

FIGURE J-39

Copying information from the contact_us.htm page to a new page

Information copied from the contact_us.htm page

New contact_us.htm page

5. Save the file as **contact_us.htm**, replacing the original file.

6. Select the Welcome heading, use the Browse for File button ☐ in the Property inspector to set the source to contact_us_head.gif, then compare your screen to Figure J-40.

7. Repeat Steps 1–6 to transfer the information from the products.htm page to a page based on the main_elements template, then save it as **products.htm**, replacing the original file.

8. Preview the two pages in your browser, close your browser, then close any open pages.

You created two new pages for the contact_us and products pages based on the main_elements template by copying and pasting the information from the existing pages and pasting them on the new template-based pages, then overwriting the existing pages.

USE TEMPLATES TO UPDATE A SITE

What You'll Do

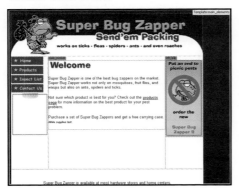

 In this lesson, you will make a change to the main_elements template, then update the site so that all pages and linked templates reflect the change.

Making Changes to a Template

If you create a successful site that draws large numbers of faithful viewers, your site will probably enjoy a long life. However, like everything else, Web sites need to change with the times. Your company might decide to make new products or offer new services. It might get purchased in a leveraged buy-out by a multi-million dollar conglomerate. When changes occur in your company, on a large or small scale, you will need to make changes to your Web site's appearance and functionality. If your Web site pages are based on a template or group of templates, you will have a much easier time making those changes.

You use the same skills to make changes to a template as you would when creating a template. Start by opening the template from the Files panel or Assets panel, then

Using Macromedia templates

If you are a licensed Dreamweaver user, you can take advantage of the large collection of beautiful templates that Macromedia creates for the exclusive use of its customers. The wide-ranging templates are a great starting point for many different types of Web sites—from weddings, to clubs, to professions, and even special events. To preview and download the templates, go to *www.macromedia.com/software/ dreamweaver/download/templates/*.

add, delete, or edit content as you would on any non-template-based page. You can turn locked regions into editable regions using the New Editable Region command. To change an editable region back into a locked region, select the region, click Modify on the menu bar, point to Templates, then click Remove Template Markup.

Updating All Pages Based on a Template

One of the greatest benefits of working with templates is that any change you make to a template can be made automatically to all nested templates and pages that are based on the template. When you save a template that you have made modifications to, the Update Template Files dialog box opens, asking if you want to update all the files in your site that are based on that template, as shown in Figure J-41. When you click Update, the Update Pages dialog box opens and provides a summary of all the files that were updated.

FIGURE J-41
Update Template Files dialog box

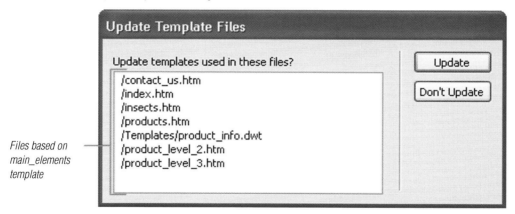

Files based on
main_elements
template

Make changes to a template

1. Open the main_elements template.

2. Click the insertion point in front of the word hardware in the page footer, then type **most**, as shown in Figure J-42.

3. Open the index page.

   The text in the page footer did not change because you have not yet saved the template and updated the site.

4. Close the index page.

You opened the main_elements template and edited the page footer.

FIGURE J-42

main_elements template with edited page footer

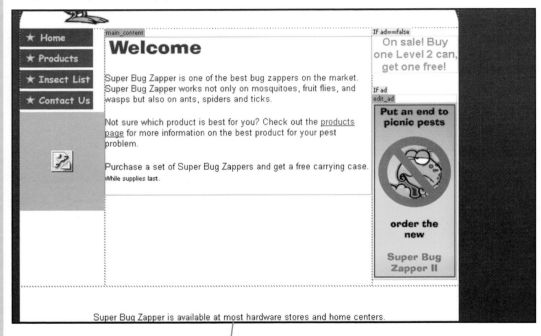

The word most is
added to the footer

FIGURE J-43

Update Pages dialog box listing files that were updated in the Super Bug Zapper Web site

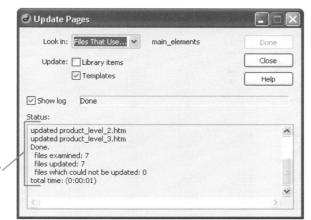

Summary of all files that were updated

Update all template-based pages in a site

1. Return to the main_elements template (if necessary), click **File** on the menu bar, then click **Save All**.

   The Update Template Files dialog box opens.

2. Click **Update** to open the Update Pages dialog box, shown in Figure J-43.

   The Status area shows that seven files were examined and seven files were updated.

3. Click **Close**.

4. Open the index page, then compare your screen to Figure J-44.

   The footer on the index page and every other page in the Web site now show the edited footer text.

5. Close the index page, the main_elements template, and all other open pages.

You saved the main_elements template and used the Update Template Files dialog box and the Update Pages dialog box to specify that all pages in the site be updated to reflect the template modifications.

FIGURE J-44

Index page with template changes incorporated

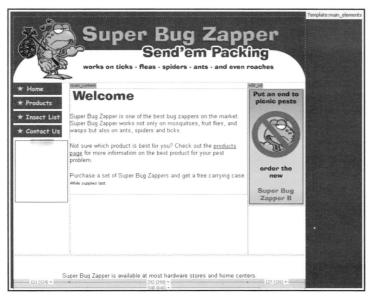

Create templates with editable and optional regions.

1. Open the Blooms & Bulbs Web site that you created and developed in Chapters A through I, then open the master_gardener page.
2. Save the master_gardener page as a template called **master_gardener**.
3. Select the Ask our Master Gardener heading and all the content below it, including Southern Living (do not select the Top of Page text), then define this selected area as an editable region named **master_content**.
4. Delete the "Top of Page" Flash text to set the insertion point, then insert a table that has one row and two columns, no borders, no cell padding, no cell spacing, and a width set to 100 percent.
5. Insert an optional region in the first cell of the table named **master_tip**. Delete the text master_tip from the table cell.
6. Insert master_gardening_ tip.gif from the chapter_j assets folder in the first cell of the master_tip optional region, add alternate text, then drag the right border of the first table cell to the left to align with the right edge of the graphic.

Enhance and nest templates.

1. Insert an editable optional region in the second cell of the table named **tips**, then click the **Advanced tab** of the New Optional Region dialog box to use the master_tip parameter.

2. Use the Property inspector to change the name of the new editable region to **edit_tip**.
3. Type **It is best not to water in the evening.** in the edit_tip editable region, then format this text using the following attributes: Font: Arial, Helvetica, sans-serif, Size: 3.
4. Save your changes, then close the page.
5. Create a new page based on the master_gardener template, then save the new untitled page as a template named **product_listing.dwt**.
6. Select the Ask our Master Gardener heading, then type **Available Products**.
7. Delete all of the content below the Available Products heading in the master_content editable region.
8. Insert a repeating table below the Available Products heading with the following settings: Rows: 2, Columns: 2, Width: 100 Percent, Border: 1, Starting row: 2, Ending row: 2, Region name: **product_list**, Cell padding: 0, and Cell spacing: 0.
9. Type **Product Name** in the first cell of the first row, type **Price** in the second cell of the first row, type **Enter product name here** in the first cell of the second row, then type **Enter price here** in the second cell of the second row.
10. Adjust the table cells so that each cell is approximately 50% of the table.
11. Format the text using the following attributes: Font: Arial, Helvetica, sans-serif, Size: 3, and Alignment: Align Center. Format the text in the top row as Bold.

12. Set the background color for the top row of the table to #CCFF99 (light green), then make the cell background color for the top row of the table an editable attribute. Specify the label as **Cell background color**, then set Type to Color.
13. Place the insertion point under the Available Products heading, insert flower.gif from the assets folder, then center-align it.
14. Make the SRC attribute for flower.gif an editable attribute. Specify the label as **Flower picture**, then set Type to URL.
15. Save your changes, then close the template.

Use templates to create pages.

1. Create a new page in the Blooms & Bulbs Web site that is based on the master_ gardener template.
2. Delete the Ask Our Master Gardener heading and the text below it in the master_content editable region.
3. Open the tips page, use the Copy command to copy all content below and including the Planting Tips heading, attach the blooms.css style sheet, then close the tips page.
4. Open the untitled page, then paste the content you copied from the tips page.
5. Save the page as **tips.htm**, overwriting the existing tips page, then close the page.
6. Create a new page based on the product_listing template, then save the page as **product_list.htm**.

13. Create a new document based on the recipe_card template, then enter the recipe title as **Grandmothers Rolls**.

14. Copy all the information from the rolls.htm file to the new rolls file, then save the new file as **rolls.htm**, overwriting the original rolls file (after you are sure that you copied the information correctly). The recipe will serve 10 people. Remember to include the optional introduction to the recipe.

15. Repeat Steps 13 through 16 for the mushroom_caps.htm file, but hide the intro region, then title it **Mushroom Caps**. The recipe will serve 8 people.

16. Save all files, preview the recipes page in your browser, compare it to Figure J-47. close the browser, and close all open pages.

FIGURE J-47

Completed Project Builder 2

Macromedia offers registered users of Dreamweaver the benefit of downloading and using professionally designed templates from their Web site. There are a wide range of templates that are appropriate for different kinds of organizations and events. Figure J-48 shows an example of a template that would be suitable for a site about an inn.

1. Connect to the Internet, then go to *www.course.com*. Navigate to the page for this book, click the Online Companion, then click the link for this chapter.

2. Spend some time exploring the templates on this site by previewing each one and opening each page.

3. Think of an idea for a new site that you would like to create. The site can be for a club, organization, event, or any topic or person that interests you. Draw an outline and a sketch of the site, including the content that will be on each page.

4. After you have completed your sketch, look through the Macromedia templates available at the Online Companion, then choose an appropriate template for your site. (*Note*: Skip to Step 9 if downloading files is not permitted.)

5. Download the template and copy the folder that contains the template files to a folder on your computer or external drive.

6. Use Dreamweaver to define a new site with an appropriate name that uses the site folder you downloaded as the root directory. Specify the Images folder as the default folder for images.

7. Open the site, then modify the pages of the sample site to match your site sketch. Replace any placeholder graphics, text, and other elements with content that is appropriate for your site's subject.

8. Save all pages in your site, preview them in a browser, print out each page, then close your browser and close all open pages.

9. If you are unable to download files, choose an appropriate template from the site and print out each page. Mark up each printed page, indicating how you would modify the template elements or replace particular elements with content appropriate for your site.

FIGURE J-48
Source for Design Project

In this assignment, you will continue to work on the group Web site that you created in Chapters A through I. Depending on the size of your group, you can assign individual elements of the project to group members, or work collectively to create the finished product.

You will continue to enhance your Web site by using templates. You will first create a template from one of your existing pages and define editable and optional regions in it. You will also insert a repeating table and set editable attributes for specific elements. You will then apply the template to a page and add content to the editable regions.

1. Consult your storyboard and brainstorm as a team to decide which page you would like to save as a template. You will use the template to create at least one other page in your site.

2. Work as a group to create a sketch of the template page you will create. Mark the page elements that will be in locked regions. Identify and mark at least one area that will be an editable region, one area that will be an optional region, and one area that will be an editable optional region. Your sketch (and your template) should also include a repeating table.

3. Assign a team member (or several team members) the task of saving the selected page as a template, then defining the editable regions in it.

4. Assign a team member the task of adding the optional regions and editable optional regions that you planned in your sketch.

5. Assign a team member the task of creating a repeating table that has one editable attribute.

6. Assign a team member the task of making any necessary formatting adjustments to the table to make sure it looks attractive, and then saving the template. This person should then create a new page based on the template, using the same name of the page

on which the template is based, so that the earlier version of the page is overwritten.

7. Assign a team member the task of applying the template to another existing page of the site, making sure to delete all repeating elements contained in the template.

8. Meet as a group to review the template(s) and the template-based pages, and offer constructive suggestions for improvements. Use the check list in Figure J-49 to make sure you completed everything according to the assignment.

9. Assign a team member the task of making any necessary changes.

10. Save your work, then close all open pages.

FIGURE J-49
Group Project check list

Web Site Check List
1. Does your template include at least one editable region?
2. Does your template include at least one optional region?
3. Does your template include at least one editable optional region?
4. Does your template include a repeating table?
5. Are all links on templates-based pages document-relative?
6. Do all editable regions have appropriate names?
7. Do all links work correctly?
8. Does the repeating table have an editable attribute?
9. Are all colors Websafe?
10. Do all pages view well using at least two different browser settings?

CREATING INTERACTIONS USING BEHAVIORS

1. Change text using behaviors.

2. Swap images and create pop-up windows and menus.

CHAPTER K
CREATING INTERACTIONS USING BEHAVIORS

Introduction

Dreamweaver MX 2004 makes it possible to create visually dynamic Web pages that contain interactive elements without writing a line of code. You can create many interactive elements on your Web pages using behaviors.

In this chapter, you will import a new Web site that promotes and sells a line of insecticide products. You will also use behaviors to make text appear in a layer, a text field, and the status bar when the mouse pointer is positioned over a link or image. Finally, you will use behaviors to create pop-up windows and menus, and to **swap** an image, which is similar to creating a rollover effect.

Using Animations and Interactive Elements Effectively

Because Dreamweaver makes it easy to create animations and interactive elements, you might be tempted to create lots of them. However, be aware that too many animations and special effects could distract and annoy your viewers and cause them to leave your site. Make sure that you have a good reason before you add sounds, pop-up elements, or animations to a page. Also, make sure that the graphics you choose for your animations and interactive elements are appropriate for the content and design of the site. If your site is promoting a serious topic such as world hunger, or is marketing a buttoned-down organization such as a law firm, you should avoid adding frivolous graphics that could detract from the message of the site.

Tools You'll Use

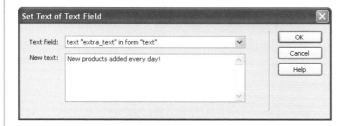

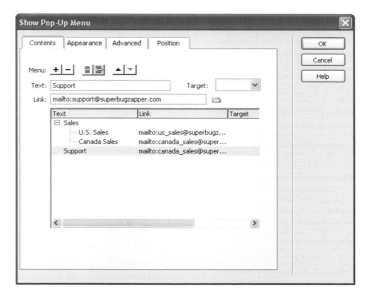

CHANGE TEXT USING BEHAVIORS

What You'll Do

In this lesson, you will create and name an empty layer and then use the Set Text of Layer behavior to make specified text appear in the layer when the mouse pointer is positioned over a certain link. You will also use the Set Text of Status Bar behavior to make customized text appear in the status bar. Finally, you will use the Set Text of Text Field behavior to make text appear in a text field.

Using Behaviors to Change Text

There are several behaviors that can be attached to links or objects that will cause text to appear in various ways on a page. Using behaviors, you can set the text of a layer, change the text in the status bar, and display text in a form field.

Changing Text in a Layer

Sometimes you might want certain text to appear on a page only after a viewer has positioned the mouse pointer over a particular link or object. Making text appear in this way can help keep your page clear of unnecessary text, and can also draw attention to information related to a specific link. To do this, you first need to create and name an empty layer on the page where you want the text to appear. Next, select the link that you want to act as the trigger for displaying the text. Finally,

choose the Set Text of Layer behavior and use the Set Text of Layer dialog box to specify the text that you want to appear in the layer.

Changing the Text of the Status Bar

By default, the status bar in a browser contains information about the current state of what is displayed on screen. For instance, if you position the mouse pointer over a link, the status bar will display the URL for that link. You can customize the text that appears in the status bar so that when a viewer selects an object or positions the mouse pointer over an object or link, the status bar will display text that is related to that object. For instance, rather than the status bar displaying the URL for a link, you could specify that it display a description of the link.

Displaying Text in a Form Field

You can also attach a behavior to a link to make specified text appear in a form field when the mouse pointer is positioned over a particular object or link. The process is similar to that of changing text in a layer, except that you use the Set Text of Text Field behavior. First, create a new text field. Next, select the object or link that you want to serve as the trigger for the text, then choose the Set Text for Text Field behavior to open a dialog box where you will specify the text that you want to appear. Figure K-1 shows an example of a Set Text behavior. As you roll your mouse over one of the navigation buttons, a short description of that link appears above and to the right of the navigation buttons.

FIGURE K-1
Example of a Set Text behavior

Mouse rolled over master plan navigation button

Change text in a layer

1. Open the contact_us page in the Super Bug Zapper Web site.

2. Click **Modify** on the menu bar, point to **Templates**, then click **Detach from Template**.

3. Click the **Insert bar list arrow**, click **Layout**, click the **Draw Layer button** 🔲, then draw a new layer that is approximately 2½ inches wide and 1½ inches high to the right of the Contact Us heading.

4. Select the layer, name the new layer **support**, set the background color of the layer to white, then compare your screen to Figure K-2.

5. Click **Window** on the menu bar, then click **Behaviors**.

6. Select the info@superbugzapper.com link, click the **Add behavior button** ＋, on the Behaviors panel toolbar to open the Actions menu, point to **Set Text**, then click **Set Text of Layer** to open the Set Text of Layer dialog box.

7. Type **Support is open Monday through Friday, 5:00 AM to 5:00 PM (PST).** in the New HTML text box, then click **OK**.

8. Save your changes, preview the page in your browser, position your mouse pointer over the info@superbugzapper.com link, compare your screen to Figure K-3, close your browser, then close the contact_us page. When the mouse rolls over the link, the layer appears and remains visible regardless of whether the mouse stays over the link.

You created and named a new layer on the contact_us page. You then added a behavior to display text in the support layer when the mouse pointer is positioned over the information link.

FIGURE K-2
New, empty layer on contact_us page

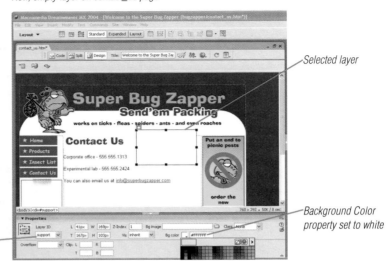

Selected layer

Background Color property set to white

Layer ID property set to support

FIGURE K-3
Viewing layer text on the contact_us page in Internet Explorer

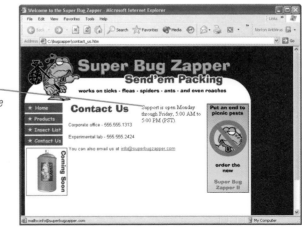

Layer text triggered by position of mouse pointer over link

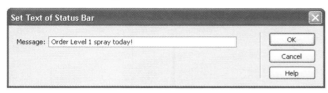

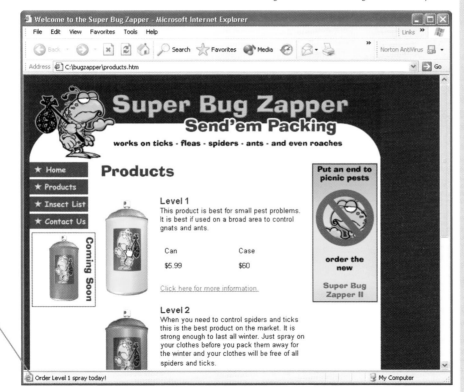

Status bar text triggered by position of mouse pointer over yellow can

Add text to the status bar

1. Open the products page in the Super Bug Zapper Web site.

2. Select the yellow can image on the page, click the **Add behavior button** +- on the Behaviors panel toolbar to open the Actions menu, point to **Set Text**, then click **Set Text of Status Bar**.

3. Type **Order Level 1 spray today!** in the Message text box, compare your screen to Figure K-4, then click **OK**.

4. Using the same method as in Steps 2 and 3, set the text of the status bar for the blue can image to **Order Level 2 spray today!**

5. Set the text of the status bar for the red can image to **Order the ultimate in pest control!**

6. Save your changes, preview the page in your browser, position the pointer over the yellow can, then compare your screen to Figure K-5.

7. Position the pointer over the blue and red cans to test the status bar message, close your browser, then close the products page.

You attached the Set Text of Status Bar behavior to the images on the products page so that a marketing message will appear in the status bar when the mouse pointer is positioned over each image.

Change the text of a text field in a form

1. Open the index page in the Super Bug Zapper Web site.

2. Click to the right of the Welcome heading to set the insertion point, then click the **Text Field button** 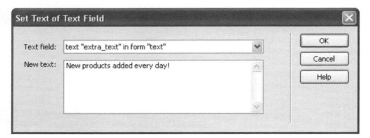 in the Forms category of the Insert bar.

   An alert box opens, asking whether you want to add a form tag.

3. Click **Yes**.

4. Select the form, then use the Property inspector to name it **text**.

5. Select the text field, use the Property inspector to name the text field **extra_text**, then set Char width to **55**.

6. Select the products page link in the second paragraph, click the **Add behavior button** in the Behaviors panel, point to **Set Text**, then click **Set Text of Text Field**.

7. Type **New products added every day!** in the New text text box as shown in Figure K-6, then click **OK**.

(continued)

FIGURE K-6
Set Text of Text Field dialog box

8. Save your changes, preview the page in your browser, position the mouse pointer over the products page link, compare your screen to Figure K-7, close your browser, then close the index page.

You added a text field to the home page. You then attached the Set Text of Text Field behavior to the products page link to specify that a marketing message appear in the text field when the mouse pointer is positioned over it.

FIGURE K-7
Viewing the form text in Internet Explorer

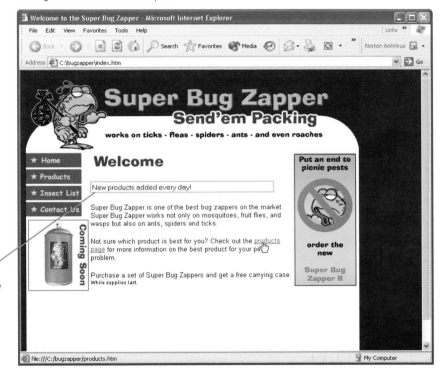

Text in text field triggered by position of mouse over link

SWAP IMAGES AND CREATE POP-UP WINDOWS AND MENUS

What You'll Do

 In this lesson, you will use the Swap Image behavior to add a rollover image to the products page. You will also add a pop-up window to the home page that contains an ad for a product. Finally, you will add a pop-up menu to the contact_us page that allows viewers to choose from a list of e-mail contacts.

Creating Interactive Elements Using Behaviors

You can use behaviors to create many interesting and dynamic effects that keep your viewers engaged in your Web site. You can create rollover effects using the Swap Image behavior. You can also use behaviors to create pop-up windows and menus.

Swapping Images

You have already learned how to create rollover images using the Insert Rollover Image dialog box. You can achieve similar rollover effects using the Swap Image behavior. By attaching this behavior to an object, you can specify that a new object appear when the mouse pointer is positioned over the original object. The Swap Image dialog box is used to specify the name and location of the image you want to swap.

Creating Pop-Up Windows

Sometimes you might want to allow a viewer to click a link on a page that will open another window showing a larger view of the link. You may have encountered this while shopping on the Web. For instance, if you've ever ordered clothes from a Web site, you might have clicked a small image of a shirt to view the same shirt up close in a larger window. What's handy about this is that you can make the pop-up window the exact size as the image. To create a pop-up window, select the link you want to serve as the trigger, then choose the Open Browser Window behavior from the Actions menu of the Behaviors panel. This opens the Open Browser Window dialog box, which is used to name the pop-up window, specify the URL that you want to display in it, and set the window's dimensions and other attributes, such as whether to include scroll bars and a status bar.

Creating Pop-Up Menus

If you want to let your viewers choose an item from a long list that links to a URL, you might want to add a pop-up menu to your Web page using the Show Pop-Up Menu behavior. This behavior lets you create, edit, and format a Fireworks pop-up menu in Dreamweaver. Fireworks is a powerful graphics program that is part of Macromedia Studio MX 2004. In order to use the Show Pop-Up Menu behavior, you must have Fireworks MX 2004 installed on your computer. Using this behavior, you can create beautiful pop-up menus without writing any program code. Figure K-8 shows an example of a pop-up menu featured on the Macromedia support Web site.

To use the Show Pop-Up Menu behavior, you must first select an image. This behavior can only be attached to images. Next, use the Actions menu in the Behaviors panel to choose the Show Pop-Up Menu behavior, which opens the Show Pop-Up Menu dialog box. Use the four tabs of this dialog box to specify the contents, appearance, position, and other attributes of the menu. The Contents tab lets you specify the names of each menu item. You can indent menu items under other menu items to create a hierarchical structure. The Appearance tab is used to specify either a vertical or horizontal menu layout, and to set the fonts, colors, and formatting of the menu items in both the **up state** (the state when the mouse pointer is not positioned over an item) and **over state** (the state when the mouse pointer is positioned over an item). Use the Advanced tab to set cell padding and spacing and to specify border properties. Use the Position tab to specify the position of the trigger image from which you want the menu to open.

FIGURE K-8

Example of a pop-up menu

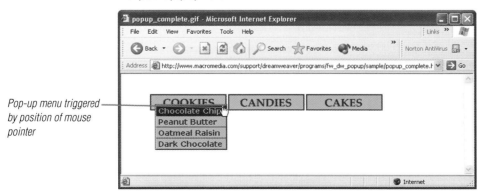

Pop-up menu triggered by position of mouse pointer

Swap images

1. Open the products page, then click the **yellow can image**.

2. Open the Actions menu on the Behaviors panel, then click **Swap Image** to open the Swap Image dialog box.

3. Click **Browse** next to the Set source to text box to open the Select Image Source dialog box, navigate to the assets folder of the Super Bug Zapper Web site, click **can_yellow_over.gif** as shown in Figure K-9, then click **OK** (Win) or **Choose** (Mac) to return to the Swap Image dialog box.

4. Click the **Preload images check box** to select it (if necesary), click the **Restore images onMouseOut check box** to select it (if necessary), then click **OK**.

   TIP Checking the Preload images check box ensures that the rollover effect happens quickly, with no delay.

5. Save your changes, preview the page in your browser, position the mouse pointer over the yellow can, compare your screen to Figure K-10, close your browser, then close the products page.

You used the Swap Image behavior to create a rollover effect for the yellow can shown on the products page.

Preview of swapped-in image in Select Image Source dialog box

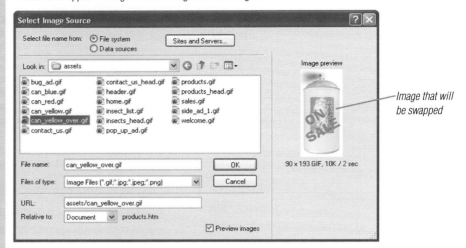

Image that will be swapped

Swapped-in image on the products page shown in Internet Explorer

Swapped-in image on the products page shown in Internet Explorer

Creating Interactions Using Behaviors

Open Browser Window dialog box

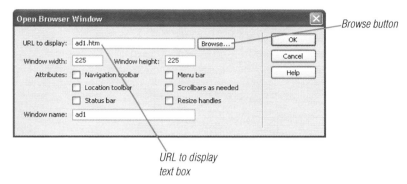

Browse button

URL to display
text box

Pop-up window containing ad1 page in Internet Explorer

Pop-up window

Create a pop-up window

1. Open the contact_us page of the Super Bug Zapper Web site.

2. Click above the banner at the top of the page so that only the body tag appears in the tag selector, open the Actions menu in the Behaviors panel, then click **Open Browser Window**.

3. Click **Browse** next to the URL to display text box, click **ad1.htm** located in the bugzapper root folder, then click **OK** (Win) or **Choose** (Mac).

4. Type **225** in the Window width text box, type **225** in the Window height text box, verify that none of the Attributes check boxes are selected, type **ad1** in the Window name text box, compare your screen to Figure K-11, then click **OK**.

5. Save your changes, preview the page in your browser, compare your screen to Figure K-12, close the window containing the ad1 page, then close your browser.

You attached the Open Browser Window behavior to trigger the opening of the ad1 page when the contact_us page is opened in a browser.

Create a pop-up menu

1. Click to the right of info@superbugzapper.com, press **[Enter]** (Win) or **[return]** (Mac), insert sales.gif from the assets folder of the Web site, then type **Sales heading** as alternate text.

2. Open the Actions menu in the Behaviors panel, then click **Show Pop-Up Menu** to open the Show Pop-Up Menu dialog box.

3. Type **Sales** in the Text text box, then click the **Add item button** **+** .

4. Type **U.S. Sales** in the Text text box, click the **Indent item button** , type **mailto:us_sales@superbugzapper.com** in the Link text box, then click the **Add item button** **+** .

5. Type **Canada Sales** in the Text text box, type **mailto:canada_sales@superbugzapper.com**, then click the **Add item button** **+** .

6. Type **Support** in the Text text box, click the **Outdent item button** , type **mailto: support@superbugzapper.com** in the Link text box, compare your screen to Figure K-13, then click **OK**.

7. Save your changes, preview the page in your browser, close the pop-up menu, position the mouse pointer over the Sales and Support link to view the pop-up menu, point to **Sales**, compare your screen to Figure K-14, then close your browser.

You added a pop-up menu to the contact_us page that contains four menu items.

Outdent item button

Add item button

Indent item button

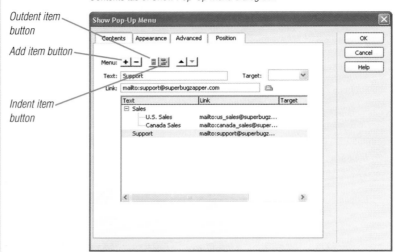

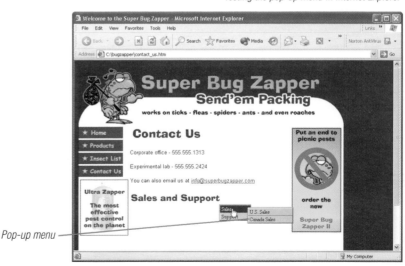

Pop-up menu

FIGURE K-15

Appearance tab of the Show Pop-Up Menu dialog box

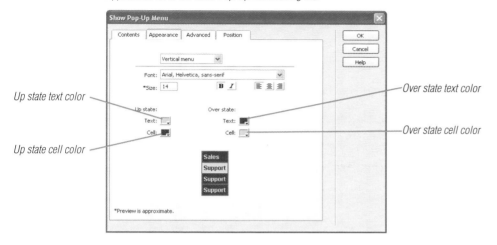

Up state text color

Over state text color

Up state cell color

Over state cell color

FIGURE K-16

Viewing the formatted pop-up menu in Internet Explorer

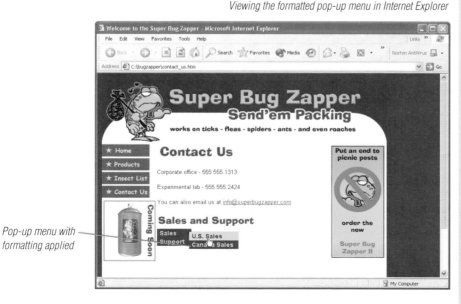

Pop-up menu with formatting applied

Format a pop-up menu

1. Click the **Sales and Support graphic** on the contact_us page, then double-click the **Show Pop-Up Menu behavior** in the Behaviors panel to open the Show Pop-Up Menu dialog box.

2. Click the **Appearance tab**, verify that Vertical menu is selected, set the Font to Arial, Helvetica, sans-serif, set the Size to 14, then click the **Bold button B**.

3. Set the Up state Text color to #FFFF33 (yellow), set the Up state Cell color to #660000 (maroon), set the Over state Text color to #660000, set the Over state Cell color to #FFFF33, then compare your screen to Figure K-15.

4. Click the **Advanced tab**, set the Cell padding to 5, then make sure the Pop-Up borders check box is not checked.

5. Click the **Position tab**, click the **Below and at left edge of trigger button** ▢, then click **OK**.

6. Save your changes, preview the page in your browser, position the mouse pointer over the Sales and Support link to view the pop-up menu, point to **Sales**, point to **U.S. Sales**, compare your screen to Figure K-16, close your browser, then close the contact_us page.

You changed the fonts and colors of the text on the pop-up menu. You also added cell padding, specified that no borders appear around the cells, and changed the position of the open menu in relation to the trigger.

Change text using behaviors.

1. Open the Blooms & Bulbs Web site that you created and developed in Chapters A-J.
2. Open the plants page.
3. Insert a new layer that is approximately 3 inches wide and ¾ inches high just below the Drop by to see our Featured Spring Plants heading on the featured_plants page frame. Drag the layer so that it appears centered under the heading, and insert line spaces as necessary to fit the layer between the heading and the paragraphs below.
4. Name the layer **text**, then set the background color of the layer to white.
5. Attach the Set Text of Layer behavior to the top photograph, specifying the text as **Blooms mid-May through August**.
6. Attach the Set Text of Layer behavior to the middle photograph, specifying the text as **Blooms February through early May**.
7. Attach the Set Text of Layer behavior to the bottom photograph, specifying the text as **Blooms mid-May through August**.
8. Attach the Set Text of Status Bar behavior to each of the navigation bar buttons on the top_frame page, using the following text for each button, as appropriate: Home—**Go to Home page**; Plants—**Go to Plants page**; Workshops—**Go to Workshops page**; Tips—**Go to Tips page**; Ask Cosie—**Go to Ask Cosie page**.
9. Cut the last paragraph of text on the page.
10. Insert a text field below the third paragraph.
11. Name the form **greeting**, name the text field **message**, set the Char width property to **40**, then set the Type property to Multi line.
12. Attach the Set Text of Text Field behavior to the bottom photograph, then paste the paragraph text that you cut in Step 8 in the Set Text of Text Field dialog box.
13. Save your work, preview the page in your browser to test the behaviors, close your browser, then close the page.

Swap images and create pop-up windows and menus.

1. Open the master_gardener page, then insert a line break after the Ask Our Master Gardener heading.
2. Insert iris.jpg from the assets folder of the Web site in the new line you inserted below Ask our Master Gardener.
3. Attach the Swap Image behavior to the iris.jpg, then set the source to the tulips.jpg located in the assets folder of the Web site.
4. Open a new, untitled page, then save the file as **popup.htm** in the root folder of the Blooms & Bulbs Web site.
5. Insert blooms_bulbs_popup_ad.gif from the chapter_k assets folder, add Popup ad as alternate text, title the page **Dicount on the new bulbs**, place the insertion point in the opening body tag, switch to Design view, place the insertion point in the body tag, then save and close the popup page.
6. Open the plants page (if necessary), switch to Code view, then click another place on the page so that only the <body> tag is showing in the tag selector.
7. Attach the Open Browser Window behavior, specifying popup.htm as the URL to display. Set the Window width to 390, the Window height to 200, and the Window name to **popup**.
8. Save all, preview the plants page in your browser, make sure the popup.htm page opens, test to make sure the layer, status bar, and text field text appear, compare your screen to Figure K-17, then close your browser and the plants page.
9. Open the master_gardener page.
10. Insert experts.jpg from the chapter_k assets folder directly below the iris.jpg that you inserted in Step 2.
11. Attach the Show Pop-Up Menu behavior to the experts.jpg image. In the Show Pop-Up Menu dialog box, add the following menu items with associated links: **Vegetable Gardening** (link: **mailto:vegetables@blooms.com**), **Weed Control** (link: **mailto:weeds@blooms.com**), and **Flowers** (assign no link to this menu item).
12. Add the following three menu items and links indented below the Flowers menu item: **Annuals** (link: **mailto:annuals@blooms.com**), **Perennials** (link: **mailto:perennials@blooms.com**), and **Bulbs** (link: **mailto:bulbs@blooms.com**).

13. Format the menu items using the following settings: Vertical menu, Font: Arial, Helvetica, sans-serif, Size: 14, Bold, Up state Text color: white, Up state Cell color: #006633 (green), Over state Text color: #006633, Over state Cell color: white.

14. Set the Cell padding to 5, then specify that no border appear.

15. Set the position of the menu to Top right edge of trigger.

16. Save your changes, preview the page in your browser, test the menu to make sure all items appear as specified, test to make sure the images swap correctly, then close your browser and all open pages.

FIGURE K-17
Completed Skills Review

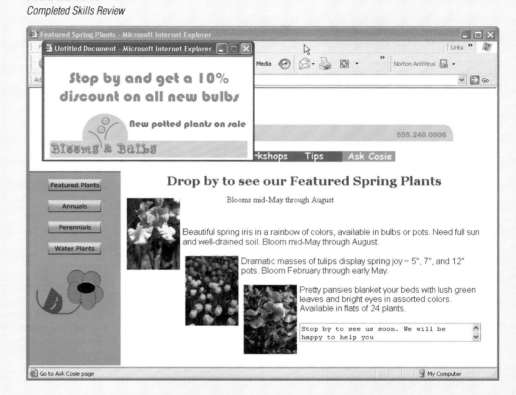

In this Project Builder, you will continue your work on the Rapids Transit Web site that you began in Project Builder 1 in Chapter A. Mike Andrew, the owner, has asked you to create an animation that will draw viewers' attention to the week's rental special. You decide to create a new, brightly-colored animated layer that will invite viewers to position their mouse pointers over the image of the kayak to see the weekly special. You will then attach the Set Text of Layer behavior to the kayak image, so that information about the weekly special will appear in the animated layer when the mouse pointer is positioned over it. You will also use the Set Text of Status Bar behavior to add customized text to the status bar.

1. Open the Rapids Transit Web site that you created in Chapters A–J, then open the rentals page.
2. Draw a layer below the table that is approximately 3 inches wide and ¾ inches high. Center the layer as best you can under the table. Name the layer **special**, then set the layer background color to white.
3. Attach the Set Text of Layer behavior to the image of the kayak using the text **Get $2.00 off any rental!**
4. Attach the Set Text of Status Bar behavior to the image of the kayak using the text **We have all your rental needs.**
5. Save your work, preview the page in your browser, make sure that the animation works correctly and that you can drag the layer, position your mouse pointer over the kayak image, then view the text layer.
6. Close your browser, then close the rentals page.
7. Open the before.htm page, then add the following sentence to the end of the paragraph about the seasons: **Spring is also nice, with fresh green foliage and cascading waterfalls.**
8. Attach the Swap Image behavior to the buffalo_fall.jpg image, then set the source to the spring_falls.jpg file located in the chapter_k Data Files folder.
9. Save your work, then preview the page in your browser to check the swap image behavior, as shown in Figure K-18.
10. Close your browser, then close the page.

FIGURE K-18
Completed Project Builder 1

In this Project Builder, you will continue your work on the Jacob's Web site that you started in Project Builder 2 in Chapter A. Chef Jacob would like to draw viewers' attention to his dessert specials. You decide to create a pop-up window that will display two different ads for desserts. You also decide to use the Set Layer Text behavior to show descriptions of the desserts when the mouse pointer is placed over them.

1. Open the Jacob's Web site.
2. Open a new, untitled page, then save it as **popup1.htm** in the jacobs root folder.
3. Insert jacobs_popup1.gif from the chapter_k assets folder on the popup1.htm page.
4. Title the page **Friday special**, then save and close the popup1.htm page.
5. Open a second, untitled page, then save it as **popup2.htm** in the jacobs root folder.
6. Insert jacobs_popup2.gif from the chapter_k assets folder on the popup2.htm page.
7. Change the background color of the page to black, title the page **Free dessert**, then save and close the popup2.htm page.
8. Open the after_theatre.htm page, attach the Open Browser Window action, using the onLoad event, to the photograph of orange slices, specify the URL to Display setting as popup2.htm, set the Window width to 390 and Window height to 200. Name the window **oranges**.

9. Attach the Open Browser Window behavior to the body tag. Specify the URL to display setting as popup1.htm, set the Window width to 390 and the Window height to 200. Name the window **popup**.
10. Draw a new layer next to the cheesecake photograph that is approximately 2½ inches wide and 1½ inches high, name the layer **text**, then set the layer background color to white. Attach the Set Text of Layer behavior to the first two dessert photos on the page, using appropriate descriptive text for each photograph.
11. Save your changes, then preview the page in your browser. Position the mouse pointer over the two photographs to make sure that the appropriate text appears in the layer and that the popup window opens and displays the correct page. Compare your screen to Figure K-19.
12. Close your browser, then close all open pages.

FIGURE K-19
Completed Project Builder 2

Figure K-20 shows the home page of ISITE Design's Web site, a site that was created using Macromedia Dreamweaver, and was named Macromedia site of the day. This site showcases the work of the ISITE design firm, and also provides information about the company.

1. Connect to the Internet, navigate to the Online Companion, then select a link for this chapter.
2. Spend some time exploring the site so that you are familiar with it.
3. What animations do you see, and how are they used to enhance the viewer's experience?
4. Do you see any rollover images? If so, describe them and comment on their effectiveness.
5. Do you see any examples of the Set Text of Layer behavior? If so, where do you see it implemented, and how effective is it?
6. Do you see any examples of the Set Text of Navigation Bar behavior? If so, where? If not, where would you recommend this behavior be implemented?

7. Based on the content and design of this site, what kind of corporate culture does this company have?

8. Write a short paragraph to summarize how the site incorporates interactivity and comment on its effectiveness.

FIGURE K-20
Source for Design Project

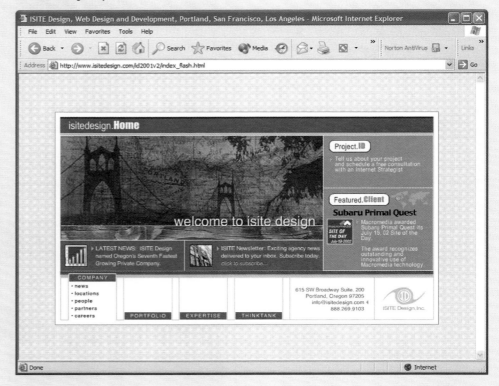

In this assignment, you will continue to work on the group Web site that you created in Chapters A through J. Depending on the size of your group, you can assign individual elements of the project to group members, or work collectively to create the finished product.

You will continue to enhance your Web site and make it more interactive by adding animated layers, pop-up windows and menus, and by attaching the Set Text behaviors to images to make specified text appear in layers, the status bar, and text fields.

1. Consult your storyboard and brainstorm as a team to decide the page or pages to which you would like to add the following elements: pop-up windows, pop-up menus, and rollover images. Also, decide as a group how and where to use the Set Text behaviors to draw viewers' attention to important information. As you discuss where and how to implement these various elements, you can choose to work with existing pages or create new ones.

2. Discuss as a group whether you will need additional graphics for any of the new features that you plan. If so, assign a team member the task of obtaining appropriate graphics.

3. Assign a team member the task of using the Set Text behaviors to add customized text to layers, text fields, and the status bar, according to the group decisions made in Step 1.

4. Assign a team member the task of creating at least two pop-up windows.

5. Assign a team member the task of creating a pop-up menu. The pop-up menu items can be linked to other pages in the site, other pages outside the site, or e-mail addresses. The pop-up menu should be formatted to match the color, fonts, and design of the site.

6. Assign a team member the task of using the Swap Image behavior to create rollover effects.

7. Assign a team member the task of using the Link Checker panel to check for broken links and orphaned files.

8. Meet as a group to preview all the pages and offer constructive suggestions for improvements. Use the Group Project check list in Figure K-21 to make sure you completed everything according to the assignment.

9. Assign a team member the task of making any necessary changes.

10. Save your work, then close all open pages.

FIGURE K-21
Group Project check list

Web Site Check List

1. Does your site include at least one pop-up menu?
2. Does your site include two pop-up windows?
3. Does your site include rollover images?
4. Do all animations work correctly?
5. Does all text that you set using the Set Text behaviors appear correctly?
6. Do all images have appropriate alternate text?
7. Do all links work correctly?
8. Are there any unnecessary files you can delete?
9. Are all colors Websafe?
10. Do all pages view well using at least two different browser settings?

CHAPTER L

USING STYLES AND STYLE SHEETS

1. Create and use inline styles.

2. Work with external CSS style sheets.

CHAPTER I
USING STYLES AND STYLE SHEETS

Introduction

In Chapter C, you learned how to create, apply, and edit Cascading Style Sheets (CSS styles). Using CSS styles is the best and most powerful way to ensure that all elements in a Web site are formatted consistently. The advantage of using CSS styles is that all of your formatting rules are kept in a separate or **external** style sheet file, so that you can change the appearance of every page to which the style sheet is attached by modifying the style sheet file. For instance, suppose your external style sheet contains a style called headings that is applied to all top-level headings in your Web site. If you decide that you want the headings to be red to make them more prominent, you could simply change the color attribute to red in the style sheet file, and all headings in the Web site would change instantly to red. You would not need to format the content of the Web site at all.

You can also create **inline** CSS styles, which are styles whose code is located within the HTML code of a Web page. The advantage of inline styles is that you can use them to override an external style. For instance, if all headings in your Web site are red because the external style applied to them specifies red as the color attribute, you could change the color of one of those headings to blue by creating and applying an inline style that specifies blue as the color attribute. However, in general, you should avoid using inline styles to format all the pages of a Web site; it is a better practice to keep formatting rules in a separate file from the content.

If you think a large segment of your viewers will be using older browsers (earlier than 4.0), then you should not use CSS styles to format your Web site.

In this chapter, you will create and apply inline styles and work with external CSS style sheets to format the Super Bug Zapper Web site.

FIGURE L-4
New CSS Style dialog box with settings for .description style

*Click to specify
an inline style*

FIGURE L-5
CSS Style definition for .description dialog box with Type settings specified

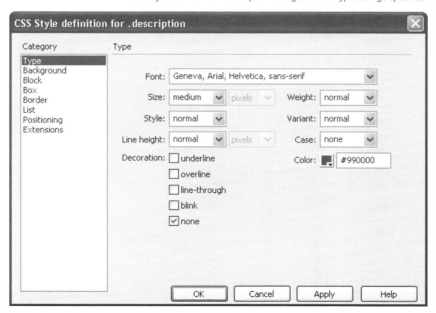

Create a custom style

1. Open the Super Bug Zapper Web site, open the insects page, click **Window** on the menu bar, then open the CSS Styles panel, (if necessary).

2. Click the **New CSS Style button** in the CSS Styles panel to open the New CSS Style dialog box.

3. Type **.description** in the Name text box, verify that the Class option button is selected, click the **This document only option button**, then compare your screen to Figure L-4.

4. Click **OK** to open the CSS Style definition for .description dialog box, which has the Type category selected.

5. Set the Font to Geneva, Arial, Helvetica, sans-serif; set the Size to medium; set the Style to normal; set the Line height to normal; set the Decoration to none; set the Weight to normal; set the Variant to normal; set the Case to none; set the Color to #990000, then compare your screen to Figure L-5.

6. Click **OK**.

   The description style appears in the CSS Styles panel.

   TIP Click the plus sign (Win) or the triangle (Mac) next to <style> in the CSS Styles panel if you do not see the description style.

You created a new inline style named .description and defined the formatting for it.

Apply a custom style

1. Select the text Super Bug Zapper works on the following insects:.

2. Use the Property inspector to change the font to Default Font and the size to None.

   You must remove manual formatting before applying a CSS Style.

3. Click the **Style list arrow** in the Property inspector, click **description** as shown in Figure L-6, then deselect the text.

   The selected text now appears in maroon and has the description style applied to it.

4. Select the text Super Bug Zapper works on the following insects:, click the **Style list arrow** in the Property inspector, click **None** to remove the description style from the selected text, then deselect the text.

5. Select the text Super Bug Zapper works on the following insects:, click the **Style list arrow** in the Property inspector, click **description**, deselect the text, then compare your screen to Figure L-7.

You used the Property inspector to apply the description style to selected text. You then used the Property inspector to remove the description style, and then reapplied the style.

FIGURE L-6

Applying the description style using the Property inspector

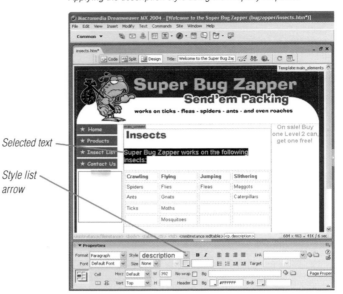

Selected text

Style list arrow

FIGURE L-7

Text with description style applied

Description style applied to text

FIGURE L-8
CSS Style definition for .description dialog box with modified type settings

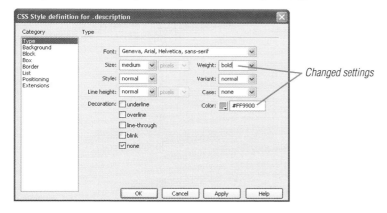

Changed settings

FIGURE L-9
Insects page after changes made to description style

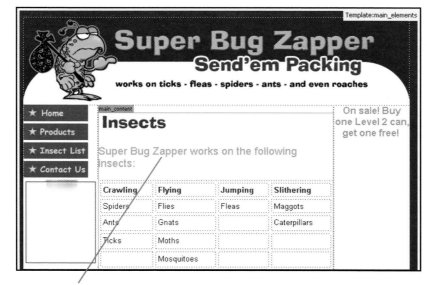

*Text with description style
now appears in bold orange*

1. Click the **description style** in the CSS Styles panel, then click the **Edit Style Sheet button** .

2. Change the color to #FF9900, change the Weight to bold, then compare your screen to Figure L-8.

3. Click **OK**, deselect the text, then compare your screen to Figure L-9.

   The text with the description style applied to it automatically changed to reflect the changes that you made to the style.

You made formatting changes to the Type category of the description style. You then saw these formatting changes reflected in text with the description style applied to it.

Redefine an HTML tag

1. Click the **New CSS Style button** 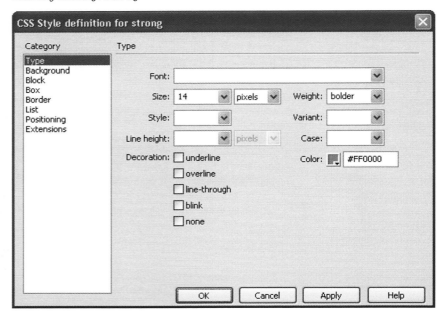 in the CSS Styles panel to open the New CSS Style dialog box.

2. Click the **Tag option button**, click the **Tag list arrow**, scroll down, click **strong**, then click the **This document only option button**.

   The strong tag is the tag that controls bold formatting.

   > TIP   To scroll quickly to the tags that begin with the letter s, type s after you click the Tag list arrow.

3. Click **OK** to open the CSS Style definition for strong dialog box, set the Size to 14 pixels, set the Weight to bolder, set the Color to red (#FF0000), compare your screen to Figure L-10, then click **OK**.

   Notice that the ad text on the page changed to red because it is formatted in bold and contains the strong tag.

4. Using Steps 1-3 as a guide, create a new CSS style that redefines the h2 HTML tag, set the Size to 14 pixels, the Style to normal, the Weight to bold, and the Color to #FF9900, then click **OK**.

   (continued)

FIGURE L-10
Redefining the strong HTML tag

FIGURE L-11
Insects page with h2 style and strong style applied to selected text

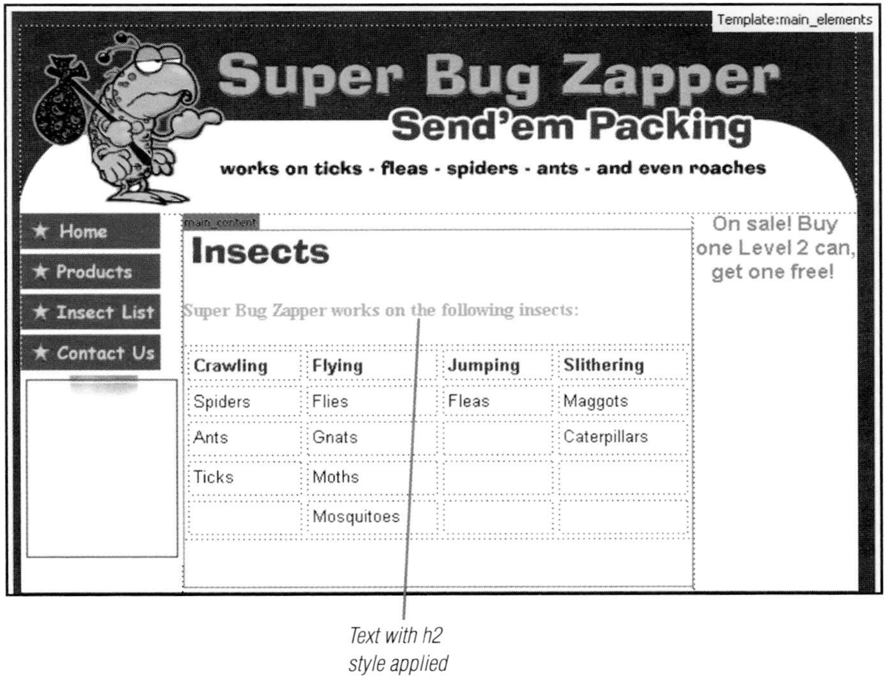

Text with h2
style applied

5. Select the text Super Bug Zapper works on the following insects:, click the **Style list arrow**, then click **None** to remove the description style from the selected text.

   You must remove a style from text before applying another style; otherwise the new style will not be applied.

6. Click the **Format list arrow** in the Property inspector, click **Heading 2**, deselect the text, then compare your screen to Figure L-11.

   The h2 style is applied to the selected text.

   TIP   You can tell which tag takes precedence by its position in the tag selector. Tags with greater precedence are positioned to the right of other tags in the tag selector.

You used the New CSS Style dialog box to redefine the strong and h2 HTML tags. You also applied the styles to selected text.

Edit an inline style

1. View the styles for the insects page in the CSS Styles panel, then compare your screen to Figure L-12.

2. Click the **strong style** in the CSS Styles panel to open the CSS properties panel, change the color to #990000.

   The ad text changes to maroon because it contains the strong tag.

3. Edit the h2 style to change the color to maroon (#990000), then compare your screen to Figure L-13.

You used the CSS Styles panel to change the color settings for the strong and h2 inline styles.

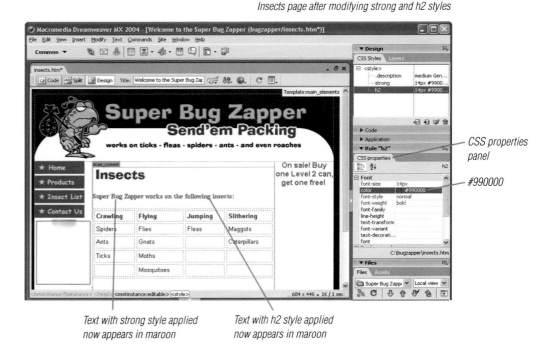

CSS properties panel

#990000

Text with strong style applied now appears in maroon

Text with h2 style applied now appears in maroon

Delete an inline style

1. Click the **description style** in the CSS Styles panel to select it.
2. Click the **Delete CSS Style button**, then compare your screen to Figure L-14.

   The description style is removed from the CSS Styles panel. If any text on this page had the description style applied to it, the style formatting would be removed from the text.

   > TIP You can also delete an inline style by right-clicking (Win) or [control] clicking (Mac) the style in the CSS Styles panel, then clicking Delete.

3. Save your changes, then close the insects page.

You used the CSS Styles panel to delete the description style.

FIGURE L-14

CSS Styles panel after deleting description style

WORK WITH EXTERNAL CSS STYLE SHEETS

What You'll Do

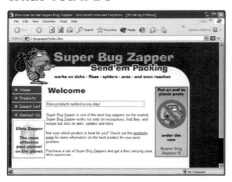

In this lesson, you will attach the super_bug_zapper style sheet to a page in the Super Bug Zapper Web site. You will then make a formatting change in the style sheet and see that change reflected on the page. You will also add hyperlink styles and custom code to the super_bug_zapper style sheet. You will then attach the super_bug_zapper style sheet to a template. Finally, you will delete a style from the super_bug_zapper style sheet.

Using External CSS Style Sheets

If you want to ensure consistent formatting across all elements of a Web site, it's a good idea to use external CSS style sheets instead of HTML styles or inline styles. Most Web developers prefer to use external CSS style sheets so they can make changes to the appearance of a Web site without changing any content. Using inline styles requires you to make changes to the styles on each page, which takes more time and leaves room for error and inconsistency.

Attaching an External CSS Style Sheet to a Page or Template

One of the big advantages of using external CSS style sheets is that you can attach them to pages that you've already created. When you do this, all of the rules specified in the style sheet are applied to the HTML tags on the page. So for instance, if your external style sheet specifies that all first-level headings are

formatted in Arial 14-point red bold, then all text in your Web page that has the <h1> tag will change to reflect these settings when you attach the style sheet to the page. To attach an external style sheet to a page, open the page, then use the Attach Style Sheet button in the CSS Styles panel to open the Attach External Style Sheet dialog box, shown in Figure L-15. Use this dialog box to browse for the external style sheet file you want to attach, and to specify whether to link or import the file. In most cases, you should choose to link the file so that the content of the page is kept separate from the style sheet file.

If all the pages in your site are based on a template, you can save an enormous amount of time and development effort by attaching an external style sheet to the template. Doing this saves you from having to attach the style sheet to every page in the site; you only have to attach it to the template file. Then, when you make changes to the style sheet, those changes will be reflected in the template and will be updated in every page to which the template is attached when you save the template.

Adding Hyperlink Styles to a CSS Style Sheet

You can use an external style sheet to create styles for all links in a Web site. To do this, open the style sheet so it appears in the document window, then click the New CSS Style button to open the New CSS Style dialog box. Click the Advanced option button, then choose one of the selectors from the Selector list, as shown and described in Figure L-16. After you choose a selector and click OK, the CSS Style definition dialog box opens, which you can use to specify the formatting of the selected link. However, not all browsers recognize link styles.

Adding Custom Code to a CSS Style Sheet

You can make changes to a style sheet by changing its code or adding code directly into the style sheet file. To do this, open the style sheet file so that it appears in the document window, click where you want to add code, then type the code you want. For instance, you can add code to the body tag of the style sheet that changes the colors of a viewer's scroll bar to match the colors of your Web site.

FIGURE L-15
Attach External Style Sheet dialog box

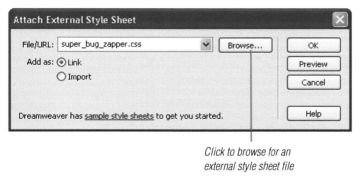

Click to browse for an external style sheet file

FIGURE L-16
New CSS Style dialog box with Selector list displayed

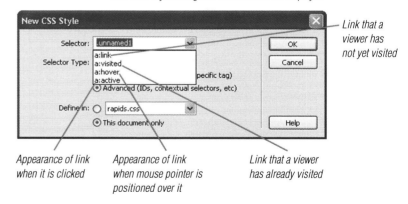

Link that a viewer has not yet visited

Appearance of link when it is clicked

Appearance of link when mouse pointer is positioned over it

Link that a viewer has already visited

Attach a style sheet to an existing page

1. Open the index page.

2. Click the **Attach Style Sheet button** ⬚ in the CSS Styles panel to open the Attach External Style Sheet dialog box, then click the **Link option button** (if necessary).

3. Click **Browse** to open the Select Style Sheet File dialog box, navigate to the chapter_l Data Files folder, click the **super_bug_zapper.css** file, compare your screen to Figure L-17, then click **OK** (Win) or **Choose** (Mac).

   A dialog box opens, asking if you would like to copy the super_bug_zapper.css file to the root folder of the Web site.

4. Click **Yes** to open the Copy File As dialog box, then click **Save** to copy the file to the root folder and return to the Attach External Style Sheet dialog box.

5. Compare your screen to Figure L-18, then click **OK**.

   The super_bug_zapper.css file appears in the CSS Styles panel, with the body style indented below it.

   TIP If you don't see the body style, click the plus sign (Win) or the triangle (Mac) next to super_bug_zapper.css in the CSS Styles panel.

You attached the external style sheet file super_bug_zapper.css to the index page. You also copied the super_bug_zapper.css file to the root folder of the Web site.

FIGURE L-17
Select Style Sheet File dialog box

FIGURE L-18
Attach External Style Sheet dialog box

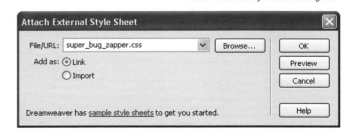

FIGURE L-19

Modifying the a:link style

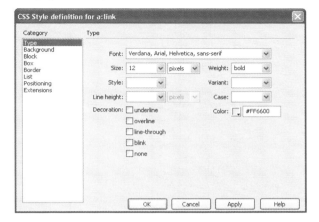

FIGURE L-20

Index page after modifying a:link style

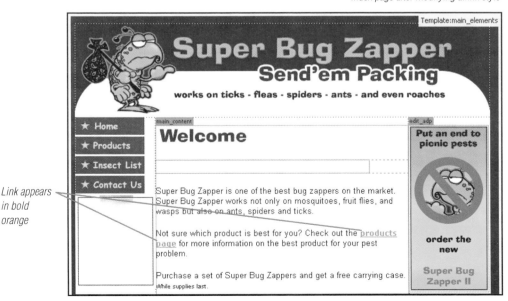

Link appears in bold orange

1. Click the **Refresh button** on the Files panel toolbar.

2. Double-click the **super_bug_zapper.css** file in the root folder in the Files panel.

   The super_bug_zapper.css file opens in the document window.

3. Click the **New CSS Style button** in the CSS Styles panel to open the New CSS Style dialog box.

4. Click the **Advanced option button**, then click the **This document only option button**.

5. Click the **Selector list arrow**, click **a:link**, then click **OK** to open the CSS Style definition for a:link dialog box.

6. Set the Font to Verdana, Arial, Helvetica, sans-serif; set the Size to 12 pixels; set the Weight to bold; set the Color to #FF6600; compare your screen to Figure L-19, then click **OK**.

   The super_bug_zapper.css page now contains new code that reflects the type settings you specified for the a:link style.

7. Save your changes, switch to the index page, then compare your screen to Figure L-20.

   The products page link in the paragraph text now appears in bold orange, reflecting the formatting changes that you made to the a:link style. Not all browsers support link formatting.

You opened the super_bug_zapper.css file and made modifications to the a:link style using the CSS Style definition dialog box.

Add hyperlink styles

1. Switch to the super_bug_zapper.css file.

2. Click the **New CSS Style button** ⊞ in the CSS Styles panel to open the New CSS Style dialog box.

3. Click the **Advanced option button**, then click **This document only option button**.

4. Click the **Selector list arrow**, click a:hover, then click **OK** to open the CSS Style definition for a:hover dialog box.

5. Set the Font to Verdana, Arial, Helvetica, sans-serif; set the Size to 12 pixels; set the Weight to bolder; set the Color to #990033, then click **OK**.

   The super_bug_zapper.css page now contains new code that reflects the font specifications you set for the a:hover style.

6. Save your changes, switch to the index page, save it, preview the page in your browser, position the mouse pointer over the products page link, then compare your screen to Figure L-21.

   The products page link in the paragraph text now appears in bold maroon, reflecting the formatting changes that you made to the a:hover style.

7. Close your browser.

You opened the super_bug_zapper.css file and then made modifications to the a:hover style using the CSS Style definition dialog box.

FIGURE L-21
Index page after modifying a:hover style

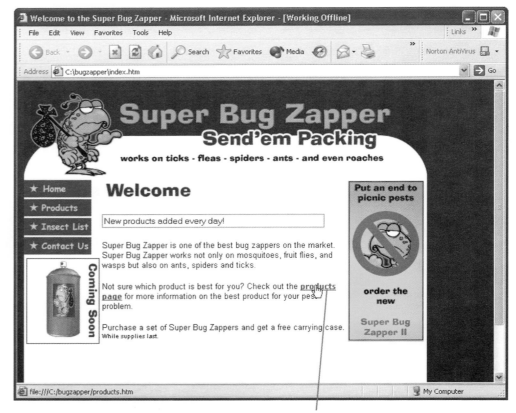

Link appears in bold maroon after changing a:hover style

FIGURE L-22

Adding custom code to the super_bug_zapper.css file

```
1  body {
2      font-family: Arial, Helvetica, sans-serif;
3      font-size: large;
4      text-decoration: none;
5      color: #000000;
6      scrollbar-track-color:#000000;
7
8  }
9  a:link {
10     font-family: Verdana, Arial, Helvetica, sans-serif;
11     font-size: 12px;
12     font-weight: bold;
13     color: #FF6600;
14 }
15 a:hover {
16     font-family: Verdana, Arial, Helvetica, sans-serif;
17     font-size: 12px;
18     font-weight: bolder;
19     color: #990033;
20 }
21
```

— New code added

FIGURE L-23

Index page in Internet Explorer after adding custom code to the super_bug_zapper.css file

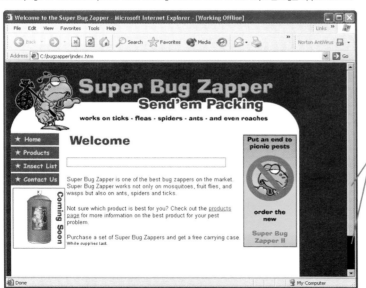

Scroll bar now appears
in orange and black

Add custom code to a style sheet (Win)

1. Switch to the super_bug_zapper.css file. If you are using a Macintosh, please proceed to the next page.

2. Locate the body tag code on the page, then click to the right of the semicolon in line 5 to set the insertion point.

3. Press **[Enter]** (Win) or **[return]** (Mac) to move the insertion point to line 6.

    TIP   A pop-up menu may appear that is not necessary for this step.

4. Type **scrollbar-track-color:#000000;** then compare your screen to Figure L-22.

    Make sure to type the semicolon (;) at the end of the line of code.

5. Press **[Enter]** (Win) or **[return]** (Mac) to position the insertion point on line 7, then type **scrollbar-face-color:#F7AB4B;**.

6. Save your changes, switch to the index page, preview the page in your browser, then compare your screen to Figure L-23.

    Your scroll bar now appears in black and orange, reflecting the custom code you added to the super_bug_ zapper.css file.

7. Close your browser, then save and close the index page.

You opened the super_bug_zapper.css file and added custom code to specify that the face of the scroll bar and the scroll bar track appear in orange and black to match the colors of the Super Bug Zapper Web site.

Use a style sheet with a template

1. Open the main_elements template, then click the **Attach Style Sheet button** 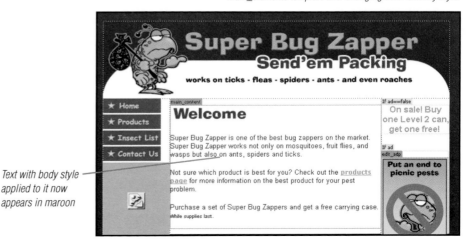 on the CSS Styles panel to open the Attach External Style Sheet dialog box.

2. Click the **Link option button**, click **Browse** to open the Select Style Sheet File dialog box, navigate to the root folder of the Web site, click the **super_bug_ zapper.css** file, click **OK**, click **OK** (Win) or **Choose** (Mac), then click **OK** to close the Attach External Style Sheet dialog box.

3. Save your changes, update all other files in the Web site, then close the Update Pages dialog box.

4. Switch to the super_bug_zapper.css file, click (Win) or double-click (Mac) **body** in the CSS Styles panel, then click **color** in the CSS properties panel.

5. Change the color to #660000, then compare your screen to Figure L-24.

6. Open the main_elements template, view the change to the body text color, then compare your screen to Figure L-25.

   > TIP If the individual product pages do not reflect the body text change to the CSS settings, remove all manual formatting from each page, then save each page.

7. Switch to the super_bug_zapper.css file, select #660000 in line 5 of the code, type **#000000**, then save your changes.

You attached the super_bug_zapper.css style sheet to the main_elements template. You changed the body text color in the super_bug_zapper.css style sheet and viewed the change in the main_elements template. You then changed the body text color back to black.

FIGURE L-24

super_bug_zapper.css file after making change to body style color

```
1  body {
2      font-family: Arial, Helvetica, sans-serif;
3      font-size: large;
4      text-decoration: none;
5      color: #660000;
6      scrollbar-track-color:#000000;
7      scrollbar-face-color:#F7AB4B;
8  }
9  a:link {
10     font-family: Verdana, Arial, Helvetica, sans-serif;
11     font-size: 12px;
12     font-weight: bold;
13     color: #FF6600;
14 }
15 a:hover {
16     font-family: Verdana, Arial, Helvetica, sans-serif;
17     font-size: 12px;
18     font-weight: bolder;
19     color: #990033;
20 }
21
```

New color reflects changes made in CSS Style definition dialog box

FIGURE L-25

main_elements template after changing color of body style

Text with body style applied to it now appears in maroon

FIGURE L-26
Selected a:link code in super_bug_zapper.css file

```
1  body {
2      font-family: Arial, Helvetica, sans-serif;
3      font-size: large;
4      text-decoration: none;
5      color: #000000;
6      scrollbar-track-color:#000000;
7      scrollbar-face-color:#F7AB4B;
8  }
9  a:link {
10     font-family: Verdana, Arial, Helvetica, sans-serif;
11     font-size: 12px;
12     font-weight: bold;
13     color: #FF6600;
14 }
15 a:hover {
16     font-family: Verdana, Arial, Helvetica, sans-serif;
17     font-size: 12px;
18     font-weight: bolder;
19     color: #990033;
20 }
21
```

Selected a:link code

Delete external styles from a style sheet

1. Select the a:link tag and the five lines of code below it (including color:#FF6600 and the bracket on line 15), then compare your screen to Figure L-26.

2. Press **[Delete]** (Win) or **[delete]** (Mac), then save your changes.

   Notice that the a:link style no longer appears in the CSS Styles panel.

3. Open the index page, then preview it in your browser.

   Notice that the products page text link no longer appears in orange, indicating that the a:link style has been deleted from the style sheet. Notice also that the style sheet is linked to the index page and the main_elements template. You do not need both of them.

   > TIP You can detach a style sheet from a template or Web page by clicking the style sheet file in the CSS Styles panel, then clicking the Delete CSS Style button. When you do this, the file is no longer linked to the Web page, but it is not actually deleted; it remains in its original location on your hard drive.

4. Close your browser, click the **first style sheet** in the CSS Styles panel, then click the **Delete CSS Style button 🗑**.

5. Save and close all open pages.

You deleted the a:link style from the super_bug_ zapper.css file and then saved your changes.

Create and use inline styles.

1. Open the Blooms & Bulbs Web site that you created and developed in Chapters A through K.
2. Open the featured_plants.htm page.
3. Delete the layer named text that is located just below the Drop by to see our Featured Spring Plants heading on the plants page.
4. Delete any blank lines between the heading and the paragraph text, as necessary, to improve the appearance of the page.
5. Select the text Available in flats of 24 plants in the third paragraph, then type **Bloom February through June.**
6. Create a new custom inline style named .bloomtimes on the plants page that has the following type settings: Font: Arial, Helvetica, sans-serif, Size: 14 pixels, Style: italic, Weight: bold, and Color: #FF0000.
7. Apply the bloomtimes style to the sentence Bloom mid-May through August. in the first paragraph.

8. Apply the bloomtimes style to the sentence Bloom February through early May. in the second paragraph.
9. Apply the bloomtimes style to the sentence Bloom February thorugh June. in the third paragraph.
10. Modify the bloomtimes style to change the color to dark green (#006633), the pixel size to 16, and the weight to normal.
11. Apply bold formatting to the text Beautiful spring iris in the first paragraph, Dramatic masses of tulips in the second paragraph, and Pretty pansies in the third paragraph.
12. Edit the strong style for this document only to change the size to 16 pixels and the weight to bolder.
13. Save your changes, preview the featured_plants page in your browser, compare your screen to Figure L-27, close your browser and close the page.

Work with external CSS style sheets.

1. Open the master_gardener page, then attach the blooms.css style sheet that you created in Chapter C to this page.
2. Open the blooms.css file, then use the New CSS Style dialog box to add the a:link style to the blooms.css file. Set the font to Arial, Helvetica, sans-serif; set the size to 14 pixels; set the weight to normal, then set the color to dark green (#006633).
3. Save your changes, switch to the master_gardener page, then make sure that the text links on the page now appear in green.
4. Switch to the blooms.css file, then use the New CSS Style dialog box to add the a:hover style to the blooms.css file. Set the font to Arial, Helvetica, sans-serif; set the size to 14 pixels; set the weight to bold, and set the color to light green (#66CC33).
5. Save your changes, then preview the master_gardener page in your browser and make sure that the links appear according to the settings you specified.

6. Redefine the body tag in the blooms.css file. Set the font to Arial, Helvetica, sans-serif, the style to normal, and the color to black (#000000).

7. Switch to the Style sheet file type **scrollbar-track-color:#006633;** in the line below color:#000000; in the body tag. (*Hint*: If you are using a Macintosh, skip Steps 7 and 8.)

8. Press [Enter] (Win) or [return] (Mac) to insert a new line, then type **scrollbar-face-color:#CCFF99;**.

9. Save your changes, switch to the master_gardener.htm page, preview the page in your browser, compare your screen to Figure L-28, then close your browser.

10. Attach the blooms.css style sheet to the master_gardener.dwt template.

11. Save the master_gardener template, then update all files in the site.

12. Save and close all open files.

FIGURE L-27

Completed Skills Review: featured_plants page

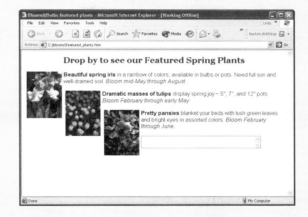

FIGURE L-28

Completed Skills Review: master_gardener page

In this Project Builder you will continue your work on the Rapids Transit Web site that you began in Project Builder 1 in Chapter A. Mike Andrew, the owner, has decided that he wants to use styles and style sheets to ensure the consistent format of elements in the Rapids Transit Web site. You will attach the rapids.css style sheet to the rapids_info template and add new styles to it.

1. Open the Rapids Transit Web site that you created in Chapters A through K.
2. Open the store_pages template, then attach the rapids.css style sheet to the template.
3. Create a new custom style named **.address** in the rapids.css style sheet with the following settings: Font: Arial, Helvetica, sans-serif, Size: 12 pixels, Style: normal, Weight: normal, and Color: #003399.
4. Apply the .address custom style to the Rapids Transit contact information located below the paragraph text. (*Hint*: Remember to remove any manual formatting first.)
5. Edit the address to change the weight to bold and the style to italic.
6. Save the template, then update all files in the site.
7. Apply the bodytext style to the description text in the store_pages template.

8. Edit the bodytext style to change the size to 14 pixels.
9. Create a new style named **.copyright** with appropriate settings of your choice.
10. Apply the .copyright style to the copyright and last updated lines.

11. Save all files, update all files, then open the store page.
12. Preview the store page in your browser, then compare your screen to Figure L-29. Your screen might look different depending on the choices you made in Step 9.

FIGURE L-29
Sample Project Builder 1

In this Project Builder, you will continue your work on the Jacob's Web site that you started in Project Builder 2 in Chapter A. Chef Jacob wants to ensure that certain text elements and text links in the Web site are formatted consistently. He has provided you with instructions for how he would like the pages to be formatted. He has also asked you to add code to the style sheet that will make the scrollbar appear in colors that match the Web site when viewed in a browser.

1. Open the Jacob's Web site that you created in Chapters A through K.
2. Open the recipe_card template.
3. Apply the .bodytext style to the optional intro text. (*Hint*: Remove manual formatting first.)
4. Apply the .subheadings style to the recipe_title text.
5. Apply the .bodytext style to the number_servings text.
6. Apply the .ingredients style to the ingredient text.
7. Apply the .bodytext style to the directions text.
8. Save the template and update the pages based on the template: rolls.htm and mushroom_caps.htm.
9. Open the rolls.htm page, check to see that the styles were applied correctly, then close the page.
10. Repeat Step 9 for the mushroom_caps.htm page.

11. Open the recipes.htm page, then preview it in your browser, checking the links for consistent formatting.
12. Redefine the HTML body tag in the jacobs.css file using the following attributes: Font: Arial, Helvetica, sans-serif. (Note: Redefine the body tag, not the .bodytext style.)
13. Add the following line of code to the end of the body tag in the jacobs.css style sheet file: **scrollbar-track-color:#660033;**.

FIGURE L-30
Completed Project Builder 2

(*Hint*: If you are using a Macintosh, skip Steps 13 and 14.)
14. Add the following line of code below the code you just typed: **scrollbar-face-color:#FFCCCC;**.
15. Save your changes, then close the jacobs.css style sheet.
16. Preview the recipes page in your browser, then compare your screen to Figure L-30.
17. Close your browser, then close all open files.

Many of today's leading Web sites use CSS style sheets to ensure consistent formatting and positioning of text and other elements. For instance, the United States Department of Justice Web site uses them. Figure L-31 shows the Department of Justice home page.

1. Connect to the Internet, navigate to the Online Companion, then select a link for this chapter.
2. Spend some time exploring the many pages of this site.
3. When you finish exploring all of the different pages, return to the home page. Click View on your browser's menu bar, then click Source to view the code for the page.
4. Look in the head content area for code relating to the CSS style sheet used. Note whether any styles are defined for a:link or a:hover and write down the specified formatting for those styles. Write down any other code you see that relates to styles.
5. Close the Source window, then look at the home page. Make a list of all the different text elements that you see on the page and that you think should have CSS styles applied to them.

6. Review the other link for this chapter. Use the Source command on the View menu of your browser window to determine whether the site uses CSS styles.

7. Print out the home page of this site, along with the source code that contains CSS styles.

FIGURE L-31
Source for Design Project

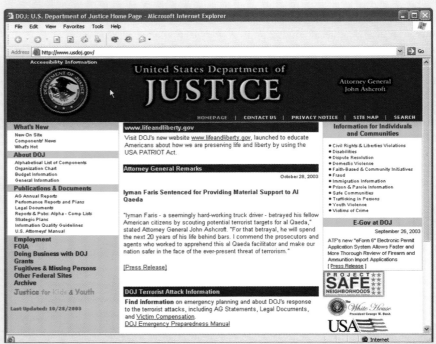

Using Styles and Style Sheets

In this assignment, you will continue to work on the group Web site that you created in Chapters A through K. Depending on the size of your group, you can assign individual elements of the project to group members, or work collectively to create the finished product.

You will continue refining your Web site by using CSS style sheets and inline styles to format the text in your Web site consistently. You will start by attaching the style sheet you created in Chapter C.

1. Meet as a group to view the pages of your Web site and write a plan in which you define styles for all of the text elements in your site. Your plan should include how you will use an external style sheet, as well as inline styles. You can use either the external style sheet you created in Chapter C, or create a new one. Your plan should include at least one custom style, one style that redefines an HTML tag, and one style that uses a selector.

2. Decide as a group whether you will attach your style sheet to individual pages in the site, or whether you will attach it to the template you created in Chapter K.

3. Based on the decision you made in Step 2, assign a team member (or members) the task of attaching the external style sheet to the template you created in Chapter K or to the individual pages of the site. Be sure to save the template after attaching the style sheet, and update all pages in the site.

4. Assign a team member the task of creating and applying the inline styles you identified in your plan.

5. Assign a team member the task of creating and applying the styles that will be added to the external style sheet.

6. Assign a team member the task of adding custom code to the body tag of your external style sheet to change the colors of the scroll bar to match the colors of your site.

7. Meet as a group to review the pages and make sure that all text elements appear as they should and look appropriate. Use the check list in Figure L-32 to make sure you have completed everything according to the assignment.

8. Assign a team member the task of making any necessary changes.

9. Save your work, then close all open pages.

FIGURE L-32
Group Project check list

Web Site Check List

1. Do all text elements in the site have a style applied to them?
2. Does your site have at least one inline style?
3. Is an external style sheet attached to each page in the site or to a template to which each page is attached?
4. Did you define and apply at least one custom style, one style that redefines an HTML tag, and one style that defines links?
5. Did you add custom code to the body tag of the style sheet to change the colors of the scroll bar in a browser to match the colors of the site?
6. Do all links work and appear according to the formatting you specified?

CHAPTER M

WORKING WITH LIBRARY ITEMS AND SNIPPETS

1. Create and modify library items.

2. Add library items to pages.

3. Add and modify snippets.

CHAPTER M
WORKING WITH LIBRARY ITEMS AND SNIPPETS

Introduction

When creating a Web site, chances are good that you will want certain graphics or text blocks to appear in more than one place in the site. For instance, you might want the company tag line in several different places, or a footer containing links to the main pages of the site at the bottom of every page. Library items and snippets can help you work with these repeating elements more efficiently.

Understanding Library Items

If you want an element to appear repeatedly, then it's a good idea to save it as a library item. A **library item** is content that can contain text or graphics and is saved in a separate file in the Library folder of your Web site. The advantage of using library items is that when you make a change to the library item and then update the site, all instances of that item will be updated to reflect the change.

Understanding Snippets

Another way to use the same content repeatedly throughout a site is to insert code snippets. **Code snippets** are reusable pieces of code that can be inserted on a page. Dreamweaver provides a wide variety of ready-made code snippets you can use to create footers, drop-down menus, headers, and other elements.

In this chapter, you will work with library items and code snippets to enhance the Super Bug Zapper Web site.

Tools You'll Use

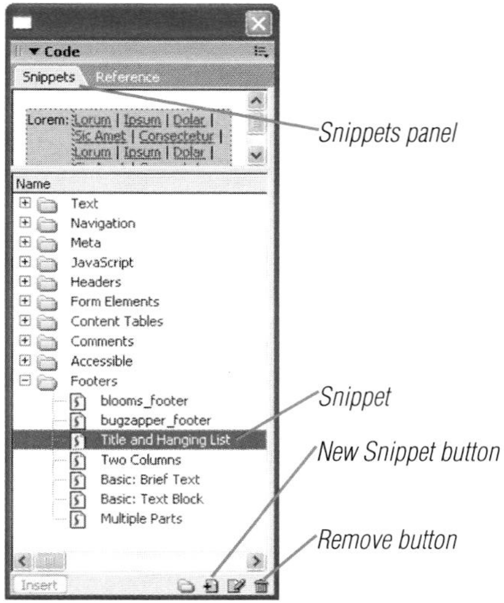

Snippets panel

Snippet

New Snippet button

Remove button

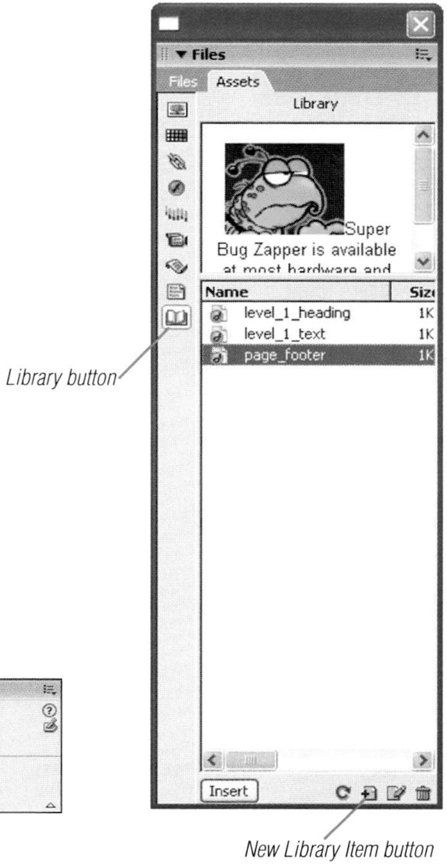

Library button

Open Library
Item button

New Library Item button

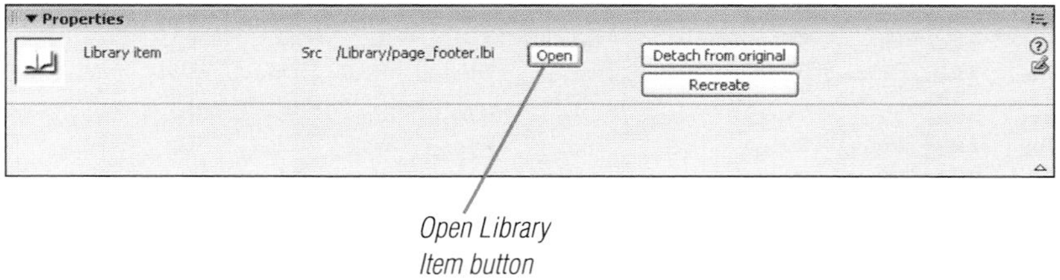

CREATE AND MODIFY LIBRARY ITEMS

What You'll Do

 In this lesson, you will create two text-based library items containing content from the products page. You will create a library item that contains a graphic in the main_elements template. You will also edit one of the text-based library items and update the site to reflect those edits.

Understanding the Benefits of Library Items

Using library items for repetitive elements—especially those that need to be updated frequently—can save you considerable time. For instance, suppose you want to feature an employee of the month photograph on every page in your site. You could create a library item named employee_photo, and add it to every page. Then, when you need to update the site to show a new employee photo, you could simply replace the photo contained in the library item and the photo would be updated throughout the site. Library items can contain a wide range of content, including text, images, tables, and sounds.

Viewing and Creating Library Items

To view library items, show the Assets panel, then click the Library button. The library items appear in a list, and a preview

of the selected library item appears above the list, as shown in Figure M-1. To save text or an image as a library item, select the item in the document window, then drag it to the Assets panel. The item that you dragged will appear in the preview window in the Assets panel and in the library item list with the temporary name Untitled assigned to it. Type a new name, then press [Enter] (Win) or [return] (Mac) to give the library item a permanent name. Library items on a Web page appear in shaded yellow in the document window. When you click a library item in the document window, the entire item is selected and the Property inspector changes to display three buttons that you can use to work with the library item, as shown in Figure M-2.

QUICKTIP

You can also view a list of available library items by expanding the Library folder in the Files panel.

Modifying Library Items

You cannot edit library items on the Web page in which they appear. In order to make changes to a library item, you need to open it. To open a library item, select the item in the document window, then click Open in the Property inspector. The library item will appear in the document window, where you can make edits or add content to it. When you are satisfied with your edits, save the library item using the Save command in the File menu. When you do this, the Update Library Items dialog box will appear, asking if you want to update all instances of the library item throughout the site.

FIGURE M-1
Library items in Assets panel

FIGURE M-2
Web page containing library items

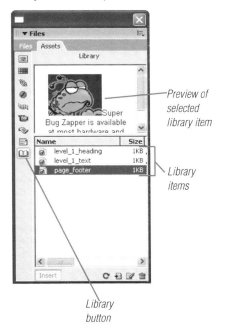

Preview of selected library item

Library items

Library button

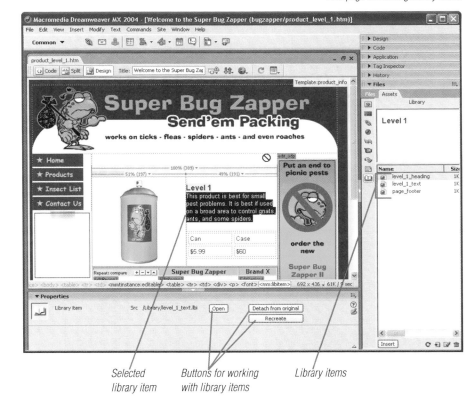

Selected library item

Buttons for working with library items

Library items

Create a text-based library item

1. Open the Super Bug Zapper Web site, then open the products page.

2. Display the Assets panel, then click the **Library button** 🕮.

3. Select the Level 1 heading in the cell to the right of the yellow spray can image, then drag it to the Assets panel.

   The Level 1 heading that you dragged is now an unnamed library item in the Assets panel.

4. Type **level_1_heading**, press **[Enter]** (Win) or **[return]** (Mac) to name the library item, deselect the library item, then compare your screen to Figure M-3.

   Notice that the Level 1 heading now has a shaded yellow background, indicating it is a library item.

5. Select the paragraph text below the Level 1 heading, then drag the selection to the Assets panel.

   The paragraph text that you dragged is now an unnamed library item in the Assets panel.

6. Type **level_1_text**, press **[Enter]** (Win) or **[return]** (Mac) to name the library item, deselect the library item, then compare your screen to Figure M-4.

You created two text-based library items from text on the products page.

FIGURE M-3

Assets panel showing new level_1_heading library item

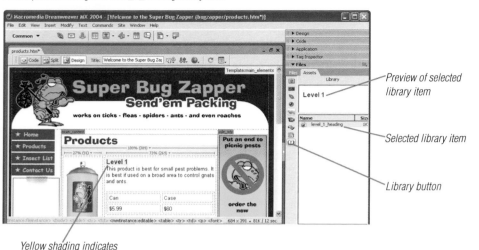

Preview of selected library item

Selected library item

Library button

Yellow shading indicates element is library item

FIGURE M-4

Assets panel showing two new library items

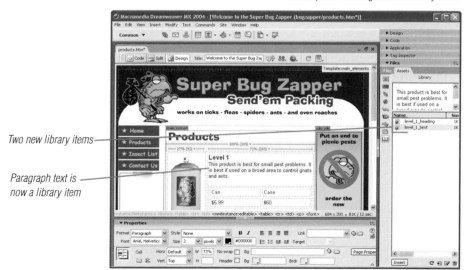

Two new library items

Paragraph text is now a library item

FIGURE M-5
page_footer library item added to Assets panel

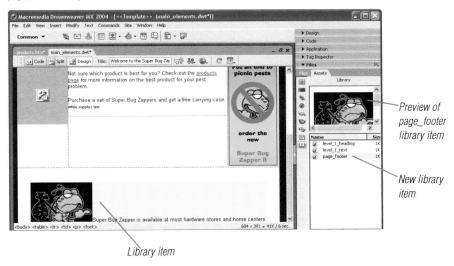

Preview of page_footer library item

New library item

Library item

1. Click the **Templates button** 🖹 on the Assets panel, then double-click the **main_elements template** to open it.

2. Click the **Library button** 🛄 on the Assets panel to display the library items in the Web site.

3. Click in front of Super Bug Zapper is available at most hardware stores and home centers. at the bottom of the page, then insert bug.gif from the chapter_m Data Files folder.

4. Type **Bug mug shot** as the alternate text, then save the file in the assets folder of the Web site.

5. Select the new graphic and the sentence that follows it, then drag the selection to the Library in the Assets panel.

   The image and text are stored as one library item and appear in the preview window at the top of the Assets panel. A new untitled library item appears selected in the library item list.

6. Type **page_footer**, press **[Enter]** (Win) or **[return]** (Mac) to name the library item in the Assets panel, deselect it, then compare your screen to Figure M-5.

7. Save your changes, then update all templates and pages in the site.

You created a library item named page_footer that contains an image and text in the main_elements template. You then saved the template and updated all templates and pages in the site.

Edit an image-based library item

1. Click the **bug.gif** image at the bottom of the main_elements template.

2. Click **Open** in the Property inspector to open the page_footer library item.

   The image and text appear in the document window. The title bar displays the filename page_footer.lbi. The file extension .lbi denotes a library file.

   | TIP You can also open a library item by double-clicking it in the Assets panel.

3. Click the image in the document window, then click the **Crop button** ⬛ in the Property inspector.

4. Click **OK** to the message warning This operation will change the original image file.

   A white dotted line (Win) or a thin mesh border (Mac) surrounds the image, as shown in Figure M-6. The white dotted line (Win) or the thin mesh border (Mac) is used to crop the image.

5. Drag the white dotted line toward the center of the image to crop the bug image to only show the bug's face.

(continued)

FIGURE M-6
Preparing to crop the bug image

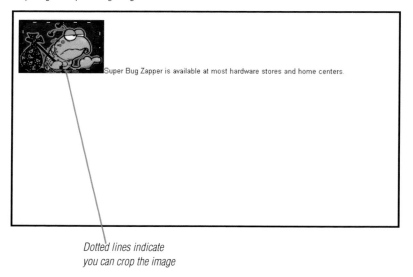

Super Bug Zapper is available at most hardware stores and home centers.

Dotted lines indicate you can crop the image

6. When you are satisfied with the crop, double-click the middle of the image, then compare your screen to Figure M-7.

7. Click the image again, then drag the **resizing
   handle** in the bottom-right corner of the
   graphic to make the graphic slightly smaller.

8. Edit the sentence to read **Super Bug Zapper
   is available at most hardware and home
   stores**.

9. Use the Property inspector to center
   the footer.

*You opened the page_footer library item, cropped
the image, then edited the text.*

FIGURE M-7
Viewing the cropped bug image

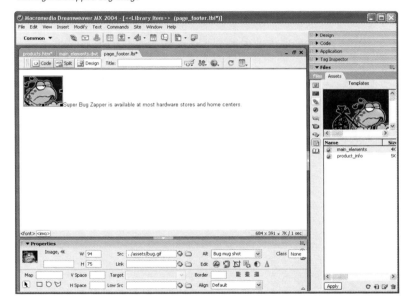

Update library items

1. Click **File** on the menu bar, then click **Save** to open the Update Library Items dialog box.

   The dialog box asks if you want to update the library item on the pages shown.

2. Click **Update** to open the Update Pages dialog box.

   This is the same dialog box that appears when you save a template. The only difference is that the Library items check box is checked.

3. Click the **Look in list arrow**, click **Entire Site**, click **Start**, then compare your screen to Figure M-8.

4. Click **Close**, then open the main_elements template.

   Notice that the footer reflects the change you made to the page_footer library item.

5. Click in front of the page footer, press **[Backspace]** (Win) or **[delete]** (Mac) twice to remove the extra line in front of the footer, then compare your screen to Figure M-9.

6. Save the main_elements template, then update all pages in the site.

You saved the page_footer library item and updated all pages in the site to incorporate the changes you made.

FIGURE M-8

Update Pages dialog box with Library items check box checked

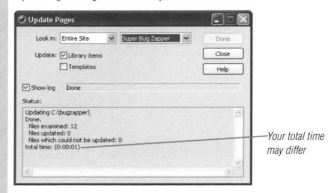

Your total time may differ

main_elements template showing updated page_footer library item

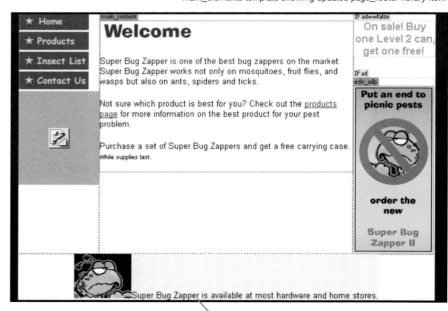

Footer shows changes made to bug image and text

Level_1_text library item after editing

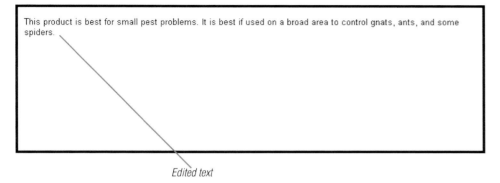

Edited text

Page reflects edits made to level_1_text library item

Text reflects
edits made to
library item

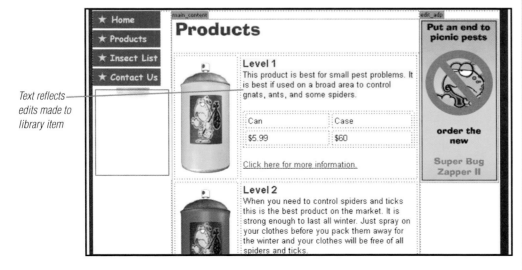

Edit a text-based library item

1. Open the products page, then click the **paragraph text** below the Level 1 heading to select the level_1_text library item.

2. Click **Open** in the Property inspector to open the level_1_text library item.

3. Select gnats and ants. at the end of the second sentence, type **gnats, ants, and some spiders.**, then compare your screen to Figure M-10.

4. Save your changes, then close the level_1_text library item.

5. Open the products page, then compare your screen to Figure M-11.

    The paragraph text under the Level 1 heading reflects the edits you made to the level_1_text library item.

You edited the text in the level_1_text library item, then saved the changes and updated the site.

ADD LIBRARY ITEMS TO PAGES

What You'll Do

 In this lesson, you will add the two text-based library items you created to the insects page and the product_level_1 page. You will then delete one of the library items and restore the deleted item using the Recreate command.

Adding Library Items to a Page

Once you create a library item, it's easy to add it to any page in a Web site. All you need to do is drag the library item from the Assets panel to the desired location on the page. When you insert a library item, the actual content and a reference to the library item are copied into the code. The inserted library item is shaded in yellow in the document window, and will be automatically updated to reflect any changes you make to the library item.

> ### QUICKTIP
> You can also insert a library item on a page by selecting the item in the Assets panel, then clicking Insert.

There may be times when you don't want content to be updated when you update the library item. For instance, suppose you want one of your pages to include photos of all past employees of the month. You would insert content from the current library item, but you do not want the photo to change when the library item is updated to reflect next month's employee photo. To achieve this, you would insert the content of a library item on a page without inserting the reference to the library item. To do this, press and hold [Alt] (Win) or [option] (Mac) as you drag the library item from the Assets panel to the document window. The content from the library item will be inserted on the page, but it will not be linked to the library item.

Making Library Items Editable on a Page

There may be times when you would like to make changes to a particular instance of a library item on one page, without making those changes to other instances of the library item in the site. You can make a library item editable on a page by breaking its link to the library item. To do this, select the library item, then click Detach from original in the Property inspector. Once you have detached the library item, you can edit the content like you would any other element on the page.

Keep in mind, though, that this edited content will not be updated when you make changes to the library item.

Deleting and Recreating Library Items

If you know that you will never need to update a library item again, you might want to delete it. To delete a library item, select it in the Assets panel, then click the Delete button. Deleting a library item only removes it from the Library folder; it does not change the contents of the pages that contain that library item. All instances of the deleted library item will still appear in shaded yellow in the site unless you detach them from the original. Be aware that you cannot use the Undo command to bring back a library item. However, you can undelete a library item by selecting any instance of the item in the site and clicking Recreate in the Property inspector. After you recreate a library item, it reappears in the Assets panel and you can make changes to it and update all pages in the site again. Figure M-12 shows the Property inspector with Library item settings.

FIGURE M-12

Property inspector with Library item settings

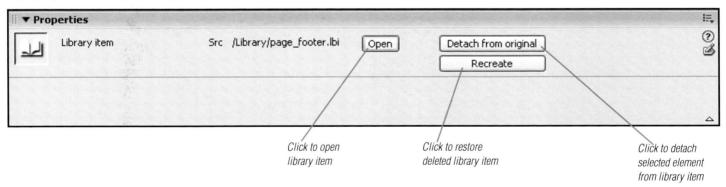

Click to open
library item

Click to restore
deleted library item

Click to detach
selected element
from library item

Add a library item to a page

1. Open the insects page.

2. Click below the insects table in the main_content editable region to set the insertion point, type **Recommended products:**, then press **[Enter]** (Win) or **[return]** (Mac).

3. Format the Recommended products: text using the following attributes: Font: Arial, Helvetica, sans-serif, Size: 2, Bold, and Color: maroon (#990000).

4. Open the Assets panel (if necessary), then drag the **level_1_heading library** item from the Assets panel to below the Recommended products: text you just typed, then deselect the heading.

   The Level 1 heading now appears where you dragged it. Notice that it is shaded in yellow, indicating it is a library item.

5. Click to the right of the Level 1 heading, press and hold **[Shift]**, then press **[Enter]** (Win) or **[return]** (Mac) to place the insertion point on the line below the Level 1 heading.

6. Drag the **level_1_text library** item from the Assets panel to the line below the Level 1 heading on the insects page, deselect the text, then compare your screen to Figure M-13.

(continued)

FIGURE M-13
Insects page with library items added

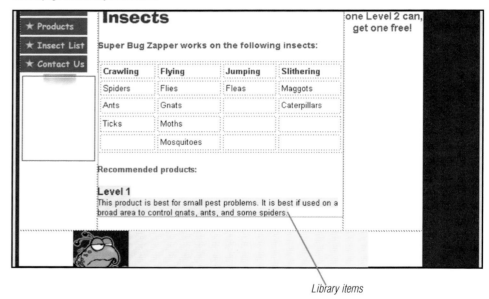

Library items

7. Open the product_level_1.htm page, then delete the Level 1 heading and the text below it.

8. Drag the **level_1_heading** library item to the same position on the page as the deleted text.

9. Drag the **level_1_text** under the level_1_heading.

   You replaced the existing heading and text with the two new library items.

10. Close and save all open pages.

You added the level_1_heading and level_1_text library items to the insects page and the product_level_1 page.

Creating library items

Although you can create library items with graphics, text, or a combination of the two, you can only use items that contain body elements. For instance, when editing a library item, the CSS Styles panel will be unavailable because style sheet code is embedded in the head section, rather than just the body section. Likewise, the Page Properties dialog box will be unavailable because library items cannot include a body tag attribute such as text color.

Make a library item editable on a page

1. Open the insects page, then click the **Level 1 heading** on the insects page.

   The Property inspector displays three buttons relating to library items.

2. Click **Detach from original** in the Property inspector.

   A dialog box opens, warning you that the item will no longer be automatically updated when the original library item changes.

3. Click **OK**.

   Notice that the heading no longer appears in shaded yellow, indicating it is no longer a library item.

4. Select the paragraph text below the Level 1 heading, then detach this text from the level_1_text library item.

5. Change the size of the Level 1 heading to 4, deselect the text, then compare your screen to Figure M-14.

   The size of the heading is now larger. The level_1_heading library item remains unchanged.

You detached the Level 1 heading from the level_1_heading library item and the paragraph text from the level_1_text library item to make both of these text elements editable on the insects page. You then increased the size of the Level 1 heading on the insects page.

FIGURE M-14
Testing the pop-up menu in Internet Explorer

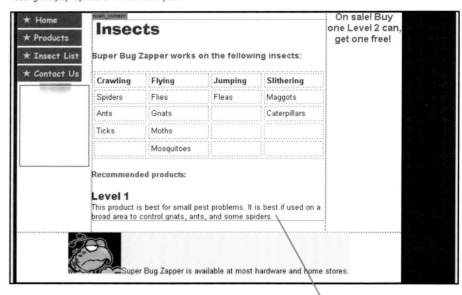

Detached library items

FIGURE M-15
Assets panel after deleting level_1_text library item

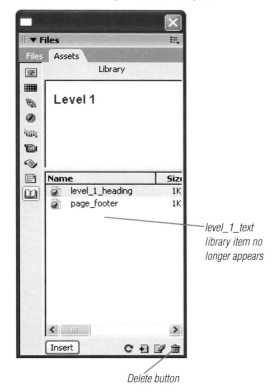

level_1_text
library item no
longer appears

Delete button

FIGURE M-16
Assets panel after recreating level_1_text library item

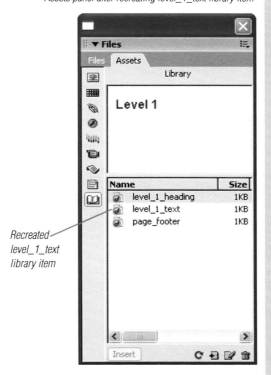

Recreated
level_1_text
library item

Delete a library item

1. Select the level_1_text library item in the Assets panel.

2. Click the **Delete button** 🗑 in the Assets panel.

   A dialog box opens, asking if you are sure you want to delete the library item.

3. Click **Yes**, then compare your screen to Figure M-15.

   The level_1_text library item no longer appears in the Assets panel.

You deleted the level_1_text library item in the Assets panel.

Recreate a library item

1. Open the products page.

   The paragraph text under the Level 1 heading still appears in shaded yellow, indicating it is still a library item, even though you deleted the library item to which it is attached.

2. Click the **paragraph text** under the Level 1 heading to select it.

3. Click **Recreate** in the Property inspector, then compare your screen to Figure M-16.

   The level_1_text library item is added to the Assets panel.

   If you do not see the level_1_text library item, recreate the site cache, then refresh the Assets panel.

4. Save your changes.

You recreated the level_1_text library item that you deleted in the previous set of steps.

ADD AND MODIFY SNIPPETS

What You'll Do

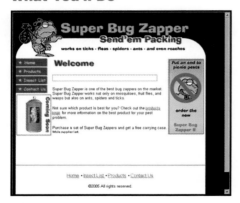

In this lesson, you will add a predefined snippet from the Snippets panel to create a new footer in the main_elements template. You will then replace the placeholder text and links in the snippet with appropriate text and links. Finally, you will save the modified snippet as a new snippet, so that you can add it to other pages.

Using the Snippets Panel

Creating a Web site is a huge task, so it's nice to know that you can save time by using ready-made code snippets to create various elements of your site. The Snippets panel, located in the Code panel group, contains a large collection of reusable code snippets organized in folders named by element type. The Snippets panel contains two panes, as shown in Figure M-17. The lower pane contains folders that can be expanded to view the snippets. The upper pane displays a preview of the selected snippet. Use the buttons at the bottom of the Snippets panel to insert a snippet, create a new folder in the Snippets panel, create a new snippet, edit a snippet, or remove a snippet.

Inserting and Modifying Snippets

Adding a snippet to a page is an easy task; simply drag the snippet from the Snippets panel to the desired location on the page. Once you position a snippet, you will need to replace the placeholder text, links, and images with appropriate content.

> **QUICKTIP**
>
> You can also add a snippet to a page by selecting the snippet in the Snippets panel, then clicking Insert.

Creating New Snippets

Once you've modified a snippet so that it contains text and graphics appropriate for your site, you might want to save it with a new name. Doing this will save time when using this snippet on other pages. To save a modified snippet as a new snippet, select the snippet content in the document window, then click the New Snippet button in the Snippets panel to open the Snippet dialog box. Use this dialog box to name the snippet and give it a description. Because the Snippet dialog box displays the snippet code, you can make edits to the code here if you wish. Any new snippets you create will appear in the Snippets panel.

FIGURE M-17
Snippets panel

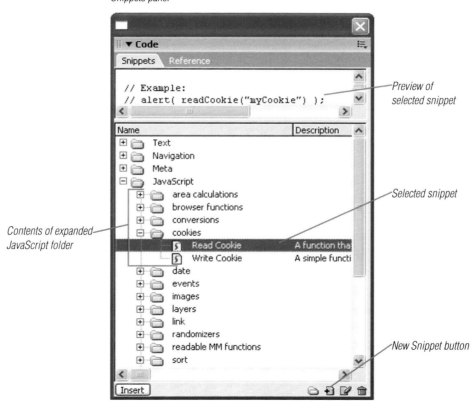

Preview of selected snippet

Selected snippet

Contents of expanded JavaScript folder

New Snippet button

Add a predefined snippet to a page

1. Open the main_elements template.

2. Scroll to the bottom of the page, select the library item that includes the bug graphic and sentence "Super Bug Zapper is available at most hardware stores and home centers.", then press **[Enter]** (Win) or **[return]** (Mac) to delete it.

3. Display the Code panel group, then click the **Snippets tab** to open the Snippets panel.

   > TIP If the Code panel group is not open, click Window on the menu bar, then click Snippets.

4. Click the **plus sign (+)** (Win) or the **triangle** (Mac) next to the Footers folder in the Snippets panel to display the contents of the Footers folder.

5. Drag the **Basic: Text Block Snippet** in the Footers folder to the bottom of the main__ elements template, as shown in Figure M-18.

6. Save your changes, then update all templates and pages in the site.

You deleted the footer in the main_elements template, then added a predefined footer from the Snippets panel.

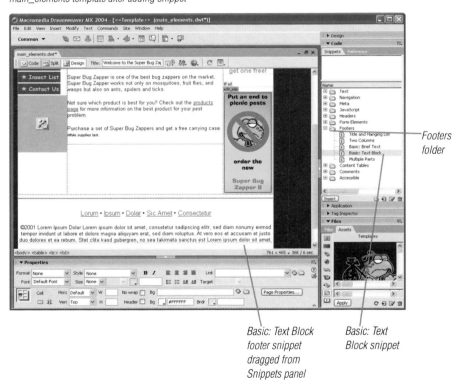

Footers folder

Basic: Text Block footer snippet dragged from Snippets panel

Basic: Text Block snippet

FIGURE M-19

main_elements template after editing snippet placeholder text

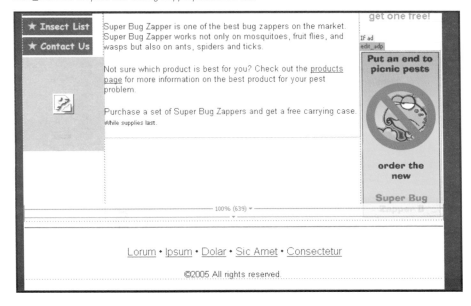

1. Click between the copyright symbol (©) and 2001 in the footer, press and hold **[Shift]**, then click to the right of the period at the end of the paragraph.

   The entire paragraph, except for the © at the beginning of the paragraph, should be selected.

2. Type **2005 All rights reserved.**, then compare your screen to Figure M-19.

3. Save your changes, then update all templates and pages in the site.

You edited the placeholder text contained in the footer snippet in the main_elements template.

Modify snippet links

1. Select the Lorum placeholder link in the bottom row of the table in the main_elements template, then type **Home**.

2. Replace the Ipsum placeholder link with **Insect List**, replace the Dolar placeholder link with **Products**, then replace the Sic Amet placeholder link with **Contact Us**.

3. Delete the Consectetur placeholder link, then delete the black dot to the right of the Contact Us link.

4. Display the Files panel, select the Home link in the footer in the main_elements template, then use the Point to File icon ⊕ in the Property inspector to set the Link property to the index page, as shown in Figure M-20.

5. Use the Point to File icon ⊕ to set the Link property for the Products, Insect List, and Contact Us links.

6. Save your changes, then update all other templates and pages in the site.

7. Preview the main_elements template in your browser, test all the links in the footer, then close your browser.

You changed the names of the placeholder links and used the Point to File icon to create links to the four main pages in the Super Bug Zapper Web site.

FIGURE M-20

Using the Point to File icon to create document-relative links in the footer

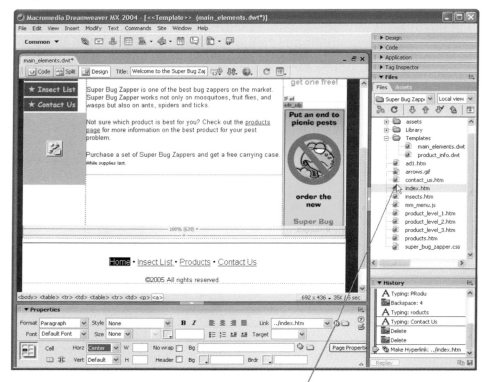

Point to File icon

FIGURE M-21
Snippet dialog box

Name—
text box

Description—
text box

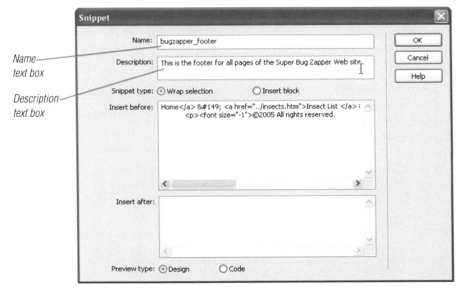

1. Select the footer in the main_elements template.

2. Click the **New Snippet button** in the Snippets panel to open the Snippet dialog box.

3. Type **bugzapper_footer** in the Name text box.

4. Type **This is the footer for all pages of the Super Bug Zapper Web site.** in the Description text box, then compare your screen to Figure M-21.

5. Click **OK**.

   The bugzapper_footer snippet now appears in the Snippets panel. You can insert it on any page by dragging it to the desired location in the document window.

6. Save and close all open pages and templates, then close Dreamweaver.

You copied the footer from the main_elements template and saved it as a snippet called bugzapper_footer.

Create and modify library items.

1. Open the Blooms & Bulbs Web site that you created and developed in Chapters A through L, then open the master_gardener template.

2. Scroll down the page until the Further Research heading and paragraph text is visible on your screen, select the text *cosie@blooms&bulbs.com*, then convert this selected text into a library item named **contact_email**.

3. Select the phone number *(555)248-0806* in the paragraph below the Further Research heading, then convert this selection into a library item named **contact_number**.

4. Edit the contact_number library item so that the last four digits in the phone number are **0807**.

5. Save and update the contact_number library item, check to make sure the phone number in the paragraph text changed to reflect your edit, then save and close the template, and update the files associated with it.

6. Open the tips page, then insert flower.gif from the assets folder of the Web site under the Planting Tips heading, adding appropriate alternate text.

7. Convert the flower.gif image to a library item named **flowers**.

8. Open the flowers library item, select the flower.gif image, copy the image, then paste it twice so that the flowers library item contains three flower images.

9. Save and update the flowers library item, close the flowers library item, then save the tips page.

Add library items to pages.

1. Place the insertion point at the end of the first paragraph on the tips page. Type **And remember, if you have questions, call or e-mail our experts at**.

2. Insert the contact_number library item to the right of the text you just typed.

3. Type **or** to the right of the contact_number library item you inserted.

4. Insert the contact_email library item to the right of the words that you just typed, then type a period (**.**) after the contact_email library item.

5. Make the contact_email library item editable on the page, select cosie in the address, then type **tips**, so that the e-mail address is changed to *tips@blooms&bulbs.com*.

6. Delete the flowers library item.

7. Recreate the flowers library item.

8. Detach the tips.htm page from the template, then modify the navigation bar to change the down state to reflect the tips navigation element, rather than the Ask Cosie navigation bar element.

9. Save your changes, preview the tips page in your browser, compare your screen to Figure M-22, close your browser, then close the tips page.

Add and modify snippets.

1. Open the master_gardener template.

2. Scroll to the bottom of the page so that the Top of Page Flash button is visible.

3. Insert the Basic: Text Block snippet, located in the Footers folder of the Snippets panel, at the bottom of the page, below the Top of Page Flash button.

4. Replace the paragraph text below the placeholder links with the following text: **Copyright 2004. Thank you for your business!**
5. Replace the placeholder links in the footer with links to the home, plants, workshops, tips, and master_gardener pages.
6. Create a new snippet from the footer you just inserted. Name the snippet **blooms_footer**, then give it an appropriate description.
7. Save your changes, update all pages in the site, preview the master_gardener template in your browser, then compare your screen to Figure M-23.
8. Test the links in the footer to make sure they work, close your browser, then close the master_gardener template.

FIGURE M-22

Completed Skills Review: tips page

FIGURE M-23

Completed Skills Review: master_gardener template

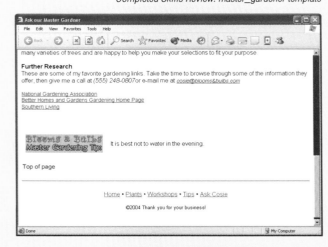

In this Project Builder you will continue your work on the Rapids Transit Web site that you began in Project Builder 1 in Chapter A. Mike Andrew, the owner, has asked you to add the Rapids Transit address and phone number to every page of the Web site. He also asked you to create a new footer for every page that provides links to the main pages of the site and gives copyright information. You decide to use library items and snippets to incorporate these items.

1. Open the Rapids Transit Web site that you created in Chapters A through L, then open the index page.
2. Convert the Rapids Transit address information at the bottom of the page into a library item named **rapids_address**.
3. Add the rapids_address library items to the bottom of the before and rentals pages.
4. Open the reservations page and replace the contact information at the bottom of the page with the rapids_address library item.
5. Open the rapids_address library item, then change the color of the text to #003399 and the style to bold.
6. Copy the Mike Andrew link from the index page, then paste it at the bottom of the rapids_address library item.

7. Save and update the rapids_address library item, then look at the index page to verify that the address reflects your edits.
8. Open the store_pages template and replace the address with the rapids_address library item.

FIGURE M-24
Sample Project Builder 1

9. Save and close the store_pages template.
10. Save all pages, preview the index page in your browser, then check all links.
11. Close your browser, then close all open pages.

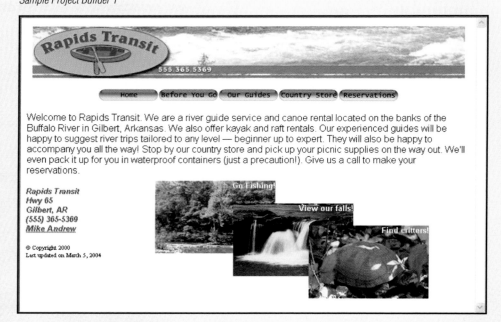

In this Project Builder, you will continue your work on the Jacob's Web site that you started in Project Builder 2 in Chapter A. Chef Jacob has asked you to create a graphic that he can use to "rate" recipes with stars. He wants the rolls recipe rated with three stars. He has also asked you to place alternate text links at the bottom of the index, menus, and directions pages.

1. Open the Jacob's Web site.
2. Open the rolls.htm page.
3. Place the insertion point to the right of the Grandmother's Rolls text, then insert star.gif from the chapter_m Data Files folder.
4. Type appropriate alternate text, then align the image to Absolute Middle.
5. Add the star image to your library, then name it **star**.
6. Edit the star library item by copying the star to make a three-star item, then save the file as **three_stars.lbi**.
7. Delete the star image on the rolls page, then replace it with the three_stars library item.
8. Save and close the rolls page.

9. Open the index page, then use a snippet to place text links at the bottom of the page to provide alternate text links to the main page of the Web site.
10. Delete all unnecessary text in the snippet, then name the snippet **jacobs_footer**.
11. Save and close the index page.

12. Place the snippet at the bottom of the menus and directions pages.
13. Save your work, then preview the pages in your browser to test each link.
14. Make necessary minor formatting adjustments, then close your browser and close all open pages.

FIGURE M-25
Completed Project Builder 2

Library items and snippets are commonly used in Web sites to ensure that repetitive information is updated quickly and accurately.

1. Connect to the Internet, navigate to the page for the Online Companion, then select a link for this chapter.
2. Spend some time exploring the pages of this site to become familiar with its elements. Do you see many repeating elements?
3. If you were developing this site, which images or text would you convert into library items? Print out two pages from this Web site and write a list of all the text and visual elements from these pages that you would make into library items.
4. Review a second link for this chapter, then print out two pages from the site.
5. Write a list of all the elements shown on the printed pages that you think should be made into library items.

FIGURE M-26

Source for Design Project

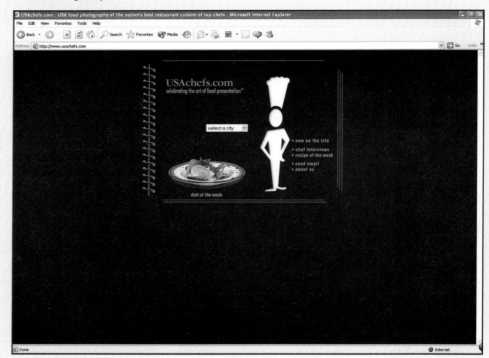

In this project, you will continue to work on the group Web site that you created in Chapters A through L. Depending on the size of your group, you can assign individual elements of the project to group members, or work collectively to create the finished product.

You will continue to enhance your Web site by using library items and snippets.

1. Consult your storyboard and brainstorm as a team to decide which text and graphic elements in the site should be converted into library items. Write a list of these items.

2. Discuss what content to include in a footer that you will add to each page of the site using a snippet.

3. Assign a team member the task of converting all the text elements you identified in your list into library items.

4. Assign a team member the task of inserting the library items that were created in Step 3 in appropriate places in the Web site.

5. Assign a team member the task of converting all the graphic elements you identified in Step 1 into library items.

6. Assign a team member the task of inserting the graphic library items that were created in Step 5 in appropriate places in the Web site.

7. Assign a team member the task of editing two of the library items that were created, then saving and updating all instances of the library item in the site.

8. Assign a team member the task of adding a footer to the Web site using one of the snippets in the Footers folder of the Snippets panel. This team member should replace all placeholder links with appropriate links to each major page in the site and should also replace placeholder text with text that is suitable for your site.

9. Assign a team member the task of creating a new snippet from the footer that was created in Step 8. This team member should also insert this snippet on the other pages of the site.

10. Save your work, preview all pages in a browser, and test all the links. Use the check list in Figure M-27 to make sure your Web site is complete.

11. Assign a team member the task of making any necessary changes, then saving and closing all open pages.

FIGURE M-27
Group Project check list

Web Site Check List

1. Have you converted all repeating text elements into library items?
2. Have you converted all repeating graphic elements, such as logos, into library items?
3. Did you save and update the library items after making edits to them?
4. Do all links work?
5. Did you add the footer to all pages in the Web site?
6. Does your copyright notice appear below the links in the footer?

MANAGING A WEB SERVER AND FILES

1. Publish a Web site and transfer files.

2. Check files out and in.

3. Cloak files.

4. Import and export a site definition.

CHAPTER N
MANAGING A WEB SERVER AND FILES

Introduction

Once you have created all the pages of your Web site, finalized all the content, and performed site maintenance to ensure that all links work, all colors are Websafe, and all orphaned pages are eliminated, you are ready to publish your site to a remote server so the rest of the world can access it. In this chapter, you will start by defining the remote site for the Super Bug Zapper Web site. You will then transfer files to the remote site and learn how to keep them up to date. You will also check out a file so that it is not available to other team members while you are editing it, and learn how to cloak files. When a file is **cloaked** it is excluded from certain processes, such as being transferred to the remote site. Finally, you will export the site definition file from the Super Bug Zapper Web site so that other users can import the site.

Preparing to Publish a Site

Before you publish a site to a remote server so that it is available to the rest of the world, it is extremely important that you test it to make sure the content is accurate and up to date, and that everything is functioning properly. If you use the Web at all, you have probably felt frustrated when you click a link that doesn't work, or have to wait for pages that load slowly because of large graphics and animations. Remember that a typical Web viewer has a short attention span and limited patience. Before you publish your site, make sure to use the Link Checker panel to check for broken links and orphaned files. Make sure that all image paths are correct and that all images load quickly and have alternate text. Verify that all pages have titles, and remove all Non-Websafe colors. View the pages in at least two different browsers to ensure that everything works correctly. The more you test, the better the chances that your viewers will have a positive experience and stay at your site.

Tools You'll Use

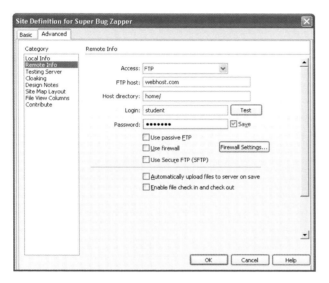

PUBLISH A WEB SITE AND TRANSFER FILES

What You'll Do

In this lesson, you will set up remote access to either an FTP folder or a local/network folder for the Super Bug Zapper Web site. You will also view a Web site on a remote server, upload files to it, and synchronize the files.

Defining a Remote Site

As you learned in Chapter A, publishing a site means transferring all files for a site to a Web server. A **Web server** is a computer that is connected to the Internet with an IP (Internet Protocol) address so that it is available on the Internet. Before you can publish a site to a Web server, you must first define the remote site by specifying the Remote Info settings in the Advanced section of the Site Definition dialog box. You can specify remote settings when you first create a new site and define the root folder (as you did in Chapter A when you defined the remote access settings for the TripSmart Web site), or you can do it after you have completed all of your pages and are confident that it is ready for public viewing. To specify the remote settings for a site, you must first choose an Access setting, which specifies the type of server you will use. The most common Access setting is FTP (File Transfer Protocol). If you specify FTP, you will need to specify an address for the server and the name of the folder on the FTP site in which your root folder will be

stored. You will also need to enter login and password information. Figure N-1 shows an example of FTP settings in the Remote Info category of the Site Definition dialog box.

QUICKTIP

If you do not have access to an FTP site, you can publish a site to a local/network folder. Use the alternate steps provided in this lesson to publish your site to a local/network folder.

Viewing a Remote Site

Once you have defined a site to a remote location, you can then view the remote folder in the Files panel by choosing Remote view from the View list. If your remote site is located on an FTP server, you will need to connect to it first by clicking the Connects to remote host button on the Files panel toolbar. If you defined your site on a local/network folder, then you don't need to use the Connects to remote host button; the root folder and any files and folders it contains will appear in the Files panel when you switch to Remote view.

Transferring Files to and from a Remote Site

After you define a remote site, you will need to transfer or **upload** your files from the local version of your site to the remote host. To do this, view the site in Local view, select the files you want to upload, then click the Put File(s) button on the Files panel toolbar. Once you click this button, the files will be transferred to the remote site. To view the uploaded files, switch to Remote view, then click the Connects to remote host button, as shown in Figure N-2. Or you can expand the Files panel to view both the Remote Site and the Local Files panes.

If a file you select for uploading requires other files, such as graphics, a dialog box will open after you click the Put File(s) button and ask if you want those files (known as **dependent files**) to be uploaded. By clicking Yes, all dependent files in the selected page will be uploaded to the appropriate folder in the remote site. If a file that you wish to upload is located in a folder in the local site, the entire folder will be automatically transferred to the remote site.

QUICKTIP

To upload an entire site to a remote host, select the root folder, and then click the Put File(s) button. Sometimes you will need to move the files you want to upload in an intermediary folder before transferring them to the remote site.

If you are developing or maintaining a Web site in a group environment, there might be times when you want to transfer or **download** files that other team members have created from the remote site to your local site. To do this, switch to Remote view,

FIGURE N-1

FTP settings in the Remote Info category of the Site Definition dialog box

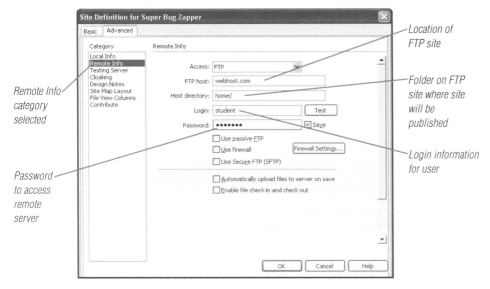

Remote Info category selected

Password to access remote server

Location of FTP site

Folder on FTP site where site will be published

Login information for user

FIGURE N-2

Files panel with Remote view selected

Click to connect to remote site

select the files you want to download, then click the Get File(s) button on the Files panel toolbar.

Synchronizing Files

In order to keep a Web site up to date—especially one that contains several pages and involves several team members—you will need to update and replace files. Team members might make changes to pages on the local version of the site, or make additions to the remote site. If many people are involved in maintaining a site, or if you are constantly making changes to the pages, ensuring that both the local and remote sites have the most up-to-date files could get confusing. Thankfully, you can use the Synchronize command to keep things straight. The Synchronize command instructs Dreamweaver to compare the dates of the saved files in both versions of the site, then transfers only the files that have changed. To synchronize files, use the Synchronize Files dialog box, shown in Figure N-3. You can synchronize an entire site or just selected files. You can also specify whether to upload newer files to the remote site, download newer files from the remote site, or both.

FIGURE N-3
Synchronize Files dialog box

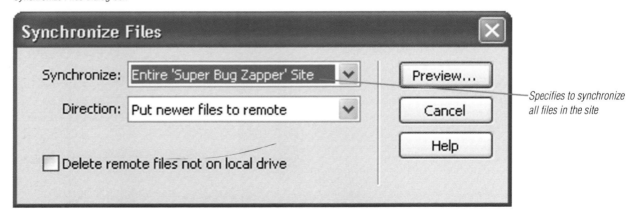

Specifies to synchronize all files in the site

FIGURE N-4

Site Definition for Super Bug Zapper Web site with FTP settings specified

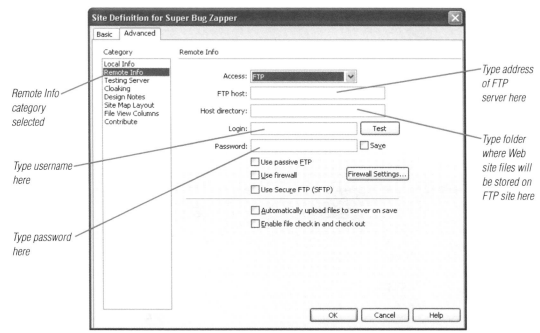

Remote Info category selected

Type username here

Type password here

Type address of FTP server here

Type folder where Web site files will be stored on FTP site here

Set up Web server access on an FTP site

NOTE: Complete these steps only if you know you can store the Super Bug Zapper files on an FTP site, and you know the login and password information.

1. Open the Super Bug Zapper Web site, click **Site** on the menu bar, then click **Manage Sites**.

2. Click **Super Bug Zapper** in the Manage Sites dialog box (if necessary), then click **Edit**.

3. Click the **Advanced tab**, click **Remote Info** in the Category list, click the **Access list arrow**, click **FTP**, then compare your screen to Figure N-4.

4. Enter the FTP Host, Host Directory, Login, and Password information in the dialog box.

   If you do not have access to an FTP site, complete the exercise called Set up Web server access on a local or network folder on Page N-8.

   TIP You must have file and folder permissions to use FTP.

5. Click **OK**, then click **Done** to close the Manage Sites dialog box.

You set up remote access information for the Super Bug Zapper Web site using an FTP site folder.

Set up Web server access on a local or network folder

NOTE: Complete these steps if you do not have the ability to post files to an FTP site and could not complete the previous exercise.

1. Using Windows Explorer (Win) or Mac Finder (Mac), create a new folder on your hard drive or on a shared drive named **bugzapper_yourlastname**. (For instance, if your last name is Jones, name the folder **bugzapper_jones**.)

2. Switch back to Dreamweaver, open the Super Bug Zapper Web site, click **Site** on the menu bar, then click **Manage Sites** to open the Manage Sites dialog box.

3. Click **Super Bug Zapper**, click **Edit** to open the Site Definition for Super Bug Zapper dialog box, click the **Advanced tab**, then click **Remote Info** in the Category list.

4. Click the **Access list arrow**, then click **Local/Network**.

5. Click the **Browse for File icon** 🗁 next to the Remote folder text box to open the Choose remote root folder for site Super Bug Zapper dialog box, navigate to the folder you created in Step 1, select the folder, then click **Select** (Win) or **Choose** (Mac).

6. Make sure the Refresh remote file list automatically check box is checked, compare your screen to Figure N-5, click **OK**, then click **Done**.

You created a new folder and specified it as the remote location for the Super Bug Zapper Web site.

FIGURE N-5

Site Definition for Super Bug Zapper Web site with FTP settings specified

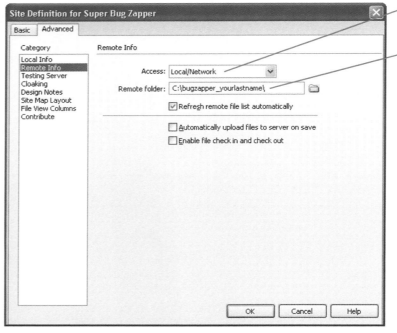

Local/Network setting selected

Local or network drive and folder where remote site will be published (your drive may differ and the folder name should end with your last name)

FIGURE N-6

Connecting to the remote site

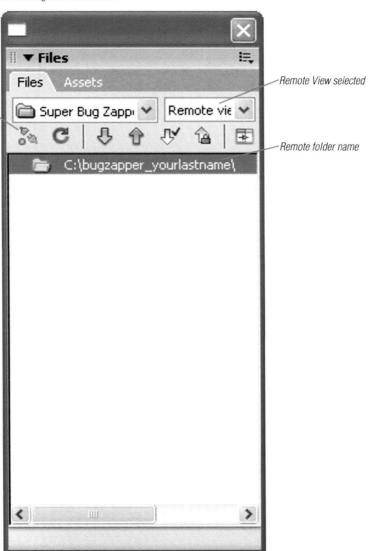

Connects to remote host button

Remote View selected

Remote folder name

Super Bug Zapp

Remote vie

C:\bugzapper_yourlastname\

1. Click the **View list arrow** in the Files panel, then click **Remote view**, as shown in Figure N-6.

   If you specified your remote access to a local or network folder, then the bugzapper_yourlastname folder will appear in the Files panel now. If your remote access is set to an FTP site, you will need to complete Step 2 to see the remote access folder.

2. Click the **Connects to remote host button** in the Files panel (if necessary).

   The Files panel changes to show the contents of the remote server that you specified as your remote host. The folder you specified should be empty, because you have not yet uploaded any files to it.

3. Click the **Expand/Collapse button** to view both the Remote Site and Local Files panes.

You used the Files panel to set the view for the Super Bug Zapper site to Remote view. You then connected to the remote server to view the contents of the remote folder you specified.

Upload files to a remote server

1. Click the **products page**, then click the **Put File(s) button** 🔼 on the Files panel toolbar.

   The Dependent Files dialog box opens, asking if you want to include dependent files.

2. Click **Yes**.

   The products page, along with all the other image files, library items, and templates used in the products page are copied to the remote server. The Status dialog box appears and flashes the names of each file as they are uploaded.

3. Click the **Refresh button** 🔁 , expand the assets folder (if necessary), expand the Library folder, then compare your screen to Figure N-7.

   The remote site now contains the products page as well as several images, two library items, and the super_bug_zapper external style sheet file, all of which are needed by the products page.

   TIP You might need to expand the bugzapper_yourlastname folder in order to view the assets folder.

You used the Put File(s) button to upload the products page, and all files that are dependent on the products page.

FIGURE N-7

Remote view of the Super Bug Zapper Web site after uploading products page

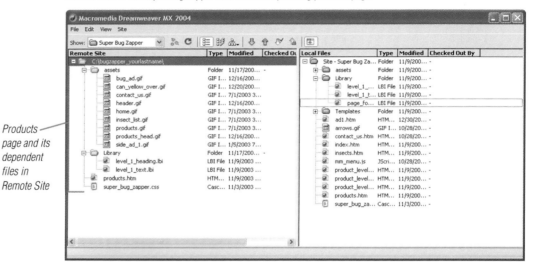

Products page and its dependent files in Remote Site

Synchronize Files dialog box

Files that need to be uploaded to remote site

Your number of files may differ

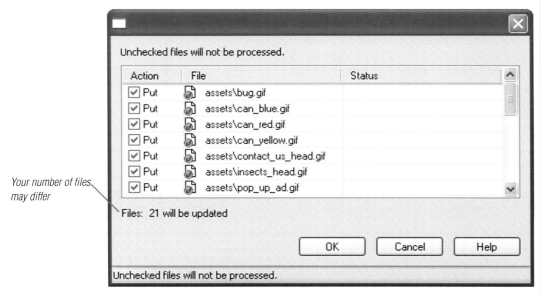

Synchronize files

1. Click **Site** on the Files panel toolbar, click **Synchronize** to open the Synchronize Files dialog box (Win) or click the **Options list arrow**, point to **Site**, then click **Synchronize** to open the Synchronize Files dialog box (Mac).

2. Click the **Synchronize list arrow**, then click **Entire 'Super Bug Zapper' Site**.

3. Click the **Direction list arrow**, click **Put newer files to remote** (if necessary), then compare your screen to Figure N-8.

4. Click **Preview**.

   The Status dialog box might appear and flash the names of all the files from the local version of the site that need to be uploaded to the remote site. Then the dialog box shown in Figure N-9 opens and lists all the files that need to be uploaded to the remote site.

5. Click **OK**.

   All the files from the local Super Bug Zapper Web site are now contained in the remote version of the site. The dialog box changes to show all the files that were uploaded.

6. Click **Close** to close the dialog box.

   > TIP   If you want to keep a record of your synchronizations, you could click Save Log, specify a location and name for the synchronization log, then click Save.

7. Refresh the Files panel to place the files and folders in order.

You synchronized the Super Bug Zapper Web site files to copy all remaining files from the local root folder to the remote root folder.

CHECK FILES OUT AND IN

What You'll Do

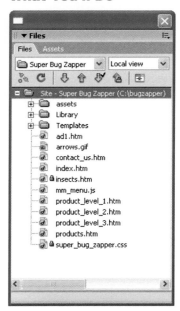

 In this lesson, you will use the Site Definition dialog box to enable the Check In/Check Out feature. You will then check out the insects page, make a change to it, then check it back in.

Managing a Web Site with a Team

When you work on a large Web site, chances are that many people will be involved in keeping the site up to date. Different individuals will need to make changes or additions to different pages of the site by adding or deleting content, changing graphics, updating information, and so on. If everyone had access to all of the pages at all times, big problems could arise. For instance, what if you and another team member both made edits to the same page at the same time? If you post your edited version of the file to the site after the other team member posts his edited version of the same file, the file that you upload will overwrite his version and none of his changes will be incorporated.

Not good! Fortunately, you can avoid this scenario by using Dreamweaver's collaboration tools.

Checking Out and Checking In Files

Checking in and out files is similar to checking in and out library books. No one else can read a book while you have it checked out. Using Dreamweaver's Check In/Check Out feature will ensure that team members do not overwrite each other's pages. When this feature is enabled, only one person can work on a file at a time. To check out a file, click the file you want to work on in the Files panel, then click the Check Out File(s) button on the Files panel toolbar. Files that you have checked out are marked with green check marks in the Files panel. Files that have been checked in are marked with padlock icons.

After you finish editing a checked-out file, you will need to save and close the file, then click the Check In button to check the file back in and make it available to other users.

When a file is checked in, you cannot make edits to it unless you check it out again. Figure N-10 shows the Check Out File(s) and Check In buttons on the Files panel toolbar.

Enabling the Check In/Check Out Feature

In order to use the Check In /Check Out feature with a team of people, you must first enable it. To turn on this feature, check the Enable file check in and check out check box in the Remote Info settings of the Site Definition dialog box.

FIGURE N-10
Check Out File(s) and Check In buttons on the Files Panel toolbar

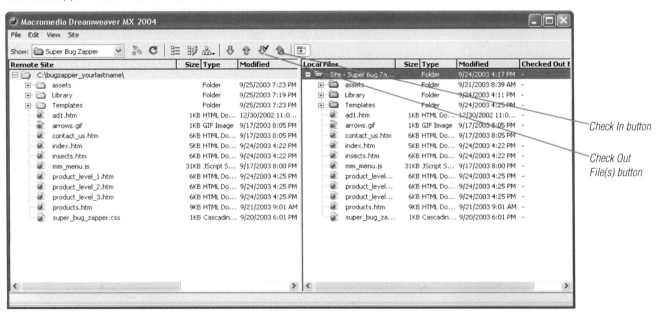

Enable the Check In/Check Out feature

1. Click **Site** on the menu bar, click **Manage Sites** to open the Manage Sites dialog box, click **Super Bug Zapper** in the list, then click **Edit** to open the Site Definition for Super Bug Zapper dialog box.

2. Click **Remote Info** in the Category list, then click the **Enable file check in and check out check box** to select it.

3. Check the **Check out files when opening** check box to select it (if necessary).

4. Type your **name** using lowercase letters and no spaces in the Check out name text box.

5. Type your **e-mail address** in the Email address text box.

6. Compare your screen to Figure N-11, click **OK** to close the Site Definition for Super Bug Zapper dialog box, then click **Done** to close the Manage Sites dialog box.

You used the Manage Sites Definition for Super Bug Zapper dialog box to enable the Check In/Check Out feature and let site collaborators know when you are working with a file in the site.

Check out a file

1. Click the **insects page** in the Local Files list in the Files panel to select it.

(continued)

FIGURE N-11
Enabling the Check In/Check Out feature

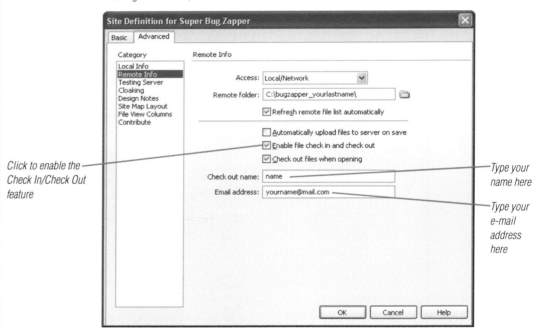

Click to enable the Check In/Check Out feature

Type your name here

Type your e-mail address here

FIGURE N-12

Files panel in Local view after checking out insects page

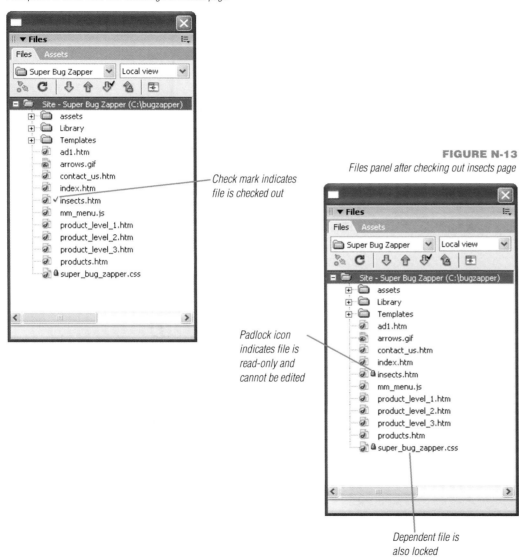

Check mark indicates
file is checked out

FIGURE N-13

Files panel after checking out insects page

Padlock icon
indicates file is
read-only and
cannot be edited

Dependent file is
also locked

2. Click the **Check Out File(s) button** 🔧 on the Files panel toolbar.

   The Dependent Files dialog box appears, asking if you want to include all files that are needed for the insects page.

3. Click **Yes**, click another file in the Files panel to deselect the insects page, collapse the Files panel, switch to Local view, then compare your screen to Figure N-12.

   The insects file has a check mark next to it, indicating you have checked it out.

You checked out the insects page so that no one else can use it.

Check in a file

1. Open the insects page, type **Cockroaches** in the table cell below Ticks on the insects page, then save your changes.

2. Close the insects page, then click the **insects page** in the Files panel to select it.

3. Click the **Check In button** 🔒 on the Files panel toolbar.

   The Dependent Files dialog box opens, asking if you want to include dependent files too.

4. Click **Yes**, click another file in the Files panel to deselect the insects page, then compare your screen to Figure N-13.

   A padlock icon appears instead of a green check mark next to the insects page on the Files panel.

You made a content change on the insects page, then checked in the insects page, making it available for others to check it out again.

CLOAK FILES

What You'll Do

 In this lesson, you will cloak the assets folder so that it is excluded from various operations, such as the Put, Get, Check In, and Check Out commands. You will also use the Site Definition dialog box to cloak all .gif files in the site.

Understanding Cloaking Files

There may be times when you want to exclude a particular file or files from being uploaded to a server. For instance, suppose you have a page that is not quite finished and needs more work before it is ready to be viewed by the rest of the world. You can exclude such files by **cloaking** them, which marks them for exclusion from several commands, including Put, Get, Synchronize, Check In, and Check Out. Cloaked files are also excluded from site-wide operations, such as checking for links or updating a template or library item. You can cloak a folder or specify a type of file to cloak throughout the site.

QUICKTIP

By default, the cloaking feature is enabled. However, if for some reason it is not turned on, open the Site Definition dialog box, click the Advanced tab, click the Cloaking category, then click the Enable cloaking check box.

Cloaking a Folder

There may be times when you want to cloak an entire folder. For instance, if you are not concerned with replacing outdated image files, you might want to cloak the assets folder of a Web site to save time when synchronizing files. To cloak a folder, select the folder, click Site on the Files panel menu bar, point to Cloaking, then click Cloak. The folder you cloaked and all the files it contains will appear with red slashes across them, as shown in Figure N-14. To uncloak a folder, click Site on the Files panel menu bar (Win) or on the menu bar (Mac), point to Cloaking, then click Uncloak.

QUICKTIP

To uncloak all files in a site, click Site on the Files panel menu bar (Win) or click the Options list arrow, point to Site (Mac), point to Cloaking, then click Uncloak All.

Cloaking Selected File Types
There may be times when you want to cloak a particular type of file, such as a .swf file. To cloak a particular file type, open the Site Definition dialog box, click the Cloaking category, click the Cloak files ending with check box, then type a file name in the text box below the check box. All files throughout the site that have the specified file extension will be cloaked.

FIGURE N-14
Cloaked assets folder in the Files panel

Red slash indicates folder is cloaked

Cloaked files

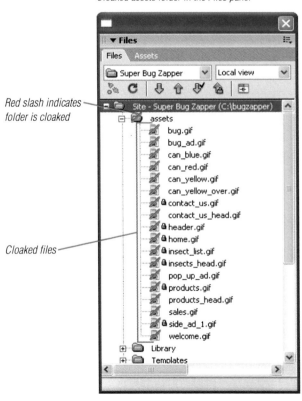

Cloak and uncloak a folder

1. Verify that Local view is displayed in the Files panel, click **Site** on the menu bar, then click **Manage Sites**.

2. Click **Super Bug Zapper** (if necessary), click **Edit** to open the Site Definition for Super Bug Zapper dialog box, click **Cloaking** in the Category list, verify that the Enable cloaking check box is checked, click **OK**, then click **Done**.

3. Click the **assets folder** in the Files panel, click the **Options list arrow** ≣▾, point to **Site**, point to **Cloaking**, click **Cloak**, expand the assets folder (if necessary), then compare your screen to Figure N-15.

   A red slash now appears on top of the assets folder in the Files panel, indicating that all files in the assets folder are cloaked and will be excluded from putting, getting, checking in, checking out, and many other operations.

   TIP You can also cloak a folder by right-clicking (Win) or [control]-clicking (Mac) the folder, pointing to Cloaking, then clicking Cloak.

4. Right-click (Win) or [control]-click (Mac) the assets folder, point to **Cloaking**, then click **Uncloak**.

   The assets folder and all the files it contains no longer appear with red slashes across them, indicating they are no longer cloaked.

   You cloaked the assets folder so that this folder and all the files it contains will be excluded from many operations, including uploading and downloading files. You then uncloaked the assets folder.

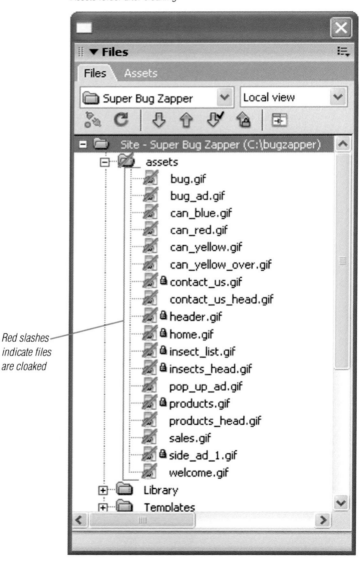

Red slashes indicate files are cloaked

FIGURE N-16

Specifying a file type to cloak

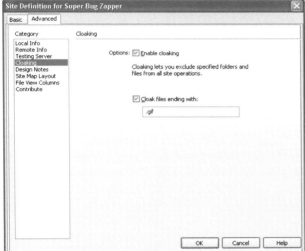

FIGURE N-17

Assets folder in Files panel after cloaking .gif files

Assets folder
is not cloaked

All .gif files
are cloaked

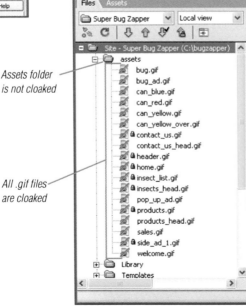

1. Right-click (Win) or [control]-click (Mac) the **assets folder** in the Files panel, point to **Cloaking**, then click **Settings** to open the Site Definition for Super Bug Zapper dialog box with the Cloaking category selected.

2. Click the **Cloak files ending with check box**, select the text in the text box that appears, type **.gif** in the text box, then compare your screen to Figure N-16.

3. Click **OK**.

   A dialog box opens, indicating that the site cache will be recreated.

4. Click **OK**, open the assets folder (if necessary), then compare your screen to Figure N-17.

   All of the .gif files in the assets folder appear with red slashes across them, indicating that they are cloaked. Notice that the assets folder is not cloaked.

You cloaked all the .gif files in the Super Bug Zapper Web site.

IMPORT AND EXPORT A SITE DEFINITION

What You'll Do

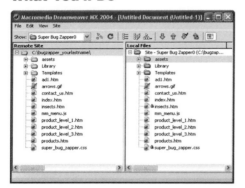

 In this lesson, you will export the site definition file for the Super Bug Zapper Web site. You will then import the Super Bug Zapper Web site.

Exporting a Site Definition

If you work on a Web site for a long time, it's likely that at some point you will want to move it to another machine or share it with other collaborators who will help you maintain it. The site definition for a Web site contains important information about the site, including its URL, preferences that you've specified, and other secure information such as the login and password information. You can use the Export command to export the site definition file to another location. To do this, simply click Site on the menu bar, click Manage Sites, click the site you want to export,

then click Export. Because the site definition file contains password information that you will want to keep secret from other site users, you should never save the site definition file in the Web site. Instead, save it in an external folder.

Importing a Site Definition

If you want to set up another user with a copy of your Web site, you can import the site definition file. To do this, click Import in the Manage Sites dialog box to open the Import Site dialog box, navigate to the .ste file you want to import, then click Open.

Export a site definition

1. Use Windows Explorer (Win) or Finder (Mac) to create a new folder on your hard drive or external drive named **bugzapper_site_definition**.

2. Switch back to Dreamweaver, click **Site** on menu bar, click **Manage Sites**, click **Super Bug Zapper**, then click **Export** to open the Export Site dialog box.

3. Navigate to and select the bugzapper_site_definition folder that you created in Step 1, as shown in Figure N-18, click **Save**, then click **Done**.

You used the Export command to create the site definition file and saved it to the bugzapper_site_definition folder.

FIGURE N-18

Saving the bugzapper.ste file in the bugzapper_site_definition folder

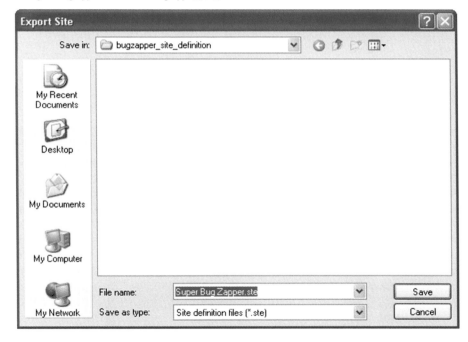

Import a site definition

1. Click **Site** on the menu bar, click **Manage Sites**, click **Super Bug Zapper**, then click **Import** to open the Import Site dialog box.

2. Navigate to the bugzapper_site_definition folder, compare your screen to Figure N-19, select Super Bug Zapper.ste, then click **Open**.

   A dialog box opens and says that a site named Super Bug Zapper already exists. It will name the imported site Super Bug Zapper0 so that it has a unique name.

3. Click **OK**, click **Done**, then click **OK** to close the message about the site cache being recreated.

4. Click **Site** on the menu bar, click **Manage Sites**, click **Super Bug Zapper0**, click **Edit**, then compare your screen to Figure N-20.

   The settings show that the Super Bug Zapper0 site has the same root folder and default images folder as the Super Bug Zapper site. Both of these settings are specified in the Super_Bug_Zapper.ste file that you imported. Importing a site in this way makes it possible for multiple users with different computers to work on the same site.

5. Click **OK**, click **Done**, then click **OK** to close the warning message (if necessary).

   TIP   If a dialog box opens warning that the root folder chosen is the same as the folder for the site "Super Bug Zapper," click OK.

You imported the Super Bug Zapper.ste file.

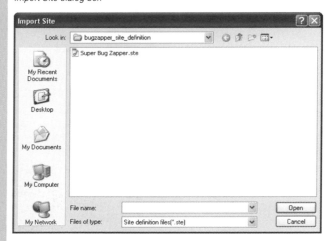

FIGURE N-19
Import Site dialog box

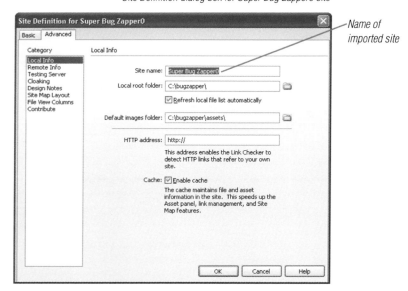

FIGURE N-20
Site Definition dialog box for Super Bug Zapper0 site

Name of imported site

1. Click the **Expand/Collapse button** 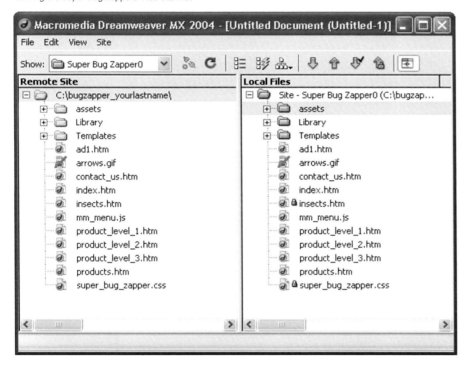 on the Files panel toolbar to expand the Files panel.

2. Expand the Site folder to view the contents (if necessary).

3. Click the **Refresh button** to view the files in the Remote Site pane.

   As shown in Figure N-21, the site looks identical to the original Super Bug Zapper site, except the name has been changed to Super Bug Zapper0.

4. Click the **Expand/Collapse button** to collapse the Files panel.

5. Close the Super Bug Zapper0 Web site.

You viewed the expanded Files panel for the Super Bug Zapper0 Web site.

FIGURE N-21
Viewing the Super Bug Zapper0 Web site files

Publish a Web site and transfer files.

1. Open the Blooms & Bulbs Web site that you created and developed in Chapters A through M.
2. Set up Web server access for the Blooms & Bulbs Web site on an FTP server or a local/network server (whichever is available to you) using appropriate settings.
3. View the Blooms & Bulbs remote site in the Files panel.
4. Upload the iris.jpg file to the remote site, then view the remote site.
5. Upload the master_gardener template and all dependent files to the remote site, then view the remote site to make sure all files were transferred.
6. Synchronize all files in the Blooms & Bulbs Web site, so that all files from the local site are uploaded to the remote site.

Check files out and in.

1. Enable the Check In/Check Out feature.
2. Check out the plants page and all dependent pages.
3. Open the plants page, change the heading size of Drop by to see our Featured Spring Plants to 3, then save your changes.
4. Check in the plants page.

Cloak files.

1. Verify that cloaking is enabled in the Blooms & Bulbs Web site.
2. Cloak the assets folder, then uncloak it.
3. Cloak all the .jpg files in the Blooms & Bulbs Web site.

Import and export a site definition.

1. Create a new folder named blooms_definition on your hard drive or external drive.
2. Export the Blooms & Bulbs site definition to the blooms_definition folder.

In this project, you will finish your work on the group Web site that you created and developed in Chapters A through M. Depending on the size of your group, you can assign individual parts of this project to group members, or work collectively.

You will publish your site to a remote server or local or network folder.

1. Before you begin the process of publishing your Web site to a remote server, meet as a group to review your Web site and make sure that it is ready for public viewing. Use Figure N-26 to assist you in making sure your Web site is complete. If you find problems, assign team members to make the necessary changes to finalize the site.

2. Assign a team member the task of deciding where to publish your site. The folder where you will publish your site can be either an FTP site or a local/network folder. If you are publishing to an FTP site, be sure to write down all the information you will need to publish to the site, including the URL of the FTP host, the directory on the FTP server where you will publish your site's root folder, and the login and password information.

3. Assign a team member the task of using the Site Definition dialog box to specify the remote settings for the site using the information that was decided upon in Step 2.

4. Assign another team member the task of transferring one of the pages and its dependent files to the remote site, then viewing the remote site to make sure the appropriate files were transferred.

5. Assign a team member the task of synchronizing the files so that all the remaining local pages and dependent files are uploaded to the remote site.

6. Assign a team member the task of enabling the Check In/Check Out feature.

7. Assign a team member the task of checking out one of the pages. This team member should also open the checked-out page, make a change to it, save the change, close the page, then check the page back in.

8. Assign a team member the task of cloaking a particular file type of the group's choosing.

9. Assign a team member the task of exporting the site definition for the site to a new folder on your hard drive or on an external drive.

10. Assign a team member the task of importing the site to create a new version of the site.

11. Close the imported site, save and close all open pages (if necessary), then exit Dreamweaver.

FIGURE N-26
Group Project check list

Web Site Check List

1. Are you satisfied with the content and appearance of every page?
2. Are all paths for all links and images correct?
3. Does each page have a title?
4. Do all images appear?
5. Are all colors Websafe?
6. Do all images have appropriate alternate text?
7. Have you eliminated any orphaned files?
8. Have you deleted any unnecessary files?
9. Have you viewed all pages using at least two different browser settings?
10. Does the home page have keywords and a description?

Read the following information carefully!!

The following files are located on the CD-ROM included with this book.

- To complete many of the chapters in this book, you need to use Data Files. These data files are available on the CD-ROM included with this book.

- All the Data Files are organized in folders named after the chapter in which they are used. For instance, all Chapter A Data Files are stored in the chapter_a folder. You should leave all the Data Files in these folders; do not move any Data File out of the folder in which it is originally stored.

Copy and organize your Data Files.

- Copy the folders that contain the Data Files to a Zip drive, network folder, hard drive, or other storage device.

- As you build each Web site, the exercises in this book will guide you to copy the Data Files you need from the appropriate Data Files folder to the folder where you are storing the Web site. Your Data Files should always remain intact because you are copying (and not moving) them to the Web site.

- Because you will be building a Web site from one chapter to the next, sometimes you will need to use a Data File that is already contained in the Web site you are working on.

Find and keep track of your Data Files and completed files.

- Use the **Data File Supplied** column to make sure you have the files you need before starting the chapter or exercise indicated in the **Chapter** column.

- Sometimes the file listed in the **Data File Supplied** column is one that you created or used in a previous chapter, and that is already part of the Web site you are working on. For instance, if the file jacobs/recipes.htm is listed in the **Data File Supplied** column, this means that you need to use the recipes.htm file in the Jacob's Web site that you already created.

- Use the **Reader Creates File** column to find out the filename you use when saving your new file for the exercise.

DATA FILES LIST

Files used in this book

Naked Macromedia Dreamweaver MX 2004

Chapter	Data File Supplied	Reader Creates File	Used In
A	dwa_1.htm contact.swf newsletter.swf services.swf tours.swf assets/tripsmart.jpg assets/trps_log.gif		Lesson 2
	dwa_2.htm assets/tripsmart.jpg	accessories.htm catalog.htm clothing.htm newsletter.htm services.htm tours.htm	Lessons 4 and 5
	dwa_3.htm dwa_4.htm assets/bloom_log.gif assets/blooms.gif	plants.htm workshops.htm tips.htm	Skills Review
	dwa_5.htm assets/rapids.jpg	guides.htm rentals.htm store.htm	Project Builder 1
	dwa_6.htm assets/jacobs.jpg	directions.htm menus.htm recipes.htm	Project Builder 2
	none		Design Project
	none		Group Project
B	dwb_1.htm packing_essentials.doc assets/tidbits.jpg assets/tripsmart.jpg		Lesson 2
	dwb_2.htm gardening_tips.doc assets/blooms.gif assets/planting_tips.jpg		Skills Review

Chapter	Data File Supplied	Reader Creates File	Used In
	none		Project Builder 1
	none		Project Builder 2
	none		Design Project
	none		Group Project
C	how_to_pack.doc		Lesson 1
		tripsmart.css	Lesson 2
	dwc_1.htm assets/tripsmart.jpg assets/giraffe.jpg assets/lion.jpg assets/zebra_mothers.jpg		Lesson 3
	assets/seamless_bak.gif assets/tile_bak.gif		Lesson 5
	dwc_3.htm gardening_tips.htm assets/blooms.gif assets/daisies.gif assets/iris.jpg assets/pansies.jpg assets/planting_tips.jpg assets/tulips.jpg	blooms.css	Skills Review
	dwc_4.htm assets/buster_tricks.jpg assets/rapids.jpg	rapids.css	Project Builder 1
	dwc_5.htm rolls.htm assets/cheesecake.jpg assets/jacobs.jpg assets/oranges.jpg assets/poached_pear.jpg	jacobs.css	Project Builder 2
	none		Design Project
	none		Group Project

Chapter	Data File Supplied	Reader Creates File	Used In
D	dwd_1.htm assets/tripsmart.jpg		Lesson 1
		top.swf	Lesson 3
	assets/nav_catalog_down.jpg assets/nav_catalog_up.jpg assets/nav_home_down.jpg assets/nav_home_up.jpg assets/nav_news_down.jpg assets/nav_news_up.jpg assets/nav_services_down.jpg assets/nav_services_up.jpg assets/nav_tours_down.jpg assets/nav_tours_up.jpg		Lesson 4
	dwd_2.htm assets/blooms.gif assets/blooms_ask_down.jpg assets/blooms_ask_up.jpg assets/blooms_home_down.jpg assets/blooms_home_up.jpg assets/blooms_plants_down.jpg assets/blooms_plants_up.jpg assets/blooms_tips_down.jpg assets/blooms_tips_up.jpg assets/blooms_workshops_down.jpg assets/blooms_workshops_up.jpg	top.swf	Skills Review
	dwd_3.htm assets/buffalo_fall.gif assets/rapids.jpg		Project Builder 1
	dwd_4.htm assets/jacobs.jpg		Project Builder 2
	none		Design Project
	none		Group Project
E	assets/headphones.jpg assets/packing_cube.jpg assets/passport_holder.jpg assets/tripsmart.jpg		Lesson 3

Chapter	Data File Supplied	Reader Creates File	Used In
	headphones.htm packing_cube.htm passport_holder.htm		Lesson 4
	dwe_1.htm dwe_2.htm assets/hat.jpg assets/hats_on_the_amazon.jpg assets/nav_catalog_down.jpg assets/nav_catalog_up.jpg assets/nav_home_up.jpg assets/nav_home_down.jpg assets/nav_news_down.jpg assets/nav_news_up.jpg assets/nav_services_down.jpg assets/nav_services_up.jpg assets/nav_tours_down.jpg assets/nav_tours_up.jpg assets/pants.jpg assets/vest.jpg		Lesson 5
	assets/tearoom.jpg assets/texas_rose.jpg assets/yellow_rose.jpg agenda.htm exhibition.htm nursery.htm tearoom.htm		Skills Review
	rental_info.htm store.htm assets/fruit_basket.jpg assets/kayak.jpg		Project Builder 1
	directions_paragraph.htm assets/signature_dish.jpg		Project Builder 2
	none		Design Project
	none		Group Project

Chapter	Data File Supplied	Reader Creates File	Used In
F	northwest folder containing these files:		
	about.htm		Lesson 1
	cables.htm		
	catalog.htm		
	docks.htm		
	index.htm		
	laptops.htm		
	memory.htm		
	Northwet.ste		
	pda.htm		
	support.htm		
	northwest assets folder containing these files:		
	layout_r1_c1.gif		
	layout_r3_c1.gif		
	other files:		
	dwf_1.htm		
	assets/pda.gif		Lesson 3
	dwf_2.htm		PB1
	assets/rapids.jpg		PB1
G	assets/layerbg.gif		Lesson 1
	assets/visor.gif		
	assets/flower.gif		SR
	assets/creek.jpg		PB1
	assets/turtle.jpg		
	assets/waterfall.jpg		
H		catalog.htm	Lesson 1
	dwh_1.htm		Lesson 3
	dwh_2.htm		Lesson 3
		laptops.htm	Lesson 3
	assets/laptop.jpg		Lesson 3
	assets/topbanner.png		Lesson 3
	annuals.htm		SR
		featured_plants.htm	
	perennials.htm		
		plants.htm	
		top_frame.htm	
	water_plants.htm		
	assets/iris2.jpg		
	assets/fuschia.jpg		
	assets/water_hyacinth.jpg		

Chapter	Data File Supplied	Reader Creates File	Used In
	gear.htm snacks.htm assets/fruit_basket.jpg assets/store.jpg	navigation.htm store.htm store_links.htm	PB1
	mushroom_caps.htm	recipe_links.htm recipes.htm navigation.htm	PB2
I	assets/cservice.swf assets/nwmemory.png assets/swmemory.png assets/chord.wav		Lesson 1 Lesson 2 Lesson 2 Lesson 3
		annuals.swf perennials.swf plants.swf water.swf	SR
	assets/flower.swf assets/flowerreverse.gif assets/chord.wav	home.swf before.swf guides.swf reservations.swf store.swf directions.swf home.swf menus.swf recipes.swf	PB1 PB2
	assets/chord.wav assets/map.swf		
J	bugzapper folder containing these files: ad1.htm contact_us.htm index.htm insects.htm products.htm	Lesson 1	

Chapter	Data File Supplied	Reader Creates File	Used In
	bugzapper/assets folder containing these files: bug_ad.gif, can_blue.gif, can_red.gif, can_yellow.gif, can_yellow_over.gif, contact_us.gif, contact_us_head.gif, header.gif, home.gif, insect_list.gif, insects_head.gif, pop_up_ad.gif, products.gif, products_head.gif, sales.gif, welcome.gif		
		main_elements.dwt	Lesson 2
		product_info.dwt	Lesson 2
	other files: assets/side_ad_1.gif		Lesson 2
		product_level_1.htm	Lesson 3
		product_level_2.htm	
		product_level_3.htm	
	assets/master_gardening_tip.gif		SR
		master_gardener.dwt	
		product_listing.dwt	
		product_list.htm	
		store_pages.dwt	PB1
		recipe_card.dwt	PB2
K		popup.htm	SR
	assets/blooms_bulbs_popup_ad.gif		
	assets/experts.jpg		
	assets/spring_falls.jpg		PB1
		popup1.htm	PB2
	assets/jacobs_popup1.gif		
		popup2.htm	
	assets/jacobs_popup2.gif		
L	super_bug_zapper.css		Lesson 2

DATA FILES LIST

Chapter	Data File Supplied	Reader Creates File	Used In
M	assets/bug.gif assets/star.gif		Lesson 1 PB2
N	There are no data files supplied.		
		Super Bug Zapper.ste Blooms & Bulbs.ste Rapids Transit.ste Jacob's.ste	Lesson 4 SR PB1 PB2

Absolute path
A path containing an external link that references a link on a Web page outside of the current Web site, and includes the protocol "http" and the URL, or address, of the Web page.

Absolute positioning
The positioning of a layer according to the distance between the layer's upper-left corner and the upper-left corner of the page or layer in which it is contained.

Action
A response to an event trigger that causes a change, such as text changing color.

Action property
Property that specifies the application or script that will process form data.

Alert box
See **popup message**.

Aligning an image
Positioning an image on a Web page in relation to other elements on the page.

Alternate text
Descriptive text that can be set to appear in place of an image while the image is downloading or when a user places the mouse pointer over the image.

Assets folder
A subfolder in a Web site in which you store most of the files that are not Web pages, such as images, audio files, and video clips.

Assets panel
A panel that contains nine categories of assets, such as images, used in a Web site. Clicking a category button will display a list of those assets.

Background color
A color that fills an entire Web page, frame, table, cell, or document.

Background image
A graphic file used in place of a background color.

Banner
Graphic that appears across the top of a Web page that can incorporate the company's logo, contact information, and navigation buttons.

Behavior
A preset piece of JavaScript code that can be attached to page elements. A behavior tells the page element to respond in a specific way when an event occurs, such as when the mouse pointer is positioned over the element.

BMP
Bitmapped file. A file format used for images that is based on pixels.

Bobby
A free service provided by CAST to evaluate Web pages and Web sites for accessibility.

Body
The part of a Web page that is seen when the page is viewed in a browser window.

Border
An outline that surrounds a cell, table, or frame.

Broken links
Links that cannot find the intended destination file for the link.

Browser
Software used to display Web pages, such as Microsoft Internet Explorer or Netscape Navigator.

Bullet
A small raised dot or similar icon.

Bulleted list
The name that is sometimes given to unordered lists using bullets.

Cascading Style Sheet (CSS)
A file used to assign sets of common formatting characteristics to page elements such as text, objects, and tables.

CAST
Acronym for the Center for Applied Special Technology.

Cell padding
The distance between the cell content and cell walls in a table.

Cell spacing
The distance between cells in a table.

Cell walls
The edges surrounding a cell.

Cells
Small boxes within a table that are used to hold text or graphics. Cells are arranged horizontally in rows and vertically in columns.

Checkbox
Form object that can be used on a Web page to let viewers choose from a range of possible options.

Child page
A page at a lower level in a Web hierarchy that links to a parent page.

Class style
See **custom style**.

Client-side scripting
A method used to process information a form collects by using the user's computer.

Clip property
Property that determines the portion of a layer's content that will be visible when displayed in a Web browser.

Cloaked file
File that is marked to be excluded from certain processes, such as being transferred to the remote site.

Code and Design view
A view that is a combination of Code view and Design view.

Code inspector
A window that works just like Code view except that it is a detachable window.

Code snippets
See **snippets**.

Code view
A view that shows the underlying HTML code for the page. Use this view to read or edit the code.

Cold Fusion
Development tool that can be used to build data-driven Web applications.

Columns
Table cells arranged vertically.

Common Gateway Interface (CGI)
Server-side application used for processing data in a form.

Contents
The Macromedia Help feature that lists topics by category.

Custom style
A style that can contain a combination of formatting attributes that can be applied to a block of text or other page elements. Custom style names begin with a period (.).

Debug
To find and correct coding errors.

Declaration
The property and value of a style in a Cascading Style Sheet.

Default base font
The font that is applied by default to any text that is entered on a page created in Dreamweaver.

Default font color
The color the browser uses to display text if no other color is assigned.

Default link color
The color the browser uses to display links if no other color is assigned. The default link color is blue.

Definition lists
Lists composed of terms with indented descriptions or definitions.

Delimited files
Database or spreadsheet files that have been saved as text files with delimiters.

Delimiter
A comma, tab, colon, semicolon, or similar character that separates tabular data.

Dependent file
File that another file needs in order to be complete, such as an image or navigation bar element.

Description
A short summary of Web site content that resides in the head section.

Design view
The view that shows the page as it would appear in a browser and is primarily used when designing and creating a Web page.

Document
A page created in Dreamweaver.

Document toolbar
A toolbar that contains buttons for changing the current Web page view, previewing and debugging Web pages, and managing files.

Document window
The large white area in the Dreamweaver workspace where you create and edit Web pages.

Document-relative path
A path referenced in relation to the Web page that is currently displayed.

Domain name
An IP address expressed in letters instead of numbers, usually reflecting the name of the business represented by the Web site.

Down image state
The state of a page element when the element has been clicked.

Download
Transfer a file or files from a remote server to a computer.

Download time
The time it takes to transfer a file to another computer.

DSL
Digital Subscriber Line. A type of high-speed Internet connection.

Editable optional region
An area in a template where users can add or change content, and that users can also choose to show or hide.

Editable region
An area in a template where users of the template can add or change content.

Element
A graphic link that is part of a navigation bar and can have one of four possible appearances.

Enable cache
A setting to direct the computer system to use space on the hard drive as temporary memory or cache while you are working in Dreamweaver.

Event trigger
An event, such as a mouse click on an object, that causes a behavior to start.

Export data
To save data that was created in Dreamweaver in a special file format so that you can bring it into another software program.

External CSS style sheet
Collection of rules stored in a separate file that control the formatting of content in a Web page. External CSS style sheets have a .css file extension.

External links
Links that connect to Web pages in other Web sites or to e-mail addresses.

Field
See **form object**

Fieldset
HTML tag used to group related form elements together.

File field
Form object that allows viewers to upload files to a Web server.

Files panel
The panel you use to manage your Web site.

Flash button object
Button made from a small, predefined Flash movie that can be inserted on a Web page to provide navigation in a Web site.

Flash text
A vector-based graphic file that contains text.

Form control
See **form object**.

Form element
See **form object**.

Form object
An object on a Web page, such as a text box, radio button, or checkbox, that collects information from viewers. Also referred to as **form element**, **form control**, or **field**.

FormName property
Property that specifies a unique name for a form.

Frame
Fixed region in a browser that can display a Web page and act independently from other pages displayed in other frames within the browser window.

Frameset
A document that contains the instructions that tell a browser how to lay out a set of frames showing individual documents on a page, including the size and position of the frames.

Frames panel
Panel in the Advanced Layout panel group that shows a visual representation of the frameset and is used for selecting frames.

FTP
File Transfer Protocol. The process of uploading and downloading files to and from a remote site.

Get
Transferring files from a remote location.

GET method
Method property that specifies that ASCII data collected in a form will be sent to the server appended to the URL or file included in the Action property.

GIF
Graphics interchange format. Type of file format used for images placed on Web pages that can support both transparency and animation.

Graphics
Pictures or design elements that add visual interest to a page.

Head content
The part of a Web page that is not viewed in the browser window. It includes meta tags, which are HTML codes that include information about the page, such as keywords and descriptions.

Headings
Six different styles that can be applied to text: Heading 1 (the largest size) through Heading 6 (the smallest size).

Height property
Property that specifies the height of a layer either in pixels or as a percentage of the screen's height.

Hexadecimal value
A value that represents the amount of red, green, and blue in a color and is based on the Base 16 number system.

Hidden field
Form object that makes it possible to provide information to the Web server and form processing script without the viewer knowing that the information is being sent.

History panel
A panel that lists the steps that have been performed in Dreamweaver while editing and formatting a document.

Home page
Usually the first Web page that appears when viewers visit a Web site.

Hotspot
An area on a graphic, that, when clicked, links to a different location on the page or to another Web page.

HTML
Hypertext Markup Language. The language Web developers use to create Web pages.

HTML style
A named set of formatting attributes that can be applied to text to ensure consistency for common text elements across all pages of a Web site.

Hyperlink
Graphic or text element on a Web page that users click to display another location on the page, another Web page on the same Web site, or a Web page on a different Web site. Hyperlinks are also known as links.

Image field
Form object used to insert an image in a form.

Image map
A graphic that has been divided into sections, each of which contains a link.

Import data
To bring data created in another software program into an application.

Index
The Macromedia Help feature that displays topics in alphabetical order.

Inline CSS style
A CSS style whose code is contained within the HTML code of a Web page.

Interactivity
Allows visitors to your Web site to affect its content.

Insert bar
Groups of buttons for creating and inserting objects arranged by category.

Internal links
Links to Web pages within the same Web site.

IP address
An assigned series of numbers, separated by periods, that designates an address on the Internet. **ISP** Internet Service Provider. A service to which you subscribe in order to be able to connect your computer to the Internet.

JavaScript
A Web-scripting language that interacts with HTML code to create interactive content.

JPEG file
Joint photographic experts group. Type of file format used for images that appear on Web pages, typically used for photographs.

Jump menu
Navigational menu that lets viewers go quickly to different pages in a site or to different sites on the Internet.

Keywords
Words that relate to the content of a Web site and reside in the head content.

Layers
Containers used to divide and arrange the elements of a Web page in a logical front to back order. A layer can contain multiple objects, all of which are managed in the Layers panel.

Layers panel
Panel in the Advanced Layout panel group that is used to control the visibility, name, and Z-Index stacking order of layers on a Web page.

Layout view
A Dreamweaver view that is used for drawing tables.

Left property
Property that specifies the distance between the left edge of a layer and the left edge of the page or layer that contains it.

Library item
Content that can contain text or graphics and is saved in a separate file in the Library folder of a Web site.

Link
See hyperlink.

List
Element on a Web page from which viewers can make a choice from several options. Lists are often used in order forms.

List form object
A form object that lets users choose one or more options from a list of choices.

Locked region
An area on a template that cannot be changed by users of the template.

Macromedia Flash Player
A program that needs to be installed on a computer to view Flash movies.

mailto: link
A common point of contact that viewers with questions or problems can use to contact someone at the company's headquarters.

Menu
Element on a Web page from which Web viewers can make choices. Menus are often used for navigation in a Web site.

Menu bar
A bar located above the document window that includes names of menus, each of which contain Dreamweaver commands.

Menu form object
A form object, commonly used for navigation on a Web site, that lets viewers select a single option from a list of choices.

Menu list
Lists that are very similar to unordered lists.

Merge cells
To combine multiple cells in a table into one cell.

Meta tags
HTML codes that include information about the page, such as keywords and descriptions, and reside in the head content.

Method property
Property that specifies the HyperText Transfer Protocol (HTTP) method used to send form data to a Web server.

Multimedia
Content that combines text, graphics, sound, animation, or interactivity to create a fully engaging experience.

Named anchor
A specific location on a Web page that has a specific name.

Navigation bar
A group of buttons, usually organized in rows or columns, that link to different areas inside or outside a Web site.

Nested layer
Layer whose HTML code is included within another layer's code.

Nested table
A table within a table.

Nested template
A template that is based on another template.

NoFrames content
Alternate content of a Web site that can be viewed without frames.

Non-Websafe colors
Colors that may not be displayed uniformly across computer platforms.

Numbered lists
Lists of items that are presented in a specific order and are preceded by numbers or letters in sequence.

Objects
The individual elements in a document, such as text or images.

Optional region
Region in a template that template users can choose either to show or hide.

Ordered list
List of items that need to be placed in a specific order, where each item is preceded by a number or letter.

Orphaned files
Files that are not linked to any pages in a Web site.

Overflow property
Property that specifies how to handle excess content that does not fit inside a layer.

Over image state
The state of a page element when the mouse pointer is positioned over it.

Over While Down image state
The state of a page element when the mouse pointer is clicked and held over it.

Panel
A window that contains related commands or displays information on a particular topic.

Panel groups
Sets of related panels that are grouped together.

Paragraph style
HTML style that is applied to an entire paragraph.

Parent page
A page at a higher level in a Web hierarchy that links to other pages on a lower level.

PICS
The acronym for Platform for Internet Content Selection. This is a rating system for Web pages.

PNG
Portable network graphics. A type of file format for graphics.

Point of contact
A place on a Web page that provides viewers a means of contacting a company.

Pop-up menu
A menu that appears when you move the pointer over a trigger image in a browser.

Pop-up message
Message that opens in a browser to either clarify or provide information, or alert viewers of an action that is being taken.

Position property
Property used to define a layer's position on a page.

POST method
Method property that specifies that form data be sent to the processing script as a binary or encrypted file, so that data will be sent securely.

Property inspector
A panel located at the bottom of the Dreamweaver window that lets you view and change the properties of a selected object.

Publish a Web site
To make a Web site available for viewing on the Internet or on an intranet.

Put
Transferring files to a remote location.

Radio button
Form object that can be used to provide a list of options from which only one selection can be made.

Radio group
A group of radio buttons from which viewers can make only one selection.

Ransom note effect
A phrase that implies that fonts have been randomly used in a document without regard to style.

Reference panel
A panel used to find answers to coding questions, covering topics such as HTML, JavaScript, and Accessibility.

Refresh Local File List Automatically option
A setting that directs Dreamweaver to automatically reflect changes made in your file listings.

Relative path
A path containing a link to a page within a Web site.

Remote server
A Web server that hosts Web sites and is not directly connected to the computer housing the local site. **Remote site**
A Web site that has been published to a remote server.

Repeating region
An area in a template whose format is repeated over and over again. Used for presenting information that repeats, such as product listings in a catalog.

Repeating table
A table in a template that has a predefined structure, making it very easy for template users to add content to it.

Resolution
The number of pixels per inch in an image; also refers to an image's clarity and fineness of detail.

Rollover
A special effect that changes the appearance of an object when the mouse rolls over it.

Rollover color
The color in which text will appear when the rollover is taking place.

Rollover image
An image on a Web page that changes its appearance when the mouse pointer is positioned over it.

Root folder
A folder used to store all Web pages or HTML files for the site. The root folder is given a name to describe the site, such as the company name.

Root relative path
A path referenced from a Web site's root folder.

Rows
Table cells arranged horizontally.

Sans-serif fonts
Block-style characters used frequently for headings and subheadings.

Screen reader
A device used by the visually impaired to convert written text on a computer monitor to spoken words.

Seamless image
A tiled image that is blurred at the edges so that it appears to be all one image.

Search
The Macromedia Help feature that allows you to enter a keyword to begin a search for a topic.

Selection style
HTML style that is applied to selected text.

Selector
The name or the tag to which the style declarations have been assigned.

Serif fonts
Ornate fonts with small extra strokes at the beginning and end of characters. Used frequently for paragraph text in printed materials.

Server-side application
An application that resides on a Web server and interacts with the information collected in a form.

Server-side scripting
A method used to process information a form collects that uses applications that reside on the Web server and interact with the information collected in the form.

Snippet
A reusable piece of code that can be inserted on a page to create footers, headers, drop-down menus, and other items.

Split cells
To divide cells into multiple cells.

Standard toolbar
A toolbar that contains buttons you can use to execute frequently used commands also available on the File and Edit menus.

Standard view
A view that is used to insert a table using the Insert Table button.

States
The four appearances a button can assume in response to a mouse action. These include: Up, Over, Down, and Over While Down.

Status bar
A bar located below the document window that displays HTML tags being used at the insertion point location as well as other information, such as estimated download time for the current page and window size.

Step
Each task performed in the History panel.

Storyboard
A small sketch that represents every page in a Web site.

Styles
Preset attributes, such as size, color, and texture, that you can apply to objects and text.

Swap
A behavior similar to a rollover effect.

Table
Grid of rows and columns that can either be used to hold tabular data on a Web page or can be used as a basic design tool for page layout.

Tabular data
Data that is arranged in columns and rows and separated by a delimiter.

Tag selector
A location on the status bar that displays HTML tags for the various page elements, including tables and cells.

Tags
Determine how the text in HTML should be formatted when a browser displays it.

Target
The location on a Web page that the browser will display in full view when an internal link is clicked, or the frame that will open when a link is clicked.

Target property
Property that specifies the window in which you want form data to be processed.

Template
A special page that contains both locked regions, which are areas on the template page that cannot be modified by users of the template, as well as other types of regions that users can change or edit.

Text area field
A text field in a form that can store several lines of text.

Text field
Form object used for collecting a string of characters such as a name, address, or password.

TIFF
Tagged image file format.

Tiled image
A small graphic that repeats across and down a Web page, appearing as individual squares or rectangles.

Top property
Property that specifies the distance between the top edge of a layer and the top edge of the page or layer that contains it.

Unordered lists
Lists of items that do not need to be placed in a specific order and are usually preceded by bullets.

Unvisited links
Links that have not been clicked by the viewer.

Up image state
The state of a page element when the mouse pointer is not on the element.

Upload
Transfer files to a remote server.

URL
Uniform resource locator. An address that determines a route on the Internet or to a Web page.

Vector based graphics
Graphics that are based on mathematical formulas.

Visible property
Property that lets you control whether the selected layer is visible or hidden.

Visited links
Links that have been previously clicked or visited. The default color for visited links is purple.

Web design software
Software for creating interactive Web pages containing text, images, hyperlinks, animation, sounds, and video.

Web-safe colors
Colors that are common to both Macintosh and Windows platforms.

Web server
A computer dedicated to hosting Web sites that is connected to the Internet and configured with software to handle requests from browsers.

Web site
A group of related Web pages that are linked together and share a common interface and design.

White space
An area on a Web page that is not filled with text or graphics.

Width property
Property that specifies the width of a layer either in pixels or as a percentage of the screen's width.

Workspace
The area in the Dreamweaver program window where you work with documents, movies, tools, and panels.

WYSIWYG
An acronym for What You See is What You Get, meaning that your Web page should look the same in the browser as it does in the Web editor.

Z-Index property
Property that specifies the vertical stacking order of layers on a page. A Z-Index value of 1 indicates that a layer's position is at the bottom of the stack. A Z-Index position of 3 indicates that the layer is positioned on top of two other layers.

Note: Page references of terms referring to Macintosh or Windows platforms that are either unique to one of the platforms or are the same but appear on separate pages will be followed with (Mac) or (Win).